Advance praise for
HELEN KELLY – HER LIFE

'A searing modern history not just of a brilliant leader but of the struggles of the union movement and the erosion of workers' rights in the modern age. Clear-eyed and powerfully written, this is a book every New Zealander should read. Much more than a biography of a brilliant leader, Macfie has crafted a compelling analysis of the carnage caused by Rogernomics and New Zealand's descent into a low-waged, unequal society'
– Kirsty Johnston, journalist, *Stuff*

'An immensely readable tale of politics, heartache and ferocious charm. This is gifted storytelling, rich in political history, immensely readable and important, a great book about a true working-class hero and perhaps the greatest political leader of our time'
– Simon Wilson, journalist, *The New Zealand Herald*

'This vivid biography of Helen Kelly, champion of people, is also an insightful portrait of our nation. It will inspire many of us to keep fighting for a fair economy and just society, which we need now more urgently than ever'
– Rod Oram, business journalist

Praise for
TRAGEDY AT PIKE RIVER MINE
by Rebecca Macfie

'A devastating account of a needless tragedy'
– Victor Billot, *Otago Daily Times*

'Macfie gets to the heart of a complex and detailed story without losing or confusing her audience … Lucid, exhaustive, enraging'
– Guy Somerset, *New Zealand Listener*

'Her prose is a perfect example of Orwell's gold standard for good writing: as clear as a windowpane ... deserves not just a prize but a medal'
– Jane Westaway, *New Zealand Books*

'If you've already read accolades for this book, they're all deserved and then some'
– Jim Eagles & Mark Fryer, *Weekend Herald*

'An astonishingly good book – hard to put down, brilliant'
– Duncan Garner, *RadioLive Drive*

'Will stand for a long time as one of the classics of New Zealand non-fiction'
– Lewis Martin, *Nelson Mail*

'Its full telling needed a business journalist of Rebecca Macfie's experience and acumen. Her account is complex yet highly readable, and sometimes shocking'
– Philip Matthews, *The Press*

'Rebecca Macfie's research is relentless and her writing style easily accessible. She creates a palpable sense of urgency and anticipation...'
– Ellen Read, *The Sunday Star-Times*

HELEN KELLY
HER LIFE

REBECCA MACFIE

AWA PRESS

First published in 2021 by Awa Press, Level Three, 67 Dixon Street, Wellington 6011, New Zealand

ISBN 978-1-927249-74-1 (paperback)
ISBN 978-1-927249-75-8 (ePub)
ISBN 978-1-927249-76-5 (Mobi)

A catalogue record for this book is available from the National Library of New Zealand.

Author photograph by Sam Brett
Cover and internal design by Neil Pardington
Typesetting by Tina Delceg
Editing by Mary Varnham
Production by Sarah Bennett
Indexing by Lee Slater
This book is typeset in Minion Pro and Independent Sans
Printed and bound in Australia by Griffin Press

MIX
Paper from responsible sources
FSC® C009448
FSC
www.fsc.org

Back cover images, clockwise from top left: Helen Kelly *c.* 1965; with Jackie Moore *c.* 1975; Helen and her mother, Cath Kelly; in action as CTU president; Helen in 2016; with Dylan Kelly *c.* 1993; in 2006; Helen with her father, Pat Kelly *c.* 1972. *Kelly family collection*; *Andrew Dart*; *NZ Herald Archives.*

CONTENTS

Author's Note

The first time I met Helen Kelly she was crossing a room with flowers. I now know this was characteristic – she loved flowers, especially peonies, and she was forever giving gifts.

It was November 2013 and we were at Unity Books in Wellington. I had been giving a talk about my book *Tragedy at Pike River Mine: How and why 29 men died*, which had just been published. The room was quite full, which surprised me. I now know why: the National Affiliates Council of the Council of Trade Unions was having one of its regular bimonthly meetings that day and Helen, as CTU president, had called an early lunch and marched everyone down to Unity.

If I had known the country's union leaders were going to be there I would have been even more nervous than I was. Pike River Coal Ltd was an incompetent operator, whose path to catastrophe was uninterrupted by either a capable regulator or an empowered union. I had described the Engineering, Printing and Manufacturing Union's presence at the mine as 'limp' and 'marginalised and irrelevant', so I didn't expect plaudits from the union movement.

But here was Helen Kelly, New Zealand's union leader, handing over an enormous bouquet of flowers. She proceeded to address the room with warmth and crispness. She talked about the failure of Pike, and about the appalling rate of death and injury in the forestry industry and the work the unions had been doing to bring it to light. The parallels between the two were obvious.

She was impressive. We agreed to talk further about forestry.

A fortnight later, attention was again fixed on Pike River. Health and safety charges against the mine's boss, Peter Whittall, had been dropped in a deal involving the payment of an unpaid debt of reparations to the families of the 29 dead and the two survivors.

The decision was so shocking and wrong as to be unbelieveable. But while many people (including me) simply felt angry and helpless, Helen started assembling her forces to challenge it in court. It was apparent that not only was she sharp on her feet, she was gutsy and determined and saw a remit for the union movement that went far beyond merely servicing fee-paying members.

We spoke often over the following months about the proposed court challenge, and about forestry. I worked for the *Listener* and wrote about both. In my first years in journalism I'd covered industrial relations, including the radical labour market deregulation of the 1990s, and had some understanding of how the position for workers had been permanently weakened by that reform. I'd known and respected many unionists over the years but Helen Kelly was something different, and not just because she was a woman leading a labour movement still dominated by men. She was a fireball of charm, grit, humour and piercing analysis, and she seemed to be succeeding against a hostile political tide in getting the idea of workers' rights and union activism back into public consciousness. As New Zealand reluctantly began to confront some uncomfortable truths – gaping inequality, child poverty, stagnant wages, jobs bereft of security or certainty – she seemed to be the kind of leader that we could do with.

Then came the news in early 2015 that she had cancer. At the *Listener* we discussed the need for an in-depth article about her. She was coming to Christchurch, where I live, and we met for lunch about three weeks after her diagnosis. Over a salad (from which she pushed aside every scrap of dried fruit – she had cut sugar from her diet as part of her cancer fight) I asked if she would be interviewed for a profile. She was non-committal. I suspect she was suspicious that the media wanted to put her on a pedestal now that she was dying. But word came back a few days later that she was willing to participate.

It turned out that the first interview took place at her hospital bedside. She had set aside most of the afternoon of March 26, but our meeting had to be cancelled because she had been rushed to Wellington Hospital that morning with a heart complication that could have killed her. I had already boarded my flight when I got the message, so there wasn't much choice but to come to Wellington anyway. The next morning she insisted she was well enough to do at least part of the interview. She sat up in bed, hooked to tubes and under close medical watch, and talked about her work, labour history, her ideas about industrial relations reform, family. She seemed in good spirits and it was easy to lose sight of the fact that she was extremely sick. She had set one condition for this interview: I wasn't to reveal that she was speaking from a hospital ward. She wasn't dead yet, and didn't want the article to come across as an obituary.

She talked about the decision that she and her long-time partner Steve Hurring had made to get married and throw a big wedding party for friends and family. She said, 'You're invited.' I'm pretty sure I hadn't been, right up until the moment the words came out of her mouth. But it was completely genuine, so my husband and I were among the 450-odd people who came together for the celebration. I now know that this spontaneous invitation was typical – she was an extrovert, and had a gift for friendship.

Helen sometimes referred to dying as a 'social event' and the rich interaction with friends and family as a non-stop 'cancer party'. In her case it was also a public event; in her last months she was constantly in the news, particularly after she started campaigning for and openly using medicinal cannabis to ease her symptoms.

When she died in October 2016, there was a deep feeling that New Zealand had been deprived of a leader who had much more to contribute, and whose absence would leave a large gap in our public discourse and our collective ability to redesign the economy to provide decent wages, a fair share, and protection from poverty.

Workers had lost a powerful voice. The Council of Trade Unions formed a small committee to think about how to recognise Helen's work. The idea of a biography evolved from there and I was asked if I would take it on. I could see the opportunity not only to tell Helen's story, but to use it to carry a wider story of economic and political change over the span of her life. Mary Varnham, the publisher at Awa Press, had been keen on a Helen Kelly biography for some time. In March 2018 we signed a publishing agreement and I left my job at the *Listener*.

Detail on reference material and supporters is at the back of the book, but it's important to say up front that I would not have been able to write this book without the extraordinary access I was granted to Helen's CTU papers and wider CTU documents, and to family archives. A huge amount of trust was placed in me by Helen's former colleagues and her family, who understood at the same time that I was independent and had to write the story as I saw it.

Journalism is a lonely business at times and as the writer I am solely responsible for what comes out the other end – including any errors – but this book rests on the generosity, time, knowledge and support of the many, many people who made it possible for me to complete it. I went in blindly thinking I knew a bit about the labour movement and that it might take me a year to write. I quickly discovered that I knew very little and it ended up taking the better part of three years. To those who put up with my endless questions, dug out documents from hard-drives and bottom drawers, participated in the hundreds of hours of interviews that form the backbone of the book, kept talking even when my questions triggered their grief, read and commented on draft chapters – my eternal gratitude.

Much of this book was written in the time of Covid-19, the pandemic that had killed two million people by mid-January 2021 and turned the global economy on its head. In New Zealand we were the 'team of five million', embracing the power of collective action by staying home to save lives. During our strange, anxious period of lockdown, suddenly it was clear to everyone who mattered most to the functioning of society: those who went out every day to care for the sick and the old, stack the supermarket shelves, harvest the crops, keep the lights on and the water running, clear away the garbage, scrub the hospital floors – those very often rewarded with wages demonstrably less than is required to live a decent life in this country.

Helen Kelly would have seen this rupture as a massive organising opportunity, a chance to fight for fair pay and better conditions, for reciprocity and respect. She would have been demanding, persistent and sometimes annoying, and she would have helped us reframe our thinking about what is possible, and what is just.

I hope this story of her life and times helps inspire others who share the simple values of fairness, equity and care for the vulnerable to get organised, and to be a bit more demanding, persistent and – if necessary – annoying too.

Prologue

A dark-haired figure in a black jacket, black A-line skirt, black low-heeled boots and black tights holds the attention of a large crowd on the front lawn of New Zealand's Parliament.

'John Key thinks working people are skivers! Throw sickies! Are slackers! Are liars who don't deserve to be protected and have fairness at work!' she belts through the public address system. 'The government thinks it's time to kick working people. Within the same month of giving themselves a big fat tax cut, they decide it's time to remove your work rights!'[1]

Two years after the world's economic system has been brought to the brink of collapse by greed and the unshackled power of financial markets, New Zealand's wage workers are paying for the crisis through reforms advanced by the centre-right government of Prime Minister John Key. Public services are being whittled back, goods and services tax increased, protections against unfair dismissal curtailed, access to trade union representation made more difficult. Over 250,000 people are jobless.

Around the country, 22,000 workers are on the streets protesting against the changes, gathering under fluttering union banners in towns and cities from Kaitaia in the far north to Bluff in the south.

It is a good day for the trade union movement, and a good day for its first woman leader, Helen Kelly. Her thick hair blows about in the wind and a fine forefinger drives home her points. She has a handful of notes but barely glances at them. Her speech is quick, plain and fervent. The 4000-strong crowd responds with cheers and affirmation.

'Today your presence is showing Key that we will not put up with this! We will campaign until we win those rights back, and no government dares touch them again!'

It is October 20, 2010. The massive nationwide turnout to the Council of Trade Unions' Fairness at Work rallies is heartening for Kelly, three years into her role as the organisation's president. She worked hard on a collaborative relationship with Key after his government was elected in 2008 in the midst of the Global Financial Crisis. But the prospects for a pragmatic partnership have been dissolved by the government's aggressive reforms.

After the crowd disperses, the CTU's small staff regroups at its office in Willis Street, a central city street in the New Zealand capital. Kelly and a colleague pop out to buy chips and dips to share while they debrief on the day's events. The 'National Day of Action' has been an enormous logistical effort; everyone is exhausted, but satisfied that the long-planned rallies have gone so well.

It is a relief for Kelly to be focused again on Key's planned workplace reforms. She has spent much of the previous few weeks mired in delicate backroom negotiations to resolve a difficult dispute involving the country's actors, the film-maker Peter Jackson and the Hollywood behemoth Warner Bros. Thankfully, a solution has been sorted out that will allow the parties to save face and move forward. There is to be a meeting of actors that night at an old church next to the CTU's office to explain the settlement.

The dispute concerned Jackson's next epic, a series of three films based on the J.R.R. Tolkien fantasy *The Hobbit*. The *Hobbit* project had long been beset by delays and financial challenges but it was finally going ahead. It was widely expected to match the success of Jackson's three *Lord Of The Rings* films, which had been among the most profitable movies ever made.[2]

The Media, Entertainment and Arts Alliance (MEAA) – a trans-Tasman union of which New Zealand Actors' Equity was a branch – had demanded that the Hollywood producers negotiate a collective agreement with New Zealand actors on the production. Unlike their international peers, New Zealand actors didn't work under union contracts and were increasingly aggrieved that their pay and conditions seemed to be getting worse, despite the growth and international success of the New Zealand film sector. In the global film industry, New Zealand casts and crews had become known as 'Mexicans of the South Pacific'.

The local branch of the MEAA had previously tried and failed to get New Zealand screen producers to negotiate collective agreements that provided actors with better protections and a fair share of the spoils from successful productions. The prospect of *The Hobbit* being made in New Zealand by Warner Bros. offered an opportunity for leverage: the union would be dealing with a huge US studio accustomed to collective bargaining with actors' unions, and the production was reported to have a budget as high as US$500 million.

And this time the MEAA had the backing of the international actors' unions. The absence of enforceable union contracts for actors had made New Zealand an outlier in the global film industry. Unions such as the US Screen Actors Guild and UK Actors' Equity wanted that to change. In June 2010 the International Federation of Actors – the global grouping of performer unions – had decided to tell its members not to sign up to roles on *The Hobbit* until the producers sat down with the MEAA and negotiated a collective agreement for the New Zealanders.[3]

All of this had rumbled away out of the public gaze until late September 2010, when Jackson went public. He accused the MEAA of 'bully boy' behaviour motivated by a 'grab for power' over the New Zealand film industry. Jackson, a national hero on account of the *Lord Of The Rings* films and knighted earlier that year, claimed the union's action could lead to *The Hobbit* being made in Eastern Europe. Jobs for thousands of New Zealand film production workers were at stake.

In any case, he asserted, it would be illegal under New Zealand's competition law to bargain collectively with the local actors because they were all self-employed contractors – a legal interpretation contested by lawyers for the MEAA.[4]

By the time Jackson spoke out, government ministers were already being briefed on the situation and meetings arranged with the celebrated director. The dispute posed a 'serious threat' to future big-budget international film production in New Zealand, public servants advised Chris Finlayson, the minister for arts, culture and heritage. 'It is recommended that you seek Sir Peter's views on how this threat to future large budget productions can be resolved.'[5]

Jackson, with his immense popular support and political connections (he had recently completed a review of the New Zealand Film Commission for the government) had seized control of the narrative. The MEAA, which naïvely thought it could keep its negotiating gambit quiet, had been spectacularly gazumped.

As president of the CTU, Helen Kelly had come to the union's aid. Her objective was to find a way to settle what had rapidly become a highly polarised dispute.[6] Whatever she may have thought of the strategy being pursued by the local and international unions, there was a vital point of principle that needed to be defended, not just for the actors, but for the wider union movement – the right of workers to bargain collectively for their pay and conditions.

By October 20, Kelly had helped facilitate the bones of a deal. It would establish a pathway for future negotiations between the union and the film industry, and enable local actors to withdraw their threatened industrial action. The international actors' ban was being rescinded. Jackson knew that, and so did the government.[7]

As Kelly and her colleagues snacked on chips and reflected on the day's rallies, phone calls started flooding in. One was from Kelly's brother Max, a former film production worker. That afternoon he had received a text: 'If you want to save your job on The Hobbit come to Stone St Studio.'

Stone Street was a large production hub in the Wellington suburb of Miramar, co-owned by Jackson and his close associate Richard Taylor of Weta Workshop. Those who had turned up had been told the worldwide actors' ban was still in place, 'hundreds, if not thousands of jobs will be lost', and it was 'doubtful the industry itself will survive'.[8] Fired up by this information, the gathered workers had grabbed placards bearing anti-union slogans, jumped into their cars, and headed for the Willis Street church where the actors were due to meet that evening.

Arriving in the city, they marched to the church, loudly chanting 'Whipp go home! Whipp go home!' Their target was Simon Whipp, the Australian representative of the MEAA. They had been told Whipp was out to 'completely unionise' the New Zealand film industry and gain control of actors' contract negotiations, thus putting the entire sector at 'serious risk of collapse'.[9] The protesters – by then numbering about a thousand – had clearly accepted the line that the actors' union was the enemy. The dispute was no longer about a group of workers seeking an industrial negotiation with their bosses. It had spun into a battle *among* workers.

When word of the protest reached the CTU's office, a decision was made to call off the actors' meeting for fear of a dangerous confrontation.

There was good reason to be concerned about safety: venomous abuse was targeted at local actors' union representatives as the dispute wore on.

Vicious calls poured into the CTU.[10] Robyn Malcolm, an actor who had taken on the mantle of media spokesperson, received an emailed death threat.[11] The union's office in Auckland received emails dripping with bile and contempt. One read: 'You wankers will be remembered in history as the people who killed the New Zealand film industry. Fuck you very much.' Others said: 'If you don't like the money you're making … go back to sucking dicks on street corners'; 'I don't like actors. They are selfish, careless arseholes …'[12] The office had to be evacuated because it was felt Frances Walsh, the local organiser, was not safe working there alone.[13]

Although Helen Kelly had become involved only after the international actors' ban had been decided on and the dispute was entrenched, some never forgave her. Five years later, when the world heard the news that she had terminal cancer, an email arrived from an 'unelected representative' of the New Zealand film industry wishing her a 'long and painful death'.[14]

With the actors' meeting cancelled, Whipp, Malcolm, Walsh and another actor, Jennifer Ward-Lealand, headed to the CTU office. It was Malcolm's first meeting with Kelly and she was impressed by her apparent fearlessness, despite the angry workers chanting on the street below. Kelly went down to talk to the crowd, trying to explain that the dispute had been settled and the international actors' boycott was being withdrawn. If the movies ended up being made somewhere other than New Zealand, she said, it wouldn't be the fault of the actors' union; it would be because Warner Bros. could get better tax breaks elsewhere.

It was a futile effort. She was shouted down with cries of 'Bullshit!' and 'Lies!'[15] The mood was ugly, remembered fellow unionist Tom Ryan.[16]

After a few minutes the crowd marched off in the direction of Parliament, where they were addressed by Richard Taylor beside Wellington's historic war memorial cenotaph. They ended their protest with chants of 'Thank you, Richard!' and 'Thank you, PJ [Peter Jackson]!'

Kelly believed the film workers were being manipulated for political and commercial ends. She suggested to Malcolm that they head to the Matterhorn bar – where she thought many would go after the march – to again try to explain the union's side of the story. The two women talked and argued with antagonists throughout the evening. The conversations were cordial but robust. They failed to change any minds. By the end of the night, when Auckland-based Malcolm, Whipp and Walsh walked back to their hotel, the mood of civility had vanished. They were harassed by a group who followed and videoed them, repeatedly demanding of Whipp, 'Why are you targeting *The Hobbit*, Simon?'

The actors' union had been completely out-manoeuvred. Plans were underway for Warner Bros. executives to come to New Zealand the following week. The government would meet them to see if *The Hobbit* could be 'saved'. At the same time as Kelly and Malcolm were debating with protesting film workers at the Matterhorn, an adviser to minister of economic development Gerry Brownlee was emailing a studio representative to assure him that the Hollywood executives would receive VIP treatment, including Crown cars and Diplomatic Protection Squad security. 'We will make them very welcome in our country,' wrote the aide.[17] That night, Jackson issued a public statement claiming Warners were on their way to New Zealand to make arrangements to move *The Hobbit* out of New Zealand.

The dispute was over. The MEAA had guaranteed there would be no industrial disruption, and the international actors' ban was being lifted. Yet the following days were marked by hysterical media attention, fuelled by Jackson's claims of looming disaster. A radio announcer told Kelly she appeared to have 'lost *The Hobbit*'. She retorted that Jackson was behaving like a 'spoilt brat'.[18] Jackson described her on national television as clueless; Brownlee – who had chaired a key meeting to resolve the dispute – accused her of lying.[19]

When Kelly picked up her daily paper, *The Dominion Post*, on October 21, the front page shouted '*The Hobbit* looks headed overseas' over a story reporting that Jackson blamed the unions for the likely loss. The next day, the film-maker was again on the front page, looking glum and saying, 'We may as well not live here.'[20]

Vitriol poured into Kelly's inbox. One emailer called her 'a stupid little woman'; another described her as 'despicable' and 'Pat Kelly's sprog'.[21] The reference was to her beloved father, a unionist who had died six years earlier.

An influential business lobby group even demanded reassurance that the trade unions wouldn't 'Hobbit the Rugby World Cup', which was to be held in New Zealand the following year.[22]

Out of the fog of invective, another issue came into view. Several years earlier James Bryson, a model-maker working on *The Lord Of The Rings*, had challenged his employment status through the courts. He had ostensibly been engaged as a self-employed contractor, but when he was laid off he went to the Employment Court to claim he had been unfairly dismissed.

The claim could be heard only if Bryson was an employee. Applying well-established and orthodox legal principles, the court found that he was indeed an employee (for instance, he wasn't allowed to work for any other company and had fixed hours).[23] This meant he was entitled to the protections of employment law, such as the right to be paid at least the minimum wage and to have recourse against unfair dismissal. The Employment Court's decision had been overturned by the Court of Appeal but subsequently restored by the Supreme Court in 2005.

For five years the decision had sat as settled law. But Jackson and Warners had been privately telling the government that the Bryson case caused 'uncertainty' and they were 'spooked' by it.[24] Brownlee had been initially unmoved; he had advised Jackson that any uncertainty could be dealt with by getting legal advice.[25] Now he was suggesting the Bryson decision was such a problem for the industry that the government might have to 'clarify' the law.[26]

On October 25 – Labour Day – thousands rallied in support of *The Hobbit*, waving placards proclaiming 'Hobbits are loyal' and 'We love Middle Earth'. According to John Key, the public response showed that unions were 'out of touch with everyday New Zealanders' and 'had the weight of the country against them'.[27]

The Warners executives, who arrived in Wellington that day, got the message loud and clear that New Zealanders were on their side. They met Key the following day. Officials from Crown Law were told to be on standby at Premier House, the prime minister's residence, during the high-level meeting in case advice was needed on changing the country's employment law.[28] Department of Labour officials had that day furnished advice to the minister of labour, Kate Wilkinson, on the Bryson case and options for resolving the 'uncertainty that has arisen in the film industry'.[29] The front page of *The Dominion Post* blared: 'Hobbit fans warned we could lose it all.'[30]

The visitors from Hollywood were well rewarded for their long flight across the Pacific. On top of the existing taxpayer subsidies designed to lure big-budget films to New Zealand, the Warner executives were promised an extra $33 million. The likely total subsidy for *The Hobbit* would now be around $100 million.[31] The law would be changed immediately to exclude film production workers from the protection of employment law by stipulating that they were self-employed independent contractors.

The deal guaranteed *The Hobbit* would be made in New Zealand and would 'safeguard work for thousands of New Zealanders', Key claimed. It would 'allow us to follow the success of *The Lord Of The Rings* trilogy in once again promoting New Zealand on the world stage'.[32]

The law change was rushed through Parliament under urgency on October 28 and 29, There was no public input and no scrutiny by a select committee. It came into effect the following day.

Helen Kelly stood in the parliamentary office of Labour MP and former CTU secretary Carol Beaumont and watched as the legislation was rammed through the House. 'A sovereign country has sold its soul to a multinational,' she told reporters. She was shocked, upset and angry.[33] In Parliament's debating chamber, government members berated her involvement in the dispute and Brownlee accused her of doing 'irreparable damage' to the union movement.[34]

It had been a brutal, bruising month. People who would not previously have been able to name New Zealand's top trade unionist were now aware of Helen Kelly: she was that woman who had the effrontery to challenge the colossus that was Peter Jackson, and to advocate for workers who – as *The Dominion Post*'s editorial writer put it – had '[bitten] the hand that feeds them'.

Some unionists feared the *Hobbit* dispute had burned through precious political capital at a time when basic worker rights were under more general attack by the government. Kelly acknowledged this risk in a long letter to the prime minister on the eve of the *Hobbit* legislation: 'We realise that the *Hobbit* dispute provides a political context where the government may simply want to push through these unfair changes on the basis of your strong criticism of the role of unions,' she wrote. 'We hope you will not do this.'[35]

The November meeting of the CTU's governing body, the National Affiliates Council, was certain to witness some testy debate about how the whole thing had played out. One prominent union leader, Andrew Little of the Engineering, Printing and Manufacturing Union (EPMU) – the country's largest private sector union – had already publicly attacked the actors' union's handling of the dispute, calling it an 'absolute disaster'.[36] It was unlikely he was alone in that view.

As it turned out, only a brief mention of *The Hobbit* was recorded in the minutes of the meeting. By then the nation was grief-stricken and shocked by a genuine catastrophe. There had been a series of massive explosions in the recently opened Pike River underground coal mine on the South Island's West Coast. The first had occurred on the afternoon of November 19, 2010. Twenty-nine workers were dead; two had miraculously escaped. It was the worst industrial disaster in almost a century.

Kelly, who before the disaster knew little of the Pike project, travelled to the West Coast and offered assistance where she could to the EPMU, which had lost eleven members. As the families of the 29 men began to emerge from the glare of international publicity and consider how to get answers, and recovery of their loved ones' bodies from the mine, she encouraged them to come together as an organised group.

In the terrible days and weeks after the disaster, the mine company's top manager, Peter Whittall, was fêted in the media for his apparent compassion and clear communication. At the national memorial service held on December 2 he sat on the stage alongside the prime minister and other dignitaries. Some newspaper readers were so impressed they thought he should be named New Zealander of the Year.[37]

Kelly was outraged and said so publicly. 'He's now been called a national hero, but he's the CEO of that company and he hasn't apologised,' she said. 'That mine was open for just over a year. There are 29 miners dead. We've got to be more mature about who we honour, how we think about things, what we demand. … [T]he hard questions have not been asked.'[38]

How dare she! 'Fresh from the PR triumph of attacking Sir Peter Jackson, the CTU continues its strategy of winning over the public by targeting Peter Whittall,' harrumphed blogger David Farrar.[39] Toxic correspondence arrived in her inbox: 'My God woman,' wrote one affronted man. 'You nearly kill off The Hobbit … And now you have the insensitivity to start attacking people at Pike who are doing a job YOU know absolutly [*sic*] nothing about.'[40]

Kelly had known from childhood that abuse and intimidation came with the territory of trade union work. But there was more to it than that: something had galvanised in her. She was angry. Bloody angry. The *Hobbit* debacle and the Pike calamity were chapters in a generation-long economic and political narrative in which businesses were cast as generous benefactors and workers as supplicants who were 'lucky to have a job … Workers that make a fuss are depicted as ungrateful.'[41]

For a generation, the voice of New Zealand workers had been drowned by the chorus that demanded fewer business constraints and more freedom, a generation in which employees had become variable costs to be defrayed or outsourced for competitive advantage. Now one group of 29 had paid for that narrative with their lives, and another with the removal of basic legal rights.

Harnessing her radical heritage, the mana of her position and her charismatic ability to charm and inveigle others into her causes, Helen Kelly would spend the remainder of her life fighting a hard, stubborn, defiant and exhausting fight to create a new story for New Zealand workers.

1. Red Siren

You have to keep going. You don't win anything without a struggle. And even when you do win it, it tends to disappear unless you keep on putting in the effort. *Cath Kelly*

Growing up in Wellington, Helen Kelly had no need to chart her own youthful rebellion. In the old villa in Shannon Street, Mt Victoria, where she spent her childhood and in which she lived the last years of her life, fervent political activism was a way of life. The house was stacked with protest pamphlets, trade union journals and communist literature from New Zealand and abroad. The front room, with its panoramic view over Wellington's harbour and city centre, was a smoke-filled hub for activists and organisers. Helen and her brother Max were raised from the cradle on their father Pat's stories of growing up poor and malnourished on the Liverpool docks, their mother Cath's tales of road-building in Tito's Yugoslavia, and the language of class struggle.

The house was a nerve centre for organising against multiple evils – the war in Vietnam, the apartheid regime in South Africa, the fascists in control of Chile, the rapacious capitalists at home who must be checked by strong trade unions.

'Our house was full of politics the entire time,' Helen said in a 2013 interview. 'We used to get woken up in the morning by my mother saying, "Arise ye workers from your slumbers." So it was completely in our blood.'[1]

It was a household that expanded readily and often to accommodate waifs, strays, fellow travellers, rank-and-file workers and neighbourhood kids. Chairman Mao's portrait was proudly on display and the government's spies were watching.[2]

When other teenagers in the late 1970s and early '80s were experimenting with alcohol and dope, sneaking out bedroom windows at night and challenging their parents' social mores and political beliefs, Helen Kelly was a straight-laced and loyal protégé of Cath and Pat Kelly's values.

Helen's mother Cath Eichelbaum had bought the house in Shannon Street in 1954, when she was a 28-year-old member of the small but active Communist Party of New Zealand. Cath was a striking dark-haired beauty – in one of its many communist-baiting headlines, *Truth* newspaper named her the 'Red Siren'.[3] Mt Victoria was a working-class suburb and the house was regarded as something of a slum. Uncarpeted floors sloped away due to decaying piles, there was no drive-on access, and it was surrounded by other run-down places. But Cath had taken one look at the magnificent view from the front window and decided to buy it. It cost £2900, a sum she had access to after she and her sisters inherited and sold the large Thorndon home of her well-to-do parents Siegfried and Vera Eichelbaum.[4]

Cath was born in March 1926, the youngest of four Eichelbaum girls, all of whom became communists despite their privileged upbringing. Siegfried was likely scandalised by their views: after he died in August 1952 his daughters discovered he had been a card-carrying member of the National Party.

'Sieg was a solid middle-class New Zealander, totally conservative in thought and deed, and increasingly outnumbered by these five females [including his liberal wife, Vera] whose line of thinking was different to his and who generally brought home boyfriends who were more of their thinking than his,' Cath's cousin Thomas Eichelbaum would remember.[5]

Siegfried was a reluctant businessman. He had trained as a lawyer but never practised, instead stepping in to help his invalid father Max, who was manager of the New Zealand branch of S. Oppenheimer &

Company, an American firm that manufactured animal casings for sausages, tennis strings and medical sutures. When Max died, Siegfried took over his role.[6]

Consignment telegrams would arrive at the elegant Eichelbaum home, notifying that a tonnage of North Island sheep's bungs had arrived at Petone, where they would be processed before being shipped to the US for the production of frankfurters, or that a shipment of American pigs' bungs had arrived in Wellington for manufacture into the fat sausages that New Zealanders preferred.[7]

Siegfried and Vera were well known in Wellington's professional and academic circles. 'Sieg' served for 29 years on the council of Victoria University College and for seven years on the senate of the University of New Zealand.[8] He was clever, witty and cultured. Gordon Dryden, a former Communist Party member who courted Cath in the early 1950s, recalled being corrected by Sieg for being off-key when humming Beethoven's Fifth Symphony at the Eichelbaum home one evening.

Dryden described the rambling two-storeyed house in Fitzherbert Terrace – later demolished to make way for the Wellington motorway – as 'one of the very nicest' in the area.[9] Among the Eichelbaum's near neighbours was the American ambassador, with whom Siegfried was good friends.[10] The last home of Katherine Mansfield before she left for England was along the street.[11]

Before marrying Siegfried in 1915, Vera had studied art in Paris, been art mistress at Chilton Saint James private school for girls in Lower Hutt, and displayed her work at the New Zealand Academy of Fine Arts before the conventions of marriage required her to desist from exhibiting. She came from a prominent New Zealand legal family, the Chapmans. Her grandfather, Henry Samuel Chapman, had emigrated from England to become a judge of the Supreme Court's southern district in 1843, and her father, Frederick Chapman, was the first New Zealand-born judge of the Supreme Court. Her uncle, Martin Chapman, founded the law firm Chapman Tripp.[12]

Vera and Siegfried brought up Cath and her sisters in an environment of security and comfort. Education was a high priority and the girls went to school at the fee-paying Queen Margaret College, over the road from the family home. All four went on to study at university or Teachers'

College. Cath was sporty and active with Girl Guides, swimming, tennis, tramping and camping. The family holidayed every summer in a rented bach at the seaside village of Paremata just north of Wellington, where they would swim and fish, and Vera would paint.

The four girls were strongly influenced by their mother's liberal tendencies and sense of social justice.[13] Vera was greatly concerned by the poverty she witnessed during the Depression years. She gave her time to charities assisting the unemployed and helped set up the Free Kindergarten Association to make it easier for mothers to earn an income. Possibly unbeknown to Siegfried, she supported Michael Joseph Savage's Labour Party at the 1935 election.[14]

Everyone in the Fitzherbert Terrace household was disturbed by the rise of fascism in Europe throughout the 1930s, particularly given the family's Jewish roots. Siegfried Eichelbaum was descended from a wealthy East Prussian Jewish merchant who had 14 children, including Siegfried's father Max, who emigrated to the United States, where Siegfried was born in San Francisco. Max later moved his family to Wellington to run Oppenheimer's New Zealand operation and over the years the links with the big extended family in Germany fell away.

But with the rise of Hitler's National Socialists in Europe, Jewish refugees started trickling into Wellington. Vera helped many of them to settle and some became friends of the household. When Cath was nine, letters addressed to Siegfried began arriving from long-lost German relatives seeking advice on immigrating to New Zealand. In 1935 news reached them that Siegfried's cousin Walter Eichelbaum, a lawyer in the city of Königsberg, had been badly affected by the Nazis' policy of barring Jews from practising their profession. That Walter had suffered a severe head injury while serving in the German army in the First World War, and that he had renounced his Jewish faith, was of no consequence – he now had no way to support himself, his Christian wife Frida and their young son Thomas.

For the next two and a half years Siegfried kept Walter informed of the New Zealand government's policy towards the immigration of Germans. At first there was no hope. Siegfried put his cousin's case to officials at the Customs Department, who advised that while 'a number of Germans had in recent years come here, since then strict regulations had come into force, under which further immigration from Europe was absolutely stopped'.[15]

There followed a brief period of openness under the 1935 Labour government before the door was again slammed shut to all but British subjects. It is clear from the excruciatingly patient and sometimes mundane correspondence during 1936 and 1937 – which included details on the cost of living in New Zealand and the merits of bringing linen and furniture from Germany – that neither Walter nor Siegfried had any notion of Hitler's crazed determination to eliminate Jews nor of the unimaginable horrors to come.

Eventually Siegfried made a personal call on the Labour government's minister of customs, Walter Nash, who in March 1938 granted approval for Walter, Frida, Thomas and Walter's nephew Peter Brinkman to come to New Zealand. By that time their lives were hanging by a thread and it is unlikely they would have got into the country if not for Siegfried's intervention.[16] They arrived in July, having been forced to leave behind Walter's elderly widowed mother Sophie in Berlin. Siegfried was required to sign a bond guaranteeing they would not be a burden on the state.

Other relatives wrote to Siegfried with pleas for assistance. 'I ask you with all my heart to help us, as we don't know anybody all over the world who could do anything for us,' wrote a desperate cousin in December 1938. 'You are our last and only hope.' He was forced to reply that he had exhausted his influence because of his frequent approaches to government officials on behalf of Walter's family and the 'numerous other relatives who have written to me, with the same request, but without my being able to achieve any success'.[17] The full extent of the casualties suffered in the Holocaust by the extended Eichelbaum family is unknown, but at least 12 perished.[18]

Thomas Eichelbaum was seven when he arrived with his parents into the welcoming arms of Siegfried, Vera and their daughters. Walter and Frida struggled in New Zealand, where anti-German sentiment was strong and Walter's law qualification was not recognised. He worked for years as a labourer in a woolstore before getting work as a government legal clerk.[19] Thomas trained as a lawyer, working for many years in the family firm, Chapman Tripp, and would become a reforming and empathetic chief justice.

With the war still raging and American soldiers enlivening Wellington's social life, Cath left Queen Margaret College in 1943 with a testimonial from the headmistress remarking on her 'very good ability and ... quick, eager, active and questioning intelligence ... She is independent in outlook, quick in sympathy, with a strong sense of fair-play ... I judge that she will bring a rich humanity to whatever work in life she undertakes.'[20]

She went up the hill to Victoria University to study for a Bachelor of Arts and continued to excel at swimming – in part because of the dogged determination that would later characterise her political activism. With the university sports coming up but the Thorndon swimming pool closed for the winter, she would climb over the wall to continue her training. The unattended pool became increasingly filthy and littered with fallen leaves and dead rats. Her only concession to the putrid conditions was to swim with her eyes open. 'At least they weren't live rats,' she told her friend Pat Webster years later.[21] Her reward was a University Blue.

She was a member of the Student Christian Movement, a progressive group that had some dealings with the university's Socialist Club. The war years had instilled in her a hatred of fascism and racism but she wasn't yet drawn to the communist movement, which reached the peak of its popularity in New Zealand during the last two years of the Second World War. She was hanging her hopes for humanity on God rather than politics: 'I thought that Christianity could change the world and make it better. That's why I was attracted to religion. Brotherly love was in short supply.'[22]

It was a trip to Yugoslavia in 1948, when she was 22, that convinced Cath the solution to the world's ills lay with communism. After graduation she had gone to England in early 1947, travelling with the family of a close friend. Accustomed to the rarefied life of Fitzherbert Terrace, she disapproved of the drinking, gossip and flirtations on the six-week journey aboard the *Dominion Monarch*. She spent a year training to be a teacher at the Institute of Education – part of London University – and was periodically invited to meetings of the British Communist Party.

When she finished her training she joined a programme, run by the National Union of Students, that was helping to rebuild war-shattered regions in Europe. She elected to join a work brigade headed for a village halfway between Zagreb and Belgrade. The Soviets had split with Tito's Yugoslavia just weeks before and Siegfried and Vera wrote her agitated letters – they were afraid war would break out and worried for her safety. But she was determined: 'I'd paid my money and it was all I had, and I wanted to go.'[23]

Cath was one of only four or five women in the group of 96, half of whom were students and the other half workers. Until then the only communists she had known were students and intellectuals, people she thought would abandon their revolutionary convictions as soon as they acquired status and wealth. Now she was cheek by jowl with British workers entrapped by their class, whose communist beliefs were the product of their families' economic struggles.

She and the other members of her work group laboured on the roads from early in the morning until driven indoors by the searing heat. They lived in huts, and with food in desperately short supply survived on a diet consisting mostly of brown bread. In the evenings there were lectures on Marxist-Leninist thought.

The ideological turning point came on a billeted visit to a middle-class family in Belgrade. The family was cultured and educated, much like her own family in Thorndon, and at first she identified with them. But as she chatted to them in German she became appalled by their narrow self-interest. They had been deprived by the new communist regime of their status and privileges, including their country house and access to the theatre, and were bitterly dissatisfied.

At the end of the visit, Cath asked them, 'What would you like to see now? How could it get better?'

'They said, "America will come again and make war on the Russians." They were prepared to have another war! There had been slaughter and a terrible war, but to get their privileges back they were prepared for that,' she would tell researcher Lesley Hall. 'I thought: that's the meaning of politics. People want what they can get for themselves, not what they can do to improve the world.'[24]

She returned to London – sleeping rough on railway benches en route through northern Italy – and decided to join the British Communist Party. She had hovered at the fringes but now it made absolute sense to her. In her short lifetime, the established capitalist order had produced the devastating poverty of the Great Depression, a disastrous world war, violent fascism and genocide, and yet the wealthy classes were still determined to hold on to their privileges.

It was a pivotal decision that launched a life of activism. She abandoned any thought of working as a classroom teacher and instead found work as a typist and went to night school to learn shorthand. She would deploy these skills over decades of radical campaigning, leaflet- and newsletter-writing and administration of activist groups.

Against a background of rising Cold War tensions and hostility towards communism, Cath was a dedicated foot soldier for the party. She sold its newspaper the *Daily Worker* outside London's tube stations and on roadsides on freezing mornings. On Sundays she would go door to door, seeking recruits and attempting to counter the anti-Soviet rhetoric that had displaced post-war gratitude to the Russians for their role in defeating Hitler.

For a radical young woman London was exciting. She attended talks, demonstrations and rallies, pasted up posters and painted graffiti on walls. She got arrested at a protest against German rearmament, and campaigned against the Korean War, which broke out in 1950. She went to communist education groups and worked for a time in a left-wing bookshop, and for the communist-dominated Fire Brigade Union. She attended concerts and speeches by her idol Paul Robeson, the African American singer, actor and civil rights activist.[25]

Siegfried worried about the consequences of his daughter's activism. On one occasion he arrived in London after a business trip to the US to discover she had just been on a deputation to the American embassy against the Korean War. Cath cast fierce judgement on what she saw as her father's selfish reaction: 'He didn't like it because he might be in trouble. He thought he'd never get another visa for America after that.'[26]

In early 1952, after five years away, Cath reluctantly returned home to Fitzherbert Terrace as Siegfried was ill with leukaemia. He would die about six months later. Thirteen months after this, her mother, Vera, would die of breast cancer.

She got a job as a shorthand typist in the Department of Māori Affairs and joined the Communist Party of New Zealand and other activist groups, including the Progressive Youth League and the Wellington

Peace Council, of which she became secretary. From the early 1950s she was increasingly interested in, and horrified by, events in Vietnam, where the French were fighting a losing US-funded battle to retain control of their colony. In the aftermath the country was divided into the communist north and anti-communist south, and the conditions set for the terrible war that was to come. Her nascent interest in Vietnam's struggle was to strengthen through her years of protest against the war and develop into a life-long humanitarian involvement in the country.[27]

Cath's activities in Wellington's left-wing network were of considerable interest to the security services, who regarded her as a 'well-indoctrinated and active communist who would constitute a security risk in any position where she might have access to secret information'.[28] The snooping was at times farcical. In an account of his life undercover in the 1950s, the former spy George Fraser described attending the 'sumptuously furnished' Eichelbaum drawing room in Fitzherbert Terrace, where Cath and her sister Margaret ran meetings of the Communist Party's Wellington city branch. 'In the huge and elegant drawing room, rank-and-file branch members drew up strategies for street marches and poster pasting, with political discussion mainly led by Comrade Cath. She was a striking beauty who would turn the head of any red-blooded male, but it was her sometimes searing attacks and plans for retribution on the conservative politicians in the nearby Parliament Buildings which drained that blood away,' Fraser wrote. 'There was even a post-revolution commitment among the group to "stringing up those Labour Party lapdogs of American imperialism" on the telegraph poles which at that time lined the main thoroughfare to Parliament.'[29]

Fraser wrote of his decision to carry a .22 starting pistol to provide some protection in case his cover was blown. The weapon could 'discharge eight deafening shots in rapid fire. It also looked remarkably like the real McCoy'. He carried it in his pocket to the next party meeting at the Eichelbaum home, but when he slumped back on an 'ornately decorated and cushioned settee' the pistol dropped out of his pocket and slid down the back of the couch. As members continued their discussion about circulation figures of the party newspaper, *People's Voice*, he managed to manoeuvre the weapon back into his pocket, only to have it slip out again when a comrade thumped back down on to the sofa in the midst of a vigorous debate. This time the gun disappeared into the bowels of the furniture. Fraser managed to recover it later in the night and escape with his cover intact.

More often, however, the spies observed and recorded prosaic details of Cath's life of activism: attendance at Progressive Youth League camps and tramps, at Peace Council public meetings and socials, and at Communist Party education classes and meetings.[30]

As in London, Cath Eichelbaum was a hard-working and committed party member. She served as secretary of the Wellington city branch, went as a delegate to district and national conferences, and wrote leaflets. She door-knocked and canvassed, and sold the *People's Voice* on Cuba Street, in factories and in working-class pubs. Anyone who bought a paper was followed up, in a bid to engage with them about the party's ideas and to establish a permanent readership.

George Fraser may have been alarmed by her revolutionary fervour, but Cath knew that life in New Zealand was far too comfortable and prosperous for there to be any prospect of armed struggle against the capitalist state. 'There were rich and poor, but the gap between them was not so great. People could get jobs ... If they weren't getting enough [money] they could organise through their union or go down the road and get another one.'[31]

She saw the party's role, and her task as an acolyte, as encouraging workers to 'understand that this capitalist system would not work for them. But we didn't think we were going to do that in a hurry – we hoped we were a sort of a force leaning towards the understanding of the capitalist system'.

It must have been thankless work much of the time, but she did it with a steely sense of duty. 'You couldn't say you enjoyed canvassing or selling [the *People's Voice*] but I never stopped to say, "Do I like doing this?" because I thought it had to be done. It was an attitude I had. There were other people, particularly the men who worked in trade unions, who wouldn't canvass because they hated it ... But I used to think, "If it's got to be done, you do it." I didn't stop and think, "Oh, I'd rather be home today."'

On one occasion, when she went into a Wellington pub with party newspapers tucked under her arm, a naval rating came up behind her and set them alight. 'The whole bar turned on him and gave him a bad time,' she told Hall. She was unharmed, but the young man incurred the stony wrath for which she later became known in left-wing circles. 'I turned on him like an angry mother, which always frightens men I think. We put the paper out and carried on.'[32]

Her loyalty to the party didn't falter despite incessant hostility towards communism from both Labour and National politicians, declining membership, internal schisms and the departure of her three sisters from its ranks. Allegiance carried a personal toll – she was barred from some public service jobs because of her affiliation and surveillance was a fact of life.[33]

She stuck with the party, too, when many others quit following the denunciation of 'Uncle Joe' Stalin – who had died in 1953 – by First Secretary Nikita Khrushchev in a speech to the 20th Congress of the Soviet Union in February 1956 in which he attacked Stalin's reign of terror and cult of personality. At first, members of the New Zealand party discounted the reports of Khrushchev's speech and attributed the stories to capitalist propaganda. When confirmation of Stalin's murderous record came through Communist Party channels, they descended into infighting and accusations.

A few months after the Khrushchev revelations came another event that sent shockwaves through communist parties worldwide. Soviet tanks rolled into Hungary in November 1956 to crush a popular revolution and restore communist rule. Three thousand citizens were killed and 200,000 fled as refugees. It was the last straw for some New Zealand party activists, including Gordon Dryden, who had become increasingly disillusioned while working as a journalist on the *People's Voice*.[34] Others were expelled for criticising the Soviet action in Hungary. They included the party's one-time general secretary Sid Scott, who had dared to publish his views in the 'capitalist' *New Zealand Herald*, and Wellington stalwart Connie Birchfield, who had campaigned as a Communist Party candidate in national and local elections over almost two decades.[35]

The events in distant countries, over which Cath and other New Zealand activists had no control, were not enough to shake her conviction. She told Hall that she never strayed from the beliefs that had drawn her into the party – 'the principles of equality, of no exploitation of man by man, of the ownership of the means of production'.[36]

Cath also became an activist in her union, the Public Service Association (PSA). She was a delegate, a member of the Women's Committee, and part of Kōrero, an unofficial left-wing ginger group that pushed progressive policies and worked to get sympathisers on to the union executive. Its influence in the PSA drew persistent attention from the security services and *Truth* newspaper.[37]

In 1955 Cath became a key player in the PSA's campaign for pay equity in the public service. Despite New Zealand women being the first in the world to achieve the right to vote, by the 1950s the country was lagging internationally in its treatment of women in the workforce. Her friend and fellow party member Rona Bailey had been prominent in the fight for equal pay from the 1940s but progress was halting.

Cath's involvement began at a lunchtime meeting of PSA members in February 1955, when 200 women voted unanimously to support any attempts to introduce equal pay and opportunity for women in the public service. Among those elected on to a 12-person committee to mount a new campaign were Cath and Margaret Brand.[38] The two women and later their families became close friends.

'We held lunchtime women's meetings in all the government departments to convince women they were worthy of equal pay,' Cath later told her friend Anne Goodman. 'The level of activism was great … Buffet teas were a big organising tool. We would invite a speaker and sell tickets. It amused us that here we were, non-respectable women, doing such a respectable task as having a buffet tea.'[39]

By now, Cath had a Gestetner machine at her house, which enabled her to 'run off leaflets … in the dead of night'.[40]

One of the campaign's key supporters was Bill Sutch, a prominent and controversial public servant who was then economist at the Department of Industries and Commerce.[41] Sutch's analysis showed the assumption that men needed higher pay because they had dependents to support was mostly false. The majority of men didn't have dependents while many women did, including elderly parents.

The turning point in the campaign was the case of a Dunedin public servant. Jean Parker was a clerk in the Inland Revenue Department who had been appointed to the position of section leader in charge of eight staff. The disparity between men and women in public service pay scales was such that, even with her experience and responsibility, she earned less than what a male cadet could earn.

After the PSA successfully appealed to the Public Service Appeal Board, the Public Service Commission instructed the IRD to reduce Parker's pay and responsibilities. This set the equal pay campaign alight. Women's groups around the country were outraged and there was a snap debate in Parliament. However, four more years of political prevarication followed before the prime minister, Walter Nash, introduced the Government Service Equal Pay Bill in the dying days of the second Labour government.

The bill was the product of deft work by PSA general secretary Jack Turnbull. Years of procrastination by Nash's government meant time was running out to get legislation through Parliament before the general election on November 26, 1960, so Turnbull worked with Crown Law officials to draft a bill while Nash was out of the country. Cath later told historian Mark Derby that the prime minister was presented with the bill on his return as a 'virtual fait accompli'.[42]

With his government holding a majority of just one seat in Parliament and facing likely defeat at the polls, Nash insisted there be no publicity about the impending introduction of the bill.[43] Consequently, after years of intensive campaigning and organising, the women who had done so much to create this historic achievement almost missed the moment when equal pay for public servants was codified into law. On the night of October 25, 1960, after the radio broadcast from Parliament had gone off the air, Cath and her co-campaigners received excited phone calls. 'On the night it went through we were all in bed. ... Somebody rang round and said, "It's in the House, it's being debated now." So I sprang into a taxi, which I never did at an ordinary time,' Cath told Derby.[44]

They got there in time to witness Keith Holyoake's National Party vote to support the bill, allowing it to pass unanimously.

Cath had helped bring about a far-reaching breakthrough for New Zealand women, yet she refused to identify herself as a feminist. She saw everything through the lens of class struggle: feminism was regarded as a bourgeois diversion and an erosion of class solidarity. 'I see the class issue as the major issue,' she told Hall. 'The capitalist class oppresses the working class, men and women.'[45]

During the 1950s, the house in Shannon Street was a hub for left-wing parties and communist meetings. Ken Douglas – a young rising force in the union movement and president of the militant Wellington Drivers' Union – was inducted into the party in the front room.[46]

A fellow activist named Paul Potiki lived in the house for a time. Cath had met him through her job at the Department of Māori Affairs and he had become a convert to the Communist Party. Potiki was articulate and handsome and the relationship was serious, but Potiki was married. The couple made no attempt to hide their unconventional cohabitation. 'We became rather open about it … There were no secrets around,' Cath told Pat Webster.

Potiki's wife refused to grant him a divorce, for which Cath would later say she was grateful. 'We would have married and he would have treated me the way he treated all the women in his life – very casually and deceitfully. I had to offload him, which wasn't easy.'[47]

The transition was made gentler by the entry into Cath's life of a slightly built Communist Party member from Auckland. Pat Kelly was a Liverpudlian of Irish Catholic descent with little formal education. He was funny, loquacious and warm, and when Cath met him his leg was in plaster as a result of a serious motorbike accident.

Pat Kelly would joke that his marriage to Cath was arranged by the party.[48] Certainly the hierarchy interfered in the private lives of its members, often attempting to put a stop to behaviour deemed damaging to its already negative public profile.[49] A witness to Cath and Pat's early courting, Meg Bailey, said it was her parents, party members Rona and Chip Bailey, who conducted the matchmaking. 'They were very good at it. Apparently, it went on quite a bit. I always remember my parents peeking around doors to see what was happening.'[50]

The marriage of Cath Eichelbaum, 34, to Pat Kelly, 30, took place at the Wellington Registry Office on November 3, 1960, ten days after Pat proposed and a few days after the Government Service Equal Pay Act passed into law. The witnesses were Cath's close friend and fellow equal pay campaigner, Margaret Long (née Brand) and Pat's friend, mentor, trade unionist and fellow party member Bill Andersen. Cath took half a day off work; the registry office was next door and her colleagues discovered she had married only when one of them looked out the window and saw the small wedding party emerge.[51]

Just a few days earlier, *Truth* had published a front-page story about an alleged communist plot, involving Paul Potiki and the alluring 'Red Siren', to take over the nation's electricity system.[52]

After the wedding Pat returned to Auckland, where he canvassed for the Communist Party's candidates in the coming general election, looked for work that wouldn't impede the recovery of his injured leg, and waited for Cath to get a public service transfer north. They kept in touch through letters full of politics, organising and hopes for their life together. They had spent a total of 13 days in each other's company.

'A fair sort of morning selling 18 F.M.N. [*Fight Monopoly Now*] pamphlets and two P.V. [*People's Voice*],' Pat wrote on November 13, ten days after their marriage. The next day Cath wrote that in her impatience to get on with her new domestic life she risked 'forgetting my Bolshevik duties'.[53]

They came from opposite sides of the globe and opposite ends of the social spectrum, but they were bound by two common desires: to have a family and to continue the struggle for a better deal for the workers of the world.

2. From Bootle to Shangri-La

I made one commitment as I began to understand the world in which I lived – to serve to the best of my ability to see that no other children lived through what we went through. *Pat Kelly*

Pat Kelly was born in the Bootle docks, above the office of the Scalers' Union. His grandfather was the union's secretary, representing men who earned a wage by scraping down ships and cleaning boilers. Bootle, part of greater Liverpool but staunchly independent, was a working-class borough dominated by the seaport and heavy industry. The Kellys were surrounded by the families of dockers, seamen, scalers and labourers, many struggling to eke a living on the wharves and in the borough's warehouses and factories.

When Pat was born in November 1929, the world economy was in collapse and unemployment was becoming pervasive – as many as one in four was out of work in Bootle by 1931.[1] Pat's father, also Patrick, was a dock worker, but throughout the Depression he had no regular employment. By the time the economy began to improve, he was so ill with the bowel cancer that would kill him at the age of 39 that he was unable to work.

Like many of the families crowded into substandard, unsanitary housing along the docks, Patrick and Nora Kelly and their five children survived on parish relief, weekly loans from the local pawn shop, and the mutual support of neighbours. Hunger and deprivation also turned them into small-time enterpreneurs, occasional beggars and petty thieves.

'There was no real food in the house. There was never fruit and not much in the way of vegetables. It was mainly jam and bread. There was not so much jam – bread and margarine, and not a great deal at all,' Pat would later recall.[2]

Patrick got assistance from the Dockers Union, and also qualified for some medical help.[3] The medicine prescribed for what was then called 'yellow jaundice' was the health drink Horlicks. To garner a few extra pennies Patrick would sell the prescription back to his doctor. 'I think the Horlicks was about ninepence a jar at the time, and he used to get sixpence for the prescription, so he was actually going without what he needed to sustain him to bring the sixpence back for other purposes,' Pat remembered.[4]

Those dockers who had work were paid on Saturdays at lunchtime. Malnourished kids like Pat Kelly knew that was the time to hang around the dock gates in the hope of receiving a ha'penny, a penny, or at least a leftover sandwich from a lunch bag. 'There were lots of children in that situation. We were all brought up on the basis that you stuck together and got what you could, and of course we were all thieves.'[5]

Pat and his older brother Charlie stole lengths of timber, chopped it and sold it as bundles of firewood before the family developed the idea into a more organised and lawful enterprise. Patrick hired a handcart from the local milkman for threepence a time and negotiated a legitimate supply of wood offcuts from a nearby box factory at the rate of sixpence per cartload. Pat, Charlie and their oldest sibling Marie would stack as much wood as possible into the cart then wheel it home, where it would be chopped into lengths and bundled. The cart would be returned to the milkman, and Pat and Charlie would load the bundles into a pram and sell them door-to-door and to local shops, earning twopence for five bundles. For almost two years they were able to bring in as much as a pound or twenty-five shillings a week from their wood round, until the outbreak of war put an end to the business.[6]

All Pat knew was the weekly rhythm of subsistence. Twice a week the family would visit Stanley's pawnshop; on a Monday morning the community would meet there, 'all pawning their husbands' suits and the children's best Sunday clothes, to be redeemed the following Saturday,' Pat wrote in a series of unpublished stories about his childhood. 'It was always the same families. Whether the husband had secured any work determined the size of the "bundle".'

Just enough was pawned to see them through the week. It was a foregone conclusion, however, that if the husband owned a suit, it would be the principal item to pawn. 'My Dad's suit always went in on Monday and came out again on Saturday morning for the weekend.'[7]

The family moved several times within Bootle before war broke out in 1939. About five years were spent in a two-up two-down in a ubiquitous row of red-brick terraced houses built to accommodate workers for the docks and factories. The family was surrounded by other poor working-class families, many of whom were, like the Kellys, Catholics whose forebears had crossed the Irish Sea to escape famine or civil unrest.

Their rented house – like all the others in the area – had neither hot water nor a bath. The toilet was outside in the small backyard, and in winter the place was damp and cold. They seldom had enough cash to buy coal for heating and the children's bedding was supplemented by Patrick's and Nora's coats. Despite Nora's best efforts to keep the house clean, 'we all suffered from head and body lice and bed bugs, and not infrequently there were rats, particularly when the sewers overflowed. As kids, I think we all took this for granted.'[8]

Some families were better off, and one of Pat's enduring memories was of the quiet, practical assistance that neighbours would provide his parents. On one side was the local bookmaker, who operated his illegal business using runners to take bets on commission from punters – all of whom gambled under nom-de-plumes for fear of prosecution. The bookie's wife, Kate Cunningham, was aware of the nom-de-plume Nora Kelly used for her occasional flutter. When Kate knew things were grimmer than usual in the Kelly household she would advise Nora to write out a bet after the horse had won. Kate would pay for the bet herself and deduct it from the 'winnings' Nora collected.

On the other side of the Kellys lived the Tattersalls. There was a low wall between the backyards of the two houses, and Mrs Tattersall –

whose husband had work on the railways throughout the Depression – would leave pot of stew or a loaf of bread on the wall. Nora would collect the food, the Kelly family would eat it and wash the dishes, and Nora would return the empty pot to the wall. 'There were never a word exchanged about things having passed [*sic*],' Pat recalled. 'She [Mrs Tattersall] would never do it on a face to face because she knew it would embarrass my Mum.'

Institutional charity was less subtle. At Christmas Nora would go to Liverpool and queue up with hundreds of other mothers to receive a food parcel at the John Goodfellow Society. As children of the poor, Pat and his siblings would be invited to the annual Christmas party hosted by the local police. 'They treated us to a good spread and we always finished up with a small present – an apple, an orange and a new penny. At Christmas we also received a new guerney [woollen jersey], and a new pair of short corduroy trousers. These clothes were like a uniform identifying the poor. I hated them but I had to wear them.'[9]

Nora was sometimes forced to take drastic action to get help. Pat remembered his mother once marching him and his siblings into Bootle parish, from which she received some charitable aid, and demanding, 'I'm not getting enough, I've told you that. The father is sick and he needs assistance and help. Now, I can't look after them [the children] any more. You have them.' With that, she 'walked out and left us,' remembered Pat. 'I knew she was having them on: there was no way my mother was leaving us. But it worked.'[10]

Pat revered his parents and was proud of their struggle to provide for their children and bring some joy into their lives.[11] He recalled a Christmas shopping outing when his father selected a dozen or so toy soldiers, 'put them under his cap, and walked out with me in tow. I was amazed at how cool he was, and also the audacity of the act'.

They proceeded to another children's shop. Patrick 'cornered a shop assistant and had her pulling out every little girls' sewing set that was available. In the midst of the confusion, he passed me back a sewing set, a rather large one, and indicated for me to move away. He then brought a very small sewing set and had it put in the largest paper bag available, and on catching up with me, put the large set in the same bag and we walked out.'

Christmas that year – probably 1937 – was a happy one for Pat and his siblings as the boys unwrapped their new soldiers and the girls their sewing sets. Years later, Pat considered the shoplifting justifiable and said he would do the same if it was the only way he could provide for his own children.[12]

With fascism on the march in Europe and poverty and unemployment rampant, politics filled the air in Bootle. Pat joined with other ragged children and adults in marches around the streets, chanting slogans against Mussolini's invasion of Abyssinia and helping drive Oswald Mosley, the founder of the British Union of Fascists, out of town.[13]

There were meetings around the district seeking volunteers to fight on the side of Spain's left-wing Popular Front government, against which the army, under General Francisco Franco, had staged a coup in July 1936, and, with the support of Hitler's tanks and planes and Mussolini's troops, was fighting for total control of the country.

Some young Bootle men joined the unsuccessful battle against Franco's forces in the brutal three-year Spanish Civil War. One of those active in recruiting supporters for the Spanish republicans was Pat's uncle Owen, a prominent communist in Bootle. Owen, Patrick's twin brother, was kept at arms length by Patrick and Nora, probably because they were devout Catholics. However, he would visit, and whenever he had money to spare would press it quietly on Nora to avoid embarrassing Patrick.

Uncle Owen always looked ill-fed and poorly dressed, Pat recalled. He would give away any money he had 'to some organisation or family who, as he would say, needed it more than he did'.[14] Owen was active on the docks as a member of the Transport and General Workers Union and a leader in the National Unemployed Workers Movement, financing much of its campaigning work, which included silent marches, demands for public work schemes at union rates of pay, and increased benefits for the unemployed.[15] He was also one of the leaders of the Bootle contingent of a hunger march in which thousands of unemployed workers walked for 19 days from Liverpool to London in 1936.

Pat was almost ten when war broke out and the conflict brought him face to face with Britain's class divide when he and his mother and siblings were evacuated from their home. The docks along the Mersey

– including Bootle, Liverpool, Wallasey and Birkenhead – were Britain's lifeline, bringing food and war materiel in from the United States. This made them Hitler's number one target outside London and thousands of children, parents and teachers were moved away in September 1939.[16]

Nora and the girls were sent to stay in a home in Southport and Pat and Charlie to another, into the care of a Mrs Hartley. The boys were exposed to luxuries and largesse beyond their imagination: Mrs Hartley employed a maid, a gong was rung for dinner, and the table was laid with strange cutlery that they had no idea how to use and foods they'd never seen or tasted before. The property also had an orchard, and there was a fairground nearby. The two penniless but enterprising boys saw an obvious opportunity – they picked apples from the orchard, sold them for a few pennies, and spent their earnings on rides at the fairground. When Mrs Hartley discovered apples were missing from her trees she instructed Nora to come and collect her sons.

The family returned with some relief to the familiar deprivation of Bootle, where they were reunited with the increasingly unwell Patrick. Bomb shelters were being constructed in backyards, including the Kellys'. Most nights from August to December 1940 were spent huddled inside on bunks constructed by Patrick from timber pilfered by Pat and Charlie, reading comics Patrick had pasted on the walls and ceilings to distract his children as the bombs rained down.[17]

The first air raids occurred in August 1940. By the time the Liverpool blitz was over in January 1942 about 4,000 people had been killed, including 424 in Bootle.[18] Pat's youngest sister, Lolo Moss, remembered shrapnel coming through the roof of their house and destroying a wardrobe, but the Kelly family came off comparatively lightly, losing just one relative – the husband of one of Pat's cousins.[19]

Just before Christmas 1940 the raids intensified, and the extended family except Patrick – who had been confined to Liverpool's Walton Hospital since August – packed up late at night and took a train north-west to Wigan. There almost the entire clan moved into one dilapidated house. Pat recalled that at one stage the squalid place was home to 40 family members, and Lolo remembered four families living there. Nora and the five children were in one room; she and the three girls shared a double bed and Pat and Charlie a single bed. There was no bathroom, and washing was a production line in which mothers took turns to load water into a tin tub to scrub down their scabies-infected children.

Nora would take the train to visit Patrick at weekends and nights when she could, but Pat and his siblings never saw their father again. He died about six weeks later. Years later, in his unpublished vignettes, Pat wrote: 'My anger remains with me for the terrible life [my father] had in his short 39 years. His anguish and suffering were not of his own making. The capitalist system took no prisoners and it killed my dad as it did with many dads in those horrific times. It did it slowly and viciously and it has never to date been recognised who the murderers were.'[20]

Although Pat spent more years in Wigan than in Bootle, the hard-scrabble streets around the docks would remain his ideological touchstone throughout his adult life. Most years from about 1980 he would return from his adopted home in Wellington and retrace his childhood steps along the route where he and Charlie had plied their firewood trade as small boys, the docks where they begged for food and pennies, and the cobbled streets where he and other kids would play tops and rugby with a ball fashioned from rolled-up newspaper tied with string.

'My memories come flooding back and the anger in me almost suffocates at times when I recall those economic times and the nature of society I was brought up in,' he wrote. 'It has not changed a great deal today. We see today, as then, examples of obscene wealth and indescribable poverty. Despite all the setbacks of the working class, there will be a day of reckoning and we should exercise [towards] those that exploit and bleed the people the same compassion they have shown to us.'[21]

After Patrick's death, the hand-to-mouth struggle continued for Nora and the children. Nora worked at a munitions factory on the afternoon and night shifts, the oldest daughter Marie, aged 14 or 15, got a job in a shop, and Pat got a morning paper round and a weekend bread-delivery job. His paper round led to regular canings from the headmaster of St Joseph's Catholic School because the job invariably made him late. St Joseph's was one of three primary schools he attended in Wigan before finishing his schooling at 14 and going to work in a bakery. The brutality of its headmaster fed his growing ambivalence towards the Catholic Church, whose well-fed priests he saw with one hand outstretched for tithes from poverty-stricken families like his while the other hand provided only minimal, grudging aid.

Despite his rising rage, the example of his activist Uncle Owen and the involvement of other family members in the Merseyside trade unions, Pat was more interested in betting and beer-drinking than in politics. One of the high points of his life as a young man in post-war England was winning £2,416 on the football pools in 1949. It was an extraordinary sum of money for someone who had nothing, and according to Lolo he squandered it. He bought a car, which he rolled after a night at the pub. 'And he bought us a television. It was beautiful,' Lolo remembered. 'Not that many houses had a television set, and it was, "Oh, the Kellys have got a television!" Everyone came and watched the coronation of the queen.'[22] He spent some of his winnings on a piano for his mother, which neither she nor anyone in the family knew how to play, and paid for a cousin's wedding.[23]

Pat's bad habits with money, reckless driving and love of gambling remained with him for much of his life. Max and Helen Kelly would hear their father recite his TAB number – WYS11886987 – so often as he placed bets over the phone it was burnished into their memory.[24]

Post-war Britain offered few prospects. Food was rationed, Liverpool was war-ravaged, and Pat had little education. The choices were poorly paid work on the docks or poorly paid factory work. He had been entranced for years by the stories that his Uncle Frank, a merchant seaman with the Blue Star Line, told of his visits to New Zealand, a place Frank claimed was drenched in sunshine and where it only rained at night.[25] Since 1947, to meet a desperate labour shortage, the New Zealand government had been heavily promoting the country to prospective British migrants. 'Ten Pound Poms' could move to New Zealand provided they passed a medical test, promised to stay and work for two years in a job approved by the Department of Labour, and contributed ten quid towards their fare.

In 1954 Pat joined the exodus. That year 5611 migrants sailed from the UK to New Zealand; between 1947 and 1971, 77,000 arrived as part of the biggest assisted migration scheme in New Zealand history.[26] There was nothing left of Pat's pool winnings by the time the ship docked in Wellington on November 18 – he'd blown the last in Panama on a Dutch girl on board the ship and had to frantically cable England for the requisite ten pounds so he could disembark.

He arrived to a country that was 'magnificent'. It was 'clean, [had] beautiful buildings and streets ... healthy children, people with plenty of food, people in work, people well dressed.'

He wrote home to Nora: 'I've found Shangri-La.'[27]

It was a fair assessment. New Zealanders in the 1950s and '60s commonly claimed their country had the highest standard of living in the world, a boast that was only a modest exaggeration. International data showed New Zealanders were the third wealthiest in the world after the citizens of the United States and Canada.[28]

Pat was sent to Dunedin to work at the Methven tap factory, but quickly broke his two-year work bond.[29] He had worn thick glasses since he was a child and his lenses were being ruined by his work as a tap polisher. When he demanded safety goggles, the manager told him it was up to workers to provide their own. It was a red rag to the hot-headed young migrant: 'I finished up holding the boss over the desk. We severed the contract.'[30]

Full employment was a key government goal; when Pat arrived in New Zealand 58 people were registered as unemployed and there were 12,500 job vacancies. The number out of work remained below 1000 for most of the next decade.[31] He could afford to assault the boss and get the boot, knowing there would be work available down the road.

He got a job driving for a Dunedin carrying company, where he again had cause to complain about the conditions of work. When he took his concern to the local drivers' union official, he was told if he wasn't happy he could go back to England. 'We don't need the likes of you in this country,' he was informed.[32] He headed north to Kawerau, where he worked as a driver on the construction of a new mill being built to process pinus radiata from the vast plantations of the central plateau. Here he took the first steps in what would become a long career as a militant trade unionist. In an interview for the 1997 documentary *Ten Pound Poms*, he said he was pressured by friends to become a site delegate because the bitter legacy of the 1951 waterfront lockout meant few people were willing to take on union leadership roles. 'I was half-pie stood over by these friends of mine who were ex-watersiders, who said, "You can do it, we know you can do it, and it's your responsibility to do it."'[33]

From Kawerau he went to work on the Meremere power station construction site, where he became the chair of the union site committee. He was outgoing, energetic, full of wisecracks, and increasingly skilled at leading rank-and-file workers in their demands for better wages and conditions. His effectiveness brought him to prominence within the Northern Drivers' Union, which by 1957 was led by Bill Andersen, a veteran of the 1951 waterfront lockout and a Communist Party member. Andersen became a friend and mentor, lending Pat books on socialism and helping build his self-confidence.

Andersen also pushed him to abandon the sideline gambling business he ran at Meremere. Pat had been making £150 a week running a two-up table, although he operated it in the spirit of the Bootle bookie's wife Kate Cunningham, making sure the family of one incurable gambler didn't lose out. 'If he won, fine. If he lost, we made sure his wife got it,' he told journalist Tim Pankhurst years later. 'He never knew. I suppose it was gambling with compassion.'[34] But Andersen gave him a choice: he could either represent the workers or take their money, but not both.[35] Pat shut down the gaming table.

By late 1957 Pat had finally followed in the footsteps of his Uncle Owen and joined the Communist Party, where his anger from a childhood of brutal poverty found natural expression. 'They [the party] had workers in the highest positions and confirmed what I suppose we had been brought up with, that we hadn't been given a fair crack of the whip and that without us [workers] the world just wouldn't move.'[36] Trade unions could only do so much to address workers' problems, he believed. 'It had to have a political solution. And I saw the Communist Party of New Zealand and the whole theory and thesis of Marx and Engels and Lenin as the answer.'[37]

His involvement with the party brought him opportunities, as well as retaliation from bosses and union moderates, and surveillance. Meremere workers passed the hat around to help him attend the 1957 conference of the communist-aligned World Federation of Trade Unions in Leipzig, East Germany, after which he spent three weeks in the Soviet Union before travelling back to England to see his mother, whose health was declining.

When he tried to get work at Meremere on his return two-and-a-half months later, he was thrown off the site. His union activities at Meremere had attracted the attention of the Auckland trucking industry, which blacklisted him.[38] The Federation of Labour, under the leadership of arch anti-communist Fintan Patrick Walsh, banned him from representing the Northern Drivers' Union at the annual FOL conference.[39] He even drew the attention of the Catholic newspaper *Zealandia*, with a regular columnist on trade union affairs condemning his attendance at the Leipzig gathering and backing the FOL's ban.[40]

Community party members were expected to attend Marxist-Leninist study groups and follow the reading lists collated by party leaders.[41] Pat, who had learned little but hymns in the crowded Catholic classrooms of Bootle and Wigan, was finally receiving an education. 'When I first came to New Zealand I found it extremely difficult to put two words together. I couldn't write properly. I could not really put pen to paper at all. I had great difficulty writing home,' he told broadcaster Geoff Robinson. 'The Communist Party of New Zealand taught me to write, taught me to read and taught me to speak.'[42]

The network of Communist Party friendships brought him into the orbit of the beautiful and fervent Cath Eichelbaum. At the time of their marriage in the Wellington Registry Office in November 1960, Cath was working for the government's Vocational Guidance Service after a successful appeal against earlier being denied a role. But as far as she could make out, her superiors still objected to her radical politics and were plotting to get rid of her. She was given a compulsory transfer to Hamilton, presumably in the expectation she would refuse and have to resign.[43]

As luck would have it, Cath wanted to be shifted to Hamilton: Pat had been asked by the Northern Drivers' Union to step in as organiser for the region. But life was tough for the newly married couple in the Waikato town. The damp climate triggered severe asthma in Cath, and then tragedy struck. She became pregnant with twins and carried them to six-and-a-half months before miscarrying. The cause was placenta previa. She suffered massive blood loss and was hospitalised for months. She never saw the two baby girls. 'It was in the dead of night. Off they went in a bedpan.'[44]

By then she was 35 and fearful she would never have the family she and Pat both desperately wanted. As far as she was concerned, Hamilton was 'the end of the world – a farmers' town'; Pat was travelling constantly around the Waikato and King Country in his union role and they hadn't been there long enough to make new friends.

She desperately missed her beloved Wellington. It was time to go home to Shannon Street.

3. Union central

The young woman at work says, 'Oh, saving people again are you, Cath?' That's the way Pat and I have spent our lives. That's what I believe in doing. *Cath Kelly*

Cath Kelly wondered if there could be a more exposed place than the William Cable engineering factory in the industrial suburb of Kaiwharawhara on the outskirts of Wellington. The wind blew constantly from one direction or another – down the Hutt Valley from the north, down the gorge from the west, or up the harbour from the south. Nevertheless she went there every week, regardless of the elements, to sell *People's Voice* to the workers and hand out Communist Party leaflets opposing American military and political involvement in Vietnam and the New Zealand government's support of its ANZUS ally.[1] She was at Cable's the day before she gave birth to her daughter, Helen. She would keep up her duties there until 1969, when Helen started at Clyde Quay School.

Cath and Pat had come back to Wellington in early 1962 from what Cath regarded as 'exile' in Hamilton. Pat got a job as a truck driver, and Cath took an undemanding administrative role with the Department of Education while she recovered her health after the miscarriage of the twins. She became pregnant again. Max was born in March 1963, a week before Cath's 37th birthday. He was named after her grandfather Max Eichelbaum and her sister Mary Max, known to everyone as Max.

Helen, named after one of Pat's younger sisters, was born on Suffrage Day the following year, 1964.[2] Cath went on to have one more pregnancy, which again ended in miscarriage. They would not take any further risks. 'We had two good kids and we decided not to try again.'[3]

Cath was determined not to return to paid work while she had a young family – she didn't want to leave them with 'endless babysitters' – but continued with her party work.[4] Sometimes she would head out in the early morning with a bundle of literature before Pat went to work, and she sold *People's Voice* on Cuba Street on Friday nights. She produced a regular leaflet, 'The US War', which aimed to stir blue-collar workers into opposing the war in Vietnam. She also typed anti-war pamphlets written by others and printed them on her Gestetner.

At the time of Helen's birth, opposition to the Vietnam War was mostly limited to the Communist Party, the Campaign for Nuclear Disarmament and the Peace Council. Ever since the early 1950s, when she had learned about Vietnam's then struggle against its French colonial masters, Cath had been horrified by what she saw as an unjust war to destroy the independence of a small nation.[5] Her interest was strengthened through her friendship with Freda Cook, a peace activist and former Communist Party member who, in 1961, went to Hanoi to teach English. Cook wrote regular articles for the left-wing *New Zealand Monthly Review* in which she described the lives of ordinary North Vietnamese people under socialism, criticised the American military involvement, and condemned the South Vietnamese regime as cruel and corrupt. Her portayal was a stark contrast to the Cold War-laced commentary of New Zealand's daily newspapers.[6]

From early 1965 anti-war sentiment began to spread from the far left of the political spectrum into the mainstream. A visit in April that year by Henry Cabot Lodge, President Lyndon Johnson's special envoy, to tell the New Zealand government how much the Americans would appreciate a military contribution, triggered street protests and scuffles. Momentum continued to grow with sit-ins, vigils and rallies. By May, when Prime Minister Keith Holyoake announced that New Zealand would send troops, the Committee on Vietnam had sprung into life, organising meetings, protests, seminars, speakers, publications and fundraising.[7]

Cath did whatever she could to support the anti-war effort – painting slogans and pasting posters around the city at night (for which she was charged and fined £10), producing anti-war literature, participating in the movement's complex backroom politics and attending every rally and protest she felt was safe for Helen and Max.[8]

At first the children attended as infants still in nappies; as they got older they carried their own placards and learned to chant, 'One, two, three, four, we don't want your dirty war!'[9] Max remembered marches ending in front of Parliament, where Pat would often be holding the megaphone. He was short, always wore a cloth cap and necktie, and observed the world through spectacles as thick as milk bottles. He spoke in a heavy Liverpudlian accent and he could move a crowd. 'He was a huge public speaker,' Max remembered. 'He often addressed really large crowds of people. He had a fantastic ability to capture, and discuss, and explain.'

When Pat returned from Hamilton it hadn't been easy for him to get work in the trucking industry. Blacklisted for his militancy by the Auckland Road Transport Association, he had had to go by the name Joseph (his second name) Kelly to get a job in Wellington. At first he was employed by a furniture removal firm, but carting pianos and sofas up and down the city's steep paths and steps was not suitable work, given the lingering after-effects of his broken leg. The Wellington Drivers' Union, which was under the leadership of Pat's friend and idol Chip Bailey – the fellow Communist Party member who, with his wife Rona, had matched him up with Cath – was growing in strength, and had forged mutually beneficial relationships with some trucking companies who were worried that the emergence of big transport firms would squeeze out competitors. On sites where it was well organised, the union could even insist on being consulted about who got employed; it was this influence that helped Pat get a job as a driver with Certified Concrete.[10]

The union hadn't always enjoyed such leverage. Twelve years earlier, in 1951, it had been brought to its knees in the waterfront dispute, facing the wrath of Sid Holland's National Party government for supporting locked-out wharf workers. The brutal 151-day confrontation had occurred against the backdrop of florid Cold War rhetoric. By 1947 'socialism was becoming a dirty word, and to demand higher wages made one suspect of being part of a sinister Communist plot,' wrote labour historian Bert Roth.[11] The Federation of Labour was increasingly under the thumb of conservative forces, particularly Fintan Patrick Walsh.[12]

The fuse had been lit for the wharf dispute when the Waterside Workers' Union imposed an overtime ban in response to a pay dispute.[13] The waterfront employers ordered them to drop their ban and locked them out when they refused, bringing the wharves to a standstill. The government, determined to break the militant union, asked it to submit to statutory arbitration. When the union refused, the government cracked down hard under the Public Safety Conservation Act of 1932.[14] Sweeping emergency regulations were imposed, giving the government the power to call in the army, ban pickets, marches and meetings, tap phones and seize union funds. It was illegal to say or print anything that could encourage, incite, aid or abet the wharfies. It was unlawful even to provide food to their families. The union was deregistered.

The FOL had supported the government, publicly denouncing the wharfies as 'part of the war that New Zealand troops are fighting in Korea' and telling them to reject their 'Communist-inspired misleaders'.[15] The Wellington Drivers' Union supported the wharfies by refusing to handle any goods unloaded by the army and it too was deregistered.[16]

The waterfront dispute had ended in total defeat for the watersiders and the militant wing of the union movement and left an enduring legacy of bitterness.[17]

Neither Cath nor Pat had been in New Zealand in 1951, but as communists and working-class advocates they couldn't help but be affected by the long and complex aftermath of the dispute. Cath had returned from England to a communist movement in which people felt 'depressed and defeated'; Pat was drawn into union activism because New Zealand workers had become unwilling to put their heads above the parapet after witnessing the state and the union movement's top leaders collaborate to crush the wharfies.[18]

Recriminations and accusations flew for years between adversaries. Veterans of the confrontation, including Bill Andersen, who was blacklisted following the lockout, and Rona and Chip Bailey, who produced illegal bulletins telling the workers' side of the story and whose home was ransacked by police in search of the typewriter they used to write them, were influential comrades of the Kellys.[19] Their close friend Dan Long was one of many workers who had risked arrest to regularly give money to the wharfies.[20]

When Pat began work as a driver (and site delegate) at Certified Concrete in 1962, the Wellington Drivers' Union was still recovering from the trauma of 1951, and working towards greater democracy through development of a network of site delegates, regular delegates' conferences and stopwork meetings where workers could voice their concerns. Leader Chip Bailey's vision was of a union 'uniting and leading the workers to a fairer share of the wealth they produce'.[21] It wasn't easy work, and some employers resorted to violence to frustrate the union's efforts, Ken Douglas remembered. 'Because they knew exactly what we were about, which was developing an organisation that would lead to wage demands.'[22]

Nor was this worker-centred approach standard practice in the wider union movement. Since 1894 the relationship between organised labour and employers in New Zealand had been conducted under the Industrial Conciliation and Arbitration Act.[23] The Act would largely prevail until its last vestiges were swept aside by the Employment Contracts Act in 1991. To anyone who entered the New Zealand workforce after 1991, the industrial conciliation and arbitration regime reads like a foreign language. It is incomprehensible to those whose lives and work have been framed by the neoliberal economic and social policies that have dominated for more than a generation. The Act was designed to encourage the formation of trade unions which, once registered by the state, obtained exclusive coverage of workers in their industry and region. If a union chose to register under the Act (and most did) it gained the right to force employers to meet it in a bargaining forum overseen by state-appointed conciliators. If a deal was reached on pay and conditions, this became an 'award' with blanket coverage across all employers within its scope, regardless of whether they were part of the negotiation.

If a settlement couldn't be reached, the case would go to the Arbitration Court – a presiding judge plus worker and employer representatives – and the court would issue an award. After the Second World War the court was also empowered to issue periodic General Wage Orders, across-the-board pay adjustments to all award rates, decided upon after hearing evidence on the cost of living and the state of the economy. The government – through the Department of Labour – enforced awards. Union membership was compulsory.[24]

The system encouraged the creation of hundreds of unions, most of them small and weak. By the time Pat became an official of the Wellington Drivers' Union in 1963, New Zealand had 379 unions and 334,000 union members.[25] The flip side of this bargain between labour, capital and the state was that strikes and lockouts were illegal and the government had the power to deregister a union for engaging in stoppages – a penalty that stripped a union of its rights and allowed a new union to be registered in its place.

With the exception of the 1951 wharf lockout, the penalties were seldom invoked, and after the mid '50s not at all.[26] But until 1968 stoppages were rare, despite labour shortages, rising prices and the fact that wages increased very gradually while company profits soared.[27] In 1961 the rate of work stoppages was eight times greater in the United States, six times greater in Australia, and more than three times greater in the United Kingdom.[28]

Support from employers for the conciliation and arbitration regime waxed and waned. They favoured it during periods of industrial militancy and derided it during economic lulls, when they claimed it kept wages up.[29] The union movement, too, was ambivalent. History had shown the regime could be used as a powerful club with which to beat organised labour. Militants believed it bred tame unions full of passive members – 'an army of shadows', as historian Stevan Eldred-Grigg put it – who joined up only because the law forced them to, and that it discouraged genuine worker involvement and democracy of the kind that Chip Bailey envisaged.[30] It was possible for union officials to collect members' union dues and make no effort to hear their concerns, and for weak unions to reap the benefits of pay rises achieved in bargaining by stronger unions. On the other hand, the system meant that workers in small, scattered workplaces who would otherwise find it almost impossible to organise and bargain collectively – such as cleaners, shop workers and clerical workers – could rely on standard award pay rates.

Chip Bailey died in 1963 at the age of 42 and Ken Douglas was elected to his role as secretary of the Wellington Drivers' Union. Pat moved into Douglas's former role as the union's Wellington city organiser, a job in which he would remain for the next 13 years.

Pat and the increasingly effective drivers' union would run successful campaigns to get sick pay and tea breaks for drivers, chafe against the rigid pay relativities set by the arbitration system, sort out on-the-job skirmishes, advocate for drivers injured on the job, and draw workers into political activism against the Vietnam War and apartheid in South Africa.

'He was passionate about safety for drivers,' Helen said in a 2015 interview.[31] 'He would go out in the middle of the night and photograph crashed trucks.' By now Cath had knocked the rough edges off Pat's pugnacious manner with the bosses. In his early days as a union delegate he had been inclined to see poor working conditions and 'without really knowing the other workers or having their trust, go in and table thump and get the sack within weeks,' Cath remembered.[32] He was now a talented organiser and communicator, and a pragmatic mentor to job delegates and budding activists.

Having grown up in the impoverished tenements of Bootle knowing the power of friendship and solidarity among neighbours, he also understood intuitively that camaraderie among workers made unions stronger. Helen and Max grew up socialising at gatherings like the annual wharfies' picnic and the drivers' union party. It was Pat's job to go around employers and drum up contributions for such events for workers and their families. In union vernacular this was called 'bumming', and with his wisecracking manner and sense of mission Pat was good at it. He scaled up the Wellington Drivers' Union party into a full-blown ball featuring the Rodger Fox Big Band; breweries and other companies reliant on a cooperative workforce were pressed for contributions.[33] It was a modest price to pay for industrial peace.

By the time Helen and Max started primary school, they had been steeped in a rich marinade of protest and activism, laced with Pat's Irish craic and Cath's unyielding ideological certainty. Despite the strictures of the conciliation and arbitration system, which was designed to stop unions venturing into broader political activity and limit their role to the negotiation of wages and conditions, the boundary between human rights activism and worker advocacy was increasingly blurred. Compulsory membership meant union ranks enjoyed steady growth, and – led particularly by militant unions like the drivers and seafarers – were bringing crucial heft to New Zealand's emerging mass movements against the war in Vietnam, nuclear weapons and apartheid; they were natural partners in protest alongside churches and student activists.[34]

The house at Shannon Street was in the thick of it. 'Both Mum and Dad talked about all the work they were involved with all the time with us from the earliest age,' Helen said in 2004.[35] As they got older, she and Max were enlisted to crank the handle of the Gestetner, fold stacks of leaflets, and stuff and lick envelopes by the thousand. The house was busy with the comings and goings of adults who shared similar beliefs to their parents. If Helen or Max were uncertain as to someone's political probity, they would ask: 'Are they a goodie or a baddie?'[36] Politics – not hollow punditry about polls and personalities but active organising about what needed to be done and who should be supported – was consumed with every family meal.

Childhood at Shannon Street was, for Helen, an 'amazing adventure'.[37] She and Max would climb into a cart that Pat had knocked together from apple crates and pram wheels, and Pat would trundle them along the Wellington docks to visit the watersiders' union. While he talked politics, placed bets on the horses and had a beer they would raid the union's safe for foreign chewing gum and chocolate.[38] On Sunday mornings they'd be sent to the dairy for Pat's tobacco, *Turf Digest*, *Best Bets* and fresh white bread.

On Friday nights they would phone the Panama Hotel, hang-out for the unionists of Trades Hall, to tell Pat it was time to come home for tea.

'Half an hour before his dinner was ready to be served, we'd ring,' remembered Max. '"Is Pat Kelly there please? Dad, dinner's ready."'

'"I'll be home in twenty minutes."'

'An hour later he still wouldn't be home and we'd ring again. "Dad! Dinner's ready, it's getting cold."'

'"I'll be home soon, I'll be home soon." And two-and-a-half hours later he'd wander in.'[39]

When Pat sat down in the Shannon Street living room with his union mates – roll-your-own cigarette and beer in hand – to discuss the affairs of the working class, Helen would slide on to her father's lap and listen. When she and Max got paper rounds, Pat insisted they organise their fellow workers and ensure the Newspaper Publishers' Association's code of practice for juniors, which set minimum pay and maximum bag weights, was complied with. 'We believed in it,' said Helen. 'It was exciting.'[40]

For Cath, opposition to the war in Vietnam was an overriding concern. 'Sometimes I think we had Vietnam for breakfast, dinner and tea, because there was always something being planned,' Cath would later tell an interviewer.[41]

However, in 1967, when Max was four and Helen three, Cath began to play a central role in the Campaign Against Rising Prices (CARP). New Zealand was facing a sharp recession after a collapse in the international wool price, which accounted for a third of New Zealand's exports. There was rising inflation, and added pressure on households when the National government removed subsidies on wheat, flour and butter, increased postal, electricity and rail charges, put up state house rentals, and sharply increased taxes on tobacco, cars and spirits.[42]

CARP had been formed in Auckland in November 1966 under the leadership of unionist and former 1951 waterfront activist Flo Humphries. In Wellington, Cath attended a meeting called by the Housewives Association to discuss rising prices but concluded these 'nice women' were not up to the task. 'They weren't prepared to get into political action.' She linked up with other women associated with the union movement and a Wellington division of CARP was launched.[43]

CARP lobbied for price controls, organised protests and generated news coverage. The minister of finance, Rob Muldoon, alleged it was directed by communists. Cath retorted publicly that Muldoon saw Reds everywhere – 'soon he will be looking for them under the bed.'[44]

She kept detailed inventories of everyday prices, wrote a newsletter, published articles in union journals, and talked to women's and union groups around Wellington – fighting back against the prevailing argument that rising wages were the cause of rising food prices. Instead she blamed corporate monopolies and profiteering.[45] CARP took Woolworths to court over the state of its potatoes, led boycotts of price-inflated tinned fruit and biscuits, and campaigned to keep milk at four cents a bottle.[46]

Deceptive packaging was also in CARP's sights. Cath would take containers that had once held expensive face creams, cut them in half to expose how large they were in relation to the volume of product, and set them on cardboard with hand-written notations to use as educational displays. For years afterwards, the displays sat in the basement of Shannon Street as emblems of corporate manipulation.

Cath was the driving – some would say dictatorial – force that held CARP together in Wellington until 1979. She kept up the campaign despite suffering breast cancer and undergoing a radical mastectomy in 1973, and two years later losing her sister Mary Max to cancer at the age of 51. She enlisted Helen and Max as her foot soldiers. They slapped campaign stickers on the revolving doors at Parliament and kept watch at Woolworths to make sure the prices of old goods were not illegally marked up.[47]

Whether her efforts yielded results is a moot point: her nephew, George Rosenberg – a young lawyer who helped CARP – once told her it '"was the most unsuccessful organisation ever because prices have kept on rising". She took that rather badly. She didn't have much of a self-reflective sense of humour.'[48]

Somehow she managed to carve out time to attend carpentry lessons and build new joinery for the kitchen at Shannon Street. Max remembered his mother would periodically call out to Pat to lend a hand. 'He'd be listening through his earpiece to the races or talkback radio on his transistor, or watching TV. He was a bit of an inventor, and he'd rigged up a speaker salvaged from an old valve radio and fitted into a home-made wooden box, and had an earplug with a long cord that connected to the TV. He'd say to Mum, "Wait until the ad break!" Then he'd come and hold something up while still listening to the TV.'[49]

Pat had his own DIY projects, usually carried out with the assistance of his union mates and often with less finesse than Cath's. Along the front of the wooden villa he built a verandah with galvanised iron poles and lined with a substrate that leaked. He reconstructed and levelled the front lawn using old bottles as fill; the whole thing later collapsed when the ground became sodden in heavy rain.[50]

Helen and Max frequently vacated their bedrooms to make way for visiting comrades and international activists, such as exiled South African trade unionist John Taolo Gaetsewe, who came to stay while on a national speaking tour hosted by the union movement and funded, in part, by the proceeds of the balls and picnics Pat helped organise. 'Our house always had people staying. Workers, South African militants. Anyone who was in town and needed somewhere to stay,' Helen would recall. 'It was an open house and us kids were just squashed down the end of it.'[51]

Some who came to stay became de facto members of the family. Dave Morgan was a 23-year-old unemployed Adelaide seafarer and Australian Communist Party member in 1963 when he decided to try his luck in New Zealand. Within days of arriving in Wellington he met Pat Kelly, who was selling *People's Voice* at the Terminus Hotel. After a couple of further meetings in the same circumstances at the same drinking hole, where they continued to bond over politics and beer, Morgan was invited home.

'My own family had collapsed under alcohol and I had never met a family like this,' he remembered. 'There was love, politics and family. The attraction was their warmth, their generosity and their politics. Their politics matched mine … Pat was one of us – a drinker and a worker. A militant worker. He saw humour in most people and most things … Cath had discipline and opinions and she cared. All that stuff that was missing from my own life … I was like Monty Woolley – the man who came to stay, and stayed and stayed and stayed.

'To get my feet under the table was a fairly unique experience for me … and it was all part of what identified itself for me as love. … Pat and I had huge rapport. I think he was probably the dad I didn't have.'[52]

Eventually Morgan got his own flat, married Maggie Mason, a dental nurse and union activist, and in 1973 became president of the New Zealand Seaman's Union, where he remained for three decades as one of New Zealand's most influential militant unionists. His public reputation was as a gravel-voiced, fedora-wearing hardliner. He was also, like Pat, a dogged advocate for workers and an internationalist. His union played a frontline role in the anti-apartheid campaign, the anti-nuclear movement – in 1976 seamen joined harbour workers and watersiders in refusing to assist the nuclear ship USS *Truxtun* while it lay at anchor in Wellington Harbour – and against the military junta of Chile's Augusto Pinochet.[53]

At Shannon Street, he was part of Helen's and Max's lives from their earliest moments, not just as one of their parents' fellow travellers but as a big brother figure or a beneficient uncle bearing gifts from exotic locations. When the children had birthdays, he would dress up as a clown and chase screaming kids around the house. He was Pat's closest friend and confidante and Helen wanted to be part of their conversations. 'She knew the activities of the two prominent males in her life,' he said. 'We always made room for her.'[54]

Another who came to visit and ended up staying was Alby White. He and Helen were five when Helen befriended him at Clyde Quay School and regularly brought him home to play. Alby's family was afflicted by alcohol and conflict. For him, Shannon Street was a loving refuge, enriched by the tribe of neighbourhood kids.

Next door to the Kellys were the Moores, a hard-working couple with ten children who rented the top storey of the house and got by on Joe Moore's wages as a council dustman and night-time meat delivery driver and Cissy Moore's as a part-time relief primary school teacher. The Kelly and Moore kids had the run of each others' houses.

When Alby was seven his family went to live in Blenheim and he moved in with the Kellys; Helen's bedroom was divided in half to create space for him. Years later he learned from Helen that Cath had wanted to adopt him, but after a year and a half with the Kellys he went back to his family.[55]

Childhood was busy at Shannon Street. Cath orchestrated a tight schedule of cubs, Girl Guides, swimming, gymnastics, Scottish dancing, ballet, and kapa haka at the Ngāti Pōneke Māori Club – a tide of activity into which Cath swept not only Alby but also Jackie, Alan and Lynda Moore. 'It was like having second parents in the other house,' Jackie Moore (now Jackie Ford) remembered.

The forested reserve of Mt Victoria was their backyard and the inner-city beach of Oriental Bay a short sprint down a labyrinth of concrete stairways. The Kellys, Moores and other neighboorhood kids ran free – building forts in the bush and furnishing them with blankets and furniture hauled from home, playing war games, traversing the neighbourhood via garage roofs and backyards, and careening helmetless down the steep streets on metal-wheeled roller skates Cath had kept from her childhood.[56] 'We used to sit on them and race down Hawker Street, sometimes in pairs or triples, holding the person in front, like a conga line,' Max remembered.

Helen was an organiser and fixer. She would come up with ideas for what they should do, win consensus from the group and arbitrate disputes among her peers.[57]

In among it all, Cath's much-loved dog Sparky – a Corgi-cross acquired from Margaret and Dan Long – announced the arrival of visitors at the front door with a volley of barks and clatter of claws. The dog was notoriously vicious, and Pat was forever threatening to have him put down if he bit another person. Helen swore one of her best friends, Shelley Hopper, to secrecy after Sparky bit her, lest Pat follow through with his promise.[58]

The Kelly household was avowedly working-class, but rich with opportunities that would be beyond the means of later generations of kids with wage-earning parents. Pat's salary as a union organiser was modest, linked, like that of other Wellington Drivers' Union officials, to award rates.[59] His position was subject to election by members so there was no long-term job security. From time to time he and other officials went without pay if the union was under financial stress. However, the job came with a car, which was available for the family to use, and the Shannon Street house that Cath had brought into the marriage was the backbone of the Kellys' economic security.

There were idyllic family holidays in rustic houses at Victoria University's Taurewa research camp at the base of the 'Three Sisters' – the volcanic peaks of Ruapehu, Ngāuruhoe and Tongariro – usually with the families of Cath's three sisters. Helen and Max had ten cousins on the Eichelbaum side and Pat was the cousins' favourite uncle. His public demeanour was dour and curmudgeonly, but to family and friends he was warm, funny and kind. Some of the kids found Cath forbidding and scary, but they all loved Pat. He'd pile them into the car – entertaining them with endless jokes and yarns – and head to the frigid snow-fed Mahuia Rapids, where he would jump in and pronounce the water warm, to entice them in for their daily bath. When it was too cold, he'd toss in coins to induce them to take the plunge.

The Long family – Dan, Margaret and their children Martin, David and Miriam – were frequent companions on weekend picnics to Kaitoke in the Remutuka Forest. When Dan Long died suddenly in 1976 at the age of 53, Shannon Street wrapped its support around the bereaved family. Cath and Margaret maintained a close friendship and Pat became an emotional liferaft for David. 'He and I had always been close, but after Dad died he poured love on me. He just gathered me in,' David remembered. 'Pat was emotionally available, and able to articulate his emotions in a way that wasn't common among men of that generation.'[60]

Margaret and David (who was closest in age to Helen) joined the Kellys for camping expeditions to Totaranui in Abel Tasman National Park. Pat would cram the car and trailer with every conceivable item to make life under canvas comfortable and fun – a dinghy, lilos, a huge and heavy steel barbecue welded together by his mates in the Boilermakers' Union. One year the vehicle was so overloaded it overheated on the long descent down the Takaka Hill into Golden Bay. And while Pat's ability to roll and light a cigarette with one hand while driving was legendary, he once went off the road in the process.

In 1972 the Kellys and the families of Cath's two sisters who lived in the North Island, the Darts and the Patricks, banded together to buy a bach on the central volcanic plateau. The old railway cottage was in the village of Rangataua. It had unimpeded views of the mountains, over an acre of land and cost $680. The extended family, including Cath's oldest sister Ann Rosenberg and her family from Christchurch – up to 18 children and adults – would sometimes holiday together, serviced by one outside toilet. The Longs, various Moore kids, Alby White and other school friends would often be invited. One summer holiday saw 23 people crammed in, playing Monopoly and cards and talking politics, while outside rain poured down incessantly.

Pat would go to the Wellington dump, collect old bikes and parts and reconstruct them for use at the bach. The bikes gave the kids freedom to venture far and wide – to swimming holes, up the mountain, to Ohakune for ice creams, along logging roads. They'd often return home only as night fell. 'We'd have breakfast and be off the leash,' remembered Tom Patrick, the youngest of the cousins. 'Helen was the chief instigator. She was optimistic and assertive, even at six or seven, always full of ideas and not shy about sharing them. ... She would come up with the list of places we could go, the back roads and forestry tracks. It was a very long leash by today's standards. We seemed to fill our time without a hint of boredom. She was pure fun to be with.'[61]

In winter Cath and the children would ski at nearby Turoa or Whakapapa while Pat read his racing guides and dragged on his roll-your-owns.

Pat and Cath's relationship with the Communist Party came to a tragicomic end. They had given years of energy and commitment to the party. Cath had even gifted it the remains of her inheritance from Siegfried and Vera, a sum of about £3000.[62]

For Pat and Cath, communism was a self-evident solution to the genocide, poverty, fascism and war they had seen in their lifetimes. Their allegiance to its ideals had made them the target of surveillance, Cold War slurs and anonymous threats. But the party had been buffeted by splits in the international communist movement. After a rift opened up between Russia and China, the two communist superpowers, the Communist Party of New Zealand, uniquely among Western communist parties, aligned itself with China. The leader, Vic Wilcox, publicly praised Mao Zedong and condemned the Soviet Union as 'puny leaders of modern revisionism'.[63]

In 1966 the party split: a pro-Soviet group broke away to form the Socialist Unity Party. Among the SUP's leading players were Pat's friend and mentor Bill Andersen, as well as almost all the Communist Party's senior trade union members. Pat's boss at the Drivers' Union, Ken Douglas, helped set up the Wellington branch and became a prominent member.

The Communist Party's Auckland-based leaders fed the division with an extravagant resolution, published in *People's Voice*, that declared 'good riddance' to the SUP defectors. 'Far from deploring the loss, [party members] will be pleased that at last the Party is rid of an internal abscess fed with the infection of imperialist and revisionist ideas. The body of the Party will be healthier as a result … Our Party can now concentrate on the task of the practical work of organising the class struggle and the fight against the main enemy of mankind, US imperialism.'[64]

Cath and Pat remained with the China-aligned Communist Party, as did most of their peers in the Wellington district, including their friend Rona Bailey. China lavished attention on the tiny New Zealand party. Vic Wilcox made nine trips to China as a guest of the People's Republic and others in the party were pressured to travel there.[65] Cath told interviewer Pat Webster years later that she disapproved of the free trips, believing they 'got people into an ideological frame of mind that wasn't necessarily the result of their own thinking'.[66] However, she and Pat made separate trips to China in 1967 – a year after Mao launched the Cultural Revolution – when Helen and Max were pre-schoolers.

Pat's letters home to Cath ('my greatest comrade in arms') and the children ('little red starlets') were full of praise for developments in China. He had witnessed thousands of Red Guards on the march, visited communes and been hosted at concerts. He described the Red Guards he met as 'young heroes', the communes as 'an eye opener and brain opener to magnificent socialist enterprises', and Mao as 'a brilliant student of Marx and Lenin'.

He met with Mao for an hour and twenty minutes and came away with a prized photograph of the occasion and a signed copy of Mao's *Little Red Book*. 'The sincerity and absolute faith in theory and practice that Comrade Mao has in the peoples of China would certainly make him a Red Sun in my heart,' he wrote home from Shanghai.[67]

But the Communist Party of New Zealand was beginning to collapse under the weight of its own revolutionary delusions. According to Cath's version of events many years later, by the late 1960s the party's top figures were 'big-noting' to the Chinese by portraying New Zealand as ripe for revolution, with young people already 'fighting in the bush'.

Things became more farcical with the establishment by the party's national leadership of an underground wing, into which they inadvertently recruited a government spy, who blew the lid on the secret 'parallel' party in *Truth*. The leadership was by then also denouncing trade unions and CARP as agents of the capitalist establishment, guilty of lulling the working class into believing the system could be reformed to their benefit. They declared the rise of youth radicalism and the massive protests against the Vietnam War were signs of widespread revolutionary ardour, with Wilcox claiming in early 1970 that 'the revolutionary New Zealand people, particularly the youth who will build the future, are already taking mighty steps forward'.[68]

Cath came to regard the party's leaders as 'basically drunks with very strong opinions'.[69] For Pat, the view that party members should not be trade union officials was unacceptable. Unions were the 'real shield of the working class' and the union movement was an 'arena out of which socialist consciousness will develop and out of which the forces for change will come'. Notwithstanding his wistful depiction of China's revolutionary zeal in his 1967 letters home, he knew his adopted country was so far off revolution that 'we hadn't even bothered to order the wood for the barricades, let alone build them'.[70]

Accusatory statements and resolutions flew between Wellington and Auckland. In August 1970 the conflict came to a head when the party's ruling coterie expelled or suspended the entire Wellington district – some 70 or 80 people, a quarter of the party's membership.[71]

In Wellington sales of *People's Voice* virtually collapsed. The newspaper that Cath and Pat had spent so many hours selling on windswept street corners now vilified them as part of the 'Manson-Bailey gang'. (Sometimes the term of abuse was broadened to 'Manson-Bailey-Goddard-Kelly-Smith-Stanton-Quinn-Austin-Harvey revisionist clique'.)[72]

Cath had been a party member for 22 years in the UK and New Zealand, and Pat for 13 years, but it was all over in a hail of fractious dogma. 'We were all betrayed with this rubbish,' Cath would say. 'It was a sad end to lots of hard work and idealism and study … They [the Communist Party] left me rather than I left them.'[73]

Cath used to joke to Helen and Max that she and Pat had been thrown out 'for socialist leanings'. But the expulsion did not dilute their commitment to the central tenets. 'The idea that social idealism, that you worked for the general good not just for your own self-interest, and the idea that people should not be allowed to exploit other people, and the ideas of peace and racial equality and so on – we didn't move away from that. We just saw that [the Communist Party] was not the vehicle we could support,' she would tell Lesley Hall.[74]

The rump of the Communist Party continued to descend into irrelevance, with further waves of expulsions and denunciations. The sacking of the Wellington district spawned a number of new left-wing bodies, including the Marxist Leninist Organisation, of which Rona Bailey was a founding member. The SUP achieved a greater presence in the capital. However, Cath and Pat remained politically unaligned for seven years before finally throwing in their lot with the Labour Party. By then Helen and Max were entering their teenage years, and Prime Minister Rob Muldoon was casting an increasingly autocratic shadow across New Zealand's political, civic and economic life.

4. The militants' daughter

I've always thought of myself as a trade unionist, from a very early age. That meant someone who belonged to this movement called the unions.
Helen Kelly

A less resilient child might have retreated from the constant thrum of politics, organising and scheming that went on in the Shannon Street household, but Helen absorbed her parents' politics and argued their corner at school and among her friends. From a young age she identified herself as part of the union movement and assumed she would follow Pat and Cath into a life of activism. She imagined herself outstripping their efforts and fancied that she might one day become New Zealand's first female prime minister. Her high school friends saw her as so capable and reliable that this would likely come to pass.[1]

Cath marked out her daughter early on as someone who was likely to go far. In the bathroom she had labelled twin towel racks for the children: 'H.M. [Helen Margaret] Kelly, PM', and 'M.P. [Max Patrick] Kelly, MP'.[2]

Helen was outgoing and seemingly self-assured, and other kids were drawn to her sunny gregarious nature. She made friends easily. One of the many with whom she formed a lifelong bond was Helen Kinsella. The two met at the age of ten at Hataitai School; Cath had moved Helen and Max to the school because she disapproved of an experiment at Clyde Quay School with syndicated classes.

The two Helens would meet at 7.30 a.m. at McDonald's on Courtenay Place, board a bus and do circuits of the city before school, all the while 'jabbering away to the bus drivers'.[3] They went on to Wellington High School – a liberal, socially diverse, co-ed college – in 1978. Max was a year ahead and Helen's cousin Tom Patrick was in the same year as her. Tom had struggled after the death in 1975 of his mother, Cath's sister Max, to cancer when he was ten, and the Kellys had become his rock. Tom found Helen's presence at the school comforting. 'I didn't take to secondary school very enthusiastically or successfully,' he said. 'Pat would have encouraged [Helen] to look out for me, I suspect, and seeing her was always reassuring. … Her group [of friends] was quite tight and formidable, all bright, strong-willed and confident. To see her smiling and happy always made me think everything would be all right.'[4]

Helen and her friend Helen Kinsella became members of a dedicated student group that ran the backstage operations of the school's 1500-seat auditorium. The crew were distinguishable by their bohemian uniform: black nylon bomber jackets with mock wool lining. Running lighting and sound and preparing the large venue for school and public performances was a serious and skilled undertaking. The gang was led by Stephen Blackburn, the son of notable New Zealand arts personalities Ken and Vi Blackburn and another whose friendship with Helen would endure through her life.[5]

Blackburn remembered the backstage years as influential for those involved. The crew had the only set of keys to the hall, giving them a private place to bond and talk. In the crew's room there were sofas, and a kettle to make coffee; they could be in the hall fixing and preparing equipment from early in the morning until late at night. Backstage responsibilities often came ahead of class attendance. In the diaries Helen kept as a teenager, she sometimes recorded entire days spent setting up the hall for shows, although Blackburn recalled she was more conscientious than others about turning up to classes.

She didn't come from a theatre background, but Helen was a central figure in the crew. 'She was always the mediator, always the one making sure the group was holding together,' Blackburn said. 'It was a very flat non-hierarchical group. There was an incredible level of mutual respect for each other. … Helen was never bossy. It was more an inquisitive openness, wanting to engage with people, and that bonded everyone to her.'[6]

The long period of industrial relations calm following the 1951 waterfront dispute was now a faded memory. The economy was in crisis, unemployment was rising, and workers were going on strike in record numbers in pursuit of higher wages to keep abreast of inflation. Having come to power in 1975 on an ugly campaign of union-bashing and red-baiting, the National Party prime minister Rob Muldoon was governing in an increasingly polarising, ad hoc and interventionist manner.

Against a background of mounting political antagonism and broiling protest over nuclear ship visits and apartheid in South Africa, the backstage group would sit around drinking instant coffee and debating, with Helen consistently promoting a pro-union position against those who felt individual enterprise was being undermined by strong-armed unionists. 'Politically we were on opposite sides of the fence,' remembered one backstager, Rob McKeen. 'We had endless debates about unions. But it was always fun, never mean-spirited … She did listen and she would try and show you the errors of your ways.'[7]

'She was articulate, and very assured speaking in front of people,' remembered another Wellington High friend, Tom Docherty. 'She could stand up and talk to the class. She wouldn't get into an argument if she didn't know how to present it. … She was measured and didn't get personal. She was very clearly left-wing and she always took the Labour side.'[8]

Throughout high school Helen remained close to Pat and Cath, and her diaries suggest clashes with them were rare. In her fourth-form year she recorded the ordinary preoccupations of a teenage girl – tiffs among friends, whether this or that boy liked her and she him, clothes, shopping, Saturday sport, school discos that were either 'fun' or 'slack'. She was heartbroken when her friend Shelley Hopper, whom she had known since she was five, moved to Australia with her family. She wrote long letters and fretted when Shelley didn't write back quickly enough. Despite their separation, the two would remain close.

Alison Saunders, another lifelong friend from Wellington High, remembered Helen's striking resemblance to the 'Macleans girl' who starred in a toothpaste ad of the era – a dark-haired young woman who leapt out of bed in the morning with a dazzling smile. 'That was Helen as a teenager. With her dimples in her cheeks, she was just clean and fresh and intelligent and motivated. And she was happy. She had a great personality. She was always smiling, always sparkling. People were very drawn to that.'[9]

When they were 14, the two went to Christchurch to stay with Cath's oldest sister Ann and her husband Wolfgang Rosenberg, prominent left-wing figures. While there, they hit on the idea of knitting tiny beaded brooches on toothpicks and selling them around the city. 'For two weeks we knitted on toothpicks into all hours of the night,' remembered Saunders. 'We came back with hundreds of dollars.'[10]

Although Helen rarely wore makeup and she and Saunders disagreed with it on principle, she was willing to dress in fishnet stockings, a tight satin skirt and top and heavy make-up so Saunders could photograph her for a flyer advertising the brooches.

The pair then came up with another venture, hosting children's birthday parties. For several years from the age of 14, they would travel to houses around Wellington dressed as clowns – Helen was 'Ding', Saunders 'Dong' – organising food and games and entertaining children with juggling acts.

At the age of 15 Helen developed an obsession with citizen band radio. She spent hours at night on the set Pat bought for her, talking to guys who were identifiable only by a first name and a number (Richard 3580; Willie 4451; Tony 3813).

There was an expectation at Shannon Street that everyone would work hard. Helen worked at McKenzies department store, in a toy shop and an ice-cream parlour, at a private hospital and as a cleaner. Whatever the job, she'd join the union. 'When they found out who my father was [the employer] would give me a five-page pay slip,' she recalled years later.[11] If Pat needed a hand at Trades Hall, where he was now leading the Wellington and Taranaki Caretakers, Cleaners and Lift Attendants and Watchmen's Union, Helen would go there after school.[12] The building was a familiar haunt: while waiting for Pat to finish work, she and Max would often watch TV in the flat of the caretaker Ernie Abbott, who was a good friend of Pat's and a Cleaners Union comrade.

Helen had a reputation around school for being rather 'square'. She worried constantly about friends who were taking risks with sex and drugs, or were in serious conflict with their parents. Nevertheless, Max recalls her telling him at school one day that she was off to try marijuana. By then he'd read the anti-drug book *Go Ask Alice*, was firmly opposed and threatened to snitch to their parents. He doubts she followed through. The backstage group drank at parties but seldom to excess. Helen didn't smoke. When she started dating, she chose 'good, decent individuals', Max said.

Her behaviour may have been moderated by the fact Pat and Cath's public profile attracted more than enough stress without her adding to it. The household endured abusive phone calls, intimidation and even a bomb threat.[13] In May 1979 she noted in her diary that someone had phoned the house threatening to throw a Molotov cocktail at Pat. 'I hate these sorts of phone calls, they really scare me. He couldn't care less,' she wrote. In a later entry she noted: 'Three abusive calls last night. Quite a joke really.'[14]

As a prominent unionist, Pat was a particular focus and his car was repeatedly attacked outside the house. The tyres were let down, oil was poured over it, and one occasion it was spray-painted from top to bottom, with the word 'Commo' scrawled across the boot.[15] Pat and Cath assured Helen and Max that people who made brash threats were unlikely to follow through with violent action, but they were sufficiently worried about the possibility of a break-in that they rigged up a panic switch at the foot of Helen's bed; it was to set off an alarm in the house of their next-door neighbours, Keith and Lorraine O'Neill.

Helen told film-maker Tony Sutorius in 2016 that as a teenager she was 'proud to be associated with my mum and dad'.[16] She was happy around the table of Cath's salon, joining political discussions and 'soaking up information like a sponge', remembered Don Swan, who was drawn into the Shannon Street network as an anti-Vietnam War and anti-apartheid campaigner and then as a Cleaners Union organiser.[17] Although Helen occasionally wrote angrily in her diary about Pat's drinking and her frustration when Cath barred her from doing something, friends who spent time at the house never saw her in conflict with them. 'She had an amazing relationship with both her parents,' Blackburn observed.

Activism came naturally. She was a member of an anti-nuclear group, leafleting the school whenever a protest was scheduled in Wellington and marching with her peers into the city centre. When the Springboks arrived in the bleak depths of the 1981 winter, she was better informed than the average teenager. By then Shannon Street had hosted Andrew Molotsane, a South African trade unionist brought over by the union movement to educate New Zealanders on the scourge of apartheid and to build pressure on Muldoon to cancel the tour. 'The pig made a statement on TV tonight about the Springboks,' Helen wrote in her diary on July 6, 1981.'It looks like they are coming.' [18]

She joined several Wellington anti-tour protest marches, including on July 25, the day protesters on the field in Hamilton forced the match against Waikato to be abandoned. 'We blocked the whole motorway,' she noted. One day during the tour, when she and Kinsella went into a café her anti-tour protest badge provoked a rude comment from the proprietor. They walked out 'telling him to get stuffed'.

She noted with distress in her diary four days after the Hamilton match was called off that police had struck peaceful protesters in Wellington's Molesworth Street with batons. It was the first time batons had been used against the anti-tour movement and Rona Bailey was among the victims. 'What pricks,' Helen wrote. 'I'm scared about what could happen now.' She was upset when her boyfriend's father suggested anti-tour protesters 'should be flattened'. When she remonstrated that she was part of the anti-tour movement, he told her she 'should be flattened too'.[19] Pat and Cath forbade her from demonstrating when the Springboks played the All Blacks in Wellington.

Eventually there was a crackdown at Wellington High on the amount of class time members of the backstage group were skipping. Several quit school in protest at the start of the sixth form, but Helen stayed on, leaving at the end of the sixth, in 1981.[20] Her organising skills were noted with approval by the school principal, T.K. Royal. 'She is a good student and a fine person who shows real initiative and responsibility in getting things done. ... We know she will succeed,' he wrote on her leaving certificate.[21] Decades later, many in the backstage group remained in touch, despite widely varying political views and career paths ranging from finance and consulting to small business and the arts.

While Helen had largely kept to the straight and narrow, her brother Max drifted off the rails. Where Helen liked to be in control, Max was, by his own account, reckless. When he was 16, he lost an eye while fooling around with friends and a gas-powered slug gun. He fought terribly with his father. Pat's beer drinking was part of the rhythm of life at Shannon Street, but by his teens Max had come to hate it. He clashed with Pat over the things he wanted to do, such as get a motorbike. Pat forbade this, even though Helen was allowed one at the same age.

When he was about 16 he abandoned his anti-drug views, having tried dope and discovered a liking for it. He became tied up with Wellington's post-punk drug scene – the fashion for torn jeans, op-shop clothes and bizarre hairdos would have strained Pat and Cath's patience – and spent time on the dole. A job lugging mail bags at the Public Service Garage left him with a back injury and several years on ACC, much of which he spent living up at the bach at Rangataua.

Max thought of Helen as his 'big little sister'. 'She had a big personality and kind of slipped into that family mould of a high degree of self-sacrifice for the betterment of others.'[22] But she wasn't invulnerable. Her diary entries reveal she was tender-hearted and sensitive to slights. Her emotions were unguarded. She fell in love easily and wanted to be loved. During her high-school years she had two long-term boyfriends. Both relationships ended in months of hurt and confusion. 'Can't bear to be alone,' she wrote just after her 18th birthday, towards the end of a year in which she had cried buckets of tears and often wondered when her heartache would ease.

Pat and Cath's political convictions hadn't changed since their expulsion from the Communist Party in 1970 and they remained active: Cath's CARP work was a priority, and in 1976 Pat had taken on the enormous challenge of building up the docile Cleaners Union into an industrial force. In 1977 they decided they could no longer sit on the political sidelines. They did what they would have once have considered unthinkable and joined the Labour Party. 'Muldoon was at his worst, attacking everybody who showed the slightest bit of left-wing thinking,' Cath told her friend Anne Goodman. 'We thought we should learn the lesson of Germany, where all the left had fought each other while the Nazis, the fascists, got into power. The people of the left should stick together, even if they are not ideologically as one. We thought the Labour Party was the only viable organisation.'[23]

Having decided to throw in their lot with Labour, they would invest as much commitment and passion in it as they had in the Communist Party. Cath became president of the Mt Victoria branch and secretary of the electorate committee for Wellington Central, and was a big supporter of Fran Wilde, the progressive young woman who took the seat for Labour in 1981. Pat exerted his influence through Labour's affiliates' council, the umbilical cord that connected the party to its trade union roots.

Helen shared her parents' new political conviction. She sold Labour Party raffle tickets at school, scrutineered for the party on polling day in 1981, door-knocked and helped at fundraising fairs. The association with Labour drew a broader network of people into the Kelly household. Among them was a young dental nurse and party activist who had moved to Wellington from Hamilton and was recruited by Cath to serve as Mt Victoria branch secretary. Annette King became part of Cath's salon, coming often to Shannon Street for Sunday lunches. 'We'd sit round the kitchen table talking politics, Pat would be smoking like a train and Paul Robeson would be playing in the background,' King remembered. She and Cath became close. Cath's thatch of dark hair had gone grey and King would dye it for her while they gossiped and talked politics. Helen babysat King's daughter, Amanda.[24]

Pat's move to the Cleaners Union had opened up a new sphere of influence and introduced a fresh cohort of young radicals to Shannon Street. Many of these people would be union elders, mentors and critical advisers to Helen when she rose to lead the movement three decades later.

Some thought it had been an odd move for a militant like Pat to go from the Wellington Drivers' Union, which operated at a choke point in the economy and could exercise serious power by shutting down critical transport links, to an insipid outfit dominated by low-paid women working in scattered worksites, a union utterly dependent on compulsory membership and the system of conciliation and arbitration. But over the following years Pat would apply the organising model he had learned from Chip Bailey – building a workplace delegate system, running stopwork meetings where workers could talk about their problems and priorities, producing a lively journal that reflected members' concerns and informing them what the union was doing in their interests, and leading strikes for better pay.

When he took over as secretary – at the urging of the vice-president Ernie Abbott – the union was an exemplar of the complacency that the conciliation and arbitration system enabled.[25] His predecessors had made no attempt to encourage grassroots activism. There were no meetings of members and scant communication. Indeed, his predecessors hadn't even attempted to enforce compulsory membership – when he took over numbers were capped at 600, enough to pay the union secretary and part-time administrator and cover the rent at Trades Hall. When workers tried to join the union, they were told it was full and turned away. Pat told interviewer Pat Webster that when he arrived and asked to see correspondence from members, he discovered there wasn't any because his predecessor had thrown it all in the bin.[26] Pat's predecessor allegedly responded to a request from one long-standing union member to see him by saying, 'Good, I'll send him a photo.'[27]

Pat put in huge hours – often meeting workers in the middle of the night as they cleaned and kept watch in the capital's high-rise buildings – to build the membership and win their confidence. Cath helped out voluntarily, and their friend Don Swan worked for free for several months in Palmerston North until the union was able to employ him as an organiser.

Through her work with CARP, Cath had got to know Hazel Armstrong, a young lawyer and feminist. Unable to get a job in the male-dominated legal profession after she graduated in 1974, Armstrong had gone to work for the New Zealand Clerical Employees Association, producing its magazine *Paper Clip*. Cath was a regular contributor, writing under the CARP banner about the cost of living, and promoting the idea of a 'social wage' that would be guaranteed to cover the cost of health, education, clothing and food.

Armstrong and her partner Bob Kerr, an artist and illustrator, were absorbed into the Kelly household. Many in Wellington's left-wing networks found Cath forbidding, judgemental and prone to fierce grudges, but Armstrong adored her and the two became close. On Sunday evenings she and Kerr would walk over to Mt Victoria from their home in Roseneath for Cath's specialty dinner of chicken and roast potatoes. The conversation would range across current affairs, international human rights battles, left-wing strategy, strikes and disputes, and family. Dave and Maggie Morgan and their daughter Jenny would often be present.

At Cath's instigation, Pat recruited Hazel Armstrong as Wellington organiser for the Cleaners Union, signing up members, meeting them in their workplaces (often in the middle of the night), checking their payslips to make sure they were getting their entitlements, working alongside Pat on award negotiations, and writing and producing the union's journal, *Advance*. 'Throughout that time of working for Pat, I regarded him and Cath as my parents,' Armstrong remembered. 'That's how it worked. Pat was boss, the father figure.'

There were differences over strategy. Pat insisted on control from the top; Armstrong believed in giving more autonomy to workplace delegates. But they were united by a drive to 'get the best deal for workers in the capitalist framework. The Shannon Street philosophy was that capital is powerful, they will make you be a child chimney sweep if they can get away with it, so you have to have equal power in the union movement to counteract the negative forces. It was about the dignity of work. [Pat] taught me that every job is skilled, that cleaning is a skilled job. The job of the union was to empower workers and represent their interests. He was a brilliant strategist. He taught me that it's very easy to start a dispute and much harder to stop it.'[28]

Another absorbed into Shannon Street during Helen's and Max's teens was Peter Cranney. In 1978 Cranney came under Pat's influence while he was working as a cleaner and union delegate in Wellington high-rise buildings. Five years older than Helen, he would later become a highly effective lawyer representing workers and unions, and one of Helen's most influential confidantes and co-campaigners.

'Pat was into organising the members,' Cranney said. 'To my mind, that meant that he believed in equality. He thought people should be organised, should be strong. If you were a toilet cleaner he didn't think for a minute you were inferior. Helen was the same and that was one of her big strengths. There were always rank-and-file workers coming in and out of the house. It was a language of struggle, of battle.'[29]

Some of the struggles were long and hard but brought significant wins. In 1979, the women who cleaned the New Zealand Army base in the small central North Island town of Waiouru went on strike for nine weeks. They had previously been employed directly by the Defence Department and received state sector rates, but when the work was handed over to a private cleaning contractor the company sought to pay them at the much lower private sector cleaners' award.

There was an important principle at stake: why should workers take a pay cut simply because their work had been contracted out? It was a perennial problem for women in the cleaning industry, which was increasingly dominated by private sector contractors, most of them foreign-owned. Pat and the union had gone into battle over the issue several times previously but this one, involving the army and a workforce in a harsh remote location, had added gravitas. *Advance* reported: 'If they could knock over Waiouru, [private contractors] must have thought the rest of the state contracts would be easy pickings.' The workers 'understood they were fighting for a principle bigger than themselves'.[30]

The family bach at Rangataua became the base of operations. Don Swan lived there during most of the strike, with Pat, Hazel Armstrong and Peter Cranney coming up from Wellington to provide support. The workers set up a picket on State Highway One and blocked attempts to bring in scab labour. The army camp was declared 'black' – a signal to other workers not to cross the line. Deliveries of meat, fresh goods, petrol and beer were blockaded.

As freezing weather gave way to summer, the contractor backed down. The 33 female cleaners and their union had won. It was a rousing endorsement of Pat's philosophy as he'd expressed it in *Advance* earlier that year: 'We need a movement of activists – all union members must become active. Any other philosophy means handing the working people on a plate to the boss.'[31] A newspaper cartoon depicted a military tank stopped in its tracks by a cleaning woman with a mop and bucket.

Within a decade of taking over leadership of the previously moribund union, Pat would achieve the unthinkable – a pay rise of over 30 percent for private sector cleaners, taking them to within a whisker of the rates paid to tradesmen under the metal trades award. 'We have lifted all our members out of the low-paid section of the workforce,' he wrote after a seven-year campaign to get all cleaners paid at the same rate, regardless of whether the employer was a school, a government department or a private contractor.[32] When the Arbitration Court decided on the pay rise in 1986, Chief Judge Jack Horn commented that he found it 'strange indeed' that workers would be paid different wages for work that was 'substantially similar'.[33]

Don Swan remembered Pat's performance as he advocated for his members in the court. 'He said, "How would you like to have to go and clean up shit that's scattered up the walls of toilets, and [clean up] toilets that are flooded with shit and rubbish everywhere?" … He used to shame them by using these sorts of analogies and personalising it.'[34] Pat Kelly, the militant unionist, turned out to be an outstanding operator of the conciliation and arbitration system, although the regime by then was in its death throes.

Throughout Helen's teenage and early adult years, Pat was at the peak of his influence and operating on multiple fronts, although he never succeeded in his ambition to get on to the powerful ruling executive of the Federation of Labour.[35] While still with the Wellington Drivers' Union he had become the lead negotiator for the various unions that covered workers at the massive car assembly plants in Hutt Valley and Porirua, and he continued to build his power base at the factories after he moved to the Cleaners Union.

Thousands of workers were employed in the car plants, where boxes of 'completely knocked down' parts would arrive from overseas, to be assembled into vehicles for the New Zealand market.[36] In the 1970s and early '80s the plants were hotbeds of union militancy, and magnets for bright young radicals who had abandoned their university studies and middle-class prospects to join the proletariat; they were part of a worldwide left-wing movement known as the 'Turn to Industry', inspired by the idea of helping to radicalise and organise the working class.

Several of these young activists came under Pat's influence in his role as union convener and as president from 1977 of Wellington Trades Council, the district council of the Federation of Labour. The trades council was a raucous vibrant outfit that attracted big crowds to its monthly meetings, coordinated industrial action, raised funds to support striking workers, and brought international human rights activists to New Zealand to talk to workers.

Peter Cranney spent five years at the General Motors plant in Petone before joining Pat as a full-time Cleaners Union organiser in 1984. 'Pat was an internationalist,' he recalled. 'He was heavily involved with the trade ban on Chile, heavily involved in the anti-apartheid movement, brought in speakers from the Philippines, South Africa, Chile ... We had anti-apartheid committees in all the factories. We had delegates' committees. Everyone was organised, even the rubbish collectors. Pat used to say, "Get them into the water, they will learn to swim."... He was a big personality and worked very hard.'[37]

Strikes were common at the car plants. No one cared about the legalities. 'In those days we didn't even think of that,' Cranney said. 'We would just walk off. We had so much power, the employer wouldn't dare to threaten us legally ... We would walk into the boss's office and put our feet on the table.

'Sometimes Pat did that. But he was a good unionist in that he knew you had to build relationships with bosses. He said, "You can't just fight, you've got to talk." He did thousands of deals with bosses and knew some of them very well.'

Funds were constantly being raised for activist causes and Pat excelled at extracting support from employers. 'For example, we'd have a South African visitor coming,' Cranney said, 'and we'd need grog and food for the function. Pat would ring DB Breweries and say, "Lion Breweries have agreed to give me 60 dozen. Can you match it?" They'd say, "No problem, Pat." Then he'd ring Lion and say, "DB have said they'll give me 60 dozen." Then he'd send some of us to Gear to get meat. ... He'd ring a bakery in Newtown and say, "We need a couple of trays of bread" and they'd say, "Yep, come on out." We'd make as much money as we could at the function and then give it all to the [visiting activist] to take back.'

In the 1970s and early '80s, a time of peak union power, the cost to employers of pitching in with the requested goods would likely have been less than the cost of defying a request. The backscratching was mutual. The employers knew they could call on a trustworthy unionist like Pat, a man who had control of his union, to help them sort out an awkward employment issue or quietly redeploy a hopeless worker.

Another who came under Pat's influence while working in the car factories and who would figure in Helen's later rise to union prominence was Robert Reid. Born into a National Party family in Dunedin, Reid rejected his conservative roots as a teenager, got involved in the anti-Vietnam War and anti-apartheid movements and became a committed socialist. In 1974 he abandoned his university studies to work at the General Motors components plant in Petone; he would stay there until made redundant in 1984.

Pat thought too many unions had not just abandoned class struggle and worker activism but were deliberately suppressing it, Reid recalled. He was willing to defy the union hierarchy and harness his regional power base and the enthusiasm of protégés like Reid and Cranney to change that. He didn't care about treading on the toes of unions he thought were too conservative, including the powerful Engineers Union, to which Reid belonged. 'For example, Pat would give us letters with basically no legal status at all, signed by him as president of the Wellington Trades Council, to give us right of entry into any workplace in the Hutt Valley. Any workplace. We were trying to build a movement. Vietnam had subsided and so it was anti-apartheid and moving towards the Springbok tour, and it was about a whole resurgence of working-class struggle in general. ... So we would take time off work – Pat would even arrange that [with the companies] – and go out and organise workers around the Hutt Valley. He'd arrange for us to be paid by the Wellington Trades Council for the lost wages.'[38]

John Ryall, another who dedicated his life to the union movement after joining the 'Turn to Industry' and would become part of Helen's network of influential confidantes, also came under Pat's wing while working in the car assembly industry. His union, the Storeman and Packers, wasn't interested in grassroots activism or nurturing effective delegates. Pat was the opposite, and Ryall found his oratory persuasive from the first time he heard him in full flight during wage negotiations.

'Despite the employer representatives having all sorts of degrees, etc, Pat could still get the better of them with his speeches about economics and politics, and he had a large group of active delegates who would lead a strike at a moment's notice,' remembered Ryall. 'As president of the Wellington Trades Council, he knew he could bypass [conservative] union officials and could also depend on the motor plant delegates to organise hundreds of members to march against nuclear warships, apartheid, the Springbok tour, the SIS Bill.

'He impressed on us that we had to be disciplined,' said Ryall. He didn't always adhere to his own rule book, however. Before one march, he called his troops in and harangued them about the need to behave peacefully, 'and then in the next morning's paper there's a photo of him across the front page trying to belt someone over the bonnet of a car.'

Pat's vision of a socialist future was expressed not just through stirring speeches, strikes and protests, but through practical and personal action, said Ryall. 'Pat had a good heart for people in distress and would help all sorts of waifs and strays that came into his life and the life of his children. On two occasions when I was a delegate at New Zealand Motor Corporation he phoned me up and told me that he had managed to get the company to employ a youngster who had been in trouble. He wanted me and the other delegates to keep an eye on him, give him support, make sure he didn't get sacked and to report to Pat if he wasn't turning up to work. … He was always interested in families, was very conservative when it came to respect for the family and making sure that the wives and husbands of organisers were being treated well and that the union work was not putting stress on these relationships.'[39]

'They were forever bailing people out,' remembered Cranney of Pat and Cath. 'Helen was the same.'[40]

By 1981, Pat – assisted by able lieutenants like Hazel Armstrong and Don Swan – had built the Cleaners Union into a fighting force of 4000 members. Women who scrubbed toilets and mopped floors in the middle of the night had industrial power and Pat was prepared to deploy it where necessary. When the cigarette-maker Rothmans changed its cleaning contractor, his members there went on strike for nine days to ensure existing staff were taken on by the new outfit. When it became known the police had used Wellington South Intermediate School as a control centre at the height of the Springbok tour, the union placed a ban on cleaning the school hall. When some workers 'scabbed' during a cleaners' strike at Television New Zealand's studios at Avalon, they were condemned by the union and the executive moved to take steps to have them removed from the industry.[41]

Pat saw his members as troops in a class war in which they would ultimately be victorious. Swan remembered one of his favourite lines, frequently directed at employers across the bargaining table: 'Workers will be making history while you are being crushed by the wheel of history.'[42]

These were days of mounting union militancy and industrial conflict, not just in New Zealand but through most of the developed world.[43] Strikes, rare during the 1950s and '60s, were commonplace by the '70s and '80s. And while the union movement was a vital partner in the mass protests against apartheid, nuclear weapons and other causes – which undoubtedly helped to force permanent social and policy change – most strikes were over wages, conditions and management practices.[44] Union confidence in the aging conciliation and arbitration system had been permanently damaged in 1968, when the Arbitration Court ordered there would be no pay rise under its General Wage Order that year because of the nation's economic difficulties.[45] Workers were outraged. With inflation running at five percent they were effectively being told to accept a pay cut for the good of the country. Although the Federation of Labour – led by the conservative ex-plumber Tom Skinner – and the Employers' Federation formed a united front to go back to the court and extract a five percent pay rise, the infamous nil wage order was the beginning of the end for the arbitration system. The FOL condemned it as protecting employers' interests, and unions increasingly chose direct bargaining and strikes as their preferred methods.

New Zealand's post-war prosperity melted into a series of crises, including the two oil shocks of the 1970s, the loss of Britain as a guaranteed buyer of farm produce when it joined the European Union, and the collapse of commodity prices.[46] Every year there were hundreds of strikes. In 1976, Pat's first year at the Cleaners Union, over 200,000 workers were involved in stoppages. In 1979, the cleaners who picketed the Waiouru army base were a mere ripple in a tidal wave of unrest: that year 158,000 workers were involved in 523 different strikes.[47]

Strategically important sectors were the most strike-prone. The meat industry accounted for between a third and two-thirds of working days lost to strike action between 1978 and 1984. In 1978, a year when there were 153 meat industry strikes, blood flowed on the streets when drought-stricken Southland farmers, angry at the stoppages that were delaying the killing of their stock, drove 1300 sheep into the streets of Invercargill and slaughtered them.[48] Transport, manufacturing, pulp and paper, and construction workers were also heavily represented in strike data.

Year after year, the pattern continued. Inflation reached 18.4 percent in mid 1980. It was eating away at workers' earning power, fuelling on-going militancy. Muldoon, on the other hand, blamed rising wages, even though his own policies – including his 'staggeringly reckless' universal national superannuation scheme, increasingly generous subsidies for farmers, and 'Think Big' programme of debt-funded energy projects – were pouring petrol on the inflationary fire.[49]

Muldoon had come to power pledging to protect the country from 'the gangster union boss who does not believe in our system and wants to see it destroyed'. He kept up his public attacks, accusing the unions of ballot rigging, illegal use of funds, intimidation, forgery and theft.[50] While the government and the union movement were locked in a cycle of combat and mistrust, unemployment rose to levels not seen since the Depression.

Muldoon made increasingly desperate efforts to hose down the pressure for wage rises. In 1979 his government passed the Remuneration Act, which empowered it to reverse wage increases agreed in bargaining between unions and employers. Pat called it 'fascist to the ninth degree'.[51] The union movement staged a one-day national strike when the Act was used to reduce an eleven percent pay rise negotiated by drivers.

Helen, who turned 15 the day the strike started, marked the occasion in her diary: 'A general 24-hour strike has been called starting from 12pm Wed 19. Dad is really pleased. … The whole of Thursday there should be nothing working at all. It will be quite fun.'[52]

The labour movement won. The matter was referred to the Arbitration

Court, which decided on a rate of increase just a fraction below the level originally agreed in negotiations.

The government tried to use the Remuneration Act again the following year, when striking workers at the Kinleith pulp and paper mill in Tokoroa achieved a deal for a 20.5 percent pay rise. Muldoon tried to limit it to 18 percent. Again, the union movement united in opposition and workers around the country were levied to support the Kinleith workers, who were on strike for 80 days. Again, the unions won the battle, with the government agreeing to reinstate the original pay rise, although not before Muldoon descended into a round of communist bashing, accusing the Socialist Unity Party of masterminding the whole situation and publishing the names of 32 unionists alleged to be SUP members.

Pat described Kinleith as the most significant victory the working class had had.[53] But the unions were losing the war. After years of holding their own in what had become an industrial relations battleground, unionists were shocked when 50,000 people, led by a 22-year-old sales representative named Tania Harris, marched down Auckland's Queen Street on March 2, 1981. The focus of their outrage was militant unionists, particularly 'pommies' like Pat Kelly. The banner was 'Kiwis Care'. 'We must pull together, not apart!' Harris urged the assembled crowd, while voices rang out against 'commos' and 'stirrers'.

Cath, writing to Ann and Wolfgang Rosenberg in Christchurch, described the Auckland marchers darkly as 'Aryan youth'.[54] Helen, then 16, observed with considerable prescience: 'Talk about bad news for the unions.'[55]

Muldoon rejected the strengthening view in business circles that the labour market should be deregulated but was happy to use the union movement as a whipping boy. His allegations that militant unionists were destroying the country found a sympathetic audience, including some workers. After Helen left Wellington High School at the end of 1981 and went to work as a forecourt attendant at a service station in Wellington's Tinakori Road, she sparred with two fellow workers who agreed with the prime minister's narrative against the 'wrecker' unionists.[56]

New Zealand's industrial relations system was breaking down under the strain of inflation and an economy no longer delivering the prosperity that been the norm during the post-war decades. But efforts to come up with a reformed model were stymied by officials and government.[57] By 1982 over 60,000 people were out of work and inflation was flaring to 17 percent.[58] Muldoon proposed a five percent pay rise combined with tax cuts. The FOL rejected the proposal. Against all advice from officials, on June 11 Muldoon declared a 12-month freeze on wages, prices, rents and professional charges.

Pat called it 'a joke'. Business, he said, was treating the price freeze with contempt, while the wage freeze was 'tight as a drum. The thrust of the regulations is to skin workers alive whilst the other sectors of the economy continue on their merry way. … The government's action has pushed the trade union movement against the wall and has succeeded, in my view, in creating a climate of fear and intimidation amongst certain sections of trade union leaders'.[59]

Helen, earning $150 a week pumping petrol at the garage, noted the prime minister's desperate new measure to control inflation. 'Muldoon has put a wage freeze on, the bastard. It's war again I guess.'[60]

Just down the road from her workplace, pressure was building among frustrated officials at the Treasury for more far-reaching economic changes. Employer groups who had long supported the arbitration system as a guarantor of industrial calm were turning to more radical proposals. Workers continued to strike in huge numbers to defend incomes that were shrinking as a result of the freeze.[61] The number of unemployed kept rising. As Helen Kelly entered adulthood, New Zealand seemed grounded by an oppressive fog of desperate measures, vitriol and blame.

5. Terror and revolution

We've got a Labour government. Yay!
Helen Kelly, 1984

Helen was rehearsing a play on the Karori campus of Wellington Teachers' College when word came through of an explosion at Trades Hall. Someone had been killed.

It was the evening of March 27, 1984, and the college drama group, of which Helen was an enthusiastic member, was working on *The Birthday Party* by Harold Pinter. Helen had a leading role as Meg Boles, a boarding-house operator. By then she was also president of the college students' union and student representative on the college's governing council. These roles that occupied much of her time.

A member of the administrative staff came into the rehearsal room and asked to speak to her. Her face went white as she received the news. Her body seemed to crumble with shock.[1]

She and Max knew Trades Hall in Vivian Street like the backs of their hands: throughout their school years they had often gone there at lunchtime and after school. They knew most of the unionists who worked there. The building's caretaker Ernie Abbott, who lived in a flat on the top floor, was their friend. He would give them the bottles he had gathered from around the building and they would redeem them for cash at the dairy over the road. Often they would wait for their father in Abbott's flat, watching TV or playing with his dog, Patch II.[2]

It was clear to Helen's close friend Clare Leniston, who was at the rehearsal, that her first thought was that Pat could be the victim of the blast. Helen knew Pat was in Trades Hall, involved with meetings relating to Muldoon's wage freeze. For years she had lived with threats to her father and Leniston knew fear over his safety ate away at her.[3]

Helen was 19 and in her second year at teachers' college. She was still living at home, intimately observing the cut and thrust of union organising, soaking in Pat's and Cath's socialist interpretation of New Zealand's economic ailments. A general election was due later that year; Shannon Street was committed to getting the Labour Party in and Muldoon's loathed government out.

The battle against the freeze had dominated Pat's work, like that of the wider union movement, since it came into effect. What had begun as a 12-month ban on wage negotiations and an exemption-riddled freeze on prices had, by early 1984, become a freeze on wages alone. Muldoon had been unable to find a way out of his desperate gambit. He refused to allow wage bargaining to resume until the Federation of Labour, Employers' Federation and government reached agreement on a new wage-fixing regime. After more than a year of talks, consensus remained elusive.

The normally fractious and splintered union movement had acted with unusual unanimity against the freeze, coordinating protest rallies that attracted some 90,000 workers in towns and cities across the country. In Auckland alone, 60,000 turned out.[4] The FOL had repeatedly called for a $20-a-week pay rise to relieve the economic strain on workers; instead, Muldoon granted an $8 General Wage Order, due to come into effect on April 1.[5] On March 26, the first strike in a FOL-backed 'right to bargain' campaign against the freeze had begun.[6]

Rubbing salt into the wounds, Muldoon had coupled the wage freeze with tax cuts that gave significant gains to the higher paid but little or nothing to the low paid; some even ended up paying more tax.[7] At a time when thousands of workers were being thrown out of work, he had also capped the amount that could be paid in redundancy.

There could be little doubt as to the purpose of the government's policies. Shortly after the freeze was announced, the minister of energy,

Bill Birch, had told a business group the intention was to lower real wages. More jobs would become available if workers accepted lower pay, he said. 'Whether voluntary or otherwise, the willingness of employed labour to accept more moderate wage increases is essential to overcome the underuse of our labour force.'[8]

By the start of 1984 almost 70,000 New Zealanders were officially unemployed – or, to borrow Birch's phrase, 'underused'.[9] Industrial relations were chaotic and Muldoon resorted to bluster and abuse. Some of his signature 'Think Big' projects, including the expansion of the Glenbrook steel plant and the Marsden Point oil refinery, were beset by strikes. Muldoon called striking boilermakers at Marsden Point 'industrial thugs' in one dispute, and threatened to bring in 1951-style emergency powers in another. Striking Invercargill meat workers were called stirrers, agitators and fermenters who were responsible for 'mindless stoppages'. He accused some union leaders of being 'drunk with power'. The editor of Catholic newspaper *The Tablet* chimed in: some strikes, he said, were of such a nature that to participate in them could be described as 'sinful'.[10]

Over 140,000 workers had gone on strike during 1983, and 1984 was shaping up to be equally troubled.[11] The triggers were varied. Many stoppages were in protest against the wage freeze, but there were also demarcation disputes, health and safety concerns, action against the hiring of imported workers instead of locals, issues with new technology, and disputes over allowances and conditions.

From February 1984 there was a new provocation – the government had brought in voluntary unionism. There were walkouts by workers who refused to work alongside people who had resigned from their unions.[12]

After hearing the news of the explosion at Trades Hall, Helen tried to phone home but the line was engaged.[13] Ralph McAllister, the college's drama lecturer, walked with her to her motorbike, a 250cc that was far too big for her and from which she had regular spills.[14] She sped home as fast as she could. Much of the inner city was clogged by police roadblocks as a result of the blast, which had coincided with rush-hour traffic. By the time Helen burst through the door of Shannon Street, the house was chocker with shocked unionists and supporters.

Pat was safe but Ernie Abbott was dead.

As he finished tidying the building for the day, Abbott had shifted a well-worn suitcase that was sitting in the ground floor hallway, tucked against the wall behind the kiosk that served as his office. The innocuous case held a bomb armed with a mercury switch. The switch would trigger an explosion the moment the case was moved. It was packed with the equivalent of one kilogram of gelignite, and a bottle of petrol to amplify the damage.

The front of the 64-year-old's body took the brunt of the blast. Abbott was so badly burned and disfigured that he could be identified only by the tattoos on his forearms, which police matched against a photograph.[15] He was killed instantly; his watch stopped at 5.19 p.m. Miraculously, Patch II survived, suffering second-degree burns to his face.

The bomb left a scene of devastation. There was debris everywhere – doors blown off hinges, windows shattered, walls and cladding damaged – although the building structure stood solid. A car parked on the street was blasted out from the kerb.

The act of terrorism was clearly targeted at the union movement. It was a miracle the explosion hadn't happened earlier in the day and that Abbott was the only casualty. Some time between about seven a.m., when Abbott unlocked the back entrance, and seven-thirty, when Henry Stubbs, secretary of the Tramways Union, arrived at work, the suitcase had been carried into the building and placed in position. The perpetrator had used an old 60-minute stove timer to temporarily disarm the mercury switch, allowing enough time for the bomb to be transported into the building without blowing up.

The act had required skill, daring and murderous intent. The bomb was designed to kill whoever moved it.

The management committee of the Wellington Trades Council, chaired by Pat, had spent much of the afternoon meeting in a room on the other side of the wall against which the suitcase sat. They were focused on a strategy in which Cleaners Union members would take a leading role in stoppages and pickets against the wage freeze. It was hoped public opinion would be swayed by protests drawing attention to the plight of low-paid women workers.[16]

People came and went through the day, and no one moved the suitcase or thought there was anything untoward about its presence.

Henry Stubbs walked past it on his way to work at the Tramways Union's ground floor office.[17] A staff member of the Coachworkers Union, who was printing leaflets to support the industrial campaign, walked past it several times as he came and went from the printing room.[18] Two teenage girls came through the building at lunchtime, thought about taking it but decided against it.[19]

Pat noticed it when leaving the building shortly after five with Graeme Clarke, the secretary of the Trades Council; they were on their way to a regular meeting of the council, which was to be held at Fraser House, Labour Party headquarters. He considered picking it up but he had a briefcase in one hand and a bundle of the freshly printed leaflets in the other.[20]

When word of the explosion reached Pat, Clarke, Stubbs and others at Fraser House, they hurried back to find the street crammed with police cars and fire crews. A devastated Pat later returned weeping, sobbing and incoherent to Fraser House to break the news of Abbott's death.[21] Like him, Abbott was a Liverpudlian. They were mates. Abbott had been caretaker at Trades Hall since 1966, and Pat had known him since his Wellington Drivers' Union days. He was a stalwart of the Cleaners Union and had just retired as its vice-president, replaced by Pat's protégé Peter Cranney. The day before, the union had awarded him life membership. He was well liked as a kind-hearted and opinionated man, a racegoer who would donate his winnings to the Sisters of Compassion.[22] Helen and Max were extremely fond of him.

The attack struck at the heart of the union movement and the Kelly family. 'It was absolutely blood-chilling,' Helen said in an interview in 2014. 'We all felt complete devastation and fear for the first time.'[23]

A large police homicide team worked on the case, offering a $25,000 reward, but no one was charged. The police developed a psychological profile of the killer as a paranoid loner whose likely motive was extreme anti-union sentiment.[24] At Shannon Street there was fear of tarring an innocent person with the blame. 'I think we decided it wasn't really fair to speculate without real grounds,' Helen told film-maker Tony Sutorius.[25]

However, there was a widely held view that Abbott's murder had its roots in the years of anti-union invective from Muldoon and his government – right back to the 1975 general election, when the National Party had run a slick TV advertising campaign showing factories being closed by union militancy, deriding British immigrants who 'import class prejudice and industrial anarchy' and featuring dancing Cossacks who would take over New Zealand's companies and farms if the Labour government retained power.

Helen was still working part-time at the Tinakori Road garage. The workforce of mechanics was 'very split between anti-union and union ... Some of them were quite cruel – "Oh, it had to happen" – and others were totally devastated. But I think the majority of New Zealanders were shocked that it had got so far. We were shocked that it had got so far. This was a real attack on the rights of unions and workers to operate effectively in this country.'[26]

She joined 3000 unionists and supporters at Abbott's funeral at the Wellington Town Hall, sitting with a stoic expression as she listened to a succession of speakers express their grief and rage.[27] A large banner behind the lectern read: 'If blood be the price of your cursed wealth – good God we have bought it fair.'[28] Mourners gathered on the street outside to hear the service broadcast through loudspeakers.

'Ernie Abbott is the victim of an outrage that we never ever believed could happen in this country of ours,' Pat told the packed Town Hall. His voice quavered with shock and anger.

'To those people who have, over this last ten or so years in New Zealand, engaged in dividing the nation, have engaged in bashing the trade unions, who have been preaching a hatred of trade unions, or organised large marches in Auckland on the basis of hate, who have consistently and constantly since the '70s put forward this vitrolic line, this line of hatred – I say to them, you will now need to reflect. Is this what you sought to achieve? Because if you did, you have been successful – but successful in striking down an ordinary working man, an active trade unionist certainly, but striking down a man who was going about his ordinary work.'[29]

After the service the congregation marched silently behind the coffin, which was carried on the back of a ute driven by Cleaners Union organiser Don Swan. Swan took Abbott on a final circuit of Lower Cuba, Manners, Taranaki and Vivian Streets. Around the country, workers downed tools to attend memorial services. One employer, Doug Catley, whose security company was often in conflict with the Cleaners Union, wrote out a cheque for $250 and asked Pat to pass it on to Abbott's family.[30]

Like her father, Helen saw Abbott's murder as the product of a sustained campaign of anti-union rhetoric. 'What I remember around the time was this absolute anti-communist, anti-socialist, anti-reds-under-the-bed hysteria, which was designed to shut down trade unions and discredit them. It was run by Muldoon and it was vicious. People were being forced to be scared of trade unions and to see them as the threat. It got worse and worse. It was a war of words,' she told Tony Sutorius. 'I don't know if the union movement was sophisticated enough to capitalise on that and explain how we had got here. ... I think they were in disarray and shocked by it.'[31]

Remarkably, she returned to college the day after the bombing. 'Probably they're trying to get Dad,' she told friends. She said police were checking around their house and looking under cars.[32] Clare Leniston said the attack shook Helen to the core.[33]

Letters of sympathy and outrage flooded into Shannon Street and the Cleaners Union. For many, the attack was a call to action. 'We are more determined than ever to uphold the trade union principles that Ernie spent his life fighting for. Appropriate stoppage action has been arranged in his memory,' wrote Peter Cranney, on behalf of the car assembly workers of the Hutt Valley.

Some could not resist the opportunity to score points. 'If anything, it [the bombing] underlines the urgency of finding a solution to the seemingly endemic problems with New Zealand industrial relations over the last few years,' wrote Max Bradford, then a rising force in the Employers' Federation and a key proponent of the radical labour market deregulation that would be enacted seven years later.[34]

As the shock subsided, life returned to normal. The Cleaners Union moved in with the Hotel Workers Union until Trades Hall was repaired. The campaign against the wage freeze continued, with strikes in the meat industry, at Marsden Point, in paint, carpet, ice cream, chicken and chemical factories, in the transport industry and on the waterfront. In Wellington, Pat's Cleaners Union members went on strike for a month against Crothall and Company, affecting the operation of more than 20 office buildings and maintaining a 24-hour picket – where Helen sometimes provided support in the evenings – at BP House in Customhouse Quay.[35] The focus on getting Labour elected into government sharpened. And Helen continued her full and rewarding life at Wellington Teachers' College, including helping bring the production of *The Birthday Party* to the stage.

She had started teacher training at the beginning of 1983, after a year working full-time at the service station. She had been accredited University Entrance in 1981 but hadn't considered going to university, despite the strong academic heritage of the Eichelbaum family and the fact her mother had an arts degree.[36]

Her time at Wellington Teachers' College coincided with the last years of a golden era of liberal arts teaching at the institution. Students could choose from one of four majors – drama, visual arts, music and social studies. Helen chose Ralph McAllister's drama stream. For three days each week, she and about 70 other students would work with McAllister on major theatrical productions, four a year, which were performed publicly in Wellington and then taken out to schools around the North Island. The standard was so high the public performances were seen as talent-spotting opportunities for Wellington's professional theatre companies.[37] Pat and Cath were unfailing supporters and attended every production.[38]

'It was immersion in the arts,' McAllister would say of the philosophy underpinning his work with young trainees. 'Teaching skill emanated from that. Drama, and this style of learning, taught the ability to respond in the moment, which is the lifeblood of teaching. … Whenever people said, "Oh, that wouldn't work with a class" we would go out to a class and I would say, "Right, let's show them that it does work."'

McAllister believed drama could be the vehicle for teaching any subject. 'All the work we were doing in schools was devoted to getting children to make decisions for themselves. If they wanted to dig a hole in the ground and put all the rubbish of the world into it, we would dig a hole in the ground [metaphorically] and put all the rubbish in it. And all the time we would reflect on it with them, every step of the way.'[39]

He was a gifted and inspiring mentor, able to shift effortlessly between teacher, role-player and director. He could quickly exploit a negative situation within the group or in a classroom and turn it into an opportunity for learning. His approach was underpinned by clear values: children were to be treated with warmth and patience; trust lay at the core of the teaching relationship.[40]

Every week McAllister took a group of students to Porirua Hospital, where they worked with up to 100 long-stay patients with severe mental illness. Helen joined the group as often as she could. The work was demanding, rewarding and confronting, said Allan Marsden, who graduated from college before Helen but remained heavily involved. 'We wouldn't plan anything. We would just go there and work with some severely disturbed people. Ralph's method was to empower them ... I remember working with one person who demanded I become an alsatian dog. When you are working in that sort of environment your ego goes, everything goes. You come out feeling very humble.'[41]

Drama called for a high level of commitment; there were many late nights rehearsing and preparing for performances. There was no room for pretence or artifice. 'Teaching is not an intellectual process. It's about the ability to relate to people,' Marsden said. 'So what Ralph did was just take us on. He would strip us bare, and we'd take it. Because of that, our ability to relate to people has been fundamental in our lives and professions.'

Because the students worked such long intense hours together, strong bonds developed. Helen remained loyal and close to many of these people, including McAllister, throughout her life. She was also part of a group that spent many evenings hanging out at McAllister's home, drinking gin, discussing life, and being introduced to his classical collection and favourite musicals.[42]

'She was vibrant, fun and interesting, so people were attracted to her,' remembered Michelle Saban, a close friend from these days.[43] She was also active and outspoken. Her college peers assumed a life of public leadership lay ahead of her.

She was never short of male admirers, but according to Liz Baldwin-Featherstone 'there were no high heels, no make-up. There was really a whole part of her that was too scary for men. Men wanted to be her mate.'

To McAllister, Helen was 'a quiet leader. She never stood up and said, "I know best." She never lorded it over others. There was no bombast about her. I would not have called her charismatic; I think that grew with time. She was one of the group, utterly reliable, and also quite good at drinking.'

Helen wrote to McAllister – likely in mid 1985 – of her thanks and gratitude. 'You have given me my passion and it is something I would never have found without your help and loving guidance.'[44] In later life, she spoke of her college years as the period in which she gained a true education. 'No fees, full student allowances, and we could study as many papers as we liked. … The place was liberal and smelled of teaching – it was a vocation and an honour,' she said in 2010. She learned from McAllister that as a teacher 'you had amazing power and you had to use it respectfully and in the interests of the kids. We learned to understand that kids are citizens too, to whom adults owe a special responsibility to support as they grow, to trust them, never bully them or make them feel afraid of your power.'[45]

At the college she cut her teeth in politics. She had joined the students' association executive in her first year, and a month after her 19th birthday was voted in as president for the 1984 year. As president, she also represented the students on the college's governing council.

Student politics was a mix of protest, organising and partying. The minister of education, Merv Wellington, was overseeing cuts to education funding, and the students' association worked with associations at Victoria University and nationally on campaigns against the austerity measures.

The association's vice-president Parks White remembered Helen as 'schooled in this. … She really understood the organisational structures and the networking, and the need to bring people on board with you, to not alienate the opposition but be able to have a discussion and get an outcome. She was pragmatic, and mature beyond her years … very articulate, very smart, very focused.'[46]

Her methods were conservative compared with those of more rabble-rousing colleagues such as White and Kevin Ward, the association's communications officer. With Merv Wellington cutting funding, the college's principal, Margaret Malcolm, had to call for voluntary redundancies. At the same time Wellington declared it would be compulsory from the start of 1985 for all state schools to fly the New Zealand flag. This was supposed to foster national pride. Ward created a flag featuring a cartoon of the minister with corks in his ears and the Southern Cross represented by dollar signs. *The Dominion* was tipped off, and early one morning, surrounded by a large crowd of students, the flag was hoisted on the college flagpole. Helen thoroughly approved of the stunt.[47]

In their role as student leaders, Helen and Parks White were delegates to the primary teachers' union, the New Zealand Educational Institute. It was the early days of bringing together the country's blue-collar unions, represented by the Federation of Labour, and the state sector unions, represented by the Combined State Unions, into a new body, the Council of Trade Unions. Union business was routinely carried out by men in smoke-filled rooms. Periodically, an attempt would be made at the Wellington Trades Council to ban smoking in meetings, recalled Robert Reid, one of Pat's protégé's from the car assembly industry. 'And on every occasion Pat wouldn't even put it to the vote. He would just rule it out of order and then roll a smoke.' One day Helen turned up to a meeting of Wellington union delegates to discuss the proposed Council of Trade Unions. Pat was in the chair. 'Helen put her hand up and moved there be no smoking. The motion passed overwhelmingly. She succeeded in rolling her father on something we had all failed to achieve.'[48]

Meanwhile, as student rep on the college's governing council, her singular success was tabling and winning support for a motion that the college be declared a nuclear-free zone. It was carried with one dissension at a meeting on August 4, 1984.[49]

By then New Zealand was three weeks into what would become a brutal economic upheaval. Coincidentally, the nuclear issue had been the vector for a sudden change in the political climate. Muldoon had called an early election on the night of June 14, 1984 after Marilyn Waring, a young National MP, had withdrawn from the caucus and select committees in protest at her party's threat to effectively suspend democracy if Parliament passed an anti-nuclear bill introduced by Labour's Richard Prebble.[50] National had a majority of just one seat, and despite Waring's assurance that she would vote with the government on matters of confidence, Muldoon – visibly drunk as he spoke to reporters – announced he couldn't govern without an 'effective assured majority'. New Zealand, he announced, would go to the polls in four weeks.[51]

It became known as the 'schnapps election'. There was a sense of despondency across the country after years of Muldoon's divisive tactics, misuse of executive power and heavy-handed interventions in the economy. The Labour Party was being led by David Lange, a 41-year-old South Auckland lawyer and brilliant orator. It had a line-up of fresh and talented spokespeople. It was in a good position to win.

So many volunteers turned up at Labour headquarters in Fraser House that the organisers struggled to find jobs for everyone. There was a mad rush to get people enrolled, and tables were quickly set up around the city so voters could get on the rolls before they closed.[52]

Fran Wilde, the MP for Wellington Central, saw 'people for Africa. We had volunteers flooding in. Everyone wanted to get rid of Muldoon'.[53]

Unions affiliated to Labour pulled out the stops. Peter Cranney was released from normal duties at the Cleaners Union to work full-time for Cath Kelly's good friend Annette King, who was standing for Parliament in the Horowhenua seat, her first time as a candidate. Don Swan and fellow Cleaners Union organiser Mary Slater worked for Margaret Shields in Kāpiti. Cath, as chair of Labour's Mt Victoria branch and secretary of the Wellington Central electorate committee, brought her organisational skills and dogged commitment to the job of getting Fran Wilde back in.

At the college, Helen had made her left-wing views well known in her role as student president, attacking government funding for private schools 'which only children from wealthy backgrounds can attend' and advocating for a tax system that redistributed wealth. 'Personally I think it is healthy for people to give a little to help each other … Do you mind paying taxes so a mother can afford to feed her baby? I put it to you that there are some people in this country that have spent their lives taking, taking, taking,' she wrote in her column in the student newsletter *Little World* in March that year.[54]

But when it came to the snap election, she was careful not to use her position to push Labour's barrow. She was 'politically astute', said

Parks White, and instrumental in organising representatives from all parties to speak on campus.[55] Among them were two candidates for the Ohariu electorate, in which the college was located: Wellington property magnate Bob Jones, who had formed the New Zealand Party in 1983 and was attracting support from disaffected National Party voters, and a young Labour candidate called Peter Dunne.

Labour won power with 43 percent of the vote, enough to claim a simple majority under the first-past-the-post electoral system. A fifth of voters backed small parties. The most popular was Jones' party. It split the right-wing vote and helped inflate Labour's majority.[56]

Even before it formally took power, the fourth Labour government assumed a mantle of drama and change. A currency crisis had developed during the campaign, with speculators dumping the New Zealand dollar in anticipation of a post-election devaluation, a measure officials had been recommending and which Muldoon had repeatedly refused to implement.[57] After the polls closed, Treasury and Reserve Bank officials informed Lange and his senior colleagues that an immediate 20 percent devaluation was needed. They agreed but Muldoon was still technically in power. Muldoon's refusal to devalue created an economic and constitutional crisis. He finally relented, but his intransigence had made the incoming Labour leaders looked measured and capable by comparison.

However, behind the aura of competency was an unresolved ideological battle within Labour's ranks. On one side were those who backed the new finance minister Roger Douglas, and his recently adopted faith in 'New Right' economic theories of small government, flatter taxes, deregulation and market liberalisation, and those who agreed economic reforms were needed but saw a significant role for the state in export growth, industry development and job creation.[58]

Going into the election, these differences had been papered over by an ambiguous economic policy document in which the two sides agreed to disagree on what a Labour government would actually do.[59] Policy was left 'so vague that Douglas was given an almost free hand once in office', wrote political commentator Colin James.[60]

After the election Pat Kelly warned of the challenges ahead. 'The country is broke and Labour's task is immense. ... We can expect Labour to do a lot of things that cost little or no money but go a long way to bringing about a more caring society.' He looked forward to an end to anti-union legislation, a return to compulsory union membership, the closure of the South African embassy and the declaration of a nuclear-free New Zealand.[61]

Helen permitted herself to celebrate the victory in her post-election president's report in *Little World*. 'We've got a Labour Government. Yay!! No more having to take insults from Merv!'[62]

But the delight at Shannon Street was short-lived. By the end of the year a Cabinet supportive of Douglas's economic agenda was firmly in control. As minister of finance Roger Douglas was in philosophical lockstep with Treasury, where belief in the merits of untramelled market forces in all spheres of the economy and society had become the in-house culture over the previous few years.[63] New Zealand soon had a new word in its lexicon: Rogernomics.

Pat quickly foresaw falling living standards for workers and rising unemployment. By December 1984 he was predicting that 'if the present economic direction of the Labour government remains they will be out of office by 1987, or before'.[64]

The devaluation had forced up prices and eaten into workers' incomes, while higher earners would benefit from planned tax cuts. Meanwhile, the lowest paid would bear a disproportionate burden from a proposed new ten percent goods and services tax.

At the same time, the new government had started feeding New Zealand's traditional import protections into a bonfire of liberalisation that would cost thousands of jobs, including those of the car assembly workers whom Pat had helped harness into an industrial force. Douglas also had his sights on government trading agencies. In his first Budget, in November 1984, he floated the idea that they would have to perform like private companies and make a return on investment.[65]

New Zealand's financial market was soon one of the freest in the world: Muldoon's interest rate controls were gone, the dollar was floated in early 1985, and the war on inflation was waged through monetary policy. Interest rates soared – the cost of home lending reached 19 percent by September that year, en route to a peak of 20.5 percent in 1987 – which attracted foreign money, which pushed up the dollar, which drove down exporters' profits, which in turn drove them to lay off workers.[66]

There were early consolations for unions, however. The minister of labour, Stan Rodger, followed through on Labour's election promise to restore compulsory membership, telling Pat the union movement needed to take the opportunity to get itself into a stronger position for 'subsequent membership onslaughts by National'.[67] And award bargaining was permitted to start again in 1985. Thanks also to the government's progressive stance on South African apartheid and its commitment to nuclear-free policies, Pat believed New Zealand was 'regaining the image it lost as a caring nation'.[68]

Douglas's blitzkrieg of economic changes was in line with policies that had taken hold in Margaret Thatcher's Britain and Ronald Reagan's United States. But within the Labour government's first two years Douglas went 'further and faster than any other minister – certainly in democratic countries – to deregulate the economy and expose its industry to market forces', Colin James wrote.[69]

Shannon Street found itself in a determined struggle to 'bring the party back to its senses', as Pat put it. 'If we sit back and do nothing to change the direction the government has chosen, then we will deserve all we get ... The traditional base of the Labour Party, the working people, is falling away. It is being replaced with upper middle income earners and high income earners.' The government needed to be pressured to bring back price and interest rate controls and import controls, and start a programme of public investment in the economy to create jobs, he argued.[70]

By then, Pat was chairing Labour's affiliates council, coordinating the unions that belonged to the party, working hard to stop them splintering off in protest at Rogernomics and trying to harness them into an effective force on the party's left.

'He was the glue that held [the party] together,' Don Swan said. 'He would just talk people through it and tell them to be patient. He always said "the working class will prevail"'.[71] He was the numbers man at party conferences, charging around mustering the votes of affiliated unions in support of this remit or against that, albeit without success on two that stood in defiance of Rogernomics – one against the introduction of GST and the other for a 'planned, self-sufficient, socialist economy'.[72]

Margaret Wilson, the party's president from 1984 to 1987, respected Pat's analysis, which was firmly grounded in the Marxist education he'd received through the Communist Party. He was 'opinionated and pig-headed', with an 'absolute commitment' to the union movement as the best way to deliver equity for working people and a firm belief in a strong role for the state. 'He was a very good organiser,' remembered Wilson. 'He understood people quite well. He had that mixture of being quite aggressive, but then being extraordinarily kind and understanding.'[73]

Cath, too, worked aggressively against Rogernomics from within her party branch and Wilde's electorate committee. 'It was very torrid. Every monthly meeting we were passing resolutions criticising our own government and trying to get them to change,' she recalled. 'As secretary I had to write the letter and send it in. Peter Dunne was secretary of the caucus. ... Of course as soon as he read it out they'd say, "Huh, Pat Kelly's wife!" He'd write a polite reply.'[74]

Her own behaviour was not as civil. 'I recall at one regional [party] conference – perhaps '87 or '88 – getting up to speak, and being hissed by her,' Dunne recalled. 'But you took that. It was part and parcel of what was going on ... They were extraordinary times. The Labour Party was going through an intense fight for its soul.'[75]

Annette King, once a close and trusted friend, now an MP in the government of Rogernomics, was no longer welcome at Shannon Street.

In 1985 Helen was approaching 21 and keen to go overseas for a year. She wanted to celebrate her birthday in the UK and spend time with her Kelly relatives in Wigan. The Teachers' College was relaxed about students breaking into their training; she would be able to complete her diploma on her return. She had finished her stint as president of the students' union and had a good group of close friends.

Among them was Chris Wratt, a talented actor and singer who had taken several major roles under McAllister's direction. Helen's friendship with Chris had grown through the two-and-a-half years they'd been at college together – working on productions, partying, and sipping gin at the McAllister home. They had performed together in *The Birthday Party*, *Fiddler on the Roof* and *Guys and Dolls*, and in a two-part play.

Chris was good-looking and reserved. He came from a conservative

National Party-voting Marlborough family that was the polar opposite to Helen's. Like her, he had thrived in the free-thinking and creative environment cultivated by McAllister.

Helen's flight to London was booked for late July 1985. Chris and two other friends drove her up the North Island to Auckland Airport. By then they were in love. He would join her in the UK, he told her. 'I think taking her up [to Auckland] made me realise just how much she meant to me, and I quickly made up my mind to follow her,' he remembered.[76]

Helen stayed initially with her relatives in Wigan, then moved in with her cousin Mathew Dart, the son of Cath's sister Margaret. Mathew was squatting in a complex of Bonnington Square houses tagged for demolition, involved in a co-op that was working to reclaim and upgrade the buildings for community housing.

Chris drove back to Wellington, saved some money and joined Helen a couple of months later. During their time together in London they lived in a squat in Vauxhall Grove. 'It had plastic sheeting on some upstairs windows and the only running water was a cold tap in the kitchen. We flushed the toilet by filling a bucket and tipping it into the bowl afterwards,' Chris remembered.

Helen auditioned for a place at the Royal Academy of Dramatic Art but, despite weeks of rehearsing and preparation, was unsuccessful. She worked in various short-term jobs and by the end of 1985 was employed day-nannying for a family near Tottenham Court Road while Chris washed dishes in a bankers' restaurant. The couple went to countless shows, drank in pubs and got to know Pat's family in Wigan, cementing relationships that Helen would maintain through her life.

In the midst of the London winter she was confronted by a sight then rare in New Zealand. As she and Chris were sitting in a Kentucky Fried Chicken outlet she looked out the window and saw an old man eating out of a rubbish bin. 'I bought him a bag of chips. Felt really sad – nothing seems right when you see that. Everything goes out of perspective – all your own troubles. Really knocks me back,' she wrote in her diary.[77]

One night they faced a terrifying home invasion. Chris answered the door to two men, who pushed their way in, forced the couple down on the bed and ransacked the squat for money and drugs. He and Helen were unharmed but badly shaken.

In the spring of 1986 they headed off to Europe. Helen found leaving the children for whom she'd been nannying painful. She worried for their future, particularly when, a few days before they were due to leave London, news broke of the Chernobyl nuclear disaster. 'Feel really ill,' she wrote. 'Feel I can't leave my boys in this mess. What have they got to live for?'[78]

She and Chris bussed to Greece and spent six weeks in Crete, other islands and northern Greece before heading to Venice, where they met up with Cath. The three then travelled back to England via Paris. Pat was waiting for them at Wigan Station and showed them around his old haunts in Bootle. Chris began to understand the rich working-class traditions that Helen had inherited from him. 'You'd go to a family party [in Wigan] and one of the uncles would stand up and go, "Right, who's going to do their song now?" Someone would stand up and sing a song through and everyone would join in with the chorus. Pat and Cath would stand up and sing "The Red Red Robin", which was their party number. Helen loved it.'[79]

They returned to New Zealand in the second half of 1986, plugged back into their college studies and graduated in December. Helen came away with a glowing testimonial from the college's principal Graeme Oldershaw, who described her as a person of 'strong intelligence, independently minded, forthright and capable of moving happily amongst small and large groups.' Her recent travel, added to her work as student president, 'has given her a particular poise, as well as experience. She is an able and polished organiser and public speaker. Overall, she is a deeply concerned citizen of wide interests.' Her professional work had been marked by a 'vigorous and positive outlook, a high level of cooperativeness, initiative, and an enthusiasm and drive which produce excellent conditions for learning.' Her personality was such that she would 'succeed anywhere.'[80]

There was no need for the couple to go job-hunting – under the system of the day they were placed by the governing Education Board into jobs in the Wellington region. Helen got Johnsonville School and Chris Corinna School in Porirua.

Helen's cousin Tom Patrick and his siblings were again bereft. Their mother Max – Cath Kelly's sister – had died thirteen years earlier at the age of only 51 and now they had lost their father Charles, a senior executive with the New Zealand Dairy Board, at 64. Tom, the youngest, was left living alone in the family home in Wilton Road. Helen and Chris had moved home to Shannon Street on their return from the UK, but now it made sense to go and live with Tom, share meals and help him through his grief. The three lived as flatmates in the large elegant home hung with an extensive New Zealand art collection.

For the second time in his life, Helen was an emotional anchor for Tom. 'They had lots of friends,' he remembered, 'and drove around in Cath's old yellow Toyota Corolla.' Helen was bright, politically engaged and compassionate. She was also 'as funny as hell – similar to Pat but possibly slightly darker in her humour, and more blunt. If she was locking horns politically in any situation she could get really pissed off. She didn't seem to mind who noticed, because she was almost invariably better informed than her counterparts.'[81]

At Johnsonville she taught a composite class of seven- and eight-year-olds. The school principal Jean Marending thought 'Oh dear' when she heard that Pat Kelly's daughter was coming to her school. 'Everyone knew who her father was.' But Marending quickly found her to be 'a very sympathetic, caring and conscientious teacher.'[82]

Within days of arriving at the school Helen took on the role of union delegate to the NZEI. There was plenty to do: Labour's juggernaut of change was about to reach into the education system. Lange had taken over the education portfolio and initiated a radical overhaul after Labour was returned to power in the '87 election with the support of many traditional National voters and despite the party's internal divisions.[83]

Tomorrow's Schools did away with education boards and put governance into the hands of locally elected boards of trustees. Schools were to operate as autonomous units, managing their own budgets and buildings, and hiring their own staff. It was all very much in line with Treasury thinking.

Helen and Chris would spend Sunday afternoons in their respective classrooms, preparing for the week ahead. 'The kids loved her,' Chris said. 'One time they were studying the solar system, and she went in on Sunday and completely blacked out the classroom with black plastic.

When the kids came in on Monday morning it was just this dark hole with planets. She was full of energy.'[84]

Amid the intense political ferment, union involvement and classroom preparation, she found time to knit. The results were evident to the children in her class, who were intrigued by her wide range of baggy hand-crafted jerseys. Rebecca Wright was in Helen's class as an eight-year-old in 1988. 'My previous teachers were in tweed suits and shirts, so this was way out there,' she recalled. With Helen's mane of thick dark hair and guitar, on which she had mastered a few chords, 'we thought she was amazing. She was so much younger than all the other teachers. For us, she was kind of wild – super kind and warm as well.'

Her classroom style was 'fluid stream-of-consciousness, rather than a set plan of the day, She was really big on social studies. We spent a lot of our time talking about social justice, race relations, human rights, animal rights. She drilled them into us.'[85]

But beyond the classroom New Zealand was in crisis. Government agencies that had been turned into corporations required to behave like private companies were laying off tens of thousands of workers, as were manufacturers forced to retrench in the face of punishing interest and exchange rates, and tumbling tariffs that exposed them to competition from cheap imports. In the car assembly industry, which Pat knew so well, 2000 jobs had already gone and the sector was destined for extinction.[86]

Between 1985 and 1990 a fifth of jobs in manufacturing disappeared; in agriculture, hit by the rapid withdrawal of Muldoon's extravagant subsidies as well as high exchange and interest rates, one in seven jobs vanished; in construction a quarter of jobs were wiped out.[87]

One of the few areas where jobs flourished was finance – importers and traders now needed foreign exchange services, and advisers and consultants needed central city office space.[88] Share and asset prices boomed – there was talk of New Zealand as the Switzerland of the South Pacific. They would collapse catastrophically when global share markets crashed in October 1987.

By the end of 1988, 156,000 workers were unemployed or on subsidised job schemes, compared with 87,000 two years before.[89] Māori and Pasifika workers, large numbers of whom had traditionally worked in manufacturing, were savagely affected: by 1990, 22 percent of Māori men and 24 percent of Pasifika men were out of work.[90] In districts such as Hokianga, the Far North and East Cape, 'unemployment has become a way of life for whole communities. Young people leaving school no longer expect to earn a wage,' wrote journalist Simon Collins.[91]

Pat's Shangri-La – the post-war paradise of full employment and full bellies – was gone. He had predicted as much after a 1986 trip back to the UK. He had seen Thatcher's New Right policies produce a financial boom in London and the south, and poverty on a scale unknown since the Depression in the north; teenagers left school without hope of permanent full-time work.[92]

The New Right theorem embraced by Roger Douglas, Treasury officials and a rising pressure group, the New Zealand Business Roundtable, required that the labour market be exposed to the same forces of deregulation and competition as farmers, manufacturers and other sectors. Strip the unions of their statutory role, remove distortions such as minimum wages and awards, and the price of labour will rise and fall according to the laws of supply and demand, they argued.

Pat warned his union colleagues of 'powerful forces abroad, such as the Round Table Group [*sic*], Employers' Federation, National Party, and some powerful figures in the Labour Party who are demanding and pressuring government to abandon the national award system and let the market determine wage rates. … The market is not some holy cow.'[93]

He was vilified as a relic of a failed system. Lange condemned him as 'Colonel Gaddafi without the ethnic charm' and he was disliked by the Cabinet for his persistent public criticism of the government.[94] But he was aware of the need for industrial relations change and tried to influence it. Mike Smith, who dealt closely with him between 1984 and 1987 as the Labour Party's trade union liaison officer, said he was a long-term thinker. 'He had a vision for what the trade union movement could be like.'

Pat was good friends with the visionary Australian trade unionist Laurie Carmichael, a key player in the development of that country's Prices and Incomes Accord between the unions and the Australian Labor government: organised labour agreed to restrain wage demands in return for improvements in the 'social wage' through better health care, benefits and pensions. At Pat's urging, Smith invited Carmichael to New Zealand to help the unions develop a response to Rogernomics.[95]

As it turned out, the pressure for radical labour market change was forestalled for the time being. Stan Rodger, a former president of the Public Service Association, thought trade unions needed to be well funded and staffed, with adequate resources to provide legal, economic, and health and safety advice, as well as capable of delivering useful services, such as holiday homes, to members.[96] But as minister of labour he wanted wages to be freed up from the rigid relativities that meant a pay rise for one group spilled through the entire workforce. Soon after the '84 election he had scrapped compulsory arbitration and launched a two-year review of labour laws, which resulted in the enactment of the Labour Relations Act in 1987.

The Act was intended to prod the unions towards wage agreements with individual companies or workplaces, while retaining the structure of national awards, blanket coverage and compulsory union membership. Unions now had to have a minimum of 1000 members, which meant some needed to amalgamate. Rodger even stumped up with a system of soft government loans to assist this.

The state no longer enforced awards. This was up to unions. They had right of access to workplaces, and employers had to provide them with the names and addresses of workers covered by awards. The Arbitration Court was reborn as the Labour Court. Rodger also set up a state-funded trade union education organisation. 'It was all contrary to the thrust of the reforms of that government. I had to go over broken glass to get a whole lot of this stuff,' remembered Rodger.

In 1988 he ushered in the more far-reaching State Sector Act. This radically reshaped the public service and brought government workers' wage-fixing arrangements under the Labour Relations Act.[97] He had also enthusiastically supported the merger of state and private sector union bodies into the Council of Trade Unions, which was finally born, following a long gestation in October 1987.[98]

But these industrial relations reforms were a fragile compromise between Labour's competing ideological factions. By early 1988 the factions were in open combat. Lange had become increasingly uneasy about the social consequences of economic deregulation. He pushed back against Douglas's radical manifesto by cancelling the finance minister's proposal for a flat tax regime. However, a sweeping programme of privatisations went ahead, inflaming resentments on the party's left.

Shannon Street was a nerve centre of internal resistance, and the fraught state of Labour politics was the centre of attention whenever Helen and Chris came for tea. Pat battled to keep the affiliated unions inside the Labour tent. 'The big question became, "Whose party is it?"' remembered Pat Webster, who became Labour's affiliates coordinator in 1987. 'We had the unions fighting among themselves about whether to support the government. The bulk of people in the party didn't believe in what [the government] was doing. But if the unions split then the party would become what ACT [later] became. You would have to form a new party.[99] We knew that was a difficult process in the first-past-the-post system. …

'There was a sense that the unions set up the Labour Party, the Labour Party was ours, and we shouldn't be giving it away. He [Pat Kelly] took the long view.'[100]

Aware of talk of a breakaway left-wing party and knowing that some within the government would rather the party be rid of the unions, Pat made a passionate plea for solidarity. 'The party does not belong to accountants without clients, lawyers without briefs, teachers without pupils, parsons without congregations, doctors without patients,' he told the affiliates council in early 1989. 'It belongs to us. Our movement, our class founded it, nourished it and built it and we must retain it. This objective can only be retained from within.'[101]

In the end, he could not prevent the party from rupturing. He had been close to Jim Anderton, a former party president and, as a member of Parliament from 1984, a vocal opponent of Rogernomics. But in early 1989 Anderton broke away and formed NewLabour. Anderton expected Pat and the affiliated unions to follow him out of Labour. Many individual activists went with him, but no affiliated unions.[102] Pat felt bitter and betrayed by Anderton. Shannon Street remained firmly with the Labour Party.

It was a testing time for Labour's left-wing loyalists. Friendships had fractured along left and right lines from the outset of the Rogernomics experiment; now they were breaking along old Labour and NewLabour lines. Brenda Pilott, who would later lead the Public Service Association, remembered Pat as a powerful presence for those who resisted the lure of NewLabour. 'It was a very introspective time. Everyone was asking themselves, "Where do I belong? What's the right thing to do here?" Many people felt aligned politically with [NewLabour].'

Anderton's backers bristled with left-wing staunchness 'but Pat was a good foil because no one could out-staunch Pat Kelly. His working-class credentials were unassailable. … His absolute rock-solid loyalty to the Labour Party, as opposed to the people who were currently running it, made him someone we could coalesce around. You thought, if he's comfortable to stay in the Labour Party and fight for its soul from within, then that's what we can do. He had that moral leadership.'[103]

Helen absorbed and inherited her father's dogged loyalty to the Labour Party. Years later, Max – who never forgave the party for Rogernomics and argued with Pat and Cath that they ought to turn their backs on it – said he was going to give his party vote to the Greens. 'Helen said, "No you're not!"' It didn't need to be spelled out that they were a Labour household. Max complied.[104]

As the fourth Labour government disintegrated and her parents fought for its soul, Helen poured the bulk of her energy into her class of seven- and eight-year-olds. By the end of 1988 she had had two demanding years in Room Five at Johnsonville School. Jean Marending was impressed. 'Helen runs a very interesting, lively "workshop" style room,' she wrote in her mid-year review. 'Her creative approach and use of drama and music is a feature. But Helen also defines boundaries and behaviours and has created a secure, happy, friendly environment where opinions are respected.

'Her very good classroom climate and sensitive way of dealing with social incidents, e.g. stealing, relationships, etc, is good social studies in action.'[105] Her sensitivity towards children with special learning needs was particularly noted.

That year, she and Chris bought a small house in the suburb of Belmont. They paid $92,000 for the secluded walk-up, set in bush on a hill above Lower Hutt. They wanted to have a baby and agreed they ought to get married first. The wedding was in November 1988 at Fraser House. Helen wore a three-quarter length white wedding dress with choker neckline and puff sleeves, and white court shoes. Reverend Don Borrie, a veteran social justice activist and prominent Labour Party figure from Porirua, officiated before a large gathering of the couple's friends from school, college and work, Shannon Street's network of family and fellow travellers, and Chris's extended family from Marlborough. Dave Morgan was emcee and Don Swan catered the buffet meal. 'We danced the night away,' Chris remembered.[106]

In his wedding vows Chris spoke of his love for Helen's vivacity, brightness and 'unstoppable optimism' and his admiration for her 'commitment to the welfare of others – your class, family and friends'. Helen spoke of Chris's kindness and care towards children, and 'the way you spoil me when I'm depressed ... I see my needs for now and in the future as being support for any political activities I get involved in.'[107]

Helen Kelly loved teaching but she was never going to stay in the classroom. The union movement was calling. In early 1989 she answered the call.

6. The Bill

The Employment Contracts Bill has been introduced into Parliament, and it is much worse than anticipated. ... This bill must not be passed.
Helen Kelly, 1991

Helen was 24 when she took on her first job as a unionist. She was employed half-time with the Early Childhood Workers' Union and half-time with the Kindergarten Teachers Association to run training programmes for workplace delegates and members of the two closely allied unions.

The joint role seemed a perfect way to combine her love of children and interest in education with her commitment to the union movement. It also brought her into the orbit of impressive role models, women who had spent years fighting for decent pay, training and recognition for those who worked as carers and teachers of young children.

In the 1970s and '80s, access to good quality, affordable childcare had become an urgent concern for women who wanted to join the paid workforce or further their education. Lifting the wages and status of early childhood workers, whose jobs were seen as akin to mothering, to which society attached little economic value, had become a key issue for the women's rights movement.

By the time Helen started her new job in March 1989, there had been years of activism by pioneers such as Sonja Davies and Rosslyn Noonan. Davies was a veteran childcare advocate, unionist and feminist. She had campaigned since the early '60s to improve the often terrible conditions in unregulated privately owned and community childcare centres. These centres received little government funding and were staffed by poorly trained workers on abysmal wages. 'Why should those who carry out this very important work be paid less than people on an assembly line or low-paid shop assistants or clothing workers?' she had demanded in 1976.[1]

Davies was convinced it was essential to form a union if the interests of the workers and the children in their care was to be advanced. Noonan, as general secretary of the Kindergarten Teachers Association from 1976 until 1981, had helped transform that organisation into an effective industrial, feminist and professional union, challenging the traditional view of 'kindy' teaching as a brief diversion for young women between leaving school and getting married.[2]

Davies and Noonan had helped drive the establishment of the Early Childhood Workers Union (ECWU) in 1982. The new union, which covered workers in privately owned and community childcare centres, was supported by advice and funding drummed up through the Federation of Labour, where Davies – the first woman to get on to the executive – was by then vice-president, and other unions.[3] The Kindergarten Teachers Association provided ECWU's sole full-time official with a desk and office space.

Just before the 1984 election the Early Childhood Workers Union had negotiated its first award. It covered only 16 childcare centres and didn't include pay rates – this was forbidden under the wage freeze – but it did deliver improved sick leave and maternity leave, limits on hours of work and, in an important breakthrough, the right to an uninterrupted tea break. It was called the Consenting Parties Award.

Despite efforts by the Employers' Federation to frustrate negotiations, by the following year 36 employers had become Consenting Parties.[4] With the wage freeze ended, the negotiators could now reach agreement on pay, although the rates were still lower than kindergarten teachers' pay, which was, in turn, lower than that of school teachers.[5]

Then in 1986 the fledgling union achieved a hard-won national award – again, in the face of staunch resistance from the Employers'

Federation – with blanket coverage throughout New Zealand covering hundreds of mostly privately owned centres. The award provided recognition for trained staff, basic conditions such as sick leave and, in 1987, a 24 percent pay rise, although those on the lowest rate were still only five cents above the country's minimum wage.[6] With bargaining success came a growing membership, and by the late 1980s enough revenue to increase the union's organiser hours in the regions.

At the same time, academic research was proving the importance of high-quality early childhood education. By the end of 1988 the idea of a coherent, well-funded early childhood sector staffed by well-trained teachers – whether in kindergartens or childcare centres – had been embraced by the Labour government in a policy called *Before Five*.

For campaigners who had been part of the decades-long battle for equity and recognition, the release of *Before Five* was a time of great hope and anticipation. However, critical detail was still to be worked out, not least of which was how much government money would be invested and whether it would make its way into workers' wages. When David Lange, both prime minister and minister of education, introduced *Before Five*, he told the assembled early childhood representatives that gaining funding for the sector was like 'snatching raw meat out of the jaws of a Rottweiler'. It ran directly counter to the Labour government's programme of reduced spending, decentralisation and privatisation. It also defied Treasury, which was trying to steer the government away from increased involvement in the sector, dismissing the arguments for quality early childcare education as 'emotive' with 'little objective evidence of the long-term effects'.[7]

All these tensions were playing out when Helen arrived, young and keen, to be interviewed for the job of education organiser with the two unions. She stood out as the leading contender. Helen Baxter, an early childhood activist who had become national secretary of the Early Childhood Workers Union in 1986, was one of her interviewers. 'I remember her walking in, and thinking, "Wow, this woman is going somewhere." She was confident and outgoing. She gave the impression she could do anything and we believed her. … I'm a sceptic and I would normally think, "Oh yeah, but what are you going to produce?" but I found her convincing. … There was no indecision between the two unions about who was the right person for this position.'[8]

Neither the Kindergarten Teachers Association nor the Early Childhood Workers Union would have been able to employ Helen if not for the fact that her salary was funded by the government, via the Trade Union Education Authority (known by its acronym, TUEA). This body had been set up in 1986 by Stan Rodger in the face of strong opposition from the National Party and business lobby groups. Rodger believed in developing an educated workforce; his Union Representatives Education Leave Act allowed for the training of delegates during work time. TUEA funded educators, who were embedded in unions, had legal right of entry into workplaces and delivered training packages on subjects such as health and safety, the economy, biculturalism, company finances, and how to interview workers following accidents or grievances. TUEA even had its own small publishing division, and engaged experts to design ergonomic equipment for workers in the meat industry and on the waterfront.

For many workers, taking part in TUEA programmes was their first positive educational experience. Hazel Armstrong, TUEA's first employee, remembered the organisation as 'transformational. We shifted from an old school to a new school of unionisation. We were very progressive in whom we employed – we made sure we had Māori and Pasifika workers, women, young, old. It was very diverse.'[9]

In the interconnected trade union movement, Helen's prospective employers were aware of her lineage. Helen Baxter had been going to meetings of the male-dominated FOL and Otago and Wellington trades councils to plead her union's case for support and had met Pat Kelly, whom she considered 'a legend … He was the face of the union movement in Wellington.'[10] Clare Wells, a Kindergarten Teachers Association activist who had become president in 1988, had come across Pat through the smoke-filled haze of union power-broker gatherings. Linda Mitchell, a former social worker who had become general secretary of the Kindergarten Teachers Association in 1986, was friendly with Hazel Armstrong and her partner Bob Kerr.

Baxter said the fact Helen was Pat Kelly's daughter was not a factor in her being selected. But it didn't hurt that she came to the job primed by a lifetime of observation and understanding of unionism.

Linda Mitchell remembered Helen's sense of mission. 'She had a very strong idea about making the world a better place. Perhaps she thought she could do more in the union movement than as a [classroom] teacher. As a teacher it's more about the individual families you are working with, but ... the collectiveness of unions was very important to her. She thought as education organiser she would be able to influence the membership and also the public through campaigns. She was a very quick thinker and politically knowledgeable.'[11]

It was a big role for a rookie – writing, facilitating and delivering training courses for delegates and members, working on campaigns, and editing and producing two union newspapers, *KTA News* and *Roundabout*. According to Wells, Helen showed a flair for creative organising and communication from the word go. 'She was a great person for tossing around all sorts of ideas. As soon as she landed on our doorstep she was raring to go.'

Within a couple of months of Helen starting the job, and with funding to back up Lange's *Before Five* promises still to be announced, a headline-grabbing 'Babies in the Beehive' press conference was held under the banner of the Campaign for Quality Early Childhood Education, a broad coalition of early childhood, feminist and trade union activists.

While campaigners such as Rosslyn Noonan – by then national secretary of the primary teachers' union, the New Zealand Educational Institute (NZEI) – pressed the case for decent funding, wages and training, the Beehive theatrette was filled with the sound of babies and pre-schoolers. There was no doubt Helen had a hand in this. Having grown up folding leaflets and pasting stickers for Cath's CARP campaigns, watching Pat at work and supporting picket lines of striking cleaners, she had an intuitive sense of how to attract attention to a cause. And she understood the political obstacles faced by a workforce of women who worked with small children. 'She was very clear that because of who we were and what we did, we were pretty low down the pecking order for media, so you had to do something smart to get your message out,' Wells said. 'That was her MO – very canny and tactical.'

Helen's signature campaign design was the ten-day plan. 'We knew that if you had a one-hit activity you wouldn't get far, but what if you spread it out over a period of time?' She put together a series of resources – ten things you could do over ten days or ten weeks, things like writing to the newspaper, hosting an event, visiting your MP – complete with background messaging, Wells said. 'That boosted the politicisation of our members, because it made them feel confident to front up to an MP and say, "This is what's happening in my job, in my life." She was very clever in thinking about how you mobilise people.'[12]

There was an enormous amount to do and few resources. 'We shared roles a lot,' Linda Mitchell remembered. 'We were often there at night, stuffing envelopes.'[13]

There was always a mad rush to get the union journal out by deadline. Copy would be typed by a secretarial service and then Helen would often literally run through the streets to the Wellington Media Collective, where she would do the paste-up over their light table. Bob Kerr and graphic designer Dave Kent, key members of the collective, were friends and mentors of the early childhood activists.[14]

There were underlying tensions between the Kindergarten Teachers Association, whose members were state sector employees with tertiary qualifications, and the Early Childhood Workers Union, whose workers often had no recognised qualifications. Helen found it easy straddle both camps, and was able to connect the 'politics of the childcare and kindergarten sectors, which helped shift the perception each had of the other and bring the membership together to campaign for policy change and increased funding,' remembered Wells.[15]

There were sometimes blazing arguments about strategy and ideas, 'but it was never personal for her', according to Helen Baxter. 'She wasn't in it for her own personal glory. She was there to do a job and make it better for workers and teachers.'[16] She was pragmatic and productive, uninterested in 'wasting time on activities that weren't producing anything. Sometimes we'd take delegates and executive members to the pub after meetings or negotiations and say, "Wow, thank God, what a good week. We've been really busy, look at what we've achieved." She'd be social but she wouldn't waste too much time on that stuff. She was a hard worker – absolutely committed.'[17]

She was impatient, wanted things to happen quickly, and expected people to keep up. 'That was a tension,' Wells said. 'The membership was conservative. I remember saying to her on several occasions, "We need to take everyone with us. We need to keep the momentum but we can't lose people. If we lose anyone we are sunk."'[18]

The campaigning worked. In the 1989 Budget, a 125 percent increase in early childhood education funding over five years was announced.[19] Helen published the details on the front page of the first combined journal of the Kindergarten Teachers Association and Early Childhood Workers Union, which by then were committed to amalgamation. 'For many years now childcare workers have endured abominable wages and conditions of work, largely due to poor funding of the service. It's difficult to demand a better deal when you know that many parents are already unable to meet the cost of fees, and your employer is hanging out for the next staff grant to keep Inland Revenue off the doorstep. Those days are now over.'[20]

There was no room for complacency: the battle to make sure workers got a fair share of the new funding was still to be waged. But it was a remarkable moment in a long struggle, and another vivid lesson for Helen in the progress that could be achieved through good grassroots organising and persistent campaigning.

In early 1990, Helen went to the USSR for six weeks of study with the Moscow International Institute of Journalism.[21] The country was under the reforming president Mikhail Gorbachev, the Berlin Wall had come down, and the Marxist-Leninist philosophy to which her parents had devoted the bulk of their lives was falling into global disrepute.

Helen was not a journalist, but editing the early childhood union journals qualified her to attend, alongside reporters from international news outlets. She was one of twenty in a group that included participants from the Philippines, India, Nepal, Sri Lanka, Pakistan, Bangladesh, Afghanistan and Malaysia.

She recorded her experiences and thoughts in a hardbacked school exercise book. Her first few days were spent feeling homesick and out of her depth. 'I can see I will have to be assertive to make all these men treat me as an equal and not as some girl,' she wrote. 'That could be very tiresome!'[22]

These emotions gave way to indignation, frustration and concern at the state of the Soviet Union and the direction it was taking. 'Today it became clear why we are here – to help the USSR become capitalist,' she wrote on April 9, a few days into the course. The group had had a lecture that day from a prominent journalist and economist who explained that the USSR was concerned the better organised USA was set to exploit South-east Asia before the Soviets did. 'They say they want closer cooperation with Asia and the Pacific,' Helen wrote. 'I say they want closer exploitation.'

The students had then attended a press conference with Leonid Abalkin, one of the Gorbachev regime's major advocates for rapid economic reform. 'Time Mag, the New York Times, Financial Times and KTA News were all represented!' she wrote home to Pat and Cath.[23] Abalkin had explained how the country would become 'market-oriented – very scary!' she observed in her journal.

That night she tried without success to phone Chris. 'Bloody USSR,' she fumed. 'Nothing works!'

There were lectures on the history of the USSR as it was currently being taught ('Lenin is the hero, Stalin is the baddy'), on the virtues and safety of nuclear power, and on the country's 'choice of radical reform to regulated market economy'. The Soviet Union, the students were told, 'wanted to separate politics from economics'.

Out on the streets of Moscow she saw ample evidence of an economy that wasn't working. Taxi drivers wouldn't accept a job unless payment was in hard currency. 'Corruption is everywhere!' Black market money trading was commonplace but she worried about being on the wrong side of the law. 'I still have not been told if it is illegal or not – everyone offers to change money for you. The hosts of our course should tell us clearly how to buy rubles,' she wrote in exasperation.

In the shops 'the only thing appealing is the Russian dolls. There is very little food or clothing, and to buy you need to queue up, buy a ticket, and queue up again to get your doll. … Every now and then you come across a long queue and that is when something is in short supply. Today we saw a 30-long queue for Palmolive soap.'

Outside the only McDonalds, she saw a queue that went 'all the way around the block. People stood in the freezing cold.' By the end of her time in Moscow, she herself was queuing for McDonalds.'The food was not quite as good as usual, but heaven compared with this place [the hotel where the students stayed].'

Occasionally she came across shops that traded only in US dollars. 'What a change. It was like stepping out of Moscow. Colourful clothes, neat jumpers, "Can I help you?", "Would you like to try that on?"' But for the locals, she observed, 'it's the lack of basics that's worrying them. Sometimes they can't buy milk. Fresh fruit and veges are very rare.' She was shocked to see beggars in the Moscow metro: 'Small children kissing people's boots – it was pathetic.'

There were highlights among the frustrations – going to wonderful operatic and orchestral shows, learning to navigate Moscow's streets, visiting magnificent historic buildings, travelling to the towns of Vladimir and Suzdal, where 'people were dressed as if they stepped out of a folk tale' and women washed their clothes in the river.

In the back of her notebook she listed friends and family she needed to buy gifts for – a near impossible task given the empty shops. Pat and Cath, Max, Chris, her friends from college and school, Hazel and Bob (and their children Kathleen and Robin), Dave and Maggie Morgan (and their daughter Jenny), her early childhood union colleagues (and their children) – the list stretched to some 35 people. There wasn't anything for it but to accumulate Russian dolls, toy dogs, pens and wallets.

Just before her return home she noted in her journal that President Gorbachev had announced a new economic package. 'It includes huge increases in food prices from the first of July. Moscow has gone crazy. People are just stockpiling goods. Queues outside everywhere. The Moscow city council announced yesterday a ban on anyone from outside Moscow buying anything.'

She graduated from the course on May 25, 1990, with a diploma certifying that she had studied 'Theory and Practice of Perestroika in the USSR', 'Problems of Modern Journalism' and 'Russian Language and Linguistics'. She couldn't take her new qualification seriously. The course had been dysfunctional and disorganised. 'The certificate is a joke. The only one I think we really did learn about, talk and discuss was perestroika.'

New Zealand's own perestroika, meanwhile, was continuing to cause social upheaval and political mayhem. The economy was shrinking, unemployment was rising and any benefits from Labour's radical economic programme were trickling into the pockets of the well off. The poorest families had suffered a 20 percent decline in real disposable incomes between 1986 and 1988.[24] Lange had sacked his privatising minister for state-owned enterprises, Richard Prebble, in late 1988. Roger Douglas had resigned as finance minister soon afterwards. When the Labour caucus returned Douglas to Cabinet in July 1989, it had been the final straw for Lange.[25] He resigned in early August.

Pat Kelly, as chair of the Labour Party affiliates council, had made an eleventh-hour appeal to Lange to stay on as prime minister, going to visit him with Pat Webster and party president Ruth Dyson. 'Pat and he just talked; they talked like normal people, which was quite unusual, certainly for David Lange,' Dyson remembered. 'Lange did listen, but he had gone too far in his decision.'[26]

Lange was replaced by Geoffrey Palmer, a constitutional lawyer with a professorial style and little political charisma. Helen Clark, who had been brought into the Cabinet in 1987, became deputy prime minister.

When Helen returned from Russia at the beginning of June 1990, one of her first tasks was to get a union newspaper published and out to members. By then the Kindergarten Teachers Association and Early Childhood Workers Union had merged to become the Combined Early Childhood Union of Aotearoa – CECUA – with a new and upgraded publication, *Double Take*.

A general election was due and the polls were pointing to certain defeat for Labour. Helen led the front page of *Double Take* with a series of interviews with unionists about the National Party's industrial relations policies. The focus was on National's plan to return to voluntary unionism. Her interviewees included her father Pat and Helen Baxter, now CECUA's co-national secretary. 'Much of [the union's] work is for the benefit of all members collectively, and that work can only be done effectively if the union has a sound financial base,' commented Baxter. 'I am concerned about our members ... if membership becomes voluntary. Our members work in small workplaces, and are often isolated. There is also a very high staff turnover in childcare centres. We are facing a future where demands on union resources are bound to be increased, not decreased.'

'This union will live through voluntary unionism,' pronounced Pat of the Cleaners Union, which by then had 5000 members across 800 workplaces. 'We will be making history when the architects of voluntary unionism and their mates in the Round Table are history. This statement is based on faith and confidence in my class.'[27]

In the August issue, Helen led with an article titled 'National Awards – to be or not to be', which focused further on National's plans for labour market change. 'The National Party claims workers who want a union to negotiate their wages and conditions in a national award will have that option, but the practicalities and viability of this under the party's Industrial Relations policy is highly questionable.'

National's policy was for flexible bargaining, but what did that mean? she asked. 'In the Philippines, Thailand and Fiji, workers don't have awards and therefore have "flexible bargaining".' But, she argued, CECUA's members didn't need to look at the experience of workers in developing economies to find out what happened without an award system to protect pay and conditions. Childcare workers knew all too well that until just four years earlier, when they had finally achieved their national award, they were on two to four dollars an hour, with no sick leave, overtime, job protection or guaranteed lunch breaks, let alone recognition of training and experience.

She quoted Clare Wells on what free choice in bargaining arrangements would be like in practice: 'Huge pressure will be placed on workers to opt out and negotiate individually … Once some members are forced out of award coverage, the award negotiations become a farce. We would no longer have the strength to bargain on behalf of those covered by the award.'[28]

By the time Helen published the August issue of *Double Take*, moves to expose New Zealand's workforce to radical change were well advanced. Pat had predicted the Business Roundtable would be beaten by the working class in the long run, but for now the organisation was well on the way to its most significant victory. Years of careful campaigning for sweeping labour market deregulation were quietly coming to fruition.

Stan Rodger's attempt to reform the industrial conciliation and arbitration system by nudging unions and employers towards industry-

and enterprise-based collective bargaining had been under sustained attack by the Roundtable ever since his Labour Relations Act came into force in 1987. The Act was condemned as mere tinkering; the radical reform that was necessary had been 'snuffed out in the trades halls and party caucuses,' said Douglas Myers, chief executive of beer company Lion Nathan and one of the most vocal members of the Roundtable.[29]

All other spheres of the economy had been exposed to deregulation and unfettered market forces since Labour took office in 1984, and the Roundtable saw no reason for workers to be treated any differently. 'The government's failure to come sufficiently to grips with the challenges of labour market reform is one of the biggest disappointments of the last three years,' Myers said. 'Why can't a young unemployed kid in Gisborne go to an employer and say, "Give me a chance, take me on for half the going rate, let me learn and see what I am worth at the end of that time?"'[30]

In earlier years the proposition that wages should be allowed to fall to a level that would soak up the supply of unemployed workers – just as a market oversupplied with cabbages would result in cheap cabbages – would have been dismissed as the fantasy of a union-busting boss. By 1987 it was the serious policy platform of a well-organised, unified and highly influential lobby, and by 1990 intensive efforts were underway to ensure it was embedded in National Party policy.

The Business Roundtable had started out in the early 1980s as a loose grouping of chief executives. In 1986 it had been refashioned as a 'think tank' with a permanent staff.[31] Roger Kerr, a bright, energetic and articulate public servant, was hired as its full-time executive director. Kerr had already made his mark at Treasury as leader of an internal division called Economics II that drove the development of the New Right policy blueprint that underpinned Rogernomics. Roger Douglas regarded him as 'one of the best and toughest-minded thinkers in Treasury' and Kerr spent long hours in Douglas's office from 1984 onwards. Economics II was a formidable group and exerted a strong influence within Treasury. 'Most people found it easier to join them than fight them,' one Treasury staffer told journalist Anthony Hubbard.[32]

At the Roundtable, Kerr proved to be no less effective as a tireless and prolific advocate for free-market policies in all areas of the economy and public sector. He was an admirer of the Austrian economist Friedrich Hayek, regarded as the father of New Right economic theories, and believed trade unions had done 'enormous damage to the interests of workers and the unemployed and to the prosperity of nations in which they were dominant forces'. He believed 'collectivism' and the welfare state were 'deadly economic sins'.[33]

Kerr and his members gave countless speeches, wrote articles, submissions and letters, brought in overseas experts to give lectures and write reports, and commissioned books promoting further deregulation and liberalisation. The organisation spent hundreds of thousands of dollars on consultants and research; almost $400,000 was budgeted for this in 1990, with labour market reform one of the top items of expenditure.[34]

By 1990 the Roundtable's ranks included about 40 chief executives – men (there were no women) who ran companies that represented about 80 percent of the market capitalisation of the New Zealand share market, as well as several state-owned enterprises and private companies. Kerr always insisted it was not a lobby group and didn't engage in 'influence-peddling behind closed doors'; he claimed it was focused purely on the national interest.[35] But it was a hand-picked club of the country's most economically powerful people. Membership was by invitation only, extended by way of letter from the chair after prospects had been checked out by Kerr to ensure they were a good fit. The cost of membership was $30,000 a year, plus further contributions to help with specific projects. Chief executives who supported tariffs, state intervention in the economy or notions of corporate responsibility were not invited.[36]

Kerr was a superb organiser and communicator. He drove the Roundtable's agenda through meticulous planning, personal networks at the highest levels of Treasury and his like-minded members, and an evangelical belief in the case for unfettered free markets.

The organisation saw its task as creating a 'climate of opinion that enables government to make the right decisions'.[37] No criticism of the Roundtable went unchallenged, and people who spoke in opposition to its arguments were left in no doubt by Kerr – through patronising letters or eviscerating public put-downs – that their analysis was inadequate, uneducated and wrong.[38]

'They had automatic access [to the Beehive] almost at the drop of a hat,' remembered Stan Rodger. 'They used to ring my office and say, "I want to see you this afternoon." … I'd say [to my principal private secretary], "Put them off until sometime later next week" or something. I mean, I always saw them. But they marched into the Beehive – Roger Kerr – and just expected to get entrée. They were obsessive about the labour market, largely because of that brewer, Dougie Myers. And they hated me with a passion.'[39]

In the Roundtable's view, the reason New Zealand's economy was failing despite the free-market reforms driven by Roger Douglas was that the changes hadn't gone far enough, having been stalled by the political dysfunction within Labour.

New Zealand's poor productivity growth and high unemployment was, according to Kerr and his members, largely caused by an inflexible labour market in which trade unionists had used their monopoly power to restrict competition between workers and therefore push up wages. They made claims to the moral high ground, arguing that a deregulated market in which individual workers or small company-based unions negotiated freely with employers would bring dignity and opportunity to people who were out of work. 'It is certain the mountain of labour market reform is another mountain that has to be scaled if we are to reach the sunlit uplands of a more productive and fully employed economy,' enthused Myers.[40]

Helen Clark had become minister of labour in August 1989, with oversight of Rodger's Labour Relations Act. Responding to the pressure for further reform, in early 1990 she developed an amendment to allow employers with more than 50 workers to initiate company or enterprise-based collective bargaining and move out of national awards.[41] By then – thanks in part to Labour's removal of compulsory arbitration in 1984 – the pattern of industrial relations had begun to break with many of the traditions of the past, with greater flexibility beginning to emerge in the range of wage increases and hours of work in award settlements, reflecting the varying economic conditions faced by industries.[42]

Rodger had also put an end to the long-standing tradition of unions and employers settling major strikes at whisky-soaked late-night meetings in the Beehive, mediated by the prime minister or minister of labour. His hands-off approach to disputes had earned him the nickname 'Sideline Stan'.

None of this was enough to satisfy the Roundtable, which insisted the Labour Relations Act was 'a machine for job destruction'.[43] The group frequently misrepresented the industrial relations systems of more prosperous countries, such as the United States and Japan, in order to make unfavourable comparisons with New Zealand's regime, according to American employment law scholar Ellen Dannin.[44]

Free up the labour market to allow individual workers and employers to bargain directly without union interference, let employers fire workers at will, and New Zealand's economic growth rates would 'leap to a minimum of seven or eight percent per annum', Myers said in July 1990. 'My strong impression is that comprehensive labour market reform is an idea whose time has come. … There is little support for the view that the relationship between employers and workers in small firms needs government nannying.'[45]

The relationship between workers and employers was 'in the very essence cooperative', argued Kerr. It involved a redistribution of risk between employee and employer, in which employees were offered a stable price for their labour in return for the employer's right to manage. If there was an 'almighty struggle between capital and labour', it had been created by New Zealand's highly centralised industrial relations system. The ideas underpinning that system – that there was unequal bargaining power between workers and employers and that the workplace relationship had special characteristics – were 'myths'.[46]

The Employers' Federation, which represented around 13,000 companies and provided its members with award-bargaining expertise and lobbying services, was traditionally more pragmatic and conservative than the Business Roundtable. Many of its members were small businesses, and some surveys showed they had little desire for radical industrial relations reform. For many employers the award system had advantages, setting comparatively low wages and keeping pay rises below the rate of inflation, saving small businesses the bother of time-consuming pay negotiations, and ensuring a level playing field in which a competitor down the road couldn't undercut on wages.[47] Some liked awards because they kept the unions further away from the workplace.[48]

However, by 1989 the Employers' Federation's policy on industrial relations resembled the Roundtable's.[49] The two organisations waged relentless public relations attacks on unions, depicting them as privileged third parties to the employment relationship, wielding power to keep wages up and price the unemployed out of jobs. They claimed a deregulated labour market would deliver pay deals that met the needs of both companies and workers, fix New Zealand's poor productivity, and promote close workplace relationships unsullied by union bosses.

The objective was to 'return to an emphasis on the liberty of individual workers,' wrote Roundtable policy analyst Penelope Brook in a book published in 1990 as the campaign to deregulate the labour market reached its zenith. The case for reform 'rests on a recognition that human dignity and human happiness depend on the championing of freedom and individual responsibility,' she concluded.[50]

In reality, the Business Roundtable and Employers' Federation 'wanted a law that would give them complete control', Ellen Dannin wrote. The policies they promoted would lead to 'oligarchic employer control and powerless unions relegated to a peripheral role'.[51]

The National Party had promised to introduce legislation to deregulate the labour market before Christmas if it won the 1990 election. Its manifesto listed the changes it planned to bring in: voluntary unionism, allowing 'flexible bargaining arrangements', letting workers choose their own bargaining agents, giving industrial agreements the status of binding contracts, and bringing 'true democracy to the workplace with a wide range of choices'. There was scant detail as to how all this would work in practice.[52]

The party's industrial relations spokesman Bill Birch was a pragmatist, better known as the driver of the Muldoon government's 'Think Big' projects than an acolyte of free-market thinking; he had proposed changes that would deliver substantial but incremental reform. At the other end of the spectrum was Ruth Richardson, National's finance spokesperson, who was ideologically at one with Kerr, the Business Roundtable and Treasury, sharing their view that radical deregulation to allow pure freedom of contract between workers and employers was needed.[53]

Richardson railed against what she regarded as the male-dominated union movement's 'stitch up' in sectors such as the meat industry. 'If you looked at who were the big earners in the freezing works, they were the slaughtermen. And who got the dregs? They were the women who were confined to very difficult and very exacting cutting operations at a fraction of the wage. ... There was no way in the world they were going to do anything to disrupt what was blokes' bounty.'

New Zealand's industrial relations system, she claimed, was a 'job destruction machine' in which the unemployed were locked out with their noses pressed against the window. She would still hold firm to these views three decades later.[54]

The tussle between the Birch and Richardson camps continued as National headed towards the election, but Richardson had the superbly effective Kerr in her corner. The Business Roundtable had been holding regular meetings with the National Party's front bench since late in 1988 to help shape its economic and social policies. It was also running a specific work programme on labour market reform with Birch and National's caucus committee on industrial relations.[55]

By early 1990 this work had achieved 'pleasing developments in National's approach to economic policy', Kerr assured a group of his members. However, 'it does not yet look like a party that is capable of taking the range of tough decisions that are needed and of resisting strong pressure groups'.[56] There was work to be done to ensure National would hit the ground running with far-reaching reform when it became government.

Birch was a worry for the Roundtable. For instance, on the question of pay equity – which the Labour government planned to address through a new Employment Equity Act – he had talked about expanding the powers of the Human Rights Commission and giving it an employment equity role. The idea of a new state-run arbiter of gender equity was appalling to the free marketeers. In a memo to Myers, Kerr wrote that 'there was supposed to be a further National Party statement on the subject. You might inquire into the state of play ... National should take an uncompromising position on repeal, with no add-ons'.[57]

Kerr warned the National Party front bench in August 1990 that, with the economy in a 'serious predicament', massive cuts in government spending would be needed, as well as reform of education, health, transport and social welfare. In the labour market, 'complete freedom of contracting needs to be introduced, not just new options based on the current system'. The Labour Court and its precedents needed to be abolished, 'minimum wage restrictions need to be removed or at least restored to their former relativity, and access to unemployment benefits curtailed'.[58]

Three months before the election Birch brought in an employment lawyer, Paul Bell, to turn National's policy statements into practical amendments to the Labour Relations Act. Bell had previously worked for the Wellington Employers' Association, one of the four regional employer associations that came under the Employers' Federation umbrella.[59] As a hands-on advocate involved in award negotiations and disputes, he believed significant changes were needed to give employers and workers much more flexibility on pay deals and to end unions' monopoly bargaining rights, while preserving workers' rights to be represented. He researched how other countries' industrial relations systems worked, and talked to old hands from the Employers' Federation and contacts in the union movement with the aim of developing 'pragmatic' amendments that could be implemented by National within three to five months of their winning the election.[60]

At the same time, Kerr continued to do the spade work needed to herd National towards a programme of radical change. Auckland lawyer Jim Farmer was tasked to draft a completely new employment law based on pure freedom of contract.[61] Efforts to influence Birch also continued, including a Roundtable session with American legal scholar Richard Epstein, a prominent advocate of free contracting at work, to whom the Roundtable was close.[62]

The Labour Government staggered towards electoral defeat. Seven weeks before the election, Palmer was replaced by Mike Moore. It was a desperate measure but Pat Kelly commented that, while the unions were still on the back foot, 'I think Mike can turn it around'.[63]

Two weeks later Moore and the Council of Trade Unions signed an Agreement for Growth, widely referred to as the 'Compact'. For several years there had been talk of a tripartite agreement – akin to Australia's

Prices and Incomes Accord – linking wage rises to productivity, and giving the union movement a say in social and economic policy and industry development. The CTU had worked hard with an embattled and divided Labour government to set up the collaborative structures that would be needed but with scant success.[64] Now, with the general election less than six weeks away and the economy falling into deeper recession, the Moore-led government had signed a deal with the CTU to limit wage increases to two percent unless higher rises were justified by productivity gains. Inflation was running at five percent.

In return, workers were offered the hope of lower interest rates, and a promise that low-paid workers would be protected from the impact of government spending cuts, and unions and employers would be consulted on economic policy.

The Employers' Federation immediately dismissed the deal. Roger Kerr labelled it Keynesian, the highest term of abuse from the Roundtable.[65] Many unions were sceptical about the effective cap on pay rises and some were openly hostile.[66]

Helen filled the front page of the last issue of *Double Take* before the election with news of the Compact and CECUA's efforts to ensure the two percent cap on pay rises would not derail its long campaign to secure decent wages for early childhood workers.[67]

As it turned out, neither the last-ditch leadership change nor the Compact rescued the doomed Labour government. On October 27, 1990 it was swept out of office by National, which had campaigned on a promise to create 'The Decent Society' – a country where everyone would get a fair go. Richardson was appointed minister of finance, the first woman in a Western country to hold such a role. Birch was named minister of labour.

A crisis awaited the new government. Within hours of being voted in, Jim Bolger was advised he would have to make swift decisions. The Bank of New Zealand, majority-owned by the state, was in crisis and would have to be bailed out to the tune of $620 million. Further, Treasury unveiled figures revealing the government faced deficits of $3.7 billion, $4.5 billion and $5.2 billion over the following three years.[68]

Just as the 1984 currency crisis had created a climate of alarm and disruption that gave Roger Douglas licence to move beyond his mandate into a programme of radical change, the situation facing the incoming National government created a golden opportunity for Richardson. Over the following weeks she brought together a mini Budget – the 'Economic and Social Initiative' – powered by the 'very strong hand' she had been given by the circumstances. 'Speed was my friend,' she remembered.[69]

As minister of finance, she didn't limit her attention to fiscal matters. Two Treasury officials, one of whom had worked closely with Roger Douglas and was well known to the Roundtable, were appointed to work with her on a 'parallel work stream' for 'full-throated' labour market reform. In her view, there was a risk that Birch would fall short of the radical change needed. The two men from Treasury liaised with Roger Kerr, who had the Jim Farmer draft on hand. 'We effectively formed something of a triangle working together,' Richardson remembered.[70]

She quickly succeeded in shifting the centre of gravity within the Cabinet. When Birch brought his package of labour market reform to the first meeting after the election, she was ready with a counter-proposal for more radical change. She won.[71]

Having 'lost his pragmatic blueprint ... to Richardson's more ideologically pure vision', Birch embraced the new approach with enthusiasm, according to his biographer, Brad Tattersfield. Roger Kerr helped him out with the task of turning it into comprehensive new legislation.[72]

Kerr wasn't taking any chances on Birch's capacity to follow through, however. In November, a month before Richardson's Economic and Social Initiative was tabled, he wrote to Myers – by then the Business Roundtable's chair following the retirement of Sir Ron Trotter – with advice on how to handle a planned meeting with Birch. 'Basically things are going quite well. Birch has moved a long way in the right directions. How much of this is intellectual acceptance and how much is pressure from other colleagues is unclear,' he wrote. 'The Labour Department is reeling at discovering where he is at. The Farmer draft is having a big impact...

'I see the meeting as basically an occasion for you to stroke Bill and encourage him to raise his sights – "this is your moment in history", "you have the mandate", "no need to compromise", "massive support for change even though there are dinosaurs on both the union and employer side", etc. I don't see a need for much discussion of detail. Essentially what we want is for him to take the high road and enact a simple statute which would give very clear signals that the world has changed, not a complicated amendment to the Labour Relations Act which would result in much more uncertainty.'[73]

There was another opportunity to work on Birch at a rooftop party hosted by Myers' Lion Nathan in Auckland. Richardson remembered the beautiful yellow orchids that had been flown in from Singapore for the occasion. 'The guys [from the Roundtable] were as thick as thieves that night. They were saying, "The shit is hitting the fan, you may as well make the most of the opportunity." I said, "You don't need to persuade me of that." They [were] saying to Birch, "Look, now is your golden opportunity."'[74]

Kerr was pleased with the results of his lobbying. He wrote to Jim Farmer on December 5, thanking him for his input and advising that his draft labour law was having a 'big effect in policy circles. We should see the returns for this and other past efforts in the next couple of weeks. My expectation is that much of our framework will emerge, but with some blemishes...'[75]

Officials in the Department of Labour charged with drafting a new bill were left in no doubt of Birch's commitment to radical change. 'By the time he became minister he'd been converted, I'd put it that way,' said Ralph Stockdill, head of the department's industrial relations division at the time. Stockdill considered Birch 'the main architect in the political sense', notwithstanding the ideological influence of the Business Roundtable. 'For example, we got quite clear instruction [from Birch] that the word 'union' was not to be included in that legislation. And you won't find the word 'worker' in that Act. That's how far it had gone.'[76]

Richardson's Initiative was presented to Parliament six days before Christmas 1990. The package included a radical new law, the Employment Contracts Bill, tabled by Birch. The Bill shredded almost 100 years of industrial relations practice, and cast individual workers and the companies that employed them – whether multinational corporations, state-owned enterprises or neighbourhood dairies – as equal parties in the sale and purchase of labour. It was due to come into effect on May

1 – May Day – the international day of celebration for labourers and the working class.

At CECUA, Helen had put the December 1990 issue of *Double Take* to bed before the Bill was tabled. On the front page she had carried more warnings about voluntary unionism and the prospect of awards without blanket coverage. Like the rest of the union movement, she had significantly underestimated the scale of change to come.

The Bill contained no recognition of trade unions. The default workplace relationship would be an individual employment contract. Workers could engage a bargaining agent – which could be a union or anyone else – to negotiate for them. These representatives had to get specific authority from each individual and they had no right of access to workplaces to talk to workers.

The Bill allowed for collective employment contracts, but only if the employer agreed to negotiate. An employer had no duty to bargain, let alone reach agreement. The blanket coverage that underpinned national awards – ensuring all employers in a sector had to pay the same minimum wage rates and conditions – was gone. Awards currently in existence would be atomised into individual contracts the moment they expired. Employment contracts that were 'harsh and oppressive' could be struck down as illegal but Richardson – backed by Birch – had insisted that officials set a high legal threshold for any worker trying to prove a case under that provision.[77]

The consequences were clear: hundreds of thousands of workers currently on collectively negotiated awards – such as office, shop and early childhood workers in small, scattered and hard-to-organise workplaces – would inevitably end up on their own, attempting to bargain one-on-one with their bosses. With the economy in recession and over 210,000 people jobless, any notion of equal bargaining power between workers and employers was fanciful.

Richardson's ambition was 'joined-up' reform. The Employment Contracts Bill was just one part of a pincer movement. The other was to take an axe to the welfare state. At the same time as the union movement's ability to organise workers was being dramatically undercut, the level of state assistance for those out of work or in need of support would be slashed.

Richardson's package cut the adult unemployment benefit by ten percent and imposed a six-month stand-down for anyone 'voluntarily unemployed without good and sufficient reason', who lost their job through misconduct, or who refused an offer of 'suitable employment or training'. Sickness beneficiaries' payments were cut by 17 percent. The age for youth benefits was raised from 20 to 25, resulting in a cut of almost 25 percent for those affected. Widows and single parents had their benefits cut by nine to 16 percent. Scheduled inflation adjustment to benefits was cancelled. The universal family benefit was abolished, with some of the savings directed into a tax credit for low-income households.[78]

It was all designed to shift New Zealand to what Richardson called an 'enterprise culture'. 'We are determined to help thousands of New Zealanders break out of the pattern of permanent dependency on the state, and achieve a permanent and substantial reduction in the financial and human cost of welfarism,' she told Parliament.[79]

The idea was to widen the gap between what a person would be paid on a benefit and what they would be paid in a job, and therefore sharpen the incentive to look for work; previous benefit levels were allegedly 'a barrier to self-help'.[80] The Christmas package was 'about attitudinal change as much as … economic change', Richardson told political commentator Colin James. The implication was that workers' indolence was the problem, not the fact that tens of thousands of jobs had been wiped out by economic restructuring and recession, and that unemployment was at eight percent of the workforce and rising.

The new world of reduced benefits and freedom of contract at work was about carrot not stick, according to Richardson. 'The huge carrot is in being in charge of your own destiny in an industrial relations sense … What we were [previously] was a low wage, low-skill, high unemployment society. And that is a direct product of an industrial relations regime with a lot of statutory sticks'.[81]

The package also included a raft of reviews of government spending, including four on early childhood education. The sector was restricted by 'ridiculous rules and regulations', which she had frozen. She changed the rules to allow kindergartens to charge parents fees, saying there was ‘no way’ she was going to put more government money into ‘statutory monopolies’.[82]

After the Christmas break, Kerr wrote to his members that the Employment Contracts Bill ‘reflects a substantial payoff for the efforts invested by NZBR members over the last five years’. The task now was ‘to attempt to improve some of its weaker features, to support the government in defending its policy approach, and to encourage employers to take advantage of the wide opportunities it opens up’.[83] He wrote to Richard Epstein that, despite ‘blemishes’, there was ‘no question that the Bill is a major breakthrough and that we are getting close to a world of free contracting. … The labour movement has reacted like stunned mullets.’[84]

At CECUA, Helen put out a January 1991 edition of *Double Take* that was filled with shock and foreboding – a reaction, as Kerr had observed, that was shared by the wider union movement.[85] Council of Trade Unions secretary Angela Foulkes recalled a meeting immediately after the Bill was introduced. ‘Nobody could understand legislation that gave them no role, that didn’t recognise them, didn’t have them registered.’[86]

National’s labour market changes were ‘much worse than anticipated’, Helen reported in *Double Take*. ‘It provides CECUA members and workers throughout New Zealand with one of the greatest ever threats to their wages, conditions and job stability.’[87]

The hard-won funding and quality gains for early childhood education promised by Labour in the *Before Five* package were also now in jeopardy. In a front-page editorial, Clare Wells described the situation as devastating. ‘The changes in early childhood policies, along with the industrial reforms, will make life extremely difficult for all of us in early childhood. If the changes go ahead, employers will have the ability to employ whoever they like at whatever price. … The stand-down period for the unemployment benefit means that people will take on jobs for whatever price offered.’

But, Wells continued hopefully, ‘the changes have not yet happened. We still have time to influence the government, and that we must’.[88]

For workers in early childhood centres, with hundreds of employers, blanket coverage had been the essential tool in improving their historically appalling wages and conditions. Helen Baxter remembered feeling that the Employment Contracts Bill had undone a decade of hard work 'with the stroke of a pen'.[89]

The women of CECUA faced an enormous task – attempting to hold their awards together before the new law blew them into thousands of individual employment contracts; coordinating with other unions on protest action; running stopwork meetings to explain the changes to workers; mobilising parents; lobbying MPs; writing submissions; distributing leaflets.

The workload was phenomenal, with many 12-hour days. Helen had seen her father on the front lines all her life and now she was alongside him, fighting the same fight.

The union movement participated in a week of action in early April. At least 300,000 workers joined rallies, marches, stopwork meetings and strikes. Members of all of the education unions – including CECUA and school cleaners and caretakers from Pat's Cleaners Union – went on strike for 24 hours in opposition to both the Bill and Richardson's swathe of cost-cutting education sector reviews. It was the first time these unions had acted in concert.

Bill Birch said they should be 'ashamed' for setting an 'appalling example' to children and inconveniencing families.[90] Helen swiped back in a comment piece on the front page of *Double Take*. 'Constant claims by the minister of labour, Bill Birch, that the unions are feeding misinformation to their members about the Employment Contracts Bill, causing unnecessary fear and reaction, must be seen by the 80,000 education sector members taking part in action as an insult to their ability to draw their own conclusions. What mysterious type of ability do we have, that Mr Birch hasn't mastered yet, that enables us to fool everyone so convincingly?

'CECUA members,' she continued, 'know this bill must not be passed. To stop it, further action will be needed. … Keep the pressure on in your local area. You're doing an amazing job!'[91]

Amanda Coulston was a teacher trainee at Helen's old stamping ground, Wellington Teachers' College. 'She came into our office one day at the student building. She said, "There's this terrible piece of legislation coming through that will affect all teachers and it's called the Employment Contracts Bill,'" Coulston remembered. 'She was very determined. She conveyed a sense that nothing is impossible, everything is possible, and swept us along in that. And she was hilarious and had an answer for everything.

'There was no way we could not get involved. We organised buses to [protests] in town, had bands and hangi and organised kits on the Employment Contracts Bill to get information out to students. She stood behind us on all of that ... It politicised all of us.'[92]

Under pressure from the wave of protests, Birch circulated a pamphlet to every household in the country. It contained a list of questions and answers designed to allay fears about the Bill: 'My wages – could they be reduced at the whim of my employer? No'; 'My penal rates – could my penal rates and overtime be cut out? No.' The public was assured that current pay and conditions could be altered only if workers agreed.[93]

Some unions engaged in a fire sale of conditions in order to get their awards settled before the law came into effect. The logic was that this would buy time to shore up their membership and prepare for a hostile regime. In some cases, those settlements came at the cost of the very penal and overtime rates that Birch had promised would be safe from cost-cutting employers.[94]

In the meantime, the CTU was coming under increasing pressure to oppose the Bill more aggressively. Pat was among those attempting to mount a strong counter-attack. Birch's proposed law had been likened to the industrial relations regime introduced in Chile following the Pinochet coup in 1973, which he had been heavily involved in protesting against.[95] In April 1991 he told the Cleaners Union executive he was trying to organise a delegation to meet with overseas union groups, in the hope of getting backing for an international trade union boycott of the kind that had been mounted against the Pinochet regime. Already, he said, he had received messages of support for such action.[96]

But the union movement was, as ever, fractious and divided – between militants and moderates, between state and private sectors, between those who had stuck with Labour during Rogernomics and those who had quit to follow Jim Anderton, between those who believed modern unions needed to work with business to lift the economy and those who believed there could never be détente between labour and capital. The fracture lines made for an intricate and complex tapestry of alliances and rivalries.

The Council of Trade Unions had been led from its inception in 1987 by Ken Douglas, Pat's comrade from Wellington Drivers' Union days and a leading light in the Soviet-aligned Socialist Unity Party – a group seen by some in the union movement as too conservative and by others as dangerous communists. The merger of the Federation of Labour and Combined State Unions to form the CTU had been supposed to achieve a single, unified voice for working people but it was far from it. Some groups refused to be part of the new organisation, fearing it would be dominated by large conservative public sector unions that would dilute the influence of smaller blue-collar unions. The Seamen's Union, led by Pat's best mate Dave Morgan, was among those who stayed out, along with unions representing railway workers, printers, plumbers, timber workers, boilermakers, carpenters, and clothing workers. The CTU was pushing a strategy of union restructuring and amalgamations, with the goal of consolidating to a small number of large industry-based unions that would have the scale and resources to be strategic partners with industry and government in skill development, productivity, research and market development, helping to create jobs and opportunities rather than scrapping for wage rises in a stagnant economy.

This strategy was controversial within the union movement. Some thought it was anathema to the union cause and would corrode pay and conditions. Left-wing commentator Chris Trotter even described the CTU's emphasis on international competitiveness and productivity gains as 'strikingly similar to that of the Business Roundtable'.[97]

After the Employment Contracts Bill was tabled, the CTU leadership had sounded modest and cautious. Ken Douglas had spoken of stoppages, or lesser measures such as rallies and 'minor disruptions'.[98] He continued to promote the Compact, even though the National government had no interest in it and the employers' lobby had rejected it.[99] 'We are entitled to be confident that we can achieve a significant change in the direction of the focus of this legislation,' Douglas stated two months after the Bill was introduced.[100]

However, the forces behind the radical programme had made it clear they didn't think the unions were entitled to anything. Within the union movement many thought the battle wasn't about winning amendments to the Bill: they needed to dig in for a long struggle to defeat it.

All of these frictions were playing out when delegates representing 449,000 workers and 39 unions came together for a special affiliates meeting on April 18, 1991 to decide what to do about the existential threat the Employment Contracts Bill presented to the union movement. Helen Kelly was present as a delegate from CECUA, along with Helen Baxter and vice-president Miriam Macpherson.

As delegates filed in the airforce was busy overhead, airlifting passengers and cars between Wellington and Picton. Seafarers on the Cook Strait ferries, led by Dave Morgan, had been on strike for over a week to pressure their employer, the state-owned New Zealand Railways, to renew their award.[101] The government had sensed an opportunity to recruit public support for its radical labour law by sending in troops to rescue passengers stranded by a vital transport link that had long been a political caricature of excessive union power, featherbedding and industrial strife.[102]

Ken Douglas had already stated publicly that he would not be calling for a nationwide general strike. In comments reported by the New Zealand Press Association, he had told a meeting of unionists in Hokitika 'there has to be an answer other than just leading a protest parade'. He opposed a hard line against the new law, telling his West Coast audience that 'a national strike to try and stop the Bill is negative, because the government has the machinery to pass it. The Employment Contracts Bill is bad law. It will be changed by this government because it is unworkable.'[103]

At the meeting, the CTU national executive tabled a three-page recommendation setting out how it thought the union movement should respond to the Bill. It included a proposal for a 'national day of activity on April 30, ranging from lunchtime meetings to a duration of 24 hours'.

The Compact was a central feature of the executive's presentation. It stated that there was 'a growing recognition of an alternative route to economic reconstruction based on the principles of the growth agreement, as opposed to the bankruptcy of the Douglas/Richardson formula of monetarism and deregulation'. The CTU would have to be 'at the forefront of the argument for a more stable and equitable and effective programme of economic recovery'.[104]

The Employment Contracts Bill was due to be reported back to Parliament from the Labour Select Committee within days. It would be law within a month. It was a declaration of war on organised labour. New Zealand unions would have fewer rights than in any other country in the developed world.[105] Yet the Council of Trade Unions appeared to be holding out for a new era of tripartite consensus.

Rick Barker, a member of the council's national executive and head of the Service Workers Federation, an alliance of hotel and hospital workers' unions and the Cleaners Union, was upset that Douglas had publicly ruled out a general strike without prior consultation. Like-minded people, including Pat Kelly, agreed that Barker would make a call at the special affiliates meeting for a national strike. Even if the Employment Contracts Bill couldn't be stopped from coming into law, Barker believed it was better to have a struggle and lose than meekly surrender. 'We thought, if we don't do anything we are doomed to fail … People felt that by not taking a clear stance against the government, the rank and file would look negatively on us for just surrendering,' Barker remembered.[106]

But Ken Douglas saw the arguments for a nationwide stoppage as 'stupidity' and the response of union leaders who wouldn't be able to get their members out as 'emotional'. 'I'm not about to say to workers that I'm going to lead them into a fight that I already know we are not going to deliver on. That doesn't develop confidence in the union movement, that just bloody demoralises people,' he told journalist Gordon Campbell in June 1991.[107]

Angela Foulkes believed the Bill was unfixable. 'To have a victory you would need to have the whole Bill withdrawn and new legislation introduced and we could never have done that. We could have gone on strike until hell froze over and we wouldn't have done that.'[108]

Motions and amendments were batted about at the meeting and there was lengthy debate. 'The tension was palpable,' Barker remembered. The big state sector unions were opposed to a strike; the vote hung on the position of the large Engineers Union and on Douglas's stance.[109]

Pat Kelly made a plea across the conference room floor 'to try and get Ken to shift his position,' Barker recalled. 'There have been calls for a general strike, calls coming from the floor,' Pat reportedly said. 'I believe it is being sought by the working people now. We can't ignore their calls.'[110]

The delegates from CECUA were among those who spoke in favour of a general strike.[111] 'We had led our members this far and we felt we would be letting them down if we didn't support nationwide industrial action,' remembered Baxter. 'Of course, we knew that we wouldn't get all our members out, but we knew we'd get some of them out, especially if a whole lot of other unions were joining them.'[112]

Barker's motion for a 24-hour national work stoppage was defeated. Among the unions that voted it down were the Public Service Association, the New Zealand Educational Institute, the Post Primary Teachers' Association and the Financial Sector Union.[113] Instead, a 'day of action' would go ahead on April 30. It would be up to unionists in each region to decide what to do.

The CTU's failure to lead a general strike against the Employment Contracts Bill created divisions and bitterness within the union movement that would last for a generation.

Five years later Helen appeared in a feature-length documentary about the impact of the changes spearheaded by Roger Douglas and Ruth Richardson. Her comment on the outcome of the vote at the special affiliates meeting was restrained and diplomatic, perhaps because by then she was employed by the New Zealand Educational Institute. 'My feeling at the time was that we should have organised some sort of public disruption. It wasn't done, I think, because we had been working under Labour and we lacked that really strong leadership and direction.'[114]

Two days after the CTU special conference, CECUA held a meeting of its elected representatives. Helen and other union staff attended. Many were shocked that there would be no general strike.[115] The minutes suggest a harried and confused discussion, with people uncertain how to proceed in their protest against the Bill in the absence of a centralised plan and clear leadership: 'Not confident that this won't be a fizzer'; 'Reluctant to ask workers to act in some regions because they need guarantee that others are acting. Members have already heard that the CTU was not calling a national strike'; 'Maybe leave it to members in regions – members may be frustrated that they have not been called on nationally by the union.'[116]

Some 50,000 people around the country turned out to protest against the Bill on April 30. Sixteen thousand marched in Auckland. A similar number gathered at Parliament, in what Wellington police said was the biggest protest since the 1981 Springbok tour. Thousands rallied in New Plymouth, Napier, Christchurch, Greymouth, Timaru and elsewhere. Bus drivers, meat workers, journalists, pulp and paper workers, clothing workers and Auckland high school teachers went on strike.[117]

Parliament took urgency to pass the Employment Contracts Act. The Labour Select Committee – chaired by new National MP and former Employers' Federation advocate Max Bradford – had heard hundreds of submissions, the majority opposed to the Bill. Bill Birch, pragmatist turned zealot, declared at the third reading in Parliament that New Zealanders were 'thirsty' for the kind of bargaining arrangements the new law would allow. Bradford called it a 'watershed' in industrial history.

Labour MP Michael Cullen called the Bill 'narrow, bigoted, stupid … freedom for the rich to oppress the poor … freedom for the powerful to oppress the powerless'. For those in dispersed workplaces and for the low-paid – particularly women, Māori and Pacific Islanders – it was, Cullen said, 'freedom to say "yes" to employers' demands'.

His caucus colleague Graham Kelly, a former trade union leader for shop workers, called the Bill an attempt to 'break the trade union movement' that would lead to the low-paid becoming lower-paid.[118] The Labour Party pledged to repeal it.

It came into effect on May 15, not May Day as originally planned.

The Business Roundtable and its allies at the Employers' Federation had got most, although not all, of what they wanted. Stockdill and his officials at the Department of Labour worked hard to ensure the specialist legal institutions were retained, in the face of pressure from Treasury and the Business Roundtable for them to be scrapped and employment disputes handled by the ordinary courts. The Labour Court – criticised by Kerr for importing notions of fairness into employment matters – was rejigged as the Employment Court, and an Employment Tribunal established to help resolve disputes.[119] The statutory minimum wage survived, and all contracts had to include personal grievance procedures.

Still, it was an impressive achievement in political organising by the New Right. A veteran mediator of industrial disputes, Walter Grills, would later describe the Employment Contracts Act as a 'political coup'.[120] The Roundtable did not give up agitating for the law to be cleansed of its impurities.

At CECUA, the effects of the new regime were swiftly felt by Helen, her colleagues and members of the union. Hundreds of employers who had previously been bound by the national award simply refused to negotiate. Some 1500 early childhood workers, for whom the award had provided a minimum floor, were on their own – as they had been just a few years earlier – attempting to negotiate one-on-one with their employers. Wages and conditions were eroded.[121]

It was a terrible time, Clare Wells remembered, 'Everyone felt very deeply but what could you do? It was very hard.'[122] There was no choice for the union but to focus its efforts on supporting workers covered by the collective contracts the union managed to retain with community childcare centres and other union-friendly employers.

Two days after the Employment Contracts Act came into effect, newspapers reported on the latest survey of the richest people in the country. Lion Nathan's Douglas Myers, one of the Roundtable's loudest advocates for labour market deregulation, was the wealthiest individual for the second year running, with $300 million.[123] A few weeks later, the number of New Zealanders without jobs reached 253,000. Ruth Richardson described the figures as 'an awful transition' but a necessary part of turning the economy around.[124]

The new era quickly produced stories from the bargaining front line. The CTU set up a Doomsday Register. Within days it had evidence of workers being told to take pay cuts or be sacked, new workers being employed on individual contracts at lower rates, and workers being asked by their employer to sign forms quitting their union, which would now be 'powerless over anything that an employer may decide to do'.[125]

Rick Barker recalled one of the first phone calls he received. It was from the head of the Hotel Association, with whom his union had recently negotiated triple-time wages for workers on Christmas Day, a deal that shared with employees the exorbitant prices hoteliers were able to charge customers. 'He rang and said, "Well, Rick, you can kiss that goodbye." All those things were just swept away.'[126]

The union movement that Helen had been born into, and which she saw as her life's work, had been dealt a near mortal blow.

7. Freedom at work

As soon as the Employment Contracts Act came in everything changed in this place ... things have gone from bad to worse.
Berice Edwards, supermarket worker, 1994

Helen was three months pregnant when the Employment Contracts Act came into effect. It had been a torrid first trimester, helping drive the union's campaign against the Bill, meeting with members to explain its significance, getting *Double Take* out, and delivering training sessions to delegates, organisers and workers. In amongst it all she took up knitting again – including, to the chagrin of feminist colleagues, in meetings.[1]

The frenetic pace kept up for the rest of her pregnancy. Ruth Richardson had set up 19 reviews into the education sector in her Christmas package. By July 1991 the women at CECUA were still speculating on the likely outcomes for early childhood education. In the meantime, they kept up campaigns: writing letters to MPs, lobbying, making submissions and organising street protests to try to protect the *Before Five* gains in early childhood funding, training and quality.

On July 30, Richardson stood in Parliament to deliver her infamous 'Mother of All Budgets'.[2] Building on Labour's six years of radical change and her December Economic and Social Initiative, she committed

New Zealand even more deeply to the New Right path of privatisation, corporatisation and a reduced role for the state.

The health system would be radically restructured. Public hospitals would become Crown Health Enterprises and compete for funding. Half the population would face greater medical bills, with new charges for GP and hospital treatment.

Tertiary students would face stringent parental means-testing for allowances, and a student loans scheme would be introduced.[3]

State house rents would move to market rates, with the poor assisted through an accommodation supplement. Benefits would be frozen and access tightened.

The welfare state was being redesigned to 'within an inch of its life'.[4]

Richardson claimed her Budget was 'about the sort of society we will become a generation into the future' and would 'end decades of chronic overspending' by the state. 'We have … charted a path to the future. … The 1990s will be New Zealand's decade, the decade in which we rediscover the energy and self-confidence we had of old. The decade in which we become a true enterprise society.'[5]

For the early childood activists who had battled for years for progress and recognition, the 'Mother of All Budgets' was a major setback. Richardson cut early childhood centres' funding for children under two by almost 40 percent, and introduced bulk funding for kindergartens, which had been regarded by many in the sector as the flagship of free, high quality, state-provided early childhood education. As far as CECUA was concerned, leaving kindergartens to decide how to spend their allocated funding would inevitably lead to pressure on teachers' pay, conditions and professional development, and make it easier for the government to reduce or freeze funding because it had distanced itself from how the money was spent.[6]

In *Double Take*, Helen reported on CECUA members' outrage at Budget decisions that would lead to lower child:staff ratios in early childhood centres, higher fees, reduced access for parents, redundancies for workers and fewer places for children under two. She quoted the fighting words of Clare Wells at the organisation's first annual conference: 'CECUA members have fought long and hard for quality early childhood education. There is no way, after all these years of struggle, that we will concede.'[7]

Helen was born on September 19, 1964, 18 months after her brother Max. Her mother Cath Kelly was distributing communist literature to Wellington workers up until the day before she gave birth to Helen. Her father Pat Kelly (seen here) was an organiser with the Wellington Drivers' Union. *Kelly family collection*

Helen's mother Cath was the youngest of Siegfried and Vera Eichelbaum's four daughters. Siegfried's father Max had emigrated from Germany to the United States (where Siegfried was born) and then to New Zealand in the 1890s. Vera was a member of a prominent legal family, the Chapmans; her father and grandfather were judges of the New Zealand Supreme Court. Cath joined the Communist Party in Britain in 1948. *Kelly family collection*

Cath was close to her three sisters and their families holidayed together. From left, Ann Rosenberg, twins Mary (Max) Patrick and Margaret Dart, and Cath, *c.* December 1963, at the Wellington home of Max and Charles Patrick. *Kelly family collection*

Both Pat and Cath Kelly were strongly opposed to the Vietnam War. In this photo from October 1967 Pat demonstrates with (from left) Adrian Webster, Conrad Bollinger and Ormond Burton. *Kelly family collection*

The Communist Party of New Zealand aligned itself with China. Pat and Cath made separate visits to the country in 1967, and Pat (far right), along with Hugh McLeod, editorial board chair of *People's Voice*, met with Chairman Mao Zedong. The party later descended into infighting and the Kellys, along with the entire Wellington district, were thrown out in 1970. *Kelly family collection*

ABOVE LEFT There was a constant flow of visitors to the Kelly household in Mt Victoria's Shannon Street. The two Kelly kids and the Moore children next door had the run of each other's houses. Jackie Moore and Helen are here aged about three. *Kelly family collection*

ABOVE RIGHT Helen and Max, aged seven and eight, watching television at Shannon Street. Helen would remember her childhood as a great adventure. Pat would often pile Max and her into a cart made from apple boxes and old pram wheels and trundle them along the waterfront to visit the Watersiders Union. *Kelly family collection*

Victoria University's Taurewa research camp was the venue for family holidays in the early 1970s. Back row: Cath and Pat Kelly, Charles Patrick, Wolfgang Rosenberg, Jim Dart, Margaret Dart, Max Patrick, Ann Rosenberg. Middle: Mathew Dart, Ben Patrick, Rachel Patrick, Jeremy Dart. Front: Max Kelly, Tom Patrick, Helen Kelly, Angus Patrick, Vera Rosenberg. Missing cousins are George Rosenberg, Bill Rosenberg and Andrew Dart. *Rachel Patrick collection*

Pat was a favourite uncle, regaling Helen and Max's cousins with jokes and taking them to swimming holes. This photo was taken near Whakapapa Village in January 1970, during a family holiday at Taurewa. From left: Cath, Rachel Patrick, Helen, Vera Rosenberg and Pat. *Rachel Patrick collection*

Helen with Pat Kelly at the family bach at Rangataua. In 1972 Pat and Cath had banded together with relatives to buy an old railway cottage for holidays in the central North Island settlement. *Kelly family collection*

ABOVE Helen and Alby White (front centre) became friends as five-year-olds at Clyde Quay School and Alby often went on Kelly family holidays and outings, such as this trip to Raumati Beach, Kāpiti in 1970. Alby also lived with the Kellys for about 18 months. *Kelly family collection*

LEFT The children spent happy days at Ruatiti Domain near Raetihi. There was a rapid they could lilo, tube or swim down, although the occasional dead sheep or cow was discovered in the water. In this photo, c. 1973, Max has his arm around Alan Moore, and Alby White and Helen are sitting. *Kelly family collection*

By the time Helen was in her early teens, Pat Kelly, seen here on May 3, 1979, was a prominent and controversial union leader. *Stuff*

Pat became secretary of the Cleaners Union in 1976. In 1979 members at Waiouru army base staged a nine-week strike to prevent pay cuts by a new contractor. Cartoonist Eric Heath depicted their win in this image, published October 18, 1979. *Evening Post Collection, Alexander Turnbull Library/courtesy of the Heath family*

Cath Kelly with teenagers Max and Helen, c. 1980. *Kelly family collection*

By the late '70s industrial relations were chaotic as the national wage-fixing system came under strain, inflation rose, the economy faltered, and prime minister Rob Muldoon accused militant union leaders of wrecking the country. On March 3, 1981, 22-year-old Tania Harris led 50,000 people in an anti-union march down Auckland's Queen Street. *NZ Herald Archives*

Pat Kelly addresses demonstrators protesting at Parliament against the Muldoon government's intention to introduce youth rates to industrial awards, September 24, 1983. *Stuff*

Sixty-four-year-old Ernie Abbott died instantly at 5.19 p.m. on March 27, 1984 when he picked up a suitcase that had sat in the hallway at Trades Hall since the morning. The caretaker, he was closing the building for the day. Many thought the bomb was intended for Pat Kelly, who had been earlier meeting in an adjacent room. *Alexander Turnbull Library, Wellington*

Pat Kelly with Paddy Flanagan, national secretary of the Textile and Woollen Mills Workers Union, and a police officer outside Trades Hall after the bombing. *Paul Estcourt/ NZ Herald Archives*

Thousands joined Ernie Abbott's funeral procession as it made its way around the streets of central Wellington. No one has ever been charged with his murder. *Alexander Turnbull Library, Wellington*

A memorial seat for Abbott was made by the Wellington branch of the Carpenters Union from wood recovered during the clean-up of the building. Here, Pat Kelly is seen looking at the seat during the dedication a year after the bombing. *The Evening Post/Alexander Turnbull Library, Wellington*

Rob Muldoon had been prime minister for nine years when he announced a snap election for July 14, 1984. The Kelly household joined the successful campaign to get their party into power. The fourth Labour government immediately faced a currency crisis brought on by Muldoon's refusal to devalue. This would help create the environment for adherents of New Right economic thinking to launch rapid and far-reaching changes. *TVNZ/Eyewitness News*

The radical changes initiated by finance minister Roger Douglas created deep divisions within Labour. Despite the tensions, Labour was re-elected in 1987. Here Douglas and the prime minister, David Lange, celebrate the win. Within a few months Lange would seek to put a brake on Douglas's plans. By the end of 1988 the government would be dysfunctional. *Stuff*

Helen took her first union job with the Kindergarten Teachers Association and Early Childhood Workers Union in 1989. The two unions were engaged in a long struggle to improve pay and conditions for teachers of very young children. Here, Helen crouches in the middle of the front row at a KTA training course, Wallace House, Lower Hutt. *NZEI Te Riu Roa*

Helen and fellow teachers' college graduate Chris Wratt married in 1988. Their son Dylan was born on November 6, 1991. *Kelly family collection*

Jim Bolger (second from left) led the National Party to victory on October 27, 1990. Ruth Richardson (left) became minister of finance. On December 19 Richardson's 'Economic and Social Initiative' cut welfare benefits, and the Employment Contracts Bill was tabled by minister of labour Bill Birch (third from left). The Bill wiped out the national award system and rested on the assumption that workers and employers were equal participants in a free market for labour. Simon Upton (right) was minister of health, environment, research, science and technology. *Phil Reid/Evening Post Collection, Alexander Turnbull Library, Wellington*

Unions led large protests against the Bill, including unprecedented joint strike action by the education unions on April 4, 1991. Both Helen and Pat believed the Council of Trade Unions should have led more aggressive resistance, including a national strike, but this was voted down. This Wellington protest was on April 30. The Employment Contracts Act came into effect on May 15, 1991. *John Nicholson/Evening Post Collection, Alexander Turnbull Library, Wellington*

Helen and Chris moved into a house in McIntyre Avenue, two doors along from Pat and Cath, in 1992. 'Granny' and 'Da' were able to play a big role in the life of their only grandchild, Dylan, here aged about two. Helen and Chris would later separate. *Kelly family collection*

Joanna Beresford was one of many female unionists who would influence Helen's career. Under Beresford's leadership of the primary teachers' union NZEI Te Riu Roa, Helen co-led negotiations for the entrenchment of pay parity between primary and secondary teachers. A deal was reached in 1998, a rare win for workers during the period of the Employment Contracts Act. *Joanna Beresford collection*

Dylan, Chris and Helen on the McIntyre Avenue steps. The photo was taken by artist and friend Bob Kerr as a Christmas present from Cath and Pat in 1999. *Kelly family collection*

Members were called to campaign against the Budget measures. This triggered a wave of activism, including street theatre, broadcasting the early childhood message on megaphones in quiet suburbs, recording workers' experiences and sending the cassette tapes to MPs, and running surveys on the impact of the funding cuts on centres.

The campaigning was noticed. When minister of education Lockwood Smith turned up in Parliament with a grazed face and stitches in his lip after tripping on a fence on his farm, David Lange quipped, 'Hello, he's been visiting kindergartens again.' Helen plastered a montage of media headlines across the front pages of *Double Take*.

Helen developed training sessions on the Employment Contracts Act, the new early childhood policies, workers' rights and campaigning methods. Janette Kelly, a former kindergarten teacher who had been hired in 1990 as a CECUA organiser based in Auckland, often saw Helen in action. 'She was smart, really smart,' she remembered. Although a relative newcomer to a union with a heritage of activism, Helen was, she said, 'incredibly self-assured, mature beyond her years and savvy'.

Like Linda Mitchell and Clare Wells, Janette formed a close and lasting friendship with Helen. 'She was incredibly charismatic, witty and clever and fun to be around. I used to watch her with delegates and she'd have them eating out of her hand. She'd be scribbling things down – her brain went faster than her hand. She would dream up things, think outside the box. She was very unconventional.'[8]

Her humour could be brutal. 'Even though she worked for a union that was predominantly women, she wasn't touchy-feely. I remember her talking about "the bosses getting rich while you [the members] are worrying about the parents not being able to afford a fee increase". And saying, "You're doing without a pay increase. You lot need to get some backbone and toughen up."

'She'd be encouraging us to sing: "Don't be too polite girls." I think class understanding was so much stronger in her.'[9]

Jane Benefield was a CECUA organiser in Wellington, working out of the same office as Helen. 'She always had a great gift with people. She had a cool head but a kind of sympathetic, empathetic heart. ... She had self-confidence without being patronising or arrogant. I think the members really liked and respected her.'

The CECUA office was a place of robust debate. 'We sometimes argued passionately about issues. We respected each other's points of view and right to express them even when they diverged. Helen was really good at getting to the crux of issues. … She was not only astute but also pragmatic in dealing with unwelcome situations and looking for ways on from them.'[10] Benefield and Helen often disagreed, particularly over Helen's strong support for a proposal that CECUA amalgamate with the primary teachers' union, the New Zealand Educational Institute, which Benefield feared would lead to the marginalisation of early childhood workers' concerns.

CECUA managed to retain its benchmark Consenting Parties multi-employer collective contract for workers in non-profit community and council childcare centres, although with fewer employers. But the job of organising in the burgeoning privately owned childcare industry, which tended to pay lower wages and whose representatives had no interest in collective bargaining, was exhausting, remembered Benefield.[11]

'We no longer had right of access [to workplaces], and we no longer had an award to offer [workers]. The workload just went crazy. We'd be waiting outside childcare centres at five or six at night with pamphlets. We'd say, "If you want to talk to the union, come to such and such a motel." No one ever came. It was so disheartening. Everything we had built up for the most powerless and exploited section of our early childhood worker members was just slowly leaking away. I remember it being a time of mourning and just trying to keep afloat.'[12]

In the midst of the industrial and political turmoil, the union had to deal with fallout from sexual abuse allegations at the Christchurch Civic Creche. Several childcare workers at the creche were arrested and one, Peter Ellis, was imprisoned after a controversial court case. At CECUA, views were divided. Some, including Helen, thought the allegations were fuelled by hysteria and that the union needed to help workers deal with the risk of false allegations as well as keeping children safe from abuse.[13]

Dylan Kelly was born in the early hours of November 6, 1991. The labour had been long and hard. The baby boy was the first grandchild both for Chris's parents and for Pat and Cath, and his arrival was heralded in that month's edition of *Double Take*.

Chris was travelling into the city each day to his job as an educator with the conservation group Forest and Bird. Helen returned to CECUA for ten hours a week when Dylan was about four months old, but spent most of his first year out of the paid workforce.

Philippa Branthwaite, who had got to know Helen as a fellow trade union educator working for the Nurses Organisation, had her first child, Jack, soon after Dylan was born. The two new mothers and babies often got together at each other's houses. 'She was totally in love with Dylan and loved being a mother,' Branthwaite remembered. 'But like probably all of us back then, we wanted and expected to have careers as well as babies. We thought we could do everything.'[14]

Late in 1992 a house two doors along from Cath and Pat in Mt Victoria came up for sale. It had the same sweeping views over Wellington that Helen had grown up with. She and Chris bought it for $122,000. For Helen it was like going home. 'It was an absolute joy for us to be back in Mt Vic almost next door to Granny and Da,' Chris remembered.[15]

Access to the house on McIntyre Avenue was up 130 concrete steps from Hawker Street or along a path through Pat and Cath's front yard. It was a run-down cottage, partly renovated but with plenty more to be done. The day the couple moved in, Helen fell through a stair tread while carrying Dylan. 'He bounced down the steps,' Chris remembered. Dave Morgan helped get the place into some kind of order, bringing in a group of seamen to hack the overgrown garden down to size.

Cath and Pat were now able to take a bigger role in Dylan's life, although by then Cath was heavily involved in supporting rural aid projects in Vietnam and Pat was still advocating for cleaners through the new Service Workers Union, which had been formed from an amalgamation of the cleaners, hotel, hospital and rest home workers' unions on the eve of the Employment Contracts Act.

Cath had not got over the injustice of the Vietnam War. 'It infuriated her that after the war ended those who had protested against it seemed to lose interest in the plight of the Vietnamese people, remembered her close friend Margaret Legerton.[16] For years a trade and aid embargo had made it virtually impossible to provide financial help to the country. Cath was part of a group inside the Labour Party that had tried to influence policy on Vietnam by putting up remits, but there was little change until David Lange handed over the foreign affairs portfolio to cabinet minister Russell Marshall after the 1987 election.

In 1989 Cath travelled to Vietnam with a small aid group, staying in rooming houses and looking for grassroots projects to support. The country was impoverished: a health clinic she visited had no medicine and villages had few resources. She returned home after a month 'feeling we weren't doing enough. The visit made me more determined,' she would tell her friend Anne Goodman.[17]

She helped set up the Vietnam Action and Information Network, which evolved into the Vietnam, Cambodia and Laos Support Network (VICALSN). She enlisted the support of the Labour Party's women's council, networked with others with an interest in the region, and raised money to support projects focused on maternal and child health and nutrition run by the Vietnamese Women's Union.

On Saturday mornings she would go around garage sales to amass knick-knacks and books for the group's annual fundraising stall at the Petone Fair. She put together a quarterly newsletter with the help of Bob Kerr and others at Wellington Media Collective, held dinners for VICALSN supporters and applied for government funding. From 1991 she was also heavily involved in a programme providing English-language training for government officials from South-east Asian countries.

In 1992 she made the first of what would become two-yearly trips to Vietnam to visit the projects her group was supporting in remote villages near the Chinese border and in the central highlands. By then she was 66 but had no intention of fading into retirement. Her involvement in Vietnam would dominate the remainder of her life.[18]

For Pat – as for other unionists – the effect of the Employment Contracts Act was a paramount concern. Against the odds, he and other cleaners' advocates managed to replace the old cleaners' award with a new multi-employer collective contract with most of the big commercial cleaning companies, who saw it was in their interests in the highly competitive contract cleaning market to avoid a downward spiral of wage costs and profit margins.[19] Initially the union even managed to hold on to penal rates for weekend and night work and wages substantially above the minimum wage, although these would be eroded over time.[20]

However, workers in other industries covered by the Service Workers Union quickly lost the protection of sector-wide minimum wages and conditions as the big awards covering rest homes, restaurants, fast-food outlets and hotels collapsed.

In the background sat a bleak job market, and the threat of Richardson's stand-down period for the dole. In one case that reached the media, a rest-home worker who was locked out for refusing to accept a pay cut was denied the unemployment benefit for two and a half months.[21]

'It was like trying to fight 3000 fires at once,' remembered John Ryall, one of Pat's protégés from the car assembly plants, who came into the Service Workers Union as an organiser of hotel and hospitality workers.[22] 'As the awards expired employers quickly called union members one by one into captive meetings to sign up individual employment agreements and withdraw from the union. New workers were then employed on these conditions. Getting access to workplaces was tough and many members thought the government had abolished unions.'[23]

Annie Newman was working as a TUEA-funded educator with the Service Workers Union when the Act came in. 'Organisers were going out to workplaces where the employer would show them to a broom cupboard, and say, "I'll let people know you are here and they can come and see you if they wish." That was typical across big hotel chains.' The message to unionists was clear: '"You are scum" and every day you fail. It was failure after failure.'[24]

By the end of 1992 union membership among cleaners had fallen by 20 percent and across the wider Service Workers Union by a third.[25] Returning to work in the new year, the union's officials faced a financial crisis. It was worsened by the fact that – as elsewhere in the workforce – employers had stopped deducting union fees, or had put workers on to individual contracts that didn't provide for union deductions.

The ensuing cost-cutting came to be known as the night of the long knives: about a third of the staff of the Service Workers Union were laid off. This further strained the ability to organise workers scattered across thousands of work sites. Those who stayed, such as John Ryall and Pat's long-time Cleaners Union colleague Don Swan, had already taken pay cuts of ten to 15 percent.[26]

By then Pat was 63. He had already resigned as chair of the Labour

Party's affiliates council and by his own account had started to slow down. His health was beginning to decline and his doctor had told him to knock off the roll-your-owns. 'It's killing me,' he told reporter Al Morrison. He wanted to spend more time with Dylan. He was now getting national superannuation and so could afford to retire, and he knew that if he didn't go someone younger would have to be laid off. But he remained involved, telling newspaper reporters he was now the union's 'rouseabout'.[27] The Service Workers Union made him a life member.

The impact of the Employment Contracts Act across the wider workforce was more severe and rapid than most had imagined. Penal and overtime rates, built up over decades of award bargaining to compensate workers for long hours, late nights and weekend work, were the first to go, especially in female-dominated workforces: retailing, hospitality and community services. By September 1992, a survey showed the span of ordinary time – the hours workers could be expected to work for ordinary pay – had been extended beyond the traditional 8.30 a.m. to 5 p.m. in 73 percent of contracts.[28] The idea that weekends were special and that workers deserved more for working them vanished for many: by 1994 a third of contracts stipulated that work on any seven days of the week would receive only ordinary pay.[29]

Business leaders applauded such evidence of workplace reform. 'The stories of improved productivity in response to the greater flexiblity allowed under the Employment Contracts Act are the sort future myths will be made from,' enthused Bankers Trust chair Alister Maitland.[30]

In the highly competitive retailing sector, the ability to stay open for longer hours without paying penal rates was a boon for shop owners. Workers got little say in the matter. The Employment Contracts Act's promise of freedom of choice and equal bargaining power proved a fiction. 'The impetus for change has primarily been in the hands of employers, who have been largely able to dictate the outcomes of bargaining,' concluded one study of the non-food retail sector. Unions that had previously been able to influence the basic pay and conditions of workers across an industry or occupation through the award system chose to focus their much-reduced resources on trying to negotiate collective contracts with big employers.[31]

For workers in supermarkets, the 40-hour week quickly sprawled over any seven days without penal rates, and the standard working day could stretch to ten hours without overtime. In some cases, employers gained the right to unilaterally change workers' hours, and meal allowances disappeared.[32]

The impact on the wages of check-out operators was studied in detail in a Masters thesis by National Distribution Union official Peter Conway, who would later become a respected economist and close colleague of Helen at the CTU.[33] Shop trading hours had been largely deregulated in 1990, bringing enormous competitive pressure on supermarkets to stay open ever longer. This was one of what Conway called a cocktail of factors pushing wages down, including the 'shock' effect of the Employment Contracts Act, massive unemployment, recession, benefit cuts and the six-month stand-down period for the dole.[34]

Analysing dozens of supermarket collective employment contracts, Conway confirmed a dramatic fall in what were already low wages. For adult part-time checkout operators, wages fell 22 percent in the first three years of the Employment Contracts Act, for part-time student workers 37.3 percent and for full-time adult workers three percent.

When the economy emerged from recession from late 1992 and unemployment started falling from its peak of 11.2 percent of the workforce, wages didn't recover. Conway's research showed that by 1997 wages for part-time adult checkout operators were 30.1 percent lower than in 1989, 44.4 percent lower for part-time students, and 11.2 percent lower for full-time adult workers.[35]

Much of the drop in pay was because of the loss of penal rates; by 1997 these had been eliminated in the industry and overtime rates for long hours were rare. Wage costs were significantly reduced.[36] The supermarkets were able to remain open all hours, and the Employment Contracts Act enabled them to push the cost on to the workforce through lower pay.

The National Distribution Union was run ragged. Membership and financial resources shrank and the workload exploded. In the supermarket industry alone, where there were previously two national supermarket awards, the union was now trying to negotiate dozens of contracts across different work sites and companies. Achieving a contract for, say, 1000 workers in a single supermarket took as much time and effort as an award that would have provided tens of thousands of workers with a comprehensive set of minimum wages, allowances and conditions. Across all the industries the union worked in, it went from negotiating 15 awards and 40 workplace agreements under the Labour Relations Act to 700 collective contracts under the Employment Contracts Act.[37]

The breakdown of standard wages and conditions across the industry fuelled a race to the bottom. 'Because bargaining was at an enterprise level and wages were one of the competitive factors for firms, individual employers were able to argue that increases would lead to higher prices, a fall in product demand and reduced employment,' Conway wrote. The union tried to negotiate contracts that would set a pattern in bargaining, but supermarkets paying higher wages would point to their competitors paying less and argue that they too had to cut labour costs.[38]

For many workers, however, there was simply no negotiation. 'As soon as the Employment Contracts Act came in, everything changed in this place,' Pak'nSave supervisor Berice Edwards wrote to the Department of Labour in 1994. 'We were told now he'd do it his way. First he got rid of the union, and some were threatened if they belonged to the union they'd be down the road. The contracts were never negotiated. We were called in one by one and given this printed document with a place to put your signature. ... Some of the young ones were not allowed to take their contracts home for their parents to read.

'The first year, all of us who already worked there got penal rates, and as people left or were sacked the new ones went on to a flat rate and there was no set amount – they were all getting different wages. Within a year there was a 90 percent rollover in staff. ... Things have gone from bad to worse and as you can guess I'm not the most popular person with the owner because I know my rights and stand up for them and let others know too.'[39]

In Pat's old union, a survey of female members carried out after three years of the Employment Contracts Act found 30 percent had taken a drop in take-home pay and 40 percent had had a drop in household income over the previous two years. Weekend penal rates had been abolished or reduced for almost half, and 40 percent had overtime rates either scrapped or cut.[40] At the same time, the union had halved from 70,000 members to 35,000.[41]

Across the wider workforce, union membership dropped like a stone and collective bargaining collapsed. Unions started to emerge as vehicles for elite, better off workers, while the huge number now on individual contracts and without collective representation were unlikely to experience anything in the way of genuine negotiation over their wages and conditions.[42]

Adding to the pressure on the earnings of low-paid workers, the Bolger government did not increase the minimum wage for four and a half years. When it was finally adjusted in 1995, it was by 12.5 cents. There was no minimum wage for workers under 20 until 1994.[43]

The poor got poorer. Since 1980 the trend had been for all but the top 20 percent of wage and salary earners to experience a drop in real incomes. After the Employment Contracts Act the decline was greatest for the lowest paid workers.[44] The CTU calculated that between 1985 and 1994 workers' share of the national economic pie had shrunk from 49 to 43 percent. That equated to about five billion dollars, or roughly $1000 a year less for every worker. This money now went to profits rather than wages.[45]

The combination of benefit cuts, loss of worker bargaining power, recession and unemployment fed increasing inequality. By 1995/96 the average income of the poorest ten percent of New Zealanders was 8.7 percent lower than in 1983/84, and the incomes of those in the second poorest decile four percent lower. Meanwhile, the richest ten percent had enjoyed an increase of more than 26 percent.[46] Demand for food parcels from the Salvation Army increased tenfold between 1990 and 1993.[47]

Ken Douglas had predicted that workers being forced against the wall in the new environment would trigger more antagonistic and even violent industrial action.[48] But strikes became rare. In the second full year of the Employment Contracts Act they were at their lowest level in 34 years. When the women at CECUA led kindergarten teachers out on strike in August 1992 – in protest at stalled negotiations and 'underhand, bullying tactics' by the government, according to Helen's reporting in *Double Take* – the stoppage was one of only 41 that year.[49]

Employers discovered a new way to impose the changes they wanted. Within the first few months of the new Act they had been given virtual carte blanche by the Employment Court to cut workers' wages and conditions unilaterally, provided they followed a simple procedure. All an employer had to do was notify its workers that it wanted to negotiate a collective contract and advise what changes in pay or allowances it sought. If workers didn't agree, the employer could – under the provision of the Act making it legal to take industrial action in support of a collective contract – simply pay them at the lower rate sought. In the meantime, the workers were obliged to turn up and work for the reduced pay, while the employer gained immediate savings and suffered no loss of production.

This was called a 'partial lockout'. It made a lie of Bill Birch's promise that workers wouldn't have their pay and conditions changed without their agreement.

The most breathtaking case was when the Society for the Intellectually Handicapped (IHC), facing a financial deficit, wanted to cut workers' wages by a third. Represented by the Community Services Union, the workers resisted. The IHC imposed the cuts, calling it a partial lockout, and told the employees to continue working as normal. The Employment Court confirmed that its action was lawful.[50] Unionists and observers of industrial relations were shocked. 'It is no exaggeration to say that making this tactic legal transformed the ECA into a non-bargaining regime,' wrote scholar Ellen Dannin.[51]

The IHC decision was just one of a cascade of early court rulings clarifying the new powers that employers had over their workers. In one case, the chief judge of the Employment Court noted that even a prolonged lockout bringing workers to their knees by 'virtually starving them into submission' might not be legally challengable under the Act.[52]

The court confirmed that the Employment Contracts Act imposed no obligation on an employer to negotiate fairly – or at all. Even where workers had authorised a union as their bargaining agent, the court ruled that an employer was free to apply direct pressure on individual employees and coerce them to join a company-sponsored union. Authorising a bargaining agent was risky for a worker anyway, because under the Act the employer had to be told of each individual authorisation. For vulnerable workers, the anonymous protection of the collective was no longer available.[53]

By 1994, the courts had begun winding back the scope of these early decisions. The full Employment Court ruled that a lockout must involve a shutdown of production, and that it was not lawful to simply cut workers' pay and conditions and expect them to continue working. The Court of Appeal overturned a key early decision giving employers power to sidestep workers' representatives and put direct pressure on the workers. But these revisions did not undo the impact of the original decisions in the crucial first years of the Employment Contracts Act, during which the partial lockout method of imposing cuts was widely threatened and imposed, and employers were at liberty to denigrate workers' unions and undermine collective action.[54]

The country's most vulnerable workers needed solidarity and support. The only way to defend workers' pay and make gains in the new environment was through sophisticated grassroots organising, but a union movement that had evolved under the old arbitration and conciliation structures had never been forced to operate that way, and it wasn't ready.

Instead it was battling for survival, and its leadership was riven with division and dissent. The two most powerful men around the top table, CTU president Ken Douglas and national executive member Bill Andersen, had fallen out. Andersen, a commanding presence in the Auckland union movement and president of the National Distribution Union, had split from the Socialist Unity Party to form the Socialist Party of Aotearoa. He and Douglas were barely on speaking terms, according to Douglas's biographer, David Grant.[55]

Douglas had moved away from the militancy of his Drivers' Union days, and the CTU had abandoned any idea of a return to national awards and compulsory membership. It argued instead for workplace reform and an economy that competed on skills. It was after cooperation and engagement, rather than confrontation.[56]

A rival grouping, the Trade Union Federation, had been formed in 1993. Dave Morgan was its president, and it included many who had rejected the CTU when it was inaugurated six years earlier. Although TUF represented only a fraction of the number of workers allied to the

CTU, it saw itself as 'defenders of genuine trade unionism' and a centre for blue-collar unions engaged in working-class struggle. It opposed globalisation and free trade agreements and campaigned hard against an ongoing reduction in import tariffs. Among its members, the CTU leaders were not forgiven for their Compact with the dying Labour government in 1990 and for failing to lead a general strike against the Employment Contracts Act in 1991.[57]

The two groups snarled at each other across the sectarian divide. CTU secretary Angela Foulkes described TUF's aims of industrial action against the Employment Contracts Act and the revitalisation of the welfare state as 'unusual and somewhat arrogant'.[58] Maxine Gay, TUF's general secretary, called the Compact 'disgraceful' and accused the CTU of 'blind acceptance of corporate unionism'.[59]

The CTU's principal protest against the Employment Contracts Act was to take a complaint to the International Labour Organisation, alleging the law breached global conventions protecting workers' rights to organise and to collectively bargain. Unions were asked to provide examples from the front line.

Despite her close relationship with Dave Morgan, Helen, as a worker for CECUA, was aligned with the CTU and helped develop CECUA's contribution to the ILO complaint. This set out the union's experience with a respected New Zealand children's charity, Barnardos. The organisation, which operated several childcare centres, had pulled out of award bargaining just before the Employment Contracts Act became law. Its workers had had no say in the matter. Their only choice was to go on to individual contracts based on the old award, or sign a Barnardos' contract that was inferior. Thirty-five workers had asked CECUA to bargain collectively on their behalf, but over a period of two years Barnardos had refused. New workers were offered only the Barnardos' contract. There was no negotiation.

Other unions supplied similar stories: pizza workers who wanted the Service Workers Union to negotiate a collective contract but whose employer refused and denied the union access to the workplace; hotel workers who were shifted from a collective contract to individual contracts and their union denied access; shop workers on contracts allowing the employer to unilaterally change hours of work.[60]

The ILO investigated, and concluded in late 1994 that the Employment Contracts Act violated key principles by failing to promote collective bargaining, and called for an amendment to allow strikes in support of multi-employer contracts. All parties claimed to have been exonerated: the government announced the Act had been 'cleared'; the Employers' Federation said the findings were a 'substantial endorsement of the fairness and value of the Act'; the CTU welcomed its conclusion that the philosophical foundations of the Act were 'incompatible with free association, promotion and encouragement of collective bargaining'.[61]

Nothing changed. The union movement continued on its path to irrelevance for most workers and its leaders continued to squabble. And New Zealand, with its textbook application of New Right theories – of which the radically deregulated labour market was a crowning feature – continued to attract interest and praise from international financial institutions and observers, including the OECD, the International Monetary Fund, *The Wall Street Journal* and *The Economist*. Not for the first time in its history, New Zealand was viewed with fascination as a social and economic laboratory.

Going to the polls in 1993, however, New Zealanders appeared less convinced. National was returned to power, but its previously large majority was reduced to just one seat. The country also voted to move to a new voting system, proportional representation: never again would a party with a simple first-past-the-post majority have the power to unleash such aggressive and far-reaching changes as New Zealand had seen over the previous decade. For the prime minister, Jim Bolger, the election result was an immediate cue to sack his radical finance minister Ruth Richardson and install Bill Birch in her place.

There was no loss of enthusiasm for the Employment Contracts Act, however. Business groups had joined in solidarity to defend the legislation. Bolger called it the glue of economic recovery and said it had retained or created more jobs than almost anything else.[62]

When the country moved into a short period of high economic growth in the mid 1990s, the Act was credited with creating 200,000 jobs. Bolger, Birch and business leaders repeatedly stated that it had boosted productivity. The claims were of dubious merit. A large proportion of the new jobs were part-time, many people were underemployed, wanting longer hours but unable to get them, thousands more workers were holding down more than one job, and only a fraction of the job growth could be attributed directly to the Act.[63]

As for the vaunted surge in productivity, the data indicated productivity had grown at a *slower* rate than in the previous five years and over the long term, and was a fraction of that experienced in Australia, which had adopted more modest reforms.[64] Economist Brian Easton concluded that the Employment Contracts Act appeared to have delivered 'very little economic benefit, if at all'.[65]

Roger Kerr, who had played a central role in the genesis of the Act and promoted it as the answer New Zealand's lacklustre productivity, scolded analysts who pointed out that the promise hadn't been delivered, saying it was too soon to judge and the critics were selecting the wrong data points.[66]

According to one academic brought in by the Business Roundtable, the Act was 'almost a model for the world. ... You are 80 percent there.' In no other advanced country, 'especially the United States, has the legislature been willing to challenge the hegemony of trade unions to such an extent,' American economist Charles Baird told a business conference held on May 15, 1996 to celebrate the Act's fifth birthday. Baird urged further reform to allow employers to sack workers at will, abolish the minimum wage, get rid of minimum holiday requirements and let workers trade their leave for extra wages, and abolish an Employment Court that insisted on seeing labour as 'special'.[67]

The Bolger-led government had also erased other avenues for state-supported collective action in the workplace. The outgoing Labour government's Employment Equity Act – which would have allowed claims of pay discrimination in female-dominated occupations to be assessed against comparable male-dominated jobs – had been scrapped soon after National was elected. A new Health and Safety in Employment Act replaced a large body of detailed and overlapping rules and laws with a permissive regime requiring employers to 'take all practicable steps' to keep workers safe. It removed any enforceable right for workers or unions to be involved in safety issues, and left it up to management whether to consult. Regulations were minimal, as was enforcement.[68]

And in 1992 the government repealed the Union Representatives

Education Leave Act and scrapped funding for the Trade Union Education Authority, the organisation that had enabled Helen Kelly to be employed by CECUA's two founding unions. The authority had been in the gun ever since Stan Rodger introduced it, and soon after National came to power Bill Birch was reminded by the employers' lobby that they wanted it gone.

'Dear Bill,' wrote Employers' Federation director-general Steve Marshall in April 1991. He attached the outline of an upcoming TUEA conference, at which matters such as workplace health and safety, the law, health policy, management strategies and 'working class identification' would be discussed. 'The structure, themes, speakers and subject headings speak for themselves,' Marshall wrote. 'As long as TUEA continues to receive government funding, we all have to accept that this sort of charade is going to continue.'[69]

The loss of the TUEA subsidy of Helen's salary put pressure on CECUA's finances, already strained by falling membership fees and rising costs. By then, momentum was building towards amalgamation with the much larger primary teachers' union, amid detailed – but ultimately unsuccessful – talks for a mega-merger of all education unions, from early childhood through to the university sector.

CECUA, with 3500 members and falling, joined the 23,000-strong primary teachers union, which changed its name to the New Zealand Educational Institute Te Riu Roa. The majority of CECUA's members had voted for the amalgamation, but it was an unhappy time for those who feared the needs of the lowest paid members of the educational workforce would be lost sight of.

The merger had been championed by Rosslyn Noonan, who knew the early childhood sector well from her years leading the Kindergarten Teachers Association and supporting the formation of the Early Childhood Workers Union. But the influence of school principals – most of them men – was strong in the NZEI, and Linda Mitchell remembered that some never accepted it.[70]

Helen was deployed into the Wellington regional office, where she worked alongside her friends Janette Kelly and Philippa Branthwaite, while Clare Wells and Linda Mitchell joined the national office. Although Helen had supported the amalgamation, her job was unsatisfying. The

Wellington office was a place of autocratic management and excessive morning teas – a far cry from the lean, argumentative and collaborative CECUA office. 'It was routine work,' remembered Janette Kelly. 'We'd been at the front of [CECUA] as staff and suddenly we were told to sit down and shut up, and it's a bunch of blokes who are principals running the show.'[71]

The job made little use of Helen's campaigning skills – attributes Rosslyn Noonan had observed the previous year when she was seconded to the NZEI to campaign on education issues in the lead-up to the election. Noonan would later attest to Helen's energy, drive and commitment, infectious enthusiasm, clear, focused thinking and ability to remain pleasant, cooperative and supportive at times of great pressure. 'She is a gifted adult educator and motivator. I have participated in seminars she has run for a very diverse range of people and marvelled at her ability to enthuse and involve them all.'[72]

Although Helen's talents were being underutilised, Branthwaite remembered a strong sense that she was already recognised as the union movement's 'bright young girl. And she acted like she was – and I mean that in a good way. She had a strong sense of confidence and a very strong sense of herself.'

While many of her colleagues saw themselves first and foremost as feminists championing the rights of a female-dominated workforce, Helen 'wasn't driven by an ideology around women's rights. She came with a sense that there were things to be fixed and we must fix them. It was about unfairness.'

Cath and Pat Kelly had opposed the emergence of women's committees inside the union movement, believing such groups would undermine working-class solidarity. This had put them offside with many feminists.[73] For Helen, too, it was concern for the working class that came first.

Dylan was enrolled in the Te Kainganui Child Care Centre in the inner-city suburb of Mt Cook. Helen had selected the centre because it was part of the Consenting Parties multi-employer collective contract and because it was run as a cooperative. She became chair of the parent-teacher committee that governed the centre. 'She was staunch about it,' remembered Philippa Branthwaite, who enrolled her son Jack in the same centre. 'She was able to see both the staff view and the parent view. She never separated her working life and her personal life – they were completely mixed together.'

Pat and Cath were now playing an intimate role in Dylan's life; there were no roads to cross to visit Granny and Da. Pat would often take his grandson on walks to Newtown or the zoo and was inclined to pronounce, 'You're the best thing in my life, wee man!'[74] Chris Wratt adored his in-laws and became close to both. The three generations would holiday together at the Rangataua bach and there were frequent dinners and lunches. 'Politics would be, of course, the main discussion point,' he remembered. 'Even I became politicised.'[75]

He and Helen did renovations on the McIntyre Avenue house. Helen's boss and confidante Linda Mitchell bought the house next door, and the two women walked to work together in the mornings and strode around the steep Mt Victoria streets in the evenings. Several years later, Clare Wells too would move into the neighbourhood. 'We used to call it the Mt Vic cabal.'[76]

It wasn't long before a more challenging opportunity came up for Helen. In late 1994 she was hired as an organiser for the Association of University Staff at Victoria University. She walked straight into a long-festering dispute.

The universities had been thrust by the education and labour market reforms of both the Labour and National governments from their traditional model of collegiality into a new era of competition and fiscal constraints. Government funding per student had fallen since 1990, student numbers were growing, and following the strict targeting of allowances brought in by Ruth Richardson, students were accumulating interest-bearing loans to pay tuition fees and living costs.[77]

At the same time, the old system of centralised pay fixing for academics was gone. University vice chancellors were now chief executives, responsible for managing staff, negotiating employment contracts and setting student fees.[78]

There had been no pay increase for staff at Victoria University for three years and workloads were increasing. Efforts by the Association of University Staff, which represented academics and general staff such as librarians, administrators and gardeners, to negotiate a pay rise were getting nowhere.

Guy Reynolds was a librarian and a member of the union's negotiating team. 'In the past the vice chancellor was first among equals. It was all about collegiality, and the feeling that in universities we don't manage each other like in the commercial world,' he said. But while both the union and the university's vice chancellor Les Holborow struggled to adapt to the new world of user-pays and employment contracts, salaries were being eroded and frustration was growing.[79]

Peter Donelan was branch president at Victoria when Helen was hired as the union's first professional organiser on campus. As the impasse over pay continued, he reached the conclusion that some kind of industrial action would be needed, but academics in New Zealand had never gone on strike. Many saw themselves as autonomous researchers and teachers who were part of the very fabric of the university, not its employees.[80]

Helen's arrival helped shunt the culture towards solidarity and action. 'She was able to come into a lecture hall of university staff, including many senior academics who were considerably sceptical, and convince them that the only way forward was to engage in industrial action,' Donelan said. Initially this involved low-level measures, such as a walkout from the Academic Board and lunchtime stoppages, which 'in Helen's mind … were more aimed at acculturating staff, especially academics, into the idea of action'.

For Reynolds, her self-confidence was infectious. 'She made you feel that anything was possible. She was always positive. If you ever saw Helen a bit uncomfortable or doubting herself she'd cover it up with laughter. … But she understood industrial relations. She understood what staff rights were. She wasn't flying by the seat of her pants.'

Nothing seemed to faze her, including being surrounded by esteemed academics. Any hint of haughtiness was cut down with a razor wit. Donelan, a mathematician, was sometimes on the receiving end, Reynolds remembered. 'Helen had this way of laughing at Pete and saying, "What are you into again? Oh, that's right, triangles." She'd reduce the whole area of mathematical specialist academic expertise to triangles. Peter would laugh; everyone would laugh.'

Lecturers and professors were hardly as vulnerable as supermarket or childcare workers but Helen framed the Victoria University dispute as a matter of justice. 'I think she saw it was an unfair situation and change needed to happen. She always felt she was arguing for the underdog. She was definitely on the side of the weaker, less powerful party.'

Negotiations for the university's general staff contract were settled in mid May 1995, but the academics rejected what they regarded as an insulting offer. They voted by an overwhelming majority to strike on May 31.

Helen arranged through Pat to use Trades Hall as a venue for members to paint placards and banners, and Pat would drop by to express his solidarity. 'We were an advantaged group compared with those Pat [had] represented as head of the cleaners and caretakers' union, but to him we were simply comrades struggling for the same workers' rights as anyone,' remembered Donelan. 'It certainly buoyed me and, I think, the others who were there.'

The day of the strike was sunny and pleasant. Those engaged in the country's first ever stoppage by academics lined Kelburn Parade with placards and gathered at lunchtime for speeches, sausage sizzles and messages of support from sister unions around the country and the world. Helen moved among the strikers giving encouragement and support.

Three months later the union's negotiating team, led by Jeff Rowe from the Association of University Staff head office, settled the academics' contract with a flat rate pay rise and improved conditions. 'Helen's presence was what made the difference,' Donelan said. 'She was passionate but never angry; she was always able to keep communication open with management, while fighting her side. I have no doubt it was her influence and positivity that resulted in our mounting a successful campaign with the almost total support of the membership.'

Success begat success. Membership of the Association of University Staff on campus grew. The contract negotiated would remain the foundation of the collective agreement at Victoria University two and a half decades later.

Reynolds took over from Donelan as branch president in 1996 and continued working closely with Helen, who by then was also studying part-time for a law degree. The marriage of academics and general staff within the union had never been without tension, but Reynolds said Helen was able to straddle both camps. 'She had this ability to be with anybody, and make them feel that she was on their side, that she could help them and effect change for them.'

It was the early days of the internet, and as a librarian Reynolds was able to connect to global sources of information. One day Helen brought Cath in to meet him, thinking he could help her hunt out new material on Vietnam. He was struck by Helen's love and care for her mother. At the same time, 'you just felt with Helen that she was one tough woman'.

She was, as ever, staunchly pro-Labour. That year New Zealanders went to the polls to vote in the first MMP election. 'She was going round saying, "Two ticks Labour"', remembered Reynolds. 'Every conversation with Helen was an opportunity to be schooled. But she'd have a huge smile on her face.'

Back at NZEI Te Riu Roa, a campaign had been running to achieve pay parity between the salaries of primary and secondary teachers. It wasn't a new idea but the decision to mount a battle for it struck a defiant note at a time when most unions were incurring constant losses, the government was imposing wage restraint across the state sector, and education spending was falling.

When the Employment Contracts Act was introduced, all the teachers' unions had come together as a united front, under the slogan 'Hold On', to defend their nationwide collective pay agreements. Joanna Beresford, who was the NZEI's assistant national secretary and known as a top negotiator, led the bargaining for the ten unions involved. The objective was to hold the line against the government's goal of fragmenting the national collectives. The unions believed this would inevitably lead to cuts in teachers' pay and conditions, making it harder to attract new recruits into the profession.[81]

By now the education sector had become a key focus of the Education Forum, a Business Roundtable spin-off. The forum was lobbying hard for teachers to be put on to performance pay and individual employment contracts.[82]

The unions were successful in retaining nationwide collective contracts, but there were no improvements in pay and conditions. By the end of 1993, primary teachers had had enough of austerity. There had been no pay rise since 1990, workloads were increasing because of the self-governing schools model brought in by David Lange, and classroom pressures were rising as a result of the stress placed on children by high unemployment and growing poverty.

The decision to launch a campaign for pay parity was 'a gigantic fightback', Beresford said. 'We decided the Employment Contracts Act wasn't going anywhere until Labour came back in, and we would fight it on equity and educational grounds.' It was part of a longer-term goal of achieving an integrated teaching service, from early childhood to tertiary, underpinned by a unified pay system.[83]

The campaign was grounded in the argument that a teacher's pay shouldn't be determined by the age of the students being taught. 'Susan', a fictional child wearing outsized shoes, became the mascot, with the slogan: 'If Susan wore size 12 [shoes] her teacher would earn a lot more!'

The campaign was about wage justice, but it was also anchored firmly in feminist analysis – almost 80 percent of primary teachers were women.

The NZEI was in a stronger position than most unions to launch such an ambitious claim. Primary teachers had the largest collective contract in the country. Well over 90 percent of teachers and principals were union members and they paid high fees, which meant the union was well resourced for a complex political battle.

Helen had not been closely involved in the early stages and initially thought the campaign had no chance of succeeding. 'She said to me, "I think you'll get sacked,"' Beresford remembered. 'She thought it was a great idea, but what a time to raise it. … Our attitude was, if we're not going to raise it now, when are we going to raise it? Our politics meant you didn't give the Tories an easy time; you didn't just wait for Labour to be reelected or for better days to come.'

Helen abandoned her scepticism when she saw the campaign's leaders, including Beresford and national secretary Rosslyn Noonan, at work. 'They knew what they were doing … and the members were buying it,' she later observed.[84]

After two strikes and convoluted negotiations, partial success was achieved in mid 1995 – about the same time Helen was corralling academics at Victoria University. The government settled a deal with the NZEI that would bring primary teachers' salaries up to the level of secondary teachers' over two years. For basic scale teachers, it meant a rise of almost 15 percent, and 19 percent for principals.

But parity wasn't locked in. As secondary teachers got increases, primary teachers again fell behind. When Helen returned to work for the NZEI in 1997, her task was to co-lead negotiations to get pay parity entrenched. She operated under the oversight of Beresford, by then the union's national secretary, and her close friend Linda Mitchell, who had been appointed assistant national secretary.

The bargaining was time-consuming, slow and frustrating. The government claimed to support the principle of an equitable pay system for all teachers, but there were constant attempts to trade that off against its wider ambition of decentralising control of school finances to local boards of trustees. It had been trying for years to get schools to accept bulk funding, under which boards would get a lump sum to cover all costs, including teachers' pay. The teacher unions had fought hard against it, arguing it would lead to the breakdown of national collective bargaining, the rise of competition among schools over teachers' salaries, and the erosion of a high-quality state education system.

In the negotiations Helen worked alongside Peter Monteith, who had cut his teeth in the union movement representing shop workers before going to work for the NZEI. 'The [government] bargaining was being effectively run out of the Beehive,' he remembered. 'And we were on a pretty short leash because of the NZEI's [hierarchical] structure.'[85]

It was a high-wire dispute: failure to achieve a deal would seriously damage the credibility of the union. Primary teachers had made it clear they regarded the entrenchment of pay parity as a priority. The slogans and one-liners – 'Susan's shoe size'; 'a teacher is a teacher is a teacher' – captured the intensity of feeling. They were prepared to go on strike again, as they had in 1994 and 1995, if the government refused or filibustered. This strengthened the arm of the NZEI negotiating team.

The government's willingness to play hardball had been made evident in April 1997, when it had forced through under urgency a law change removing kindergartens from the State Sector Act – a move that meant kindergarten teachers were no longer government employees.

It was apparently designed to thwart the goal of kindergarten teachers attaining pay parity with primary teachers.[86]

The negotiating environment was made even more complex by the toxic relationship between the NZEI and the secondary teachers' union, the Post Primary Teachers Association. PPTA leaders thought pay parity would stymie their salary claims.

Despite the tensions, Helen was always fun, Peter Monteith remembered. 'She was full of weird and wacky ideas … one of those people who'd have a bright idea, and one out of ten is brilliant and the rest is rubbish. She was a real character, a storyteller. Not around the bargaining table – that was all organised in advance and no one said anything out of turn – but in adjournments and when we worked together planning our strategy. She had a restlessness about her. Her foot would tap almost all of the time. I would try and ignore it.'

Across the table, government negotiator Suze Wilson found Helen an impressive advocate. 'She was well-organised and articulate. She understood the big picture but also paid attention to the detail. She wouldn't let anything slip. If she was unhappy about something you knew it … Even if some people found her approach a bit bracing, she certainly had their respect. If someone needed to light a fire it would be Helen. If someone needed to settle things down it would probably be Peter.'[87]

Some inside the union didn't appreciate her flippant humour and irreverence. 'She could be indiscreet, and sometimes you had to give her a little tug and tell her that it was time to zip it,' remembered Beresford, who caught a rare glimpse of vulnerability when Helen later applied for the role of assistant national secretary after Mitchell announced she was moving on.

'She'd got wind that one of the key people on the panel opposed her appointment. She walked into my office, handed me a white envelope and said, "This is my resignation." She felt if she didn't get the job she would be humiliated … She was prepared to just walk away from it.' Beresford refused to accept the letter and implored her to reconsider. Helen took the advice and got the job.[88]

A deal to entrench pay parity was finally achieved around midnight on March 4, 1998. Helen initialled each page of the document alongside the head negotiator from the education ministry. Everyone was so exhausted the magnitude of what had been achieved almost washed over them until Helen paused and said, 'You all realise what we've just signed?'[89]

Concessions had had to be made but basic scale teachers would get an eleven percent pay rise, and every time secondary teachers got an increase primary teachers would trigger the entrenchment clause and get the same deal.

The PPTA regarded the deal as a millstone on their own negotiations and hated it. Others celebrated it as a triumph for women and an inspiration for undervalued workers. Rosslyn Noonan, by then working in Brussels for Education International, the global confederation of teacher unions, called it 'one of the great negotiating victories in New Zealand trade union history'.[90]

It was a rare success in a landscape of defeat for organised labour. Fewer than one in five workers now belonged to a union, compared with over 40 percent when the Employment Contracts Act came in. Unions had all but vanished in some of the most dangerous industries. The Act had brought freedom of choice in bargaining, but mostly for employers.[91] Full-time workers were putting in longer hours, more people were working more than one job, and the 40-hour week was no longer the norm.[92]

Helen had been involved in three strikes since 1991 to advance workers' wages and conditions through collective bargaining – for kindergarten teachers, primary teachers and university academics – but collectivism had increasingly become the preserve of skilled and white-collar workers employed by big companies or government. Well over half New Zealand workers were now on individual contracts.[93] A new generation had joined the workforce in the 1990s with little concept of what collective bargaining meant, or what unions were. Despite increasing inequality, and workers' declining share of the national income that their labour helped produce – a share that had been dramatically cut during Muldoon's wage freeze, and was again shrinking rapidly under the Employment Contracts Act – strikes had become as rare as in the peaceful early 1960s.[94]

So confident was the government in its moves to decollectivise the workforce that in 1997 minister of labour Max Bradford attempted a further phase of labour market deregulation. He put the Employment Court under review, proposed a watering down of workers' protections against dismissal, and pushed for changes to the Holidays Act to allow workers to sell some of their holidays for cash – just as the Business Roundtable's ally Charles Baird had suggested.

The holidays review became a lightning rod. Unions, churches and community groups warned that vulnerable workers would be pressured to accept employers' demands for fewer holidays, and new workers would be presented with 'take it or leave it' contracts with reduced leave. Holiday rights would evaporate just as rapidly as penal rates had following the Employment Contracts Act, they predicted. A cluster of big unions – Engineers, Service Workers, Rail and Maritime, Finance Sector, PSA and NZEI – coordinated a major campaign, resulting in some of the biggest protest rallies since 1991. Bradford eventually capitulated when National's coalition partner, New Zealand First, refused to back the changes.

With the exception of vice-president Ross Wilson, national secretary of the Rail and Maritime Transport Union, the senior ranks of the CTU were, however, missing in action.[95] Discontent with the body was rising, with criticism coming as much from its own affiliates as from the rival Trade Union Federation. Its credibility as the 'voice of labour' was severely strained; in 1997 Bill Andersen had withdrawn the big National Distribution Union, and by the end of that year the CTU represented barely half the number of workers it had in 1991.

Among the unions that remained affiliated, the nature of the complaints varied. The ghost of the general strike that the CTU leadership declined to lead in 1991 still stalked the organisation. Some believed Ken Douglas and Angela Foulkes had got too close to the National government in their attempts to secure a collaborative role for the union movement. Some thought they had become remote from ordinary workers and insufficiently supportive of those who took to the picket lines for improved wages and security. Some saw the CTU's governing national executive as fractured and dysfunctional. Many were convinced the union movement would survive only if it developed a coherent strategy based on skilled, innovative rank-and-file organising.

Among those demanding change were leaders in Pat's old union. 'We were critical of the CTU because we didn't feel they were looking forward about what needed to change,' remembered Darien Fenton, who was national secretary of the Service and Food Workers Union at the time. 'I didn't feel there was any kind of strategic thinking about where we were going ... We were looking for a completely different kind of CTU that was much more activist in campaigning, and putting resources into developing the people we needed to bring forward to do that. We were saying, "We have to go back to our roots, organise workers, build power, and do it in a way that doesn't always rely on the law." ... Of course we wanted more worker-friendly legislation, but how could we ensure that the union movement is never in this position again, so that, regardless of who is the government, we can survive?'[96]

Against this mood of broiling dissatisfaction, the CTU national executive set up a review, conducted by Auckland University academic Nigel Haworth, a specialist in international labour movements. He interviewed widely among affiliated unions, politicians and the media. A sanitised report went on the CTU's files. Haworth's unvarnished findings – confirming a deep vein of criticism among some affiliates over strategy and leadership – were kept from public view.

'People thought the CTU wasn't performing anything like to the standard that it could,' Haworth would later say. '[The feeling was] that it was going through the motions, rather than providing modern trade union leadership. ... And of course some of those comments were extremely personal. They related to the succession of leadership of the CTU.'

The demand for change at the top was clear. By his own account, Ken Douglas had become disenchanted with the CTU's affiliates. He had already indicated he would not seek re-election in 1999.[97] Angela Foulkes had signalled an intention to stand as his successor but Haworth's review put an end to that.

That left two likely contenders: Ross Wilson, a lawyer who had been drawn into the union movement through his work representing railway workers injured on the job, and Rosslyn Noonan, a veteran of education unions in New Zealand and internationally.

Wilson, conscious of laying the ground for future succession, had Helen in his sights. 'She was a very lateral thinker, and spontaneous and intelligent,' he remembered.[98] He approached her to stand with him – he as president, she as secretary.

Helen was excited to be asked: she was ambitious and believed she had the capabilities to help bring about improvements for ordinary workers. Chris was supportive of her taking on the role. She rang her boss, Joanna Beresford, to let her know she had been asked to stand as number two.

Beresford 'blew a gasket'. She had been campaigning for Noonan, who she believed had the 'pizzazz and energy' needed to steer the union movement out of its crisis – not to mention become its first woman leader. She believed Helen was being used to preserve the 'male-dominant status quo, and her eyes weren't open to the implications of doing so'.[99]

Beresford told Helen that she could lead the labour movement one day. She counselled her not to play 'second fiddle' but to hold back now and get more experience of management and finances by running a union.

In the end it was clear Noonan didn't have the numbers. Helen took Beresford's counsel and declined to stand as number two. Ross Wilson became CTU president in October 1999, with Paul Goulter, who had led the Financial Sector Union, as secretary, and Darien Fenton as vice-president.

Within a few weeks, there was also a new guard at the Beehive. The wounds borne by the Labour Party as a result of the Rogernomics of the 1980s had begun to seal over, and there had been a reconciliation with Jim Anderton, who had split the party a decade earlier. Labour, which had been led by Helen Clark since 1993, and Anderton's Alliance Party had pledged to form a coalition after the November 27 election.[100] They had the numbers. The National-led government, whose coalition with New Zealand First had fallen apart, had become reliant on a ragbag of independents. It was out. A Labour-led government was in.

8. Princess Xena

We want decent incomes and decent work. It's not too much to ask.
Helen Kelly, 2007

Helen had foot-slogged to help get Labour back into power. In 1996 – at New Zealand's first MMP election – her Wellington Central electorate had been won by Richard Prebble, leader of the right-wing ACT party formed by Roger Douglas when he left Labour, disaffected.

In 1999, former Christchurch high school principal Marian Hobbs was selected as Labour's candidate for the seat. Although Hobbs had been in Parliament for three years as a Labour list MP, she wasn't intimate with her new patch. Helen took it upon herself to fix that. 'That included [Helen and Chris Wratt] taking me to a local rugby match,' Hobbs remembered. Cath issued a dictate that Hobbs was not to wear a flamboyant yellow hat she was fond of. 'So I didn't – I went in there quietly. Helen wanted me to win, and she wanted me to make connections with real people.'[1]

The electorate committee ran a superb campaign. Helen was at regular planning meetings and had the role of 'deliveries coordinator'. 'It's an arsehole job,' Hobbs said. 'You get given a whole lot of pamphlets. You have a team of about 100 deliverers and you have to make sure the buggers actually deliver and don't drop them down the back of a rubbish bin. And of course Wellington is up and down hills everywhere, and people have letterboxes in bloody strange places. She did that brilliantly. … She was so much part of that community.'

The campaign was a success; Wellington Central was one of 49 electorates won by Labour. A coalition with the Alliance was quickly sealed. The Green Party agreed to support the coalition on confidence and supply.

The election result opened the way for early childhood education to come back on to the political agenda, and for a fresh push by the NZEI for wage justice for the teachers of young children. Helen, Clare Wells and Linda Mitchell were a core NZEI triumvirate who worked closely with Labour's education spokesman Trevor Mallard to help cement the party's commitment to policies that would advance early childhood education.

They were lobbying from a solid base. Following the setback delivered by Ruth Richardson's 'Mother of All Budgets' to David Lange's *Before Five* programme, the NZEI had funded and coordinated, in consultation with community-based early childhood groups, a major project to plot out a long-term future for the sector. The final report, *Future Directions: Early Childhood Education in New Zealand*, included recommendations relating to universal funding for children, teacher qualifications and pay parity. When the report had been launched in 1996, all political parties except National had picked it up as policy.[2]

The three women were a highly effective team. 'Linda was more the academic and researcher,' remembered Mallard. 'Clare was the best person at putting stuff down on paper and [developing] strategies and longer-term organisational stuff. But if you wanted something to happen next week, Helen was the person who would corral people into doing it. She was very good at arguing the cases and … assembling the attack. To use a war analogy, other people were making the bullets and she was very good at firing them.'[3]

Mallard was a willing target. Like Helen, he was a graduate of Wellington Teachers' College and had been taught by many of the same inspirational lecturers who had influenced her. Like her, he had been president of the students' union and, in the mid '70s, involved in setting up the college's childcare centre. He had also been heavily influenced by early childhood academics at the college and by the sector's political leaders, including former Kindergarten Teachers Association president Wendy Lee and general secretary Rosslyn Noonan.

Mallard referred to Helen, Mitchell and Wells as 'the McIntyre Avenue crowd'. His discussions with them would often take place at Mitchell's house, next door to Helen and Chris's. The politics were sometimes delicate, and not just because Mallard still had work to do to get buy-in from his caucus. He was badly tainted in Cath's eyes because he had been a member of the 1984–90 Labour government that had unleashed Rogernomics. When visiting Mitchell's house, therefore, he was barred from taking the easy shortcut from Shannon Street through Pat and Cath's front yard, and instead had to walk up the steep flight of 130 stairs from Hawker Street.

He didn't dare risk Cath's wrath. 'You wouldn't take on Cath by sneaking through there because it would upset the relationship. … She was a very diminutive battleaxe, and very firm in her views and very definite.'[4]

With Mallard installed as minister of education, work began on a ten-year strategic plan for early childhood education, and on moves to bring kindergarten teachers' pay into line with school teachers'. 'Susan' had been NZEI's mascot for the primary teachers' pay parity campaign. Now the union introduced her younger sister 'Sally' to make the equivalent case for the teachers of very young children.

'Helen was absolutely passionate about early childhood education, and had a strong belief that the way you lifted the quality was to lift the quality of the workers and the pay and training, which she absolutely believed went together,' Mallard said. 'You couldn't pay people if you didn't train them, and if you trained them you had to pay them. … She was very much one of the leaders in that shift.'

Pay parity had been on the agenda for the kindergarten movement since the 1970s. Studies had shown the teachers' work was equivalent to that of primary teachers, but the National government had shut down any chance of achieving equity. The drastic move in 1997 by Jenny Shipley, the minister of state services, to throw the kindergarten service out of the state sector was effectively a message that if the teachers wanted pay parity they would have to find the extra money somewhere other than government coffers. When a job evaluation study shortly before the 1999 election showed kindergarten teachers' work was of equal complexity and difficulty to that of primary teachers, minister of education Nick Smith had responded that pay parity was not a priority and would discriminate against other early childhood services.[5]

The structural obstacles to kindergarten pay parity were removed in late 2000, when the Employment Contracts Act was repealed and replaced by the new government's Employment Relations Act, which was intended to favour collective bargaining. The kindergarten service was brought back into the state sector, where it had historically belonged as a core part of New Zealand's public education system.

By the time Mallard moved to follow through on his commitment to address pay parity, Helen had been appointed as NZEI's assistant national secretary, in charge of industrial bargaining. Lynne Bruce, a former kindergarten teacher who had specialised in early childhood education as an academic at Wellington Teachers' College, was the new national secretary, replacing the retiring Joanna Beresford.

Amanda Coulston, who had first met Helen as a teachers' college trainee in early 1991 during the campaign against the Employment Contracts Act, had been elected president of the NZEI and was vitally interested in extending the union's success with primary teacher pay parity into the early childhood sphere.[6] Clare Wells was recruited by Mallard to be his political adviser. 'We were in positions of influence,' remembered Wells.[7]

Mallard appointed Stan Rodger to chair a working group charged with figuring out how to benchmark kindergarten and school teachers' salaries. Helen was a member, along with others from the sector. With her experience of the primary teachers' parity negotiations, she was a dominant influence. 'She was the brains,' Rodger said. 'She had all the details in her head. It was essentially she and I teasing through the detail.'[8]

Helen was an exceptionally hard worker, Lynne Bruce remembered. 'When she faced the executive she had all the arguments lined up.' Bruce had known Helen since she was a child and had often visited Shannon Street with her husband, Don Swan.[9] 'She didn't suffer fools,' she said.

Helen tended to be impatient, could be dogged on a point of argument before all the background had been considered, and was sometimes frank to the point of tactlessness. 'You'd be sitting in a room, the argument or debate would be going on … and everybody would be thinking this thought. Helen would always be the one who plucked it out of the air and said it, even though it wasn't the right time and the right place. She was sharp. She said what had to be said.'

In 2002, pay parity with primary and secondary teachers was locked into the national kindergarten teachers' collective agreement, to be rolled out over four years. Pay rises of up to 61 percent were in the offing for some. It was another significant step towards equity for an overwhelmingly female-dominated workforce who had been historically underpaid. Parity for teachers in the wider early childhood education sector was also on the NZEI agenda, but it was a much more complex goal. Private childcare businesses were increasingly prevalent, there was no single national collective pay agreement, and it would be a political challenge to extract the additional funding from government.[10]

By then, family life at McIntyre Avenue had unravelled. For several years Chris had been teaching at Clyde Quay – Helen's and Max's old school – where Dylan had been since he turned five. Helen's workload and responsibilities at the NZEI had grown significantly, she was continuing to study towards her law degree, and was involved in the Labour Party's Wellington Central electorate, the Wellington industrial branch and on its policy council. She was enmeshed in the union movement, including its social life. This centred around Friday nights at the Abel Tasman Hotel.

'She was away more and home later, and we got less time together. … That was the beginning of our demise, our falling apart as a family really,' Chris said. 'But it was more than that. She became more political and I couldn't keep up with her any more. … In a way I think her relationship with Steve [Hurring] came out of that. It came out of meeting Steve and realising they had this political thing that held them together.'[11]

Helen confided in Linda Mitchell on their morning walks to work and their nightly exertions around Mt Victoria. She doted on Dylan. How would he be affected if she and Chris were to separate? What about Cath and Pat, who loved their extended family set-up? What about Chris?

'She got married very young,' Mitchell said. 'People change. She was probably much more political [than Chris] ... I listened to her, and I told her to follow her heart, really.'[12]

They tried counselling but in early 2002 Helen decided she couldn't go on. Dylan, who was ten when the separation happened, never saw his parents fight.[13] Helen and Chris rented a house in Shannon Street and took turns living there and at McIntyre Avenue so Dylan could stay in his own bedroom, but the arrangement became too painful for Chris, who would later move to the suburb of Berhampore.[14] Dylan, by then at nearby South Wellington Intermediate, lived week about with each parent.

Steve Hurring and Helen had met at a Wellington Labour Party event. Hurring worked for the Engineering, Printing and Manufacturing Union and was active in the Labour Party. His roots were in Auckland, where he was plugged into the city's left-wing network and close friends with members of a partnership that owned a 44-hectare farm on Waiheke Island.

Purchased in the early 1990s, Orapiu Grove Farm included a communal house and outdoor pizza oven, a cluster of rudimentary dwellings, a vineyard, an olive grove and regenerating native bush.[15] Its owners included Steve's close friend Steve Poletti, a University of Auckland economist, and his partner Rebecca Potts, as well as Barry Gribben, the husband of unionist and former Alliance Party MP Laila Harré, and lecturer John Stansfield, whose partner Denise Roche – also a unionist – would later become a Green Party MP. Russel Norman, another close friend of Steve's and later to become Green Party co-leader, also had ties to the farm and lived there while working on his PhD.

The place was a hotbed of political activism. The many visitors were generally, as Denise Roche put it, 'Ngāti Left', and the various Labour, Alliance and Green party allegiances made for vigorous sectarian debates. There were also old rivalries between those who had remained aligned to the Council of Trade Unions through the 1990s and those who had sided with the Trade Union Federation.

By the time Helen started visiting the farm in the early days of her relationship with Steve, Poletti was producing wine from the property's grapes. Well-lubricated protagonists would argue and poke political borax at each other late into the subtropical Waiheke nights. The topics were wide-ranging: New Zealand's involvement in the war in Afghanistan; social justice; whether Helen Clark's administration was bringing about genuine economic reform. Debate was often heated but mostly good-humoured and Helen would give as good as she got. She and Steve were tribal defenders of the Labour Party in these sessions, Poletti remembered.[16]

Somewhere along the way Helen had acquired a nickname: 'Xena, Warrior Princess'. 'I loved it. I thought it was so her,' Roche said. 'She was a ferocious advocate, but also her beautiful dimples ... and that steadfastness, the persistence and clarity and just this whole values-driven person that she was.'[17]

The arguments around the pizza oven echoed ongoing ructions on the left as it tried to recover from the Rogernomics era and the shattering of the union movement under the Employment Contracts Act. New Zealand was still adapting to proportional representation, and novel political parties were spawning regularly. By 2002 the Alliance Party was tearing itself apart and Jim Anderton formed a new Progressive Coalition. When an early election was held in July that year, support for the Alliance collapsed and Labour returned to power in coalition with Anderton's new party and support on matters of confidence from a new grouping of centrists called United Future.

Despite the fractures and squabbles, the electoral success of the centre left in the years after 1999 marked the end of the New Right revolution (more commonly referred to by then as neoliberalism). For a decade and a half, New Zealand had been the site of the Western world's most far-reaching free-market changes.[18] Among the most visible outcomes was one of the biggest and swiftest increases in inequality in the OECD. A fifth of the population was now living below the poverty line, there were entrenched disparities in health and housing, an explosion of low-paid casual work and falling real wages. Productivity was poor, the export sector was struggling, and there was a yawning current account deficit. Sweeping privatisations had delivered windfall gains to foreign investors, who now owned two-thirds of the New Zealand share market, while household debt had soared.[19]

'Fifteen years of economic reform have created a social disaster. We have an *indecent* society,' concluded *Listener* journalist Bruce Ansley in a survey of the evidence. 'What economic growth there has been has benefited only the rich.'[20]

The revolution started by Roger Douglas and continued by Ruth Richardson had failed to deliver the thriving economy promised. Yet at the same time it had been profoundly successful – New Zealand's economic structures and attitudes had been fundamentally rewired, making the revolution virtually irreversible. The assumption that deregulated markets were the best allocators of capital and resources had seeped into every crevice of policy. The idea that the private sector was always more efficient than the public sector had become an article of faith. The notion of a competent state, capable of playing an active role in the economy, had been severely undermined. And the power of global capital was such that any policies that defied these orthodoxies were liable to be punished by financial traders and investors, who could decamp in an instant to more favourable regimes.

In searching for a fresh political brand, Helen Clark's administration adopted the so-called Third Way. This was touted as a new political agenda for social democratic parties, having been embraced by Tony Blair's NewLabour in the UK and Bill Clinton's Democrats in the US. It meant retaining the core neoliberal infrastructure – the Reserve Bank Act, Public Finance Act and Fiscal Responsibility Act; borders wide open to international financial flows – while restoring the place of collective action, emphasising innovation, boosting education and research, and revitalising the welfare state.[21]

New Zealand would catch the 'knowledge wave'. The economy would thrive by turning clever research hitherto locked away in university labs and Crown research institutes into high-value exports.

Clark declared the era of neoliberal reform over, but she considered it essential to maintain the confidence of the business community. She assured the titans of commerce that 'the government doesn't intend to throw the baby out with the bathwater'.[22] For the union movement, that meant that the 'baby' of labour market flexibility – with its preponderance of individual employment contracts and weakened unions – would not go out with the 'bathwater' of the Employment Contracts Act.

The Clark government's industrial relations policy was thus a moderate correction from the extremism of the Employment Contracts Act. The Council of Trade Unions could hardly complain it didn't go further: it was the architect of the draft (the Workplace Relations Bill) that served as the starting point for the government's proposed new law.[23] It made no attempt to resurrect the award system. 'NO GOING BACK', announced a CTU information pack on its draft bill. Union membership would remain voluntary. There would be no compulsory arbitration and no exclusive rights for unions to represent categories of workers.[24]

When the minister of labour, Margaret Wilson, introduced her Employment Relations Bill into Parliament in March 2000, she was adamant it did not signal a return to the past.[25] The Bill recognised the role of unions, abandoned the language of contracts (which would now be called 'agreements'), required employers and unions to negotiate in good faith, allowed strikes in support of collective agreements covering multiple employers, provided for union entry into workplaces, banned political and sympathy strikes, and barred employers from replacing striking workers. The Alliance, wanting more far-reaching change, managed to secure a clause providing that new workers would be covered by any existing collective agreement for at least the first 30 days.[26]

But nothing in the proposed regime would automatically reverse the losses that been incurred by the most vulnerable workers under the Employment Contracts Act, nor magically organise the four-fifths of the workforce that wasn't unionised. New Zealand's labour market would still be one of the least regulated and most flexible in the OECD.[27]

That didn't stop the business community reacting to the Bill (and to the government's renationalisation of ACC, the body that administered the country's no-fault accidental injury compensation scheme) with what journalist Gordon Campbell called 'synchronised whining'.[28] The counter-attack became known as the 'winter of discontent'. A campaign led by the Employers' Federation and the National Party opposition generated florid headlines warning of resurgent unions and rampant unemployment. National launched a website devoted to attacking the Bill, which it reckoned should be called the 'Dinosaur Revival Bill' because it would take New Zealand back to the Jurassic era and wipe out the economic wonders of the Employment Contracts Act.[29]

Employers were regaled with misinformation about what the Bill meant for their businesses. Much of what was claimed was simple mischief-making. It was said, for instance, that workers would be able to strike for national awards (there was nothing in the bill that remotely resembled the old award system), and de facto compulsory unionism would return (the freedom of association rules in the Employment Contracts Act were repeated almost verbatim in the new law).[30]

The business sector threatened an investment strike and confidence plunged to historic lows. Roger Kerr, still in control of the Business Roundtable, declared the new law would 'send shockwaves through the international community investing and doing business in New Zealand'.[31] There were predictions from the ACT Party of a return to 'the industrial relations chaos of the 1980s'.[32] Headlines in the business media reduced the bill to crude shorthand: it was 'pro-union' and 'anti-boss'.[33]

In the CTU there were serious concerns that the Clark government would lose its nerve. 'At one stage Margaret [Wilson] thought Helen [Clark] was going to drop her and replace her with someone else. That's how bad it got,' remembered Ross Wilson, who worked closely on the Bill with Wilson, who lived four doors along from him in Mt Victoria. 'The government was very much under siege.'[34]

The outraged business lobby forced the government to make concessions and several lightning rod provisions were watered down.[35] Parliament passed the Act under urgency on August 16, 2000. It came into effect seven weeks later. Margaret Wilson declared the law was the work of a government that recognised the dignity of labour and the right of workers not to be treated as 'something to be bought and sold, but as [human beings] with human rights in the workplace ... The fear that has permeated the workforce in the last decade will become a thing of the past'.[36]

The new law stemmed the losses of the Employment Contracts Act era, but there was a profound realisation among the CTU's new leaders that rebuilding the union movement would require unity, grassroots organising and mobilisation around issues that mattered to workers. Peace was made with the Trade Union Federation and the National

Distribution Union, allowing the CTU to finally realise its founding ambition of being a unified voice.

New staff were recruited, including the highly respected Peter Conway as economist. Conway had worked with South Island clothing workers, North Island shop workers, and striking British miners during their bitter showdown with Margaret Thatcher in the 1980s. He produced regular economic bulletins that leaned against the dominant narrative that the economy *was* the financial markets. 'Several times a day, we hear an announcement of "and now the latest from the money markets"', he wrote in his inaugural bulletin. From now on, he said, the CTU would provide economic commentary that was 'the latest from the labour market'.[37]

Contrary to the predictions of the business lobby that the Employment Relations Act would cause industrial mayhem, strikes remained rare. However, workers in dispute with employers could rely on active and visible support from the union movement's leaders.[38]

A new union organising centre was set up in Auckland, dedicated to rebuilding capacity by training workplace delegates and putting young activists through a traineeship in which they were tutored in economics, employment law and the theory and practice of organising. The idea was to move beyond the passive 'bargaining agent' model of unionism – a worker pays a subscription in return for bargaining services – to one in which the real power lay with the workers themselves, and in their readiness to fight through collective action to defend their rights and advance their interests.[39]

The union movement was once again recognised by government as a legitimate participant in New Zealand's economic and political life. The CTU was involved in a plethora of taskforces and committees on productivity and industry development. It was funded by ACC to train thousands of workplace health and safety representatives, and by the government to develop 'learning representatives', whose role was to advocate for workplace training and support fellow workers to build their skills.

In mid 2002, Helen joined the CTU's governing National Affiliates Council in her new job as general secretary of the Association of University Staff, the union she had worked for as an organiser at Victoria University in the mid 1990s. She strongly supported the renewal efforts led by Ross Wilson, although she didn't share his strong focus on workplace health and safety. 'I would look across the room if we were having a lengthy conversation about health and safety at national council, and she would roll her eyes, and tease me a bit,' Wilson remembered.[40]

She was marked as a potential future leader for the union movement. The following year Darien Fenton was asked to make way – 'You could say I was rolled' – and Helen was elected vice-president of the CTU.[41]

Pat and Cath were there to see her voted in.[42] At only 39 she had risen further up the movement's hierarchy than Pat had ever reached. She always kept a photo from that day – she, with her hair long and without make-up, flanked by her proud parents – in her office.

By then Pat was ailing. He had had a probable heart attack when alone at the bach at Rangataua but it had been undiagnosed and untreated. There was another attack at Shannon Street. 'They were ringing Helen and saying, "Someone needs to drive Dad to the hospital,"' Max remembered. 'She was saying, "Call an ambulance!"'[43]

He needed heart surgery, but the doctors were reluctant to operate. He wasn't well enough. He was paying for decades of roll-your-owns and beer, although by then he had knocked off smoking, cut back on drinking and lost weight. He and Cath didn't have much to come and go on, apart from their national superannuation. Cath had long since given away her inheritance. Pat had sold one of his most valuable assets, his signed copy of Chairman Mao's *Little Red Book* from his visit to China in 1967, for £10,000 through Sotheby's auction house.

The following year, 2004, a surgeon agreed to operate on the 74-year-old. Pat knew it was extremely risky. At first he appeared to have come through it well. When Max visited him he was sitting up in bed. 'He said, "Maxie, I can breathe properly for the first time in years." He was overjoyed.'

However, he soon contracted a severe antibiotic-resistant infection. There was further surgery to cut away his infected sternum but he continued to deteriorate. His last weeks were spent in a monumental struggle for life, attached to a ventilator in intensive care at Wellington Hospital.

Max remembered him nodding his consent to being removed from life support. 'By then he had had enough.' He died on June 24, surrounded by Helen, Max, Cath, Dylan, Steve, Peter Cranney and Dave Morgan.

Pat's return home to Shannon Street was marked by solemnity, expletives and black humour. 'We had trouble getting [the coffin] through the front door and had to lever it upwards to take it into the second bedroom,' remembered Don Swan, who helped manhandle the coffin into the house with Helen, Steve, Cranney, Morgan and a couple of men from the funeral parlour.

When the lid was removed, Pat's milk-bottle spectacles were skew-whiff on his large nose. 'Helen turned around to these two young funeral director guys and said, "What the fucking hell have you done with his nose!" There was a stunned silence. The blood drained from the guys' faces. Dave Morgan started giggling and it broke the ice. It was pure bloody Helen.'[44]

Laid out in his suit, Pat looked a bit like a member of the Politburo. Troops of people filed through the house to bid farewell.[45]

The obituary in Wellington's *Dominion Post* featured a large photo of Pat shaking hands with Chairman Mao. The funeral at Old St Paul's was packed with unionists, activists, politicians and extended family. Morgan led the eulogies for the 'funny, generous, wise, selfless, dedicated, determined, argumentative, loving, revolutionary and inspirational Kelly … His was a useful life, well lived.'

Helen spoke last, with her close friend Linda Mitchell at her side. She told the assembled mourners she could recall Pat crying only three times: 'Once, when Ernie [Abbott] was murdered; once, when Dylan was born; and the day before he died, because he was so sick that he couldn't stand life any longer.' She spoke of the adoration between Pat and Dylan, and then turned to Cath to remind her of his immense admiration and love, and respect and pride in 'your politics and values, and the way that you've lived your life'.

Of her own confrontation with Pat's death, she said, 'It's hard for me to talk about memories of Dad as though there won't be any more. It doesn't seem right. There are so many of them and they are rich and happy. But I want more. I loved him.'[46]

By the time of Pat's death, Helen was two years into what would be a five-and-a-half year stint leading the 6000-member Assocation of University Staff (AUS). When the role came up it had had natural appeal. It was in the education sector, which she had been part of since starting at teachers' college in 1983. She had worked for the union before. As a part-time law student, she saw first-hand the mounting stresses facing university staff. And she would have had in mind Joanna Beresford's advice that she should build her skill and experience in the labour movement by leading a union.

Her CV sized up well for the job. She had played key roles in two of the most successful campaigns of recent years – primary and kindergarten teachers' pay parity. At the Combined Early Childhood Union of Aotearoa and NZEI Te Riu Roa she had sharpened her skills under the leadership of some of the most effective women in the union movement. She had proven to be an astute and pragmatic negotiator. And, as Amanda Coulston put it, she was 'unrelenting. If she believed in something she would put 120 percent into ensuring it happened'.[47]

She had impressed influential people who had come across her during those years, including Doug Martin, a former deputy State Services Commissioner turned public sector consultant. Martin had first dealt with her in 2000, when he was helping the NZEI, one of his firm's clients, make an appointment to the assistant national secretary role. He had encouraged Helen to apply for the job. She struck him as 'extremely bright. A pain in the arse – she really did corner you and hassle you. [She had] a real fire in the belly, a really committed unionist. … In that sense she stood out from the rest. She just seemed more assertive and much more stroppy. She wasn't a status quo appointment.'[48]

Nor would she be for the AUS job. Massey University academic Grant Duncan was AUS president when the union's long-serving executive director, Rob Crozier, announced his retirement. It was Duncan's job to recruit a replacement. Helen was one of two leading candidates. Duncan recalled being influenced by the advice of a key referee for both: he was told one would be a competent and reliable appointee; the other would be 'brilliant'. 'I took this message back to the [AUS governing council], and being a bunch of academics brilliant was what they liked.'[49]

Brilliant or not, Helen's appointment was controversial and unpopular with many of the union's senior staff. It was no secret that the other candidate was the 'anointed' one. Duncan was threatened face-to-face with a staff walkout on more than one occasion.

The threat wasn't carried out but a degree of white-anting against Helen continued. Some thought she was too young for the job, hadn't earned her stripes in the union movement's women's committees and didn't have much interest in identity politics. She was ambitious and driven, and some suspected she was using the job as merely a stepping stone to higher things. Others reckoned she was a show pony.[50]

'One of the things about Helen was she thought she could charm most people. She was gregarious and vivacious,' said Marty Braithwaite, the union's University of Canterbury organiser. He had got to know Helen well during her stint as an organiser at Victoria University in the mid 1990s and was one of the few senior staff who supported her appointment.[51]

Helen was aware of the opposition to her and didn't appear to let it trouble her. In any case, it was untenable to let office politics stand in the way of the development of a desperately needed industrial and political strategy to deal with a broiling sense of crisis among staff at the country's universities.

Government funding of universities had stagnated since the radical changes introduced in 1989 to '90 by minister of education Phil Goff, during the last gasp of the fourth Labour government. By one estimate, funding was 35 percent lower in 2002 than it had been two decades earlier.[52] Salaries had eroded badly. Before the Goff changes, academics' pay had been fixed by the Higher Salaries Commission and linked to that of backbench MPs. When staff were removed from that system and left to bargain directly with university chief executives – vice chancellors – that linkage had broken down.

The Clark government was touting the 'knowledge economy' but the academics whose research would be the bedrock of future high-value industries and who would be the teachers of tomorrow's skilled citizens were being paid 22 percent less than they could get in Australian universities and half what they could earn in the UK.[53] Lecturers were becoming recruitment targets for overseas universities facing staff shortages.[54]

At the same time, workloads and class sizes had increased, thanks to a drive to lift the number of tertiary-qualified New Zealanders, and to the funding model brought in during the reforms. Universities no longer received five-year grants, adjusted to take account of centrally determined salary increases. They were now funded through a subsidy attached to each student.[55] This had shrunk in real terms through the 1990s.

There was a competitive frenzy among universities for students. Vice chancellors, required to produce surpluses, were spending huge sums trying to lure school leavers with advertisements on TV, radio, online, on billboards and on the backs of city buses. An estimated $100 million worth of advertising was rolled out by universities, polytechnics and other tertiary education providers between 1999 and 2003.[56]

Restructuring and redundancies were occurring on most campuses. Morale was poor. Strikes – unheard of before the inaugural stoppage organised by Helen at Victoria in 1995 – were occurring more frequently.

One former AUS leader described New Zealand university staff as the 'peasant workers of the Knowledge Society'.[57] They were caught in a pincer between vice chancellors' need to manage their inadequate budgets, government reluctance to confront the funding problem, and political pressure over mounting student debt, which had led to a freeze on universities' ability to increase fees.[58]

Salary bargaining was a zero sum game: if staff got pay rises, something else would have to be cut and students would suffer. Thus, every year the AUS would be presented with low-ball pay offers that failed to break the downward slide. The climate of austerity didn't apply to university bosses, however: vice chancellors' salaries rose by up to 42 percent in five years, compared with less than ten percent for staff. By 2002 the highest paid vice chancellor was pulling in $380,000.[59]

The Employment Relations Act had put the possibility of nationwide collective agreements covering multiple employers back on the agenda for unions. Instead of scrapping with the vice chancellors and their HR managers university by university, why not harness the collective power of all 6000 or so AUS members to corral the bosses into two nationwide agreements – one for academics and one for librarians, technicians and other general staff?

Grant Duncan had promoted the idea of a multi-employer collective agreement (known throughout the labour movement simply as a MECA).[60] Helen – her feet barely under the general secretary's table – immediately began developing a detailed strategy.[61] 'Do we continue to negotiate within what the government "gives" to universities by way of funding increases,' she asked her members, 'or is it time to "break the link" and force government to fund universities sufficiently to enable decent salaries to be paid? The answer may well be that AUS should set its sights in the next bargaining round on achieving a MECA.'[62]

By the end of 2002 the union's national conference had backed the MECA strategy. The following year – as required under the Employment Relations Act – members at each site voted to give it the go-ahead. It signalled a significant change in style and approach for the AUS.

'Helen brought an industrial union perspective and it was a radical shift,' said Tom Ryan, a University of Waikato academic who served on the governing council for much of Helen's time at the AUS. While some were hesitant, 'she won their confidence. She came with a successful track record from the childcare sector, and she had an impressive whakapapa in terms of political know-how and activism.'[63]

Ryan said by the time the union adopted the MECA strategy, members had given up on the ability of the vice chancellors to get the government to address the chronic underfunding of their universities. '[They] had shifted from being senior colleagues to autocratic chief executives. They played it to the max. They acted tough but they were not very effective. There was a need for real leadership.' In some cases the relationship with the staff was little short of toxic. For instance, the boss of the University of Otago tried in late 2002 to sue the union over strike action taken by staff in support of their collective bargaining claims.[64]

Prising open the pincer that was constraining university pay packets would be a long game. 'Helen had a natural feel for that time frame,' Ryan said. 'Something had to give, and she understood very well that now was the time to put the pressure on' – not least because a government with which she had strong connections was in the early days of its second term, and success would rely on the application of political as well as industrial pressure.

In 2003, the union went into its first round of attempted MECA bargaining with a claim for 30 percent pay rises for academics over three years and ten percent for general staff, followed by two years of inflation-adjusted increases. The demands seemed audacious, but the ambition was to bridge the gap between New Zealand university salaries and those of other countries.

The president of the union was now Helen's cousin Bill Rosenberg – the son of Cath's sister Ann and her husband Wolfgang Rosenberg. Rosenberg worked in the University of Canterbury's IT department and was a staunch advocate for the new strategy. The pay claims might seem high, he acknowledged, but the cost of not addressing the issues would be higher still. At heart 'it is about the quality and the academic credibility and reputation of our university system,' he wrote in an op-ed in the weekly *Education Review*. 'Bargaining at individual university level has not made sufficient inroads into salary deficiencies and there has been no responsibility or obligation placed on government to provide the funding to address them. This is no longer acceptable to staff, who restrained their increasing concerns for a over a decade. National bargaining provides one means by which all parties can combine to address the issues of funding, salaries and quality.'[65]

Things didn't go well for the union at first. The vice chancellors rejected the idea of a MECA, even though the annual bargaining rounds at each university always produced very similar settlements. They insisted they needed local flexibility so that salaries were appropriate to the financial strength, size and mix of disciplines of each university. They were responsible for managing their own enterprises and were not about to relinquish their prerogative by buying into an omnibus national pay deal.

Steve Maharey, the associate minister of education with responsibility for tertiary education, was publicly sympathetic to a MECA – his government's industrial relations reforms had supposedly made it easier to achieve this kind of pay deal, after all. And he was working on tertiary education reforms aimed at more cohesion and less competition in the sector. But he ruled out the government playing any role in bargaining and refused to entertain the idea of handing over more money to the vice chancellors to fund salary increases.[66]

The union fell back to site bargaining. Strikes occurred on some campuses. There were talks about how the union, vice chancellors and government could possibly come together in a tripatite manner to discuss what to do about salaries. Efforts to find a way to turn the screws on the government for more money continued.

'Employers in the sector have no strategy for challenging the government's continued underfunding of universities; we are providing that strategy,' pronounced Helen, as she pushed the narrative that collective action and coherent national pay bargaining were the answer to the crisis.[67]

In 2005 the MECA strategy wound up in court. The University of Auckland vice chancellor Stuart McCutcheon refused to meet to discuss bargaining for a pay deal alongside other universities who were his 'competitors'. He wanted to 'prioritise [his university's] own strategic decisions' and address its 'unique financial management and risk profile'.[68]

By then Helen was working increasingly closely with Peter Cranney, who had trained as an employment lawyer during the 1990s. They decided McCutcheon's refusal raised an important question that had to be tested. Could an employer lawfully stymie a union's bid for a MECA by simply refusing to turn up? Was this a breach of the 'good faith' provisions that sat at the core of the recently strengthened Employment Relations Act?[69]

Relations between the union and McCutcheon had become increasingly hostile. As the largest university, Auckland was a key focus for the salaries campaign. Union members there voted to strike over McCutcheon's refusal to bargain for a MECA.[70] In a move that Helen regarded as a deliberate attempt to undermine the union and wreck the collective bargaining campaign, the vice chancellor offered a relatively attractive 4.5 percent pay rise to non-union members; this posed an immediate risk that union members would ditch the collective effort and take the offer.[71]

In response, she wrote to every non-union staff member on campus – via the university's email system – telling them that McCutcheon's offer was a 'direct result' of union activity, and that their non-membership was being used against unionised staff as part of 'what we believe to be an attempt to remove the union from the university. ... Your decision to join or not join the union is no longer a passive one.'[72]

Because of its wider legal significance, the union's case against McCutcheon was sent straight to a full bench of the Employment Court. The three judges quickly recognised that this was not merely a battle over strategy between two parties who both wanted salaries to increase but differed over how to get there. It was an ideological fight between a union that 'rejects a competitive and individualistic tertiary education model' and a university that regards this model as 'both irresistible and the way of the future.'[73]

The court declined to strengthen the union's hand. The university was obliged to turn up to MECA talks but it couldn't be locked into substantive bargaining. McCutcheon was slapped lightly on the hand for his tactics but no orders were made against him. He and Helen both claimed scraps of victory, but the principal outcome of the case was to underscore how limited the powers of the Employment Relations Act were in promoting sector-wide and multi-employer pay bargaining.

By mid 2005 the pressure was intense. McCutcheon's representatives turned up to bargaining as required, but refused to engage. Once again a MECA looked impossible. The union's members voted to take unprecedented national strike action.

The union now had a new president, University of Auckland business school academic Nigel Haworth. Like Helen, Haworth had close links with the Labour Party and the pair made a tight team. There had also been a reallocation of Cabinet positions. Trevor Mallard had taken over direct responsibility for tertiary education from associate minister Steve Maharey.

Mallard had been aware for some time of the mounting anxiety among senior people in the university system over inadequate salaries and funding, and of fears that the sector was at risk of long-term decline. It was election year and Haworth and his good friend Helen Kelly were in Mallard's ear. 'I was of the opinion it needed sorting,' he remembered. 'It was like an open weeping sore that had two areas of danger. One, if we couldn't get better wages and stability and an ongoing positive path as a way of resolving issues, the universities would get run down. The second thing was political. I wanted to try and get some stuff sorted in an election year, in particular, without it being an ongoing negative.'[74]

Things began to move more quickly. Mallard picked up the union's suggestion of a tripartite group to nut out a solution to the pay problem. The union inflicted two separate one-day national strikes on the universities, as well as rolling stoppages, work-to-rule actions, lightning strikes and pickets. In the middle of it all, the government announced it would scrap interest on student loans if it was returned to power.

Three weeks before the election, the union and the vice chancellors reached a truce: a so-called 'umbrella' agreement set out the terms of engagement for working together on funding and salaries through Mallard's tripartite forum. Haworth called it 'potentially the most significant bargaining development in 15 years'.[75]

The pressure was working: the warring parties were finally in the same tent.[76] By the end of that year, with a Labour-led coalition returned to power, the union was dealing with another minister. Michael Cullen was a former University of Otago academic who intuitively understood the issues. He was also minister of finance. Helen joked it was 'like mainlining the Budget'.[77]

Over the next three years, $61 million in extra money was released by the government to fund increases in university pay.[78] It still wasn't enough to address the shortfall that had compounded over the years and the vice chancellors still refused to settle a MECA.[79] But it was the first substantial boost to pay since the changes of 1989.

It would not have been achieved without effective union mobilisation. Peter Wills, a University of Auckland scientist who was branch chair and a member of the union's governing council during the period of peak industrial pressure, said without the MECA strategy and the strikes 'the vice chancellors wouldn't have felt the need to do anything; they would have kept the salaries down and blamed it on the government'.[80]

Indeed, Roy Sharp, who led the vice chancellors' group during the key period of tripatrite talks and who had high regard for Helen, went some way to acknowledging that the bosses had trailed on the union's coat-tails. The union had 'the inside running' with the government, he said, and joining the tripartite forum 'was a blatant way on our part of being able to politically get more money and so we were happy to go along with it'.[81]

Helen's influence on union members' attitudes was considerable, Wills said. 'She had that ability to get people to see things her way, and see the effectiveness of doing it her way.' She exuded confidence and resilience, and people could see she was 'willing to do the tough stuff. A lot of people had to be persuaded to some extent that it wasn't just going to backfire and leave everyone weaker than they were before. She was good at doing that. She had the personality to cajole people into being a bit braver.'

Helen, however, gave the credit to the members. 'If you, like I did at the beginning of this campaign, had any concerns about the ability of members of this union to front the media, plan and work together, stick to the national goals, take industrial action, make sensible decisions, be respectful of each other and commit to participation, these concerns proved unfounded as the campaign showed tenfold,' she told the union's 2005 annual conference, at the end of a year of high-wire activism.

As the man who was persuaded to open the funding pincer, Cullen had found Helen to be someone the government could do business with. He was familiar with Pat's flaming class rhetoric from years of attending Labour Party conferences. Helen seemed 'in many respects ... a total contrast to her father. Pat was for the battle rather than the victory, and for Helen I think it was the victory rather than the battle. She seemed to have a clear understanding of where the limits of possibilities were, but she didn't lose sight of her ultimate goals ... She was never a person who let the excellent be the enemy of the good. She would take the gains because "okay, we can make more gains next time around".'[82]

The workload for a union with a small staff had been huge. As well as the campaigning and the research effort to support the campaign, there was the normal union work of supporting members with personal grievances and responding to major reforms, including the introduction of the Performance-Based Research Fund and the Tertiary Education Commission.

Helen was also trying to modernise and grow the union. She made a point of hiring bright young organisers – sometimes over the heads of more experienced hands – and pushing them to engage one-on-one with workers in key university service areas such as call centres and libraries, listen to their concerns and win them over to the collective cause.[83] It was an approach to grassroots organising that was being strongly encouraged by the CTU leadership and the Auckland organising centre, from where she recruited several promising young unionists.

Along with Haworth, Helen pushed hard for a merger of the three unions representing workers in the tertiary education sector, including polytechnics, teachers' colleges, wānanga and private sector training establishments.[84] Universities were expanding into each others' traditional patches, polytechnics were offering degrees, and competition was driving institutions to act in their own interests rather than those of a national public education system. For Helen, bringing the unions together was about solidarity, reducing duplication, and becoming a bigger and more coherent industrial and political force for the tertiary sector and its workers. However, the merger proposal was highly controversial. Some academics argued it was being railroaded by the AUS head office, and feared it would weaken the voice of scholars and submerge their interests in a union dominated by non-academics.[85]

Helen's workload was a worry for the union's governing council.[86] She didn't draw a line between work and the rest of her life. 'You'd go to her house and she'd be lying on the sofa with her feet up, going through her emails and plotting and scheming,' said Braithwaite, who moved from Christchurch to Wellington for several years to work as her 'loyal lieutenant', driving much of the research and communications behind the salaries campaign.

'The conversation would weave in and out between work and social stuff. She just lived it. We'd go on holiday and the whole time there was plotting – "How will we get this done?" "What about that?"'[87]

In the thick of the intense industrial campaigning of 2005, Helen was finishing the last of her law papers.[88] She also needed to give Cath more support after Pat's death. She was still on the Labour Party policy council, involved in party fundraising, and in pamphlet distribution in

Wellington Central. Dylan was 14, living full-time with her and Steve at McIntyre Avenue, and would often come to the AUS office after school, or to Parliament, where Steve was working as political adviser to David Benson-Pope, a Labour Party Cabinet minister.

For Dylan, who had been soaked in politics all his life, there were plenty of attractions in hanging about Parliament. Benson-Pope became something of a surrogate grandfather. Dylan also got to witness the passage of milestone social reforms such as the decriminalisation of prostitution and the legalisation of same-sex marriage.[89]

Unknown to most in the AUS office, Helen and Steve would periodically take other children under their wing, sometimes friends of Dylan's, or kids they knew who needed a break and somewhere to stay, or the children of friends. 'If she found other people in need, especially children, she would just scoop them up and look after them,' remembered AUS staffer Suzanne McNabb.[90] She could be insistent in her generosity, and 'quite domineering', said Peter Monteith, Helen's friend and former colleague from the NZEI. Helen and Steve looked after Monteith's sons when Monteith and his partner went overseas. 'She'd say, "Of course!" It was almost an insult if you turned down an offer of help.'[91]

There were also her wider roles in the labour movement, including her duties as vice-president of the CTU and working on a taskforce set up by Margaret Wilson to develop a plan to close the gender pay gap in the state sector.

She was clearly a rising star, but in her CTU role tribal loyalties landed her in the eye of a bitter turf war. The Employment Contracts Act was gone, but the percentage of the workforce that belonged to unions had scarcely recovered.[92] There was a desperate need for renewal and innovation to reach vulnerable workers and mobilise them into collective action for improved wages. Unite Union had burst into the news in 2003 with audacious Auckland-based campaigns to organise low-paid workers.[93] The union was led by former Alliance Party operatives Matt McCarten and Mike Treen, who saw it as a project to 'organise the unorganised' in sectors that had been deunionised in the 1990s. They claimed other unions weren't making full use of the Employment Relations Act's workplace access rights to recruit new members and scoffed at the CTU's model of organising, which promoted one-on-one contact with potential members to build trust, including meeting them at their homes if necessary.[94]

'Why? It's not America,' said Treen, of this approach. 'We don't need to secretly meet in people's *homes*. No, we just march in there like we own the fucking place.'[95]

They signed up sex workers, and parked themselves in call centre hallways and at Burger King dining tables, joining people up – many of them teenagers on youth rates and unpredictable hours who had grown up not knowing what a union was. McCarten dubbed them 'Rogernomics kids'.[96]

Unite was billed as New Zealand's fastest-growing and most militant union.[97] By 2004 it had recruited members and won collective pay deals in big hotel and cinema chains, and was starting to go after the fast-food sector. It kept fees low, and grabbed attention through picket-line fracas with police and undercutting cinemas' lucrative popcorn trade by giving the stuff away for free.[98]

But they were also stomping around in others unions' terroritories – particularly that of the Service and Food Workers Union. When McCarten had first turned up with an ambition to organise café workers, the 'Servos' had welcomed his initiative. But when Unite started picking off handfuls of hospital orderlies, cleaners and security guards at sites where the Servos were already organising and negotiating collective agreements, it looked more like opportunism than innovation.[99]

Unite's aggressive approach also niggled at old tensions between Labour Party loyalists and backers of the Alliance, and poked at the fault lines that lay beneath the surface of the reunited CTU. The conflict came to a head when, after being approached by a couple of disgruntled Servo members, Unite started recruiting and organising at Auckland's SkyCity Casino. The Servos had slogged for eight years to organise the site and by 2004 had 800 members there and a collective agreement. It had won some major battles to improve workers' conditions. With support from a special CTU organising fund, the union was trying to extend its reach into SkyCity's new Hamilton casino and get a national pay agreement with the company. Unite's incursions were a major distraction and caused a serious setback to the Hamilton effort.[100]

Darien Fenton, national secretary of the Service and Food Workers

Union, was extremely angry with Unite. She considered SEA-Unite, the rival that Unite was setting up at SkyCity, to be an in-house union of the sort often referred to in labour vernacular as a 'yellow union', dominated by the employer.[101]

Helen was a member of the Servos. It was also Pat's old union. She was good friends with Fenton. She strongly disapproved of Unite's actions.

Mike Treen was aware of Helen's attitude. He had links to the farm at Waiheke and had met her there. The two wound up shouting at each other. 'Helen was always a bit of a factionalist. I think it came from her Stalinist father actually,' said Treen, himself a former member of the Trotskyist Socialist Action League. 'She was strong in her views, and even more so when she'd been drinking.' She called Unite a 'scab union' – perhaps the worst insult one unionist can hurl at another.[102]

She also sparred with McCarten, who had been a protégé of Pat in the Labour Party before he broke away to follow Jim Anderton. The pair once found themselves in the same group in a bar in Karangahape Road. 'She got into Unite. "You're a yellow union, a scab union,"' McCarten recalled.

In reply, he taunted her as a privileged union bureaucrat. 'I said, "Helen, I know you're from Wellington so you'll never understand, but this is an experiment. How do you organise the working poor? How's that going in the trade union movement? Unlike you, I come from that community, I don't have all those privileges you have down in Wellington, doing all your planning on whiteboards before you go down and have your lattes."'[103]

By the start of 2005 feelings were running high. There was talk of a motion to expel Unite from the CTU, although that wasn't the wish of the Service and Food Workers Union, which just wanted the CTU to enforce its anti-poaching rules.[104]

Ross Wilson had supported Unite's efforts to organise young and marginalised workers. He strongly opposed the move for expulsion, saying, 'If that motion is passed, I will resign as president. When Helen came in to talk to me about it and indicated she was supportive of the motion, I made the same statement to her. Well, the motion was never put.'[105]

A motion to censure Unite was put by FinSec, the Finance and

Information Workers Union. It was ruled out by Wilson and replaced with a milder version that expressed 'concern' at the SkyCity situation and urged the CTU to facilitate 'discussions' between Unite and the Service and Food Workers Union.[106] 'For me, the overriding imperative was to keep the union movement together,' remembered Wilson. 'The last thing we needed was another breakaway, or for that matter kicking out a union that was demonstrating some innovation and organising. Okay, they were stepping on established toes, but what they were doing was fundamentally good. They were working with young people in ways we hadn't seen, so why would you try and pull old demarcation lines that stemmed from a system that no longer existed?'[107]

Her attitude to Unite was, in many ways, pure Helen: loyal, passionate, unafraid of conflict, capable of dishing out and taking brutal blows.

Those in and around the AUS saw these traits and more. '[She was] a very strangely cut diamond,' observed Graeme Whimp, a senior unionist who worked at the AUS on various projects and became a firm friend and supporter of Helen.[108] Compassion sat alongside ruthlessness; generosity with hardness; discretion with tactlessness; intense focus with an irreverent, politically incorrect humour.

Her networks within the movement and in the Labour Party were strong, but she tapped into a wide range of sounding boards. 'She was not easily influenced. She had amazing capacity to draw stuff from other people,' said Whimp. 'Anyone had the potential to contribute.'

The Princess Xena label had stuck, but she didn't fit the tidy profile of a celluloid caricature. She was always working and strategising, but she also knew how to have a good time on her own terms. She was a talented shopper – of gifts for others, and boots and shoes for herself. One of her favoured modes of relaxation was watching the risqué American TV series *Sex and the City*, which she played repeatedly on DVDs. To mark the last show of the final season friends organised a party with big screens at Wellington's Concrete Bar. The place was full of unionists and political types from the beltway, as well as trusted old friends who weren't part of her activist network. They ran a pre-show quiz. Helen knew every answer, remembered Michelle Saban, a close friend from teachers' college days.[109]

She was fun to be around, but could be acerbic and abrasive – particularly after a few drinks, although she cut back on that. 'I would describe her sense of humour as wicked … combined with a razor-sharp wit,' said Bronwynn Maxwell, an AUS organiser in Auckland when Helen was hired (and one of those who had opposed her appointment as general secretary, although the two were friends and mostly got on well). Kindness was not an attribute Maxwell ascribed to Helen. Sometimes her passion and impatience compromised her judgement, she remembered.

Maxwell would sometimes joke with a colleague about 'Helen-whispering' – 'talking her down.'[110] It was unlikely to be a successful strategy. As Rosenberg put it, 'When Helen decided something, there was no stopping her.'[111]

She was fond of her own way and good at getting it. Andrew Campbell, a young former student leader when Helen hired him to work as the AUS organiser at Massey University, found she had a charm that meant 'you sort of don't even notice you are being steamrolled. It's quite a remarkable quality. You're almost happy to be told what to do.'[112]

She was a shrewd negotiator, as Erin Polaczuk quickly discovered. Polaczuk was a talented 23-year-old who had come through the CTU's organising centre. She was hired by Helen as the AUS women's officer, a newly created role that Helen had opposed, although she backed it enthusiastically once Polaczuk was in the job. Polaczuk soon found herself on the other side of the table from Helen, representing the union's employees in negotiations for their collective pay agreement. 'She always seemed to have about three different potential ways to get around an impasse. In bargaining you can get to a point where you are saying, "This is what we want" and the other side is saying, "No, you're not having it" and you're at loggerheads until someone caves. For her it wasn't so much, "No, you are not having it" as "How about options three and four?" because she had already thought ahead.'[113]

Sometimes she spoke before she thought. One year at the May Day Cup festival in Palmerston North, Andrew Campbell was in a troupe called the Real Hot Bitches; he had recently come out as gay in Wellington, but not to his family or the people he had worked with at Massey University. 'In front of a packed theatre in Palmerston North, Helen gave special mention to Andrew,' remembered Fleur Fitzsimons, who at the time was the leader of the New Zealand University Students Association and had dealings with Helen in that role. 'She said, "Well Andrew, there's absolutely no doubt about your being gay now, is there!" It was typically cheeky, but I suspect she thought afterwards, "Oops, shouldn't have done that." Just a little bit overfamiliar and overconfident.'[114]

She believed in solidarity and acted on it. When a senior figure in the Service and Food Workers Union, Luci Highfield, became ill with cancer in 2007, Helen deployed three experienced AUS organisers to fill the gap; between them they renegotiated six collective contracts. 'There was no hint of any direct outcome for AUS, just helping another union at a time they were under pressure,' said John Ryall, then national secretary of the Servos. '[It was] the best of unionism ... We do not experience that often.'[115]

At the AUS, Helen won the loyalty and admiration of some staff and the brooding resentment of others. She was open to new ideas and left people to get on with their jobs, but expected them to stick with the programme. 'She wanted the energy that she displayed shown across the whole organisation,' Haworth said. 'She wasn't a disciplinarian – you know, my way or the highway – but she had a strong sense that people were servants of the members, that the members had essentially signed off on these strategies at their annual conference and people had to basically buckle down and deliver. ... She was looking constantly for improved performance, and performance that was in tune with the strategy to grow the union, to improve its representational quality on the ground, and to deliver better outcomes in bargaining.'[116]

The changes she wanted inevitably led to casualties and clashes. In 2006 she brought in her old boss Joanna Beresford to advise on restructuring the union's staffing. A bitter split ensued when it became clear that a long-serving senior employee would be laid off. With her eye fixed on the strategy of building a large sector-wide union, Helen was similarly willing to stare down the doubters of the proposed merger of tertiary education unions – an issue that would become a key theme in a poisonous two-way battle for the AUS presidency in 2007.[117]

Ross Wilson announced in early 2007 that he would retire from the presidency of the CTU. Helen was clearly a contender for the position.

She had learned an enormous amount in her five years at the AUS; she had come into a relatively small union and overseen strong growth in membership, given it a more influential voice, achieved significant pay rises, and laid the groundwork for a complex union amalgamation.

Wilson had marked her for years as a successor. He valued her intelligence and ability to think outside the square. Yet she was tentative about the role and nervous about making public appearances. 'She was always outwardly confident and cheeky and good at relationships, but she was quite nervous really about taking on the CTU president role. She tried to talk me into staying for at least another couple of years,' Wilson said.[118]

She confided her reticence to others, too. 'She was a little scared of becoming president,' recalled Karin Currie, a trusted senior administrator at the AUS. 'I remember her saying, "I don't know if I can do this."'[119]

She sought the advice of Doug Martin, by then a ubiquitous consultant on all manner of public sector issues. She wasn't afraid of reaching outside the union movement for advice and ideas, and on this occasion she wanted the perspective of someone who was a bit more objective.[120] Martin strongly encouraged her to throw her hat in the ring.

She wasn't the only contender. Carol Beaumont, who had come up through the National Distribution Union, set up the union organising centre in Auckland and served for four years as CTU secretary, also wanted the role. Whoever succeeded, the New Zealand union movement would for the first time be led by a woman.

Numbers were done. Helen had influential backers, including the large Engineering, Printing and Manufacturers Union. As well as Wilson, other people of mana in the movement supported her, including Peter Conway and John Ryall.

For some her perceived lack of feminist credentials was a black mark; others saw her as an outgoing, appealing new leader fit for what would likely be more challenging times.[121] 'She was able to project her personality and views,' said Paul Tolich, an inveterate union power broker who represented the EPMU around the CTU top table.

There was a fair likelihood a National-led government would take power in 2008. A strong union voice would be vital. 'We don't look for stars,' insisted Tolich, of the machinations over the leadership. 'We look for capable and intelligent people who can lead and motivate. Helen was able to do that. She had a certain amount of flamboyance and turn of phrase and was very personable.'[122]

She came with the Kelly name and Shannon Street values, but without the Marxist rhetoric. She was as comfortable in a smoko room full of wharfies as with a bunch of professors. 'Everyone knew where she came from,' Tolich said.

Helen was in Berlin attending a conference of Education International, a global confederation of teacher unions, when it was announced that she was unopposed for the top job. She visited Sachsenhausen concentration camp, where thousands of political dissidents and trade unionists had perished at the hands of the Nazis.[123] She also took the opportunity to see relatives in Wigan, but felt a long way from home when a political storm broke in Wellington, in which Steve's name was broadcast in Parliament and in the media and both he and Benson-Pope lost their jobs.[124]

In taking on the leadership of the labour movement, Helen was deferring a long-held ambition to become an MP. It was election year and Marian Hobbs had announced that she was going to retire. Wellington Central, where Helen knew every street, was up for grabs.

Grant Robertson wanted to get the Labour nod for the seat. The young party activist had worked as an adviser to Hobbs and Helen Clark. He and Helen had become friendly through their electorate work. He asked her to meet him for coffee. By then it was clear she would succeed Wilson unopposed at the CTU, but the formal vote of affiliates at the biennial conference hadn't yet taken place.[125] Robertson was nervous. 'I wasn't a hundred percent that certain that Helen wouldn't flip and say, "Actually I'm not going to be CTU president, I am going to go for Wellington Central,"' he remembered.

'I said, "Helen, Marian is standing down and I want to put my name forward and I want to see if you will support me." Her response was just brilliant. She looked at me and said, "Grant, I think you know that's the job I want, but I can't do that because I am taking on this role as the CTU president. So you are taking my job but I think you'd be a good person for it so I will support you." We got out a piece of paper and wrote down a plan. [Parliament] was clearly a serious consideration in her mind, but she knew she couldn't let the union movement down in terms of taking on the CTU role.'[126]

Helen's first speech as leader of the CTU was, in any case, effectively a stump speech for Labour. 'We know the difference a government can make to the lives of working people. We know the stark difference between the current government, with its support partners, and the governments of the 1990s,' she told the October 2007 conference at which she was formally elected. 'We know in the 1990s wages decreased, rights were removed, penal rates were cut, state houses were sold, tax cuts were implemented at the expense of public services and at the expense of investment in roads and other infrastructure. We know that unemployment was high and benefits were cut. We know ACC was privatised, health and safety law was toothless, and a worker's right to strike for a multi-employer agreement was illegal. … All of us want a strong economy, but alongside that wages must increase. We want decent incomes and decent work. It's not too much to ask.'[127]

9. Working for workers

What the movement has been doing doesn't seem to work.
Helen Kelly, 2011

The previous few years had seen some significant wins for unionised workers. The movement of which Helen assumed leadership in October 2007 had barely half the membership of the pre-Employment Contracts Act era but it was in better heart than it had been through the dark years of the 1990s. A string of signature disputes and campaigns had shown that solidarity got results.

Public hospital nurses, midwives and healthcare workers had fought for and won a 20 percent pay rise in 2005 under the banner of a New Zealand Nurses Organisation 'Fair Pay' campaign, which focused on safe staffing levels, gender equity and the leakage of poorly paid workers from the profession.[1]

Unite Union – still regarded with suspicion by some other unions – had hit its stride in the fast-food sector. In late 2005 it had launched *supersizemypay.com*, an internationally groundbreaking campaign driven by a smart young volunteer, Simon Oosterman, who had come from the environmental and animal rights movements. It went after big brands such as McDonalds, KFC and Pizza Hut, throwing shame on them as exploitative low-wage businesses.

They pulled off the world's first Starbucks' strike, hit other chains with dozens of short stoppages and protests, and organised mass marches of teenage workers through central Auckland. They deployed music, comedy, street theatre and text messaging to reach their audience and recruited thousands of young members. The fast-food behemoth Restaurant Brands relented in early 2006, signing up to a collective agreement that lifted wages, phased out youth rates over two years, and gave workers more security over their hours. McDonalds resisted for longer, but by later that year it too had settled a collective agreement and undertaken to abolish youth rates. The Wendy's chain agreed to a collective pay deal in April 2007.[2]

Unite was doing what many had considered impossible – politicising and organising young workers. The story that multinational fast-food companies hired youngsters to give them a start in the workforce had been shown to be a fiction, declared Matt McCarten after the deal with Restaurant Brands was reached. 'The reason they are employed is because they are cheaper and more compliant. The ruse is up.'[3]

More traditional unions had also honed their methods. The Engineering, Printing and Manufacturing Union (EPMU) had mounted a fightback campaign in 2005 branded 'Fair Share – 5 in 05', seeking five percent pay rises to redress some of the losses incurred by workers under the Employment Contracts Act. By the end of that year, the EPMU had achieved the target in 85 percent of its collective agreements.[4]

The following year the Australian-owned supermarket giant Progressive Enterprises had gone to war with workers at its distribution centres and lost. The brutal battle between the company – which controlled nearly half of New Zealand's grocery trade – and 600 workers at three distribution sites began in August 2006, when the workers went on strike for 48 hours for a national agreement and an eight percent pay rise.[5] Progressive responded by locking them out; it called the move its 'trump card'.[6]

For four weeks the workers – members of the National Distribution Union (NDU) and the EPMU – were deprived of work and wages. But instead of being starved into submission, they became the focus of an extraordinary mobilisation of support from the wider union movement, churches, community groups and the public. Led by the NDU's national secretary Laila Harré – who had come from the successful nurses' campaign, and before that from Parliament as an Alliance MP – and aided by Simon Oosterman's communication skills, the workers' story was told through smart messaging and media work. The point was made that the chief executive of Progressive's owner, Woolworths Australia, was on $8.5 million a year – he earned more in one minute than an adult full-time supermarket checkout operator earned in an entire year.[7]

Picket lines became community hubs, with kitchens, homework tables and welfare committees. TVs were set up so that workers could see their stories broadcast on national news; there was music, karaoke and a picket-line newspaper. Helen's friend and colleague at the AUS, Suzanne McNabb, developed an 'adopt a family' scheme; supporters in other centres held concerts, rallies and other fundraising events. Some $450,000 was raised through donations and pledges to sustain the locked-out workers.

After a month, a settlement was negotiated. Although the workers didn't get a national collective agreement, the deal delivered pay parity at the three distribution centres and, for the lowest paid, an increase of almost 20 percent.[8]

Low-paid workers in the health sector had also made substantial gains through a 'Healthy Hospitals' campaign led by the Service and Food Workers Union. The wages and conditions of cleaners, orderlies, security, food service and home support workers had been eroded during the years of the Employment Contracts Act and by competitive tendering of services by district health boards. The campaign involved a significant investment by the Servos. There were public rallies, community events, campaign T-shirts and leaflets, a few short strikes, and persistent lobbying by union members at Labour Party conferences.

Eventually the government instructed the 21 district health boards to conclude an agreement that consolidated 45 separate pay deals into one national set of wages and conditions. When the union tried to extend the same deal to private sector contractors in the health sector, the biggest company – Spotless – locked out 800 workers.[9] After ten days of pressure by the union on health boards and a successful court injunction against Spotless, the company withdrew the lockout and a deal was done.

By October 2007 – after 18 months of campaigning – the Servos' 'Healthy Hospitals' effort had delivered pay rises of up to 26 percent for workers, many of whom had previously been on or near the minimum wage.[10]

The Labour-led government had delivered other gains for workers across the board – a fourth week of annual leave, 20 hours of free early childhood education, 14 weeks' paid parental leave, a 60 percent increase in the minimum wage since 1999, tax credits under the Working for Families policy. The Employment Relations Act had been amended to protect vulnerable workers, such as cleaners, orderlies and laundry workers, by ensuring that if their work was contracted to a different company they were entitled to transfer to the new employer on their existing wages and conditions. By 2007 youth rates were in the process of being scrapped and a change was in the works to ensure workers doing an eight-hour day got a paid half-hour meal break and two tea breaks – a measure decried as evidence of a 'nanny state' by the head of the Hospitality Association.[11]

Unemployment had been falling steadily for almost a decade, and by the end of 2007 New Zealand, at 3.3 percent, had one of the lowest rates in the OECD. The savage levels of unemployment among Māori and Pasifika workers at the height of the neoliberal era had eased.[12] Now many companies complained that a shortage of workers was the biggest constraint on their operations.[13]

Theoretically, wages should have surged in response to the market's signals. Theoretically, workers should have been calling the shots in bargaining and flexing their market power for a better deal. But that hadn't happened. Low wages were 'embedded' in the economy, as the CTU's economist Peter Conway put it. Even Treasury – a driving force behind the neoliberal programme of the 1980s and 1990s – had conceded that New Zealand wages had fallen dramatically compared with Australia over those years, and that employers therefore relied on cheap labour instead of investing more in capital equipment and technology that would lift productivity.[14]

Average wages had gone up, but not enough to keep up with rising grocery and house prices, and New Zealand workers were putting in some of the longest hours in the developed world.[15] Tens of thousands were leaving the country every year to work in better-paying jobs in Australia.

Without the Employment Contracts Act, employers no longer had unfettered rights over their employees, but nor had there been a restoration of workers' collective bargaining power. Successful picket-line battles such as those waged by Unite, by university staff and by hospital cleaners and orderlies were the exception rather than the rule: far fewer workers went on strike during the first eight years of the Labour-led government than during the high unemployment years of the 1990s.[16]

Most workers were still on their own, without representation or the benefits of collective bargaining. Under the more benign Employment Relations Act, the number of union members had risen to its highest level in a decade, but only 21 percent of the workforce was unionised. The new heartland of the labour movement was the public and community service workforce, which accounted for over half of all union members. In the private sector, only 12 percent were in unions, and the movement had virtually no reach at all into major industries such as farming, forestry and construction, wholesale and retail sales, hotels and cafés.[17]

The aim of the Employment Relations Act was to promote collective bargaining, but the proportion of workers covered by collective agreements had actually fallen. By 2007 only nine percent of private sector workers were covered by collectives, and just over 60 percent in the public sector. A mere five percent were covered by MECAs.[18] Yet even the OECD, which had lauded New Zealand's radical labour market deregulation in the 1990s, was starting to rethink the consequences of weakened collective bargaining. In a remarkable turnaround, economists at the Paris-based organisation concluded in 2006 that 'stronger bargaining power of trade unions is associated with lower relative poverty and income inequality'.[19]

Helen had been thinking about these issues well before she took over as leader of the CTU. She had enrolled again at Victoria University in 2007 and was working towards a Masters in Law. In her research paper she was investigating why 'the lowest paid and vulnerable workers … are missing the right to representation'. Her research was anchored in the ILO's freedom of association rules – Conventions 87 and 98 – which enshrined the fundamental rights of workers to form unions and to bargain collectively. She theorised that New Zealand labour law, including the Employment Relations Act, rested on a narrow idea of freedom of association, with the result that many workers were effectively denied the right to unionise and employers were easily able to resist collective bargaining. She asked, too, whether the ILO conventions had limited the ability of unions to represent workers by making them completely reliant for their viability on fee-paying members. Had this produced unions that worked only for *members*, and not for *workers*? If so, was that justified in a modern economy?[20]

Her own experience at the Association of University Staff had shown how difficult it was, even for a union with well-educated members concentrated in a handful of large workplaces, to achieve a MECA setting standard minimum pay and conditions for the sector. For workers in small scattered workplaces beyond the practical reach of unions – on farms or in small shops, for instance – there was no chance.

She and others in the union movement had concluded that the Employment Relations Act needed to be significantly changed to promote MECAs and industry-wide standards that established minimum pay and conditions for workers in the same sector.[21] Without that, wages would continue to be suppressed by businesses seeking to lower their costs to keep ahead of their competitors.[22]

'We don't need low wages in this country,' she told *New Zealand Herald* journalist Audrey Young. 'There's no excuse for it. People should be able to go to work, work their hours and have a decent standard of living at the end of the week.'[23]

It was a matter-of-fact comment that belied a monumental ambition – to shake up the movement she now led so that it worked for all workers, and to build the case for a law change that would stop workers' wages being eroded in a competitive race to the bottom.

She was under no illusions as to the scale of the challenge. The union movement worldwide had gone into decline as a result of the neoliberal economic model, digitisation, mechanisation and the power of global capital. Helen understood all this, said John Ryall, then national secretary of the Service and Food Workers Union. 'But she wasn't content to simply manage that decline. She believed the union movement was based on values of solidarity, and that did not just mean solidarity for those workers in unions paying union fees. It meant supporting exploited workers and their families wherever they existed.'[24]

A two-day conference of union leaders, to be held in Rotorua, had been arranged for February 2008. Helen laid out her thinking about the challenges facing the movement in a paper circulated beforehand. She had been at the helm of the CTU for four months, long enough to discover that the role was huge.[25] She had been forced to abandon her half-finished Masters' research, but had effectively carried her analysis directly into her conference paper. The paper was full of bold options but they were buried in dense academic prose. It was as if Princess Xena's sword was entangled in a thicket of scholarly journals and technocratic caution, and blunted by the nervousness she had confided to Karin Currie and Ross Wilson.

Despite 'serious and sustained efforts' the union movement was thin on the ground, particularly in the private sector. This was 'a matter for concern', she wrote. There were workers who directly benefited from union campaigning who should be members, but weren't; there were workers who were members because they were sympathetic to unions' role in advancing social equity through the likes of minimum wage campaigns; and there were workers who weren't in a union because they'd never been asked, or because joining one might make them vulnerable to an anti-union boss, or because they were juggling multiple part-time jobs just trying to stay ahead of the bills. This latter group – often low-paid, low-skilled, casual workers – may never be within reach of a union, and therefore unable to tap into support in the face of unfair dismissal or other assaults on their rights.

She scoped out the debate that she thought the union movement needed to have about reforming itself. Tentatively, she poked at the elephant in the room: what was the legitimacy of a movement that claimed to speak for workers but actively represented only a fifth of them? 'We cannot shy away from the question: why should business or government or, indeed, the broader society listen to the union movement?'[26]

The persistent reader who waded through her paper found demanding ideas that pushed towards a movement that was seen as the genuine voice for all workers, rather than merely a club for fee-paying members, 'by addressing the full range of economic and social issues with positive and innovative ideas and strategies, and by leading the debate on workforce development and the building of a better NZ for NZers'.

There was nothing here about tearing down the walls of capitalism. She talked about 'iterative discussions', 'social partnership' and the 'desirability of joint actions among organised labour, employers and government'. There were quid pro quos to be respected: any system of industry-wide pay agreements and wider union influence would 'place obligations on unions both to prove the legitimacy of this power and to show they are able to operate in a way that supports a modern workplace'.

If her paper hinted at knocking down any walls, it was those the movement had built around itself. How could unions represent marginalised and vulnerable workers who were never likely to be recruited as members 'in a way that is real, collective in the true sense of the word and legitimate'? She pointed – without a hint of regret for her earlier hostility – to Unite's success with McDonalds as a shining example of a genuine workers' movement; seven thousand had participated in that campaign, but the union collected the fees of only 400. Workers had belonged to the campaign and benefited from it without 'joining' the union in the traditional way.

What if unions rethought and broadened the whole notion of 'membership'? What if there were new ways that workers could be associated with the movement? What about the possibility of setting up a central 'holding' union for workers in hard-to-organise sectors?

The Rotorua meeting was a start. It produced a raft of recommendations hinting that the movement was open to thinking differently about how it worked for workers. Over the following months, Helen herded union leaders into four working groups: one would focus on a law change that enabled industry standard agreements and promoted MECAs; one would look at new structures and strategies fit for the modern economy; one would concentrate on developing future leaders; one would look for practical ways to reduce duplication between unions.

Helen was on all of them, as was Peter Conway, who reluctantly became CTU secretary in early 2008 after Carol Beaumont left to campaign for a parliamentary seat for Labour at the upcoming general election. Conway would probably have preferred to remain as the economist – a job he loved – but he was a senior figure in the movement and dutifully took up the role. He and Helen made for a dynamic and handsome leadership team: she creative, passionate and gregarious; he assiduous, considered and gentlemanly. Both were highly intelligent, immensely hard-working and deeply committed servants of the union movement.

Outwardly, Helen's language gradually became sharper and more confident. The four workstreams amounted to a huge programme of change for the CTU, which ran on the smell of an oily rag. She made it increasingly clear she believed a status quo union movement was not an option. 'This work will and should be contentious,' she wrote in a paper setting up the working groups. It was about 'building a strong union movement (rather than focusing on making current unions stronger)'. She expected proposals to 'demand high performance from unions'.[27] It was 'time for a whole new look at how we do things'; she wanted a movement that was 'more than the sum of unions' and had influence in the setting of every worker's wages and conditions.[28]

Privately, she wasn't enjoying the job much. 'She didn't like it at the beginning,' remembered Ross Wilson, whom Helen leaned on for advice and encouragement. 'I think there were some concerns within a number of unions about her style, that she was not concerned enough about the people around her … she was a bit out front as a president.'[29]

Gradually, proposals for change were distilled. Helen had always had a nose for sharp slogans and clever images that captured complex ideas. She had seen the power of 'Susan' and 'Sally' when they were deployed as mascots for wage justice for primary and kindergarten teachers. Now she needed an emblem of worker powerlessness in a market economy, in which the rights to unionise and negotiate pay and conditions existed in theory, but not in reality.

She landed on the 'Four Square worker from Kaitaia'. 'She needs to find a union that can represent her, sign the form and hand it to her employer, organise her workmates, hold meetings, collectively bargain (hard in a small shop), campaign and strike if needed, ratify the collective if it is achieved and maintain the organisation in the shop. This is before she gets to do something like attend the union conference and really participate!'

In the real world none of this happened: the employer set the terms of employment and the worker decided whether to take it or leave it.[30]

The Kaitaia shopworker made her first public appearance at the CTU's biennial conference in October 2009. She was the opening act in a 14-page reform plan laid out by Helen, which captured the ideas of the four working groups. It was called Union Change, and it laid out a path to a union movement 'capable of achieving improvements in the lives of working people ... including their wages and conditions, their level of influence and dignity at the workplace and their influence in shaping the political decisions of the government'.[31]

The conference endorsed the package of recommendations. They included the drafting of a new industrial relations law that would enable minimum pay and conditions to be set across whole industries, and the establishment of a new dollar-a-week union for workers in hard-to-organise sectors. The proposed new union did not have a name, but it would soon be christened 'Together'. There would also be more work done on consolidating union membership systems and legal services, as well as leadership training.[32]

It was aspirational stuff. So too was a far-reaching economic programme presented to the conference by the CTU's new economist and policy director, Bill Rosenberg.[33] It was the second time he and Helen had worked together: first, when he was president of the Association of University Staff a few years earlier; this time, as he took up the role vacated by Conway when he became CTU secretary.

By now the global economy had been more than a year in the grip of a deep crisis caused by the uncontrolled growth of toxic financial products throughout international credit markets. These complex instruments had spread like a virus, transmitted through opaque financial engineering and lightning fast transactions.[34] Very few people in the world understood how they worked.[35]

The first flicker of trouble had come in April 2007; by late 2008 massive global investment and banking outfits were being bailed out by governments, and a few left to fail. It was the biggest shock to the financial system since the Depression. The all-knowing, all-powerful market had failed utterly.[36]

At the same time, New Zealand was suffering a parallel crisis as lightly regulated and poorly governed finance companies – heavily exposed to a now teetering property market – failed, one after another. As the scale of the global crisis grew, there were fears New Zealand bank depositors would panic and rush to withdraw their money. British savers had done just that in late 2007, when news of trouble at the Northern Rock bank triggered a massive run, with customers queuing in the streets to get their money out.

In October 2008 the Clark government had been forced to hastily establish a scheme to guarantee bank deposits; Australia had done so and if New Zealand didn't follow suit there was a risk that savings would funnel across the Tasman. Announcing the scheme, Helen Clark had declared, 'A curtain is being drawn on the era of the freewheeling unregulated money traders and financiers whose greed has shaken the international financial system to its very core.'[37] Soon after, a government guarantee was introduced to stand behind the banks themselves, to help them drum up the borrowings they needed from crippled global credit markets.

The relatively easy economic times that had prevailed through the years of the Clark administration – albeit substantially underpinned by soaring house prices and loose credit – had come to a shuddering halt. New Zealand had gone into recession even before the Global Financial Crisis, and by late 2009 unemployment was at 6.5 percent. Among workers who were still in jobs, many were struggling to get by on reduced hours. Real incomes had fallen by two percent in a year, the largest drop since 1992.[38]

The crisis had exposed the dangerous folly of inadequate oversight of globally interconnected financial markets, and now ordinary citizens the world over were paying for it through joblessness, poverty, mortgage foreclosures and government austerity programmes.

For Rosenberg and the CTU, the crisis begged a new way of thinking about economic policy. It was an opportunity to re-engineer New Zealand away from its neoliberal structures and begin to design a fairer society, free of poverty, with decent wages and well-funded public services. Rosenberg's paper to the 2009 conference called for higher taxes for very high earners, a financial activities tax, reduced GST, a higher minimum wage, expansion of state housing, investment in skills, and reviews of the Reserve Bank Act, Public Finance Act and Fiscal Responsibility Act, the key laws that kept governments in a policy straightjacket.

But Helen Clark, who had railed against the greedy money merchants, was gone by then, as was her centre-left government. The general election of November 2008 had delivered a National Party-led coalition under the leadership of John Key, a millionaire with a boyish manner who had made his money as a global currency trader.

Helen and Peter Conway had decided they had no choice but to work as productively as they could with the Key regime to get the best outcomes possible for workers. They invested an enormous amount of time and effort into a high-profile 'Jobs Summit' hosted by Key in early 2009, and took a leading role in developing a scheme intended to protect jobs by allowing workers to work a nine-day fortnight.

Helen was a pragmatist and 'capable of dealing with the traditional enemies of the union movement', Ryall noted.[39] She gave Key the benefit of the doubt and thought he had a genuine commitment to jobs. He was charming and she enjoyed the seemingly easy-going relationship with him, although some of her peers in the movement warned her to tread carefully.[40]

For his part, Key respected Helen and found her engaging and trustworthy. 'She would just flat-out disagree with a lot of the things I said, but she was never spiteful about it. She was a ferocious voice for the things she believed in. … She would certainly stand her ground but she didn't do it in a way that was nasty or where she would shout you down.'[41]

National had gone into the election with an agenda to roll back workers' rights. One of its earliest moves was to change the law to allow employers with fewer than 20 staff to dismiss workers at will within their first 90 days in the job. However, Key had explicitly ruled out bringing back the Employment Contracts Act, and he didn't appear to be an ideological zealot in the mould of Roger Douglas or Ruth Richardson.[42]

Despite his government's chipping away at the position of unions

– including removing two worker representatives from the board of the Accident Compensation Commission and scrapping the pay and employment equity unit set up by Labour – there was sufficient goodwill for Helen and Conway to invite Key to address the CTU conference in October 2009, the second time that year they had offered him the floor.[43] In his speech Key tried to hunt out common ground between his government and the unions. But unsurprisingly his agenda was a world away from that which Rosenberg presented. He foreshadowed reduced investment in public services, wage suppression in the state sector, and a 'tax system that doesn't hold back people's potential or dampen their aspirations'.[44]

He finished on a note of reassurance: although National's manifesto included changing the law that protected workers' rights to meal and tea breaks, and reducing holiday and personal grievance protections, Key told the conference that employment law reform wasn't 'a driving priority' for his government.

The détente between the CTU and the Key government held for only few months more. The centrepiece of the 2010 Budget was a package of tax cuts that delivered tiny gains for low wage earners, significant gains for high earners, and pushed GST up to 15 percent.[45] The minister of finance, Bill English, called it 'a once in a generation opportunity to change the direction of this economy'. It was cheered by business interests and tax experts, but Rosenberg called it 'fundamentally unfair' – a worker on the minimum wage would get a tax cut of $4.13, while someone earning ten times that would get nearly $154 a week.[46] It also signalled serious constraints on core public services; Rosenberg calculated that health funding was more than $100 million short of what was needed just to stand still in the coming year.[47]

Two months later, it became apparent that Key's assurances at the CTU conference were hollow. On Sunday, July 18, Helen was up early to catch a flight to Auckland to join a noisy protest of several hundred workers and union leaders outside the National Party's annual conference at the SkyCity Grand Hotel. Inside, Key was announcing sweeping changes to employment law. Foremost was the extension to all employers of the right to sack workers at will within the first 90 days. The change would mean that at any given time 300,000 workers would have no protection from unfair dismissal. The government claimed it would create jobs, but there was scant evidence of this.[48]

Key also announced it would become lawful for employers to 'buy' workers out of their fourth week of annual leave. Personal grievance protections for all workers would be scaled back. Employers could require workers to present a medical certificate after a single day off sick. Unions would not be able to enter workplaces to meet with workers without employers' consent. Employers would be free to talk directly to – and potentially put pressure on – individual workers in the midst of collective pay bargaining.[49]

Outside the venue there were placards and speeches, and some protesters attempted to force their way in. As the rally was wrapping up, Helen told those gathered she'd be seeing them again soon – 'on the streets'.[50]

'Dear John,' she wrote to Key three days later, in a letter depicted by one political reporter as a 'divorce' note.[51] Not only were the changes a betrayal of trust with the CTU – Key had assured Helen and Conway that no changes to union access rights were planned and if that situation altered he would advise them – but they 'show a disregard for the working people of this country. … They paint a picture of workers as lazy, untrustworthy skivers that are out of control and need to be disciplined. Workers are painted as acting deceitfully when applying for positions (so 90 days are important), taking sickies, misusing union membership and a range of other complete generalisations that demean the people we work with every day,' she wrote. 'This is not a test of "good and evil". It is a test of fairness, decency and respect.'[52]

Having bent over backwards to collaborate with Key over the Jobs Summit, she now accused him of opportunism. 'You … said you wanted to work with the unions. Of course this was at a time of a deepening recession, but we thought it was a longer term intention.' Regarding the proposed changes to workplace rights, she assured him: 'We will campaign strongly against them.'

The focus at the CTU turned to mobilisation of mass protest, with plans for a series of rallies under the 'Fairness at Work' banner. At the same time Helen continued pushing the programme of union reform.

She was determined to develop a legal framework for industry-wide pay agreements that could be promoted into the Labour Party's policy platform for the next election.

And plans for Together, the proposed new union for the archetypal Kaitaia Four Square worker, were continuing. The CTU had already been running what was, in effect, an early trial of outreach to such workers; when the Key government rushed through the first iteration of the 90-day fire-at-will law for small employers, Helen put the word out that any worker sacked under the rule should call the CTU and their cases would be put in the hands of lawyers from the various affiliated unions. It was made clear that non-membership of a union was not a barrier to representation.

'It was radical,' said Fleur Fitzsimons, by then a lawyer with the Public Service Association. 'Helen knew that when workers lose their jobs it destroys them and their families. She saw it as a core aspect of trade unionism to protect workers and their jobs.'[53]

It wasn't easy to find ways to defend workers sacked under the 90-day rule – by definition, they had no rights against dismissal that lawyers could invoke. But in some cases it could be argued the rule had been misused. The PSA took the first of these, and Peter Cranney led the argument in the Employment Court. It involved a 33-year-old worker, Heather Smith, who had been employed for almost three years in a Stokes Valley pharmacy and was not a member of any union. When the business changed hands, she and the other workers had to reapply for their jobs and were rehired on 90-day trials. Smith was sacked a few weeks later, just before Christmas 2009. She had no idea why. 'They said I wasn't what they were looking for … I don't know – not pretty enough [or] skinny. I have lost a lot of my confidence. It's put a lot of stress on my family,' she told Helen in a filmed interview the CTU posted to YouTube.[54]

Smith's case was heard just three weeks after Key announced the extension of the 90-day rule to all employers. The court found she had been unjustifiably dismissed, that the employer had failed to deliver on undertakings to her, failed to act in good faith, and had committed 'signal failures of fair and reasonable treatment'.[55]

The case showed there were some constraints on the 90-day rule, but more importantly it showed that when unions worked for workers – not just members – they could achieve justice where otherwise there would be none. 'It was typical Cranney and Helen,' said Fitzsimons,'making the best use of the circumstances and advancing workers' rights.'

On the other hand, Helen's determination to defend the interests of non-union members sacked under the 90-day rule exposed a bedrock of resistance to the transformation she wanted to bring about. Ray Bianchi, secretary of the Northern Amalgamated Workers Union, had told her his union wanted nothing to do with her plan for unions to advocate for non-union members. 'Our members are vehemently opposed to this union using their money to encourage freeloaders,' he wrote.[56]

Helen had been the leader of the union movement for three years when – on October 20, 2010 – 22,000 workers turned out around New Zealand under the CTU's Fairness at Work banner to protest against the Key government's changes to employment law, and a broiling dispute between the actors' union and Peter Jackson over the making of *The Hobbit* mutated into a full-blown propaganda war.

At lunchtime she'd been proclaiming to a crowd of cheering workers gathered at Parliament grounds that Key was treating them as skivers and slackers who weren't to be trusted. By early evening she was attempting – in vain – to convince a 1500-strong crowd of jeering film workers that an industrial dispute over the filming of *The Hobbit* had been settled and a hugely controversial international actors' boycott of the production had been called off.

Despite her ambitious programme to reform the union movement and her staunch opposition to the government's rollback of workers' rights, Helen Kelly was not a household name. Earlier generations of New Zealanders had known the men at the helm of the old Federation of Labour – Walsh, Skinner, Knox, Douglas – but twenty years on from the decimation wrought by the Employment Contracts Act, union leaders attracted few headlines.

That changed when Helen was perceived to have challenged Jackson, a national idol. She had stepped into the dispute between the Australian-based Media, Entertainment and Arts Alliance (MEAA) – of which New Zealand Actors' Equity was a branch – and Jackson late in the piece, when it was clear things were getting out of hand and the CTU-affiliated union needed help. She had staunchly defended the actors' fundamental rights to bargain over their pay and conditions. Over the previous three weeks she had played a key role in reaching a settlement that would see future negotiations take place between the union and the industry body, the Screen Production and Development Association (SPADA).

With a settlement achieved, the international actors' boycott was being lifted. However, the MEAA had agreed that a public statement to that effect wouldn't be made until Warner Bros., the company producing *The Hobbit,* was ready.[57] As events unfolded over subsequent days, this would provide a painful tutorial for Helen in letting others take control of the narrative.

By October 20, key government and film industry figures knew the actors' boycott was being withdrawn, but the announcement had not been made. As Helen later commented, 'the only group left in the dark was the public'.[58]

In the information vacuum, film workers were called that afternoon to the Stone Street production studios in Miramar, where they were riled up by predictions of massive job losses caused by the boycott, which they were told was still in place. They were handed a lengthy flyer alleging that the MEAA was 'putting the entire New Zealand film industry at serious risk of collapse'.[59] At the end of the meeting they grabbed ready-made placards and headed downtown on an anti-union march.

Later that night, Jackson put out a statement. Warners, he claimed, was on its way to New Zealand to make arrangements to pull the production out of New Zealand. The country then went into a lather.

The morning after the march, Helen was interviewed by radio jock Mike Hosking. He told her she had 'lost *The Hobbit*', and Jackson was 'furious' with her. Her response was quick – too quick. 'Peter Jackson is being a spoilt brat, and saying that in this country I know is like something sacrilegious.'[60]

It was a throwaway remark; the words seemed to spill from her lips. In frustration, she'd deployed a rebuke she would normally use when exasperated with Dylan.[61] No matter the detailed and nuanced context she was trying to paint in the interview – the fact a settlement had been reached, the influence of the global arms race of film industry tax breaks on any decision made by Warner Bros., the right of trade unions to seek to influence pay and conditions – the damage was done. She had gone on radio and insulted a national hero. As one commentator jibed, she might as well have desecrated the grave of Edmund Hillary.[62]

Peter Conway was horrified. 'Peter's view was that it let down everything we were trying to achieve,' remembered James Ritchie, who was national secretary of the Dairy Workers Union and close to both Helen and Conway.[63]

The next day she emailed Jackson to apologise. 'You and I do have a serious disagreement on a number of issues in relation to the dispute around the Hobbit, but I do regret calling you a spoilt brat as it is not only untrue but belittling of your very strongly felt views, which I know are genuine. I just wanted to say I am sorry for that. I do think SPADA and Equity have found a way through on the industrial issues that is enduring across the industry and I am committed to making it work.'[64]

Whether she genuinely regretted the 'spoilt brat' comment, it was another costly lesson in losing control.[65] 'She never made that kind of mistake again,' Ritchie said.

Her private apology to Jackson did nothing to stem the flood of venom into her inbox from affronted New Zealanders, who now knew who she was and held her responsible for the allegedly imminent collapse of the nation's film sector.

'You should be ashamed of yourself for destroying the livelihoods of thousands of people and the NZ film industry,' emailed one stranger. 'You're evil and contribute nothing to society, you only destroy.'[66]

'There's a reason why there's a 'Sir' before Peter Jackson's name and nothing before yours,' wrote another.

'Isn't it about time to just cut bait [*sic*] instead of fucking yourself further by spewing ridiculous BS in the media?' queried one of the less coherent correspondents.

'Are you the bitch who lost the "Hobbit"?' inquired another.

'Thanks very much for wrecking the NZ film industry you short sited [*sic*] union lackey.'

'Your disgusting actions over the Hobbit film will make you and [actors union spokesperson] Robyn Malcolm the most hated people in NZ.'

'You should be deported as a traitor to NZ.'

On and on they went. She dropped them into a file labelled 'Abusive' and mostly ignored them. She assured friends and colleagues she was fine when they phoned or texted to check how she was coping. Her executive assistant, Julia London, was sure it affected her more than she let on. 'It was a very, very difficult time. It was hard on everyone in the office. Helen wasn't as hard as people would make out. She had a very soft side to her. … She maintained a staunch face for us, but privately she would have been feeling the anxiety. She inspired a loyalty that made us want to protect her.'[67]

The weekend after the union movement's nationwide Fairness at Work rallies and the anti-union march by film workers was Labour weekend. Helen and Steve had booked a trip to Christchurch to stay with Marty Braithwaite and his partner Kayleen Churton. Executives from Warner Bros. were due to land in Wellington on Labour Day, and *The Dominion Post* ran pages of anticipatory coverage. It was reported that jitters over *The Hobbit* may have dented the value of the New Zealand dollar, and a betting agency was taking punts on whether Helen Kelly would still be leading the CTU by the end of the year.[68]

While she and Steve were in Christchurch, Helen went to TVNZ's local studio for an interview with Paul Holmes, who was in the Auckland studio with John Barnett, a leading figure in New Zealand's screen industry. She might as well have climbed into a lion's den. Holmes repeatedly interrupted and talked over her. He accused her of 'preaching' when she tried to explain the settlement that had been reached. He said she was 'fantasising'. He swore. Her statement that it was 'perfectly legitimate for working people in ths country to seek to have an agreement in which they have input' met with no acknowledgement from either of the men.

'The impression people have, Helen, is that you are well out of your depth,' said the agitated Holmes. 'When Jackson calls you "clueless" and tells you to go home, this is a New Zealand-produced genius, the like of which we'll never see again. … What do you know about show business? What do you know about the film industry? What do you know about international studios? What do you know about international actors unions?'

Barnett told her she had 'really let down the actors' and had 'no credibility'. He said the president of Actor's Equity, Jennifer Ward-Lealand, and actor Robyn Malcolm – who had taken on the role of spokesperson for the union – were 'damaged goods' who would find it hard to get work because they were now seen differently by the public.[69]

Braithwaite said Helen had gone into the studio expecting a debate, and got a mauling. 'She was upset. Shattered, really, at the venom they showed. … She was tough, but there were moments like that when her vulnerability was exposed.'[70]

Within a week it was all over. The men from Warner Bros. had received a generous top-up to the already generous taxpayer subsidies for big-budget film producers. Parliament had rushed through a law change removing the rights of all film industry workers to the protection of employment law. *The Dominion Post* had headlined the moment in history when *The Hobbit* was 'saved': 'It's still our precious: NZ wins the battle for Middle Earth'.[71]

It was a comprehensive and humiliating defeat for the union movement. Strategically, the attempt by the actors' union to use *The Hobbit* as leverage to make progress on its long-standing desire for a collective agreement had been a disaster. Perhaps because the MEAA was based in Australia, there had been a failure to properly assess the political and public relations risks of challenging someone of Jackson's mana. Helen had been solid in her public defence of the actors' position, but privately she was seriously concerned that the union brand had been damaged, particularly against the background of Key's employment law changes. She even floated the possibility – quickly shot down – that Actors Equity switch from their affiliation to the MEAA and join the EPMU.[72]

But there were much larger issues, too: the spectre of Parliament writing a law to suit a Hollywood film studio; the apparent fomenting of division for commercial and political gain; the sheer ugliness of the abuse that she, Ward-Lealand and Malcolm had endured. Helen was hardened rather than chastened by the short bizarre saga. She was convinced New Zealanders had been manipulated and was determined to be able to prove it.

A few days after the Warner executives flew back to the US from their successful Wellington visit, Helen headed overseas for three weeks to attend meetings of the International Labour Organisation in Geneva and to talk to the Trade Union Congress in the UK. As she grew into her CTU role, these connections with the global labour movement were becoming increasingly important in her thinking about workers' rights and how to assert them.

When the Pike River mine blew up on the afternoon of Friday, November 19 she was still abroad. She landed in Wellington the following Sunday, three days before a second explosion that extinguished any hope for the 29 workers underground. Two workers had survived the initial blast and miraculously escaped.

With mounting fury, she witnessed the praise that was being showered on the mine's chief executive, Peter Whittall. Twice a day, the articulate Australian would speak to mass meetings of traumatised families, and address media conferences that were broadcast to a transfixed and shocked New Zealand public. He was a confident speaker and came across as honest and sincere; many thought his performance in the face of a tragedy was heroic. He was fêted as the 'man of the moment'.[73] When Helen begged publicly to differ – suggesting that, as the boss of a company where 29 workers had been killed, he should instead be apologising – a fresh torrent of abuse rushed into her inbox.[74]

By the time of the Pike River disaster she had had some exposure to health and safety issues as a CTU representative on the Workplace Health and Safety Council, a tripartite group set up while Labour was in government. She had met Whittall at a meeting of the council just six months before the mine blew up. He had come to talk about a new Business Leaders' Health and Safety Forum that he had helped establish. The chief executives in the forum had each signed a pledge taking personal responsibility for the goal of making their businesses 'zero harm' workplaces. Whittall had explained that it was all about 'leadership and accountability'.[75]

The council had failed to achieve much. It lacked power, tended to get bogged down in reports and processes, and was easily ignored by the government.[76] Helen's involvement in it had scarcely turned her into a firebrand on health and safety matters. Before the Pike tragedy she had tended to believe it was feasible for industries to self-regulate; afterwards, she took on board the perspective of Tina McIvor, the CTU's health and safety organiser, who predicted that the scrapping of strict mining regulations under the Bolger government's Health and Safety in Employment Act of 1992 would be found to be a key contributor to the disaster.[77]

Over the weeks and months following the mine disaster, she did what she could to support and encourage the well-organised committee formed by the families of the dead workers, the youngest of whom was a boy of 17, Joseph Dunbar. 'There was never a day that she wasn't furious about Pike,' remembered Dylan.[78]

There was to be a royal commission of inquiry and Ross Wilson was asked to prepare the CTU's submissions with McIvor's help. The Department of Labour was undertaking its biggest investigation ever under the Health and Safety in Employment Act. It promised to thoroughly scrutinise all the key issues: did the mine have adequate ventilation; how well was methane gas controlled; was the mine competently managed and properly funded; was its emergency response adequate.

There was profound grief, and a desperate desire to get to the truth of why a modern mine in a modern country had failed so catastrophically. The department held the power to prosecute. The police were also investigating and there was the possibility of criminal charges. Everyone was careful to avoid doing or saying anything that might impede the wheels of justice.

The families were holding on to the expectation that the bodies of their loved ones would be recovered from underground; Prime Minister Key gave them his 'absolute assurance we are committed to getting the boys out'.[79] They conducted themselves with quiet dignity and discipline.

There was an abiding expectation of accountability for the deaths of so many workers in an operation that had barely started to extract coal. Given the horrifying scale of the tragedy – one that would not have occurred if the risks underground had been properly controlled – anything short of that was simply incomprehensible.

Meanwhile, the mine's owner, Pike River Coal Ltd, had gone broke three weeks after the disaster. Receivers were working their way through the debts and trying to find a buyer.

The sadness that hung over the country was ruptured by another tragedy three months later. On the other side of the South Island, collapsing buildings and falling boulders killed 185 people in a massive earthquake in Christchurch.

They were bleak months. It had been, in many ways, a bleak two-and-a-half years. The burden of the Global Financial Crisis had trickled down through unemployment, crimped public services and tax changes that favoured the well off. Wages had been kept down while chief executives' salaries romped ahead.[80] A prime minister who had promised pragmatism and collaboration was instead stripping back workers' basic rights. Actors who had sought to negotiate a price for their skills had been intimidated and threatened. Workers who had gone to their jobs inside a black pit on a sunny Friday afternoon lay dead.

As a child of Shannon Street, Helen knew it was ultimately about power: who had it, and from whom they sought to keep it.

Five months after Pike exploded was Workers' Memorial Day, April 28, a time to honour those killed, maimed or made sick at work. Helen went to Blackball, a run-down town snuggled into the base of the Paparoa mountains not far from the Pike River mine and a place once known for its worker militancy. By then she had held senior union roles for more than a decade. Some on the left of the movement tagged her as a conservative more interested in the fortunes of the Labour Party and her own political future than workers' struggles. It was an impression hardened early on in her tenure as CTU president when she had publicly criticised a strike by junior doctors and been flayed by left-wing commentators.[81] But her speech at Blackball ought to have put paid to that caricature.

'Our job is to change the story of work in this country and demand safety and accountability,' she said. 'Workers are being consistently told that they are lucky to have a job, that they should not bite the hand that feeds them, and that the employer/employee relationship is akin to that of benefactor–beneficiary.'[82]

In the New Zealand story of work, Pike was depicted as providing jobs – doing a 'good deed, a charity of sorts. The workers were portrayed as bravely taking risks in a dangerous industry, knowing the risks but prepared to take them to get the coal out.' The true story was that the company's shareholders had invested in a project that had blown up, and had now walked away leaving 'debts and death … This model is not charitable.'

It was about far more than one badly run mine: in construction, agriculture, forestry and fishing, death and injury stalked. More than 200,000 workers were seriously harmed in New Zealand workplaces every year. This was not 'bad luck', said Helen. 'In many cases it is bad management.' Risks had been pushed down the line, particularly on to those whose work was precarious, whose access to jobs was dependent on labour-hire outfits, or who were forced to become contractors.

'While workers are depicted as beneficiaries in the relationship, any reduction in their rights and safety will be acceptable – beneficiaries should be grateful. Workers that make a fuss are depicted as ungrateful … Unions in this story are even more unwelcome. … We need workplaces where the ones causing the trouble, speaking out, objecting to unsafe practices, those that fight for the living, are the heroes and only when that happens will things really change.'

By this time she had obtained a tranche of documents under the Official Information Act revealing more detail about what had gone on in the background to the *Hobbit* dispute. The material showed beyond doubt that a settlement had been reached by the time of the anti-union film workers' march, the rushed Hobbit law change and the gifting of a souped-up subsidy to Warner Bros. She wrote a heavily annotated 11,000-word essay detailing how New Zealanders had been played. Once again, she argued, the dispute had been shaped by the dominant narrative of work and workers' rights: the actors who had sought to bargain were badly behaved ingrates who contributed 'nothing compared to the great Warners that were donating 2000 jobs to the economy'.

The CTU had been heavily criticised for its role in the dispute. She sent a warning shot to those who hoped it would retreat into a quiet corner. 'When workers are under this sort of attack, the union movement will take on anyone and we will not bow to the deference with which some parties think employers should be held in this country if it means workers will be denied their rights.'[83]

Behind the closed doors of the union movement, she was becoming impatient. The latest research showed union membership was again falling, revealing 'a movement in decline', she told CTU affiliates early in 2011. 'What the movement has been doing doesn't seem to work.'[84]

She pushed on with the Union Change programme, often in the face of disinterest and foot-dragging from affiliates. 'There wasn't a great deal of enthusiasm,' remembered Richard Wagstaff, the national secretary of the Public Service Association, who had been elected vice-president of the CTU in 2007. 'Everyone was too busy on their own thing, and the CTU Union Change agenda wasn't a burning platform for most affiliates.'[85]

Helen had shed her early caution and was willing to challenge those who failed to get on board with the programme. 'She was quite a demanding person,' Wagstaff said. 'She would push us all. It wasn't passive. If you didn't come [to Union Change meetings] Helen would say, "Where were you? You didn't turn up." She would question you and push it hard.'

One of those who strongly backed her reform efforts was John Ryall, the Service and Food Workers Union's national secretary. He was relieved to have a CTU president who was 'looking forward and not looking back to the "glory days" of unionism.'[86]

The new union, Together, was finally launched in May 2011, after being twice delayed – first by Pike and then by the Christchurch earthquake. It offered a low threshold membership to workers (and their families) who weren't in unionised sites. The need was undoubtedly there: research by Laila Harré had shown that a quarter of calls taken by the National Distribution Union, for example, were from non-unionised workers needing support.[87] The CTU's organising centre in Auckland was also constantly getting calls from desperate workers, often in sectors or situations where no union was active.[88] Helen's own inbox was full of evidence of unsatisfied demand for representation; vet nurses, franchisees, taxi drivers and others wrote asking how to join a union, how to form one, or if one existed for people like them.

The plan was for Together to start small, with existing union members joining up their friends and families for a dollar a week, and build from there. It wouldn't get involved in collective bargaining and it wouldn't accept a worker in a site where an existing union was organising. It would be a place for the 'Four Square worker from Kaitaia' and those like her to get basic support in the face of workplace bullying, sexual harassment and infringements of rights to sick leave and holidays. It would be a gateway to the union movement for thousands of workers.

Helen had big ambitions for Together. The union movement had about 360,000 fee paying members. If 50,000 of them signed up just one family member, this would generate over two million dollars a year, which could be ploughed into campaigns on behalf of vulnerable workers. It would take time to reach that point, but it was a feasible goal.[89]

Richard Wagstaff supported the concept. The PSA agreed to lead the first phase of the roll-out and make its call centre available to support Together members. The plan was that other unions would progressively join the effort.

Helen wanted all affiliates to commit to Together, but there were quiet doubts about whether it could possibly work the way she envisaged.[90] And she had invited the wrath – for the second time – of Ray Bianchi, who assured her that his union opposed what he called 'your union'. There was no barrier to any worker in New Zealand joining a 'real union', he said, and warned her off accepting membership from any workers in his union's traditional patch.

Helen tried to change his mind. 'Hi Ray,' she wrote, explaining at length why the movement needed to do something for workers on 'dodgy' contracts, or in workplaces where existing unions had neither the capacity nor plans to organise. 'Union membership is in decline,' she reminded him. 'We are trying to do something new.'[91]

There was nothing in Helen's job description that demanded she try to reinvent unionism, or convert men like Bianchi to a different way of thinking. 'She could have just stuck to the people who are currently [union] members,' Ryall said. 'If she'd wanted to have an easy life, that's the way to do it. … But that wasn't good enough for her. She was always after something extra. I think she was conscious, too, of building unionism among a new generation.'[92]

She was also putting a prodigious amount of work into drafting an alternative employment law that would drape minimum pay and conditions across whole industries. Through her connections at the ILO, she had amassed a bulging file about wage bargaining systems around the world. She was particularly interested in regimes – common in Europe – where unions could apply to have collective agreements that had been negotiated with large employers extended across entire sectors, thus establishing uniform standards for wages and conditions.[93]

At the same time, international research coming across her desk was showing a clear link between growing income inequality and declining rates of collective bargaining and trade union influence.[94] The groundbreaking 2009 book *The Spirit Level*, by British researchers Richard Wilkinson and Kate Pickett, also showed a clear link between rising inequality and declining trade unions in several countries during the 1980s and 1990s. Even the IMF, a bastion of the neoliberal experiment, was now accepting that loss of worker bargaining power was linked with growing inequality globally.[95]

By 2011 Helen had drafted a law that was anchored in the right of every worker to participate in, and benefit from, collective bargaining. Her idea was that anyone should be able to join a workplace and be protected by minimum pay and conditions negotiated between unions and employers in that sector, and not be disadvantaged by dint of working for a small employer in a small town or for an outfit that was hostile to collective bargaining.

Her proposed system would see unions come together in 'Industry Councils of Trade Unions' – clusters of unions operating in a sector. These councils would have the right to seek 'Industry Standard Agreements': once a certain proportion of a sector was covered by a collective agreement, the relevant council could initiate an industry standard agreement that extended those conditions to workplaces where no collective agreement had been negotiated. For instance, if the National Distribution Union negotiated a collective agreement with a dominant grocery company such as Progressive Enterprises, the relevant industry council of unions could seek to have that pushed out to all workers in the sector – including the emblematic Four Square worker in Kaitaia.

At first glance it looked like the old award system, but it wasn't. Under the award system some union secretaries elected to live comfortable lives without having to organise or serve their members. They could turn up to a smoke-filled room for a day or two of negotiations with their opposite numbers from the employer associations, agree on a percentage pay rise, roll the award over for another year, and then retire to the pub – all without having to seek the views or agreement of workers.

The system Helen conceived would require unions to put in the groundwork. 'She didn't want unions handed these things on a plate,' Ryall said. 'She wanted unions to gain this only if they commited to organising. She wanted unions that were big enough and capable of covering whole industries.'[96]

Workers wouldn't have to join a union. Nor would they be forced into an industry standard agreement if they preferred an individual contract – as long as their pay and conditions were no worse than the standard. She also ruled out the right to strike over industry standard agreements.

Her draft law ran to 207 pages. It was complicated, and the procedures looked time-consuming and bureaucratic. The whole package was guaranteed to be completely unpalatable to employers. Many unions weren't fussed about it either. 'My perception is that most unions didn't understand it,' Ryall said. 'Because Helen was promoting it, most people didn't oppose it, but there were a lot of people who were saying, "This is mad."'

Ryall wasn't one of them. The Service and Food Workers Union organised and bargained for the likes of cleaners and laundry workers. They did collective pay deals in big sites, but Ryall knew the cost of reaching workers scattered across countless small workplaces was impossibly high. He analysed Helen's proposed law change and thought it could work; it would bring the benefits of collective bargaining to a huge number of poorly paid workers.

Helen deployed the language of human rights to sell her draft law to the Labour Party. Ryall, a member of the party's policy council, worked to get it on the manifesto for the 2011 election. Darien Fenton, by then a Labour MP and spokesperson on industrial relations, championed it inside the caucus. The lobbying was successful: Labour promised that within its first year in office it would bring in a system of Industry Standard Agreements. The policy was virtually identical to the proposals in Helen's draft law.[97]

Employer groups were alarmed. Business New Zealand's chief executive Phil O'Reilly said it would fling the country back to 'strike-ridden National Awards'. Kim Campbell of the Employers and Manufacturers Association said it would 'take us back 50 years' to crippling transport disputes disrupting family holidays and exports left rotting on the wharves.[98]

It was obligatory huffing and puffing: in reality, no one took much notice. Labour, led by Phil Goff since shortly after the 2008 election, was polling miserably and John Key's popularity was enormous. There was virtually no chance Labour would regain power in 2011. Helen had helped shunt the party's thinking towards more far-reaching workplace reform, but it would be at least another three years before there was any prospect of her vision becoming a reality.

Helen was constantly coming into the office in the morning with a head full of new ideas. Some were good, some terrible. Peter Conway played a key role in knocking the worst or most risky on the head. Some cost money and there was a shrinking supply of that. Sue Windsor, CTU's operations and finance manager, referred to Helen as her 'contingent liability'. The Union Change programme needed investment, but there was no union growth to fund it. Affiliated unions had long resisted paying higher fees to the central body, an attitude that Helen and Peter Conway resented. At every biennial conference there would be an attempt to lift the fee – usually led by James Ritchie, who shared their view that the CTU needed more resources to do its job. Every time his motion would be voted down.[99]

Making matters worse, the contracts to train workplace health and safety and learning representatives, set up when Labour was in power, were being progressively throttled back under the Key government. Conway carried the management burden, as well as a heavy policy workload, at the CTU and it fell to him and Windsor to handle the restructuring forced by the loss of revenue. Staffing levels were reduced through attrition and redundancies – some voluntary, some forced. The CTU organising centre in Auckland was gradually wound down. The meticulous and deeply principled Conway found administering cutbacks a terrible task. 'He really struggled with that,' Ritchie said.[100]

There was little in the budget for such niceties as professional development or media coaching. Helen wanted advice on honing her ideas and getting them heard beyond the boundaries of the union movement. How could she cut through the disinterest in trade unions, embedded in New Zealand society by a generation of neoliberalism? How could she better tell the story of those whose work lives were precarious, dangerous and devoid of respect? How could she shift the dominant narrative that business was the creator of all wealth, and workers should therefore be quiet and grateful for their employers' largesse?

She contacted a respected former broadcaster, Ian Fraser, for help. He would normally have charged $250 an hour. He told her he would work with her for nothing; he had been watching her as she became more prominent and was impressed – she was beginning to look like the 'best leader the Labour Party had never had'. His pro bono assistance would be 'my investment in a decent future for this place'.[101]

They worked together on stripping back her message, clearing out union jargon, and boiling it down to raw values: equality, the right of families to earn enough to live a decent life, the place of unions as advocates for those fundamental rights. He steered her away from diversions that would dilute her message. She mentioned at one point that she was keen to campaign on cannabis law reform. 'You've got to be nuts,' Fraser responded. 'I said it might be a really nice thing to have, but when there's so much basic work to be done around the values that really matter in terms of the kind of society that we want to live in … this is playtime stuff.'[102]

She laughed and dropped it – for the time being, at least.

By then, New Zealand was ranked seventh in the OECD for income inequality. The values of individual effort and personal responsibility seemed to have become stronger than those of collective well-being and state support. People had got used to the idea that households needed two incomes and loads of debt to get by. New Zealand had become a place where a millionaire prime minister could tell struggling families it was their own fault if they needed help from food banks, and get away with it.[103] The rich were getting richer, the poor were getting poorer, and many New Zealanders didn't seem too concerned.[104]

Helen was attempting to change that, to displace the dominant narrative with one that put fairness at the centre. She worried to Fraser that she wasn't up to the task. 'Not that she was wracked with doubt, but she was hesitant. [She wondered] "is my ability equal to my ambition?"' he remembered. 'So part of the exercise was [me] saying, "You are good enough." I was doing that in absolutely good faith because I knew perfectly well that she was. I thought she was spectacularly good.'

As 2011 wore on, there was a rich flow of fresh content for her alternative narrative. 'To a report that more than 200,000 of our kids live in poverty, Prime Minister John Key responded that their needs must be balanced against the needs of other New Zealanders,' she wrote in *The Dominion Post* in September. 'To a report that two surgeons were prosecuted for avoiding thousands in tax, Peter Dunne [the minister of revenue] and others leapt to reassure other tax dodgers that there was no witch hunt. At the same time, National announced a major policy to "crack down" on benefit fraud.'[105]

There were the daily reports from the Royal Commission of Inquiry into the Pike River Mine Tragedy, which sat for months in the Greymouth courthouse. A company that had billed itself as the safe and modern face of mining was unveiled as incompetent, dishonest, and determined to keep out union influence. The mine was revealed as unsafe in design, an operation where corners were cut in a mad dash to get into production, a place so shambolic it had taken more than 40 minutes to realise there had been an explosion. It couldn't even muster assistance to meet the two survivors who, poisoned with carbon monoxide, had managed to escape.

It was all evidence of what Helen saw as a 'growing trend [that] challenges our egalitarian beliefs. I say it is time to reclaim those values,' she wrote in a *Dominion Post* op-ed.

Pat would have framed it as class struggle, but Helen knew to steer well away from that language. She kept it simple. On a Sunday morning current affairs show, when a fellow panellist asserted that corporations created the nation's wealth, she quickly responded. 'Working people create wealth as well.'[106]

Two and a half hours north of Wellington, that proposition was in dispute. Meat workers at an abattoir in the small town of Marton were under pressure to accept pay cuts of 20 percent. The CMP Rangitikei lamb-processing plant was owned by a large meat exporting company, ANZCO, which in turn was majority-owned by Japanese investors and led by its founder and chair, the recently knighted Graeme Harrison. ANZCO was one of New Zealand's largest exporters, with annual turnover of around $1.3 billion, and supplied meat to global companies such as McDonalds, Waitrose and Tesco. However, the near new Marton plant had never made a profit and the company wanted to shave 15 percent off the cost of production.

Talks with the Meat Workers Union had dragged on, despite the union offering to accept a ten percent pay cut to what were already fairly modest wages. This wasn't enough and in October the company issued a lockout notice. The plant employed 300 workers, most of whom were union members. However, by contacting workers one by one, the company convinced 200 to sign individual contracts incorporating the cuts it sought. The remaining 111 workers refused and were locked out. Terangi Wroe, a butcher whose partner was pregnant, was one of those who held out. Accepting the company's demands would have meant a $300 reduction in his fortnightly pay.[107]

The Meat Workers Union – once the bane of New Zealand farmers – was not the militant force it had been in the 1970s and '80s. Membership was declining, industry wages had stagnated, and plant closures over the years had wiped out thousands of jobs. In the negotiations with CMP the union had lacked a clear strategy, allowing the company to take the upper hand. Now that two-thirds of the workforce were inside the plant and a third picketing outside, union officials were split over whether the workers should hold out or go back. Making things even more difficult, the union's systems were antiquated, lacking even a proper database of members' contact details. The picket was disorganised, and locked-out workers who were under severe financial pressure were being offered cash inducements to accept the company's terms and go back to work.[108]

Maryann Kaka, a union delegate at the time, remembered things were getting desperate after a couple of weeks with no pay. 'We were raw. We were green as,' she said of the workers involved in the dispute. 'We were at our wits' end. We weren't getting anywhere. It's like there was no hope and there was no rainbow at the end of the line.'

Kaka rang Helen. 'I said, "We need help."' Helen drove up to Marton and met the workers. 'When she came in, it was like, oh, she was an angel,' remembered Kaka. 'She could fight but still be talking nicely.'[109]

Helen's union career had been in white-collar education unions; this was her first involvement in the meat industry. If she felt on unfamiliar ground it wasn't obvious to the workers. 'She's one of those people that when she speaks she pulls you in. It's like she's hypnotising you,' remembered Wroe. 'She knew what she was talking about. She had big words, but we could understand because how she put it in context was still simple.'

She immediately flew into action. Detailed instructions were issued: unions were to collect money for the locked-out workers; Kaka was to set up a bank account and organise a picket duty roster; contact lists for all family members were to be collated. Essential picket-line infrastructure – tent, barbecue, toilet – was soon on its way. She set up a supporters' Facebook page, drafted a newsletter for workers, made contact with Graeme Harrison, and analysed strategies to get the company back into bargaining.[110]

It was all hands on deck to salvage the best possible outcome from a bad situation. Money and supplies starting coming in from unions around the country. At the CTU, policy analyst Eileen Brown oversaw a scheme to enable unions to sponsor locked-out families. Funds were raised from the public. The dairy workers' and nurses' unions sent organisers to help on the front line with welfare and logistics. Simon Oosterman, and later another smart young organiser, Tali Williams, were deployed to drive the media campaign and organise the picket. Numbers and morale were regularly boosted by busloads of workers from other areas and representatives from other unions, as well as Helen, Peter Conway and others from the CTU office in Wellington.

Kaka, who distributed funds to families and ran the food tent, remembered Helen's capacity to keep an eye on the detail. 'She said, "If someone has a bill and they bring it to you, you pay it, because that's what's helping people to fight the fight." Helen would say, "You must ask the kids' ages, because they may need baby formula or something." We were just thinking about feeding the people, but she was thinking *who* are you feeding? What age groups are you feeding?'

It was a risky, stressful, high-stakes campaign. 'Emotions were extremely high because people had hungry families at home. It was really breadline stuff,' said Tali Williams, who was roped into organising the picket after Oosterman became unwell. She had been reluctant because she didn't feel she had the experience for the role. As usual, Helen wouldn't take no for an answer, but she was available with reassurance whenever Williams felt out of her depth. She recalled Helen frying sausages on the picket line, engaging in fraught discussions with meat workers union officials, and turning up in her white Daihatsu Charade with phone cards for workers she'd been keeping in touch with. 'This was one union, one dispute, and she's the leader of the CTU, but that was the level that she was in contact with people.'[111]

Helen continued to meet frequently with the workers. 'She had the power to get things moving … She was the driving force,' remembered Kaka. 'She used to walk into our room and just overwhelm people: "Oh wow, she's here." Anyone could go and talk to her. She would never shun anyone. … She totally understood where they were coming from. She gave that to every person she dealt with … She would slow down for that person's conversation.'

She also doled out bracing advice to union officials, whether they wanted it or not. Dave Eastlake, who was leading the union, was compelled at one point to defend the boundaries. 'I said, "Helen, I am the national secretary of the Meat Workers Union. I'll tell you what we're doing about that, you won't tell me." And she goes, "Oh okay, right." And away we went. I'm quite sure we had a much better understanding of each other from those few words on.'[112]

What had been a flagging picket on the roadside of a small country town became a story involving global brands and worker resistance. Oosterman generated a slew of headlines and started organising flying pickets targeting McDonalds, where customers were advised that their burger patties were from a company that was trying to force pay cuts on its workers. The international union movement got involved, including the big Unite union in the UK, which represented Waitrose workers. A worker from the Marton plant, Amanda Chase, was flown to London to talk to Unite and put pressure on Waitrose, which claimed to have an ethical supply chain.

In case the subtlety of the tactic was lost on the New Zealand public, Helen spelled it out. There were 'huge implications for the New Zealand meat brand. This clean, green, lovely little country we are meant to be is forcing workers into starvation, basically, or into pay cuts.'[113]

Chase's mission was successful: Waitrose told ANZCO to get back into talks with the union.[114]

Helen led the negotiations when the dispute was settled late on the afternoon of December 22, 2011. The company managed to pare back its wage bill, but the scale of the cuts was reduced to ten to 15 percent.

Over $200,000 had been raised to sustain the locked-out workers, as well as food, which Kaka remembered would arrive by the trailerload. There was also $21,500 set aside for Christmas presents for the children affected. A party for the families was organised for December 23. With the dispute settled, Helen insisted the Christmas cash be distributed that day. This presented practical difficulties and it fell to Sue Windsor and Peter Conway – who had also been heavily involved behind the scenes – to find a way to make it happen.

'The problem was the time frame and the amount of money involved,' remembered Windsor, who was in Marton on the day of the settlement. As she drove back to Wellington that night, she worked out how to get the cash into the families' hands by the next morning. The money would be transferred from the fundraising account to Helen's personal account, from where she would transfer it to her account. She would withdraw it in cash from her downtown Wellington branch first thing in the morning. Conway would meet her outside the bank and then drive north with the money in time for the party. As the bag of cash was stowed into the boot of Conway's car, Windsor advised him: 'Don't pick up any hitchhikers.'[115]

They pulled it off. The party, Kaka remembered, was 'awesome. Bloody awesome'.

The lockout had run for 65 days. It had ended with neither glorious victory nor humiliating defeat. The union movement had stood together and the employer had been forced to modify its position.

It had been a frenetically busy two months. In that time Helen had become much more familiar with the meat industry and the weaknesses of its union. A close friendship had developed between her, Terangi Wroe and his partner Tamara Barker. She became a figure of such importance in their lives that they would ask her to be godmother to their baby son Tarikopeka.

New Zealand had gone to the polls and returned John Key's National-led government to power. Helen had travelled back and forth to Marton, to Geneva for ILO work, and to Fiji, where she was detained at the airport for several hours and then deported while attempting to investigate reports that the military regime was targeting unionists.[116]

She had been down to the West Coast to join the Pike families marking the first anniversary of the mine tragedy. The Department of Labour had completed its investigation into the explosion and laid charges under the Health and Safety in Employment Act against the bankrupt Pike River Coal Ltd, drilling contractor Valley Longwall International, and the mine's once celebrated boss, Peter Whittall. Eighteen months earlier, Helen had heard Whittall speak of zero harm, of leadership and accountability. Now he complained he was a scapegoat and promised to vigorously defend the charges.[117]

The was no guarantee of accountability for the 29 dead workers, but the wheels of justice were turning.

10. Lucky to have a job

It can't be the deal that you can work Monday to Friday or longer and spend Saturday at the food bank. Work has to make a greater economic and social contribution than that, and it is not a deal that anyone I know has signed up to. *Helen Kelly, 2012*

Charanpreet Dhaliwal was 22 when he went to work late one night in November 2011 as a security guard on a West Auckland construction site. It was his first night on the job. He was due to start at 10.30 p.m. and keep watch until 5.30 next morning.

Dhaliwal had come to New Zealand early in 2010 to study information technology. His mother and brother were in India, and the expectation was that his qualification would enable him to get a good job and his earnings would help support the family. He worked a variety of part-time jobs to support himself while studying, and had done some crowd control work at the recent Rugby World Cup. But he had no experience or training to prepare him for being the sole guard on an isolated site with a history of break-ins. No such preparation was required by law.

He was offered the work after phoning to inquire about jobs with CNE Security, a small company with three full-timers and half a dozen casual workers that provided security services to several large companies and operated from the owner's house in Ellerslie. As it turned out there was work available that very night: the guard who was supposed to work at a site belonging to a large construction company, Fulton Hogan, needed time off. Dhaliwal was asked to fill in.

He got to the site at 10.15 p.m. and met the employer, Cherag Elavia, for the first time. The man he was standing in for – who himself had worked only one shift for the company – also came. Dhaliwal was 'inducted', which consisted of being shown around the dimly lit site, told how to set the alarm and fill in the logbook, and given a set of keys and a card with a phone number to call Elavia if he needed help. He borrowed the other guard's high-vis vest and safety boots. He had his own cell phone, his own small LED torch and his car to shelter in. He had not yet signed an employment agreement.

He made a log entry at 1.30 a.m. Things were 'ok'.

Some Fulton Hogan workers came across him a little after three a.m. He had probably been dead for an hour by then. Evidence would later emerge that he had approached a group of four intruders and been struck at least twice on the head, probably with a piece of 4 x 2 wood swung like a bat. The injuries were horrific. His skull was shattered and he was left lying face down across a concrete slab. His phone and wallet were taken.[1]

Reporters at Auckland's *Herald on Sunday* quickly gathered the outline of Dhaliwal's death. In a story published two days after his body was discovered, his shocked flatmates described him as a good student who was 'friendly, smart, hard-working, spiritual and open-minded'. They told the reporters about Dhaliwal's mother and brother, and that his father had passed away. A grainy photograph showed a smiling handsome young man wearing an orange turban.[2]

The *Herald on Sunday* story was the first that Helen knew of Charanpreet Dhaliwal and his death in the small hours of November 18, 2011, on his first night on the job. She and Peter Conway agreed the CTU had to follow it up.[3]

Her idea of 'following up' involved opening multiple fronts on which to fight for justice for a slain worker who, it went without saying, did not belong to any union. She and Conway, as well as the small CTU staff, were already carrying a huge workload, not least supporting the CMP workers who were still locked out at Marton. But Dhaliwal was a signal case, a member of the growing class of casual workers who took jobs where and when they could, for whatever pay and conditions the employer decreed, often with small businesses under contract to large corporations, and whose only competitive advantage was cheap labour. He was at the bottom of an economic food chain in which those who benefited from his labour had contracted out of responsibility towards him, and in which there was no possibility of negotiating for better pay or safer conditions.

If more evidence was required of the union movement's need to stop behaving as a club for fee-paying insiders and start speaking and acting for all workers, this was it.

Within a couple of days of the newspaper story Helen had established contact with Dhaliwal's flatmates and the Sikh community, which was raising money to send his body home to India. She offered the CTU's help in ensuring no stone was left unturned on behalf of his shocked and grieving mother and brother. There were serious matters to be investigated – about training and the systems that should have kept him safe – but his death was also a profound and sickening tragedy. 'As a parent of a boy the same age I can't imagine the anguish this is causing his family. I hope we are able to help in some small way,' she wrote to Daljit Singh, a representative of Auckland's Sikh community. 'We do not charge for our services,' she added. 'We are a union movement and represent workers and do not operate for profit.'[4]

There was a risk the CTU's involvement would come across as shroud-waving. In reality, Helen was shocked and felt Dhaliwal's death personally. He was only 18 months older than Dylan. He had been killed almost a year to the day after the Pike River disaster. She saw a terrible parallel with Joseph Dunbar, the 17-year old Pike victim who was on his first day underground when the mine exploded.

'As soon as she started talking about [Dhaliwal] you could see it was really important to her,' remembered Georgie McLeod, who worked for the CTU. 'She would come into our office and plonk down and talk about it. It was so outrageous to her [she thought] it must be to others as well.'[5]

Working through the Sikh community, the CTU obtained authority to act for Dhaliwal's mother Karamjit Kaur, who spoke no English and whose address – Mehal Mubrak Colony, Street 6, Back of Sonu Soap

Shop, District Sangrur, Punjab – told of modest circumstances. 'She had sold everything to get [Dhaliwal] here,' said Sammy Singh, who worked doggedly with Helen in pursuing the case.[6]

Helen deployed a CTU staff member to lodge an Accident Compensation Corporation claim on Kaur's behalf to cover funeral costs. Although Dhaliwal was killed on the job, there was no other ACC support for his mother – no earnings-related compensation was payable and he had no legally recognised dependents so there was no lump sum payout.

A few months after his death, Helen received a cheque made out to Dhaliwal for $50.05. It was his wages for the hours he worked on the night of his murder – a banal piece of paper that spoke volumes about the worth ascribed to a young worker's life. She shut her office door and cried.[7] It was, she said, was 'a very cheap death all round.'[8]

She and Peter Cranney – who were working increasingly closely on legal strategies and campaigns by this time – lodged a personal grievance on Kaur's behalf. She kept in regular contact with Detective Sergeant Murray Free, the police officer in charge of the homicide investigation. Free was struck by the force of her conviction over the case; the fact she kept the story in the media was helpful to the investigation, which initially had little information to go on and took more than six months to make an arrest.[9]

She kept the pressure on the Department of Labour, which was responsible for enforcement under the Health and Safety in Employment Act. When the department decided to prosecute Elavia's small company but refused to lay charges against Fulton Hogan, which it said had complied with its legal duties, she and Cranney looked at taking a private prosecution.[10] She was appalled to discover that avenue was blocked: if the department prosecuted any party, all other potential defendants were protected from legal action.

'It really is the most outrageous circumstances,' she wrote to Sammy Singh and Daljit Singh. 'By prosecuting CNE, the DoL is effectively stopping us prosecuting Fulton Hogan.'[11]

She pressured Fulton Hogan to pay Dhaliwal's mother $50,000 in lieu of the earnings that he would no longer provide for the family, and urged the company to work with the Service and Food Workers Union, which wanted to use the tragedy and the involvement of a high-profile employer as an opportunity to improve health and safety standards for security contractors. Fulton Hogan rejected both proposals; it had contributed towards the cost of sending Dhaliwal's body home and didn't intend to make any further payments.[12]

In every speech Helen made she hammered the tragic flaw in the economic model that allowed Fulton Hogan to take the benefit of Dhaliwal's work but avoid responsibility for his well-being.

The pursuit of Fulton Hogan was risky. Many of its employees were members of the Northern Amalgamated Workers Union, and the union's secretary Ray Bianchi was – once again – unhappy with Helen. 'The CTU action could lead to Fulton Hogan losing contracts and you losing your job,' he wrote in a newsletter to his members. He told Fulton Hogan that his union opposed the CTU action.[13]

Helen was furious that Bianchi was blatantly undermining the CTU's advocacy on Dhaliwal's behalf. She wanted him censured by the National Affiliates Council, which had voted to pursue the case and press for minimum contracting standards to protect other vulnerable workers. Peter Conway tried to convince Bianchi to fall into line. Helen went to an executive meeting of the Northern Amalgamated Workers Union; relations deteriorated further when she told them they had no organising strategy and were routinely ignoring the needs of non-union workers on building sites. There was a row at a meeting of the National Affiliates Council, which ended in Bianchi walking out. He went on to pull his union out of the central body. 'Helen Kelly and the CTU affiliates decided to put the interests of a Non-Union worker above the interests of Union Members who worked for Fulton Hogan,' he later wrote to his members.[14]

The human toll of precarious, casual work was thrown into tragic relief by Dhaliwal's death. On the other side of Auckland, parallel issues were being played out on a much broader canvas.

For months the Maritime Union of New Zealand had been in the thick of an acrimonious dispute with the council-owned Ports of Auckland over the renewal of its collective agreement. International shipping lines were playing hardball with ports as they tried to recover their losses from the Global Financial Crisis, and Auckland wanted to substantially lower its labour costs.[15] The port was profitable but the Auckland Council was demanding that it double its return on investment to an extraordinary 12 percent.

The worst of the conflict might have been avoided if MUNZ officials had not misjudged the first stage of negotiations in September 2011. The company initially offered a 2.5 percent pay rise and a rollover of the existing collective agreement.[16] Instead of accepting, the union insisted that four non-union workers whose jobs had been previously contracted out be brought back into the collective agreement.[17]

Tensions escalated from there. The company's demands for change ramped up, and while the union offered concessions it wasn't enough. The port was soon demanding 'full operational flexibility' – no more guaranteed rosters or weekends off and the right to direct any worker to do any work – in return for a ten percent wage rise. It said it needed to increase productivity to match the Port of Tauranga, where wharfies were employed by competing stevedoring contractors.[18]

The union said the company's demands would turn a skilled workforce into an army of casuals, hanging by the phone waiting to hear if they had work and unable to plan their lives.

During the last weeks of 2011, there were a series of short strikes and a lockout, and no sign of a settlement. Some wharfies peeled off to sign individual contracts on the port company's terms.

Helen and the CTU had been keeping abreast of the situation. Early in 2012, when many people were still on holiday, the dispute entered a dramatic new phase. The MUNZ workers went on strike for the fifth time, and the port announced a plan to sack 300 wharfies and contract out their work to labour hire companies.[19] It would later transpire that the company had been making plans for weeks to contract out the work, but had not revealed this publicly. 'Change has got to happen,' said Tony Gibson, chief executive of the port, which had recently lost contracts with Fonterra and a Maersk-owned shipping service to the Port of Tauranga. 'We have a business to run and clients to keep happy.'[20]

It was an aggressive move; even under the Employment Contracts Act mass sackings as a bargaining tactic had been found to be illegal.[21] MUNZ saw it as part of an overall strategy to get rid of the union from the waterfront.

Helen and Steve were on a camping holiday around the East Coast. It was a trip they had long wanted to do and one that Pat and Cath had done in their early days together. They had bought a tent, loaded up the Daihatsu Charade and hit the road after New Year. They camped at Tokomaru Bay and other beachside sites and were having a wonderful time. They were at Te Puia Springs when Helen got a call about the port crisis. That was the end of the holiday; the next morning they headed for Auckland, travelling via the small communities of Ruatoria, Te Kaha and Ōpōtiki and stopping for a night at Ōhope Beach with Helen's old friend from NZEI days, Philippa Branthwaite, and her partner.

By the time they arrived in Auckland, the port company had complete command of the public relations war. It had pushed the story that the average wharfie was on $91,000 for 27 hours a week, and brought in global consulting firm Ernst & Young to put the stamp of authority on the figures. The union protested that, in fact, only half the workforce was guaranteed full-time hours, for which they were paid $27 an hour, and did shift and weekend work; to earn $91,000 they would have to do 32 hours of overtime every week for a year. The other half were guaranteed only 24 hours a week, or were entirely casual, with no fixed hours and paid only $14 an hour.[22] Never mind – the $91,000 claim was repeated over and over by commentators who applauded the company's tactics. One said the port should 'sack the entire workforce and start again'; another invoked hazy memories of Cook Strait ferry strikes timed to inflict maximum inconvenience on decent, hard-working Kiwi families.[23] There were allegations of thuggery and bullying by union workers against non-union workers.

The port's demand for absolute flexibility was given further political momentum by a draft report of the recently established Productivity Commission into the international freight sector. Released just as tensions were escalating, the draft cited 'union activity' as a barrier to productivity improvements and said the government ought to look at whether the law needed to be changed.[24]

Helen had no need to establish her credentials with the Maritime Union when she entrenched herself at its Auckland office. Everyone knew her lineage. They were aware she had grown up at the knee of Dave Morgan, the estimable former president of the Seafarers' Union, which had merged with the Waterside Workers' Union to form MUNZ in 2002. She and the union's general secretary Joe Fleetwood, a fifth-generation maritime worker, were childhood friends; the Kelly and Fleetwood families were connected through Wellington's union network, spending time together and socialising at annual wharfies' picnics.

Helen had also proved her mettle with the Maritime Union within the first few weeks of taking over as CTU president, when the Port of Napier sought to recontract stevedoring work to a company paying lower wages. 'She came in all guns blazing on that one. She was very clever in working out what was happening, the lay of the land,' remembered Fleetwood of Helen's role in the Napier dispute, which had ended in a win for the union after a picket that effectively shut down the port for a week.[25]

Things were deeply entrenched in the Auckland dispute. A great deal was at stake. New Zealand's most important seaport was taking on the strongest branch of a traditionally militant union. In the background, the re-elected Key government was looking at another round of change that would likely lead to further erosions of workers' collective bargaining rights. A huge effort would be needed to turn things around.

Helen called in the former CTU secretary Carol Beaumont, who had not been returned to Parliament in 2011, to work with the Maritime Union. Simon Oosterman, the gifted communications strategist, was brought in help shift the public perception. Helen assessed the union's legal and bargaining strategy and found it wanting, and issued characteristically frank advice on what needed to change. 'She wasn't shy about voicing her opinion,' remembered Russell Mayn, the MUNZ branch secretary. 'But in these disputes everyone gets bossy. They're intense and there's a lot at stake. … You've got to be tough if you're going to come into a dispute that the Maritime Union's involved in and be allowed to play a high-level role. Because if you're not tough – you know, I'll be straight up – we would have just told her to fuck off.'[26]

She ran backchannels with those she thought could help alter the course of the dispute. Among them was a member of the port company's board of directors, Rob Campbell. Campbell had known Pat in his earlier life as a trade unionist; in the 1980s Campbell had been seen as the movement's rising star, until he bailed out and joined the corporate world. He was happy to meet with Helen, whom he admired, just as he had admired Pat and Cath. As they sat outside a café in Ponsonby Road, he told her the port's productivity was held back by embedded work practices, a small number of long-standing workers were resistant to change, and the impasse in bargaining was due to rigidities on the part of both the union and port management.

She listened to his comments. 'She was talking to me because she was hoping to find a constructive solution,' Campbell remembered. It would later become clear the former unionist was one of the most aggressive boardroom advocates of contracting out the wharfies' work, and keen to make the union irrelevant on the waterfront.[27]

'It was simply not in Helen's DNA to agree with me that the union had done anything wrong, that the workers had done anything wrong. I can remember Pat saying to me when I was a union official, "The worker is never wrong, Rob. He may have made a mistake, but he's not wrong."... [Helen] was looking for a solution, which would have meant concessions by the union, but there was no way she was going to strike a backroom deal and try and impose it. She was looking for a negotiated solution.'[28]

Campbell would end up resigning at the height of the dispute, but for Helen and the CTU there was no such luxury. The movement couldn't afford to lose this fight: if highly unionised Auckland wharfies were not able to hold the line against casualisation, what hope was there for the hundreds of thousands of unorganised and vulnerable workers like Charanpreet Dhaliwal, Joseph Dunbar or the Four Square worker from Kaitaia? If this battle was lost and the Auckland wharf was deunionised, what chance for other workers to retain their collective voice at work?

Efforts began immediately to counter the port's publicity machine, which was bolstered by a top-shelf PR firm, SweeneyVesty. Oosterman started publishing the stories of wharfies and their families; instead of union officials droning on about bogged-down bargaining, the public heard from ordinary workers talking about their jobs and families, about their need to know when they would be at work and when they would be home for tea, free to watch their kids' sport and go to school prizegivings. Flyers and postcards went out to Auckland's suburbs, and an artful video was made in which the partners and children of workers said their piece. 'People think it's all about money, but really it's just about family,' said one worker's son.[29] The public started to hear less about overpaid and underworked wharfies, and more about job security and the effect of casualisation on home life – the sort of issues that any fair-minded New Zealander could identify with.

Wharf workers were dispatched to community board meetings to talk about what was at stake at the port, which was owned by the people of Auckland. As the conflict rolled on through February and March of 2012, the union workers stayed out on strike for four weeks. A 24-hour picket was maintained at a park near the port entrance, with workers and supporters clad in branded turquoise 'Save Our Port' T-shirts. Family days were held where kids had their faces painted and held up placards declaring, 'All my daddy wants is a roster'. Five thousand people joined a solidarity march along the city's waterfront; the loudest and most passionate chanting came from a large delegation of meat workers, who were two weeks into a long lockout from their jobs at abattoirs owned by the wealthy Talley family. They had travelled to Auckland to stand alongside the wharfies.

The port company's move to sack the workforce and contract out their jobs was a matter of concern to the global union movement. Leaders from the 4.5 million-strong International Transport Workers Federation, the Maritime Union of Australia and the International Longshore and Warehouse Union descended on Auckland to lend moral and financial support. There were threats that any ships unloaded by non-union labour in Auckland would be blacklisted in global ports; one ship that was heading towards the docks did a U-turn at the last minute and diverted to Tauranga.[30]

The port company expressed outrage at the disruption and proceeded with its radical industrial strategy. In early March, with the wharfies still on strike, it sent out 300 redundancy notices and announced it was contracting two labour hire companies, Drake and Allied Workforce, and would be hiring a third. It was expected by the company that the sacked workers would end up re-employed by the contractors.[31]

Helen flayed the idea that the company's plan was all about productivity. In reality, it was about the port pushing risk and responsibility down the economic food chain, and would lead to a transfer of wealth from workers to the company and its contractors. She called it 'unconscionable and wrong', a race to the bottom in which workers' pay and security would inevitably be eroded by 'suitcase companies' whose only competitive advantage was low wages and poor conditions.[32]

'These suitcase companies don't bring anything. They don't bring cranes or shuttles – all they bring is labour [and] when all you have is labour, the cheapest labour price gets the work. That requires complete compliance by those workers with the price that's set in the tender. Workers are scared to raise health and safety; the contractor is not responsible for the set-out of the port and can't influence health and safety to any great degree.

'All in all it's a pretty dreadful situation, a situation that we see happening more and more to New Zealand workers,' she said in a video posted on YouTube. 'What a fight.'[33]

Helen's default setting was to run towards the bullets.[34] The Port of Tauranga, with its system of contracted stevedoring, was being held up as the exemplar of waterfront productivity that Auckland needed to match. A news reporter had dug into the idea that Tauranga's system of competing contractors and casual labour was dangerous, with workers too frightened to report accidents and near misses for fear of missing out on future work.[35] The story had drawn a stern rebuke from the Port of Tauranga.

Helen then picked her own fight with Tauranga by drawing a link in a TV interview between its contracting model and the deaths of three workers in the previous 15 months. Executives at the Port of Tauranga were furious. She was ordered to cease and desist or the company would sue for defamation. Peter Cranney replied with a stony rebuttal, pointing out that the 'link between casualisation and higher accident rates has become widely accepted'; the threats against the CTU were 'regrettable and not conducive to promoting health and safety.'[36]

Helen repeated her allegations in another media appearance. The port sent a further legal threat, although nothing came of it. She had broadcast her point to a wide audience and refused to shut up when told to; reframing the story of work was always going to mean running some risks.

At the same time, the Auckland fight was becoming increasingly filthy. Political blogs were in the ascendancy, particularly one called

Whale Oil, run by a man named Cameron Slater. It would be another two and a half years before investigative journalist Nicky Hager would expose Slater's close links with the office of Prime Minister John Key and Cabinet minister Judith Collins. In early 2012, when the port dispute was in full swing, Slater had clout and *Whale Oil* was taken seriously by many in the media. As Hager would later detail in his book *Dirty Politics*, Slater and his collaborators were cheering on the port company in its battle with the Maritime Union, and noting with approval the credentials of its recently appointed chair, Richard Pearson, as a 'union breaker' who had managed to 'seriously fuck over the unions elsewhere'.[37]

When the port leaked the personal details of a worker who had earlier taken 20 weeks' leave to care for his dying wife and had spoken out in the media about the dispute, Slater published the material on *Whale Oil* and the story was repeated by news outlets. The leak was clearly intended to intimidate: Slater afterwards boasted to a supporter that he was a 'one man union wrecking machine'.[38] The private details of other workers were also leaked by the company. The tactic ultimately backfired: Helen pursued their cases through the office of the Privacy Commissioner, and the port wound up apologising and paying tens of thousands of dollars in compensation to the workers concerned.

Slater also targeted Helen directly and repeatedly. He published blog posts calling her a 'liar' and a 'Hobbit hater'. He alleged she escalated disputes by 'using petrol to put out the fire'.[39] It was designed to deter and undermine, but it didn't get to her. She was incensed when such attacks were directed at ordinary workers, but since the Hobbit dispute she had grown a thicker skin for when they came at her.[40] And the nature of the attacks was familiar – she had many like these seen directed against her parents throughout their lives of activism.

More sinister was the involvement of a private investigation company. Maritime Union officials were aware they were being watched, and that informants were reporting from their stopwork meetings back to the port company. They were concerned enough to have their offices swept for bugs.[41]

Helen was speaking and writing frequently about the fight, dissolving the complexity with lines like this: 'The deal about work is you go to work and you earn a wage that pays your rent, buys food, buys power and allows you to sustain a decent life.'[42] Towards the end of March, the unionists' strategy appeared to be yielding results. Polling showed public opinion had become more sympathetic to the wharfies.[43] The union ended its month-long strike after the port agreed – at a conference with an Employment Court judge and recorded in a court minute – to pause the contracting out.[44] The company then locked out the workers, prompting a severe rebuke from *The New Zealand Herald* for 'sheer bloody-mindedness' and 'unnecessary provocation'.[45]

On March 27, after three months of intense conflict, Employment Court Judge Barry Travis ordered the port to halt the sacking of workers and desist from engaging contractors. It was 'seriously arguable' that the company's strategy of mass dismissals broke the law, which required it to operate in good faith towards the union. By threatening to sack the 300 wharfies, it had 'arguably' undermined the bargaining for a new collective agreement.[46]

Richard Pearson had described the company's strategy as 'bulletproof'. That now looked like hubris. Boardroom divisions blew into the open; Rob Campbell suddenly resigned because his position had become 'untenable'.[47]

The dispute was far from over. Almost three years of frustrating negotiations would follow before the collective agreement was settled. But the unionists had mounted a smart multi-pronged defence.

Helen's old sparring partner Matt McCarten credited her role in the fightback. She had been 'outstanding. If Kelly hadn't moved to Auckland and ensconced herself with the wharfies, they would not have been able to withstand the onslaught by their employer.'[48]

There was no time to pause. A thousand workers were locked out of their jobs at six Affco meat plants in rural towns around the North Island; an estimated 5000 children were affected by the loss of their families' work and wages. This was the collateral damage in a monumental battle between the Meat Workers Union and the powerful Motueka-based Talley family, which owned Affco as well as big stakes in the fishing, dairy and vegetable industries.

When the indefinite lockout was imposed on February 29, 2012, there had only been ten hours of bargaining for the renewal of the meat workers' collective agreement.[49] Talley's wanted less union influence and more flexibility at Affco, a long-established meat processing company that the family had spent a decade building a stake in, before taking full ownership in 2010.

When it came to industrial confrontation, the Talley dynasty had form. Talley's Fisheries and its director Michael Talley had the dubious distinction of meeting the high legal threshold for 'harsh and oppressive' behaviour under the Employment Contracts Act. In that case the Chief Judge of the Employment Court, Tom Goddard, had ruled that the company had induced workers to agree to a variation in their employment contracts by conveying 'with impunity' the impression that they saw themselves as 'above the law and above Parliament'. They had filled their employees' minds with 'forebodings', shown 'reckless disregard' for their rights and treated promises made 'with disdain'.[50]

In 2009, Talley's-controlled Open Country Cheese had responded to a lawful strike notice by the Dairy Workers Union by imposing a lockout; when that was found to be illegal, the workers were suspended and the plant run with non-union labour. This too was later found to be in breach of the law.[51]

Affco, previously a farmer-owned cooperative, had traditionally had good relations with the union. That changed when Talley's took control. It was 'like a cold front arriving', said Meat Workers Union organiser Roger Middlemass. He described a string of anti-union acts, such as encouraging new workers not to join and banning the union from posting information – including its financial statements – on plant noticeboards.[52]

In 2010, seasonal workers at the Affco plant in the small town of Wairoa in northern Hawkes Bay were the first to feel the frigid blast. They were told to increase production without extra pay or overtime. If they didn't agree there was no work: stock that would normally have been killed at Wairoa was trucked to other plants. Workers went for months without wages. The huge hardship this inflicted was alleviated by a fund the local union branch had built up since the 1970s, and by support from Hawke's Bay iwi Ngāti Kahungunu.[53]

For Therese Turipa, who had worked at the Wairoa plant since 2000, the arrival of Talley's as owner of the town's biggest employer marked a change in a once happy workplace. Previously 'you enjoyed going to work. It wasn't a job. You'd have three generations in one room. … It was hard monotonous work – eight hours standing – but it was a lively place. There was good energy, good wairua.'

The Wairoa experience was a sign of things to come. 'Their agenda was to smash and de-unionise the meat works,' Turipa said. Many long-serving workers left, unhappy with the direction things were taking. New workers were hired on individual agreements with higher pay. Long-standing workers were taken off jobs they had done for years and put in lower-paying roles. 'It was really petty and vindictive. When you go to work and your job is given to someone who just walked in the gate, and they're getting three percent more than what you were getting – there was no other way of seeing it.'[54]

Newcomers seeking work at Affco plants were asked if they wanted to join the union and the collective agreement, or if they wanted to sign an individual agreement. It didn't take people long to realise that if they ticked the 'union' box they wouldn't be hired, said Mike Nahu, the Meat Workers Union's national president. By the time of the 2012 lockout, union membership at the company's plants was down to about 50 percent.[55]

The Affco lockout – initially affecting 762 workers at five plants, then a further 214 at a sixth – was guaranteed to drive a wedge into the workforce: enough skilled workers were kept on to ensure the chains could keep running.[56]

Around 70 percent of the workforce were Māori, with a higher percentage at some sites. Some workers had been in their jobs for decades and many households had several members working at their local plant. Communities that relied on the works at Moerewa, Horotiu, Feilding, Rangiuru, Wairoa and Whanganui were split between those locked out and those expected to carry on working. Many who weren't locked out felt compelled to go on strike in support of those who were. Rifts formed in families and communities between people determined to resist and those who signed individual agreements and went back. If more labour was needed, specific workers would be 'unlocked' and then 'locked' again.[57] The company made it clear that workers who left the union and signed individual agreements could go back to work; for those who took up that option there was a bonus of $1000.[58]

If workers decided to look for jobs elsewhere, their options were severely limited. New Zealand, like much of the world, remained in the long shadow of the Global Financial Crisis, with unemployment still stubbornly high.

As the conflict dragged on through the autumn of 2012, the families of some 1300 workers – some locked out, some on strike – were caught up in an increasingly desperate economic struggle. A solid core of workers was united and determined to hold out; the issues at stake were fundamental to their income security in a seasonal industry in rural towns where the meat works was usually the main employer. Affco was demanding an end to long-established 'seniority' rights, which governed the order in which workers were laid off at the end of the season and taken back on at the next. Without those rights, they would have no certainty about whether they would have work from one season to the next, and no confidence about whether they could buy a car or a house. It would also leave them vulnerable to being arbitrarily dropped by the company, and make them less confident about raising health and safety issues or sticking with the union.[59]

The company also wanted control over the production tallies that determined about half of workers' pay.[60] Further, it was demanding the right to lay off anyone it considered 'incompatible' with the company, regardless of whether the worker was guilty of any misconduct or poor performance.[61]

With half the workforce inside working, and some workers under acute financial pressure peeling off to go back on individual agreements, the union was in a weak position. As winter arrived there were sick children going without treatment, power being disconnected, and parents unable to transport kids to school because there was no money for petrol. Cars were being sold and mortgages put on hold.

In the thick of an already bitter dispute, Affco poured poison into the mix by announcing it had gone to the Serious Fraud Office with a complaint against the union. It alleged tens of millions of dollars of members' fees had disappeared into a 'black hole'. This generated headlines and a fog of suspicion, but within a day the Serious Fraud Office had published a statement saying it wasn't investigating: its immediate evaluation of the information had showed no evidence of fraud.[62]

At the CTU, Peter Conway had been supporting the Meat Workers Union through the first weeks of the lockout. He was working constantly with Work and Income New Zealand to make sure locked-out workers got the emergency benefits they were entitled to, and preventing benefits being cancelled when groups of workers were 'unlocked'.

In addition, Affco's domestic and global customers had been identified and asked to both pressure the company to end the lockout and to boycott the company's products.

Simon Oosterman was pulled out of the Ports of Auckland dispute and sent in to help. As with the CMP Rangitikei dispute in Marton a few months earlier, the union's membership systems were hopelessly inadequate. Basic contact information had to be pulled together at the six sites to enable proper communication and picket-line organising.

As with the Auckland port dispute, the meat workers' struggle was branded. There were bright green T-shirts, and bright green placards printed with 'Talleys locks out families' and 'HELP Talleys Affco Workers.Com'. Picketing workers made their own handwritten placards with searing messages: 'Talleys starving our families'; 'Locked out with 3 kids to feed'.

As usual, the unionists' resources were paper-thin. The Meat Workers Union had no war chest to sustain workers through a long dispute, and the CTU struggled to raise $50,000 a week through its affiliates just to get $40 a week to each affected worker. Iwi groups became heavily involved, providing food and welfare for whānau. Paora Stanley of Ngāi Te Rangi sent food, barbecues and a mobile container to provide shelter for workers picketing at Rangiuru. The iwi's nurses were also made available. Other iwi put in similar efforts – Ngāti Kahungunu at Wairoa, Ngāpuhi at Moerewa, Tainui at Horotiu. This in turn put a strain on iwi resources.[63]

As the workers entered a third month without wages, Helen launched a nationwide public appeal. Affco responded by blaming the union for the hardship and suggesting people 'question where any donations will end up'.[64]

After the crisis at the Ports of Auckland eased at the end of March, Helen was able to devote more energy to the Affco conflict. She was appalled at the Meat Workers Union's sluggish strategy and inadequate systems and made her views clear to its leaders. She and Conway could see the potential to involve iwi leaders more deeply to create leverage with the Talleys and help resolve the dispute. She started building lines of communication, firstly through Paora Stanley at Ngāi Te Rangi, then Sonny Tau at Northland's Ngāpuhi, Ngahiwi Tomoana at Ngāti Kahungunu, Tuku Morgan at Tainui, and others. Several were former meat workers and union officials and understood the workplace issues; some led iwi businesses with connections to the Talleys through the fishing industry. As the impasse dragged on, some iwi threatened to withhold their stock from Affco works if the suffering being imposed on their whānau was not relieved.

On every platform available to her, Helen wove the battle of the Affco workers into her increasingly sharp and confident narrative about decent wages and the lack of them; security at work and the absence of it; fairness and unfairness. The narrative connected disparate stories: Charanpreet Dhaliwal's violent death on his first night at work; the 29 workers who lay dead inside the mismanaged and poorly regulated Pike River mine; the actors vilified for seeking to negotiate terms and conditions; the wharfies fighting to stop their employer turning their steady jobs into casual ones. Alongside this was the wealthy ten percent of the population who owned more than the bottom 60 percent combined.

In speeches, interviews and articles, she tried to carve out new territory for New Zealanders to start thinking differently about work. 'There is a cultural problem in this country: people think workers are lucky to have a job, shouldn't bite the hand that feeds them, and should put up and shut up'; 'The bottom line should include workers having a secure agreement about how their pay is determined. It's not much to expect.'

It was wrong, she said, that cleaners and shop workers were donating from their meagre pay packets to feed the families of locked-out meat workers, while the Talleys, whose $300 million empire was built on the resources of land and sea that once belonged to the ancestors of their Māori workers, wanted for nothing. 'What does it say about the society that makes that lawful?'[65]

On *Whale Oil*, Cameron Slater sneered at her 'snivelling, whinging, cloth cap socialist rant'. It might indeed have been hollow rhetoric if it hadn't been underpinned by Shannon Street values and by Helen's genuine affinity with working people. When she turned up to picket lines to talk to workers, there was no doubt she was tough, sincere and ready to fight alongside them.

Paora Stanley remembered scathing talk from meat workers about what they saw as the impotence of their union's leaders, but Helen was viewed in an entirely different light. 'You cannot buy mana and you cannot give yourself mana,' he said. 'Only the people can give it to you and only the people can take it away. And with Helen, you could see the people gave her mana. As a Māori I completely recognised that.'

Stanley remembered her coming to rallies at Rangiuru clad in a green lock-out T-shirt. She was an 'inspirational leader ... She didn't push herself to the front – the people put her there. There was immense respect, loyalty, appreciation for what she was doing. This was the president of the CTU coming to us, saying she gives a shit about us. As a Māori you understand all those nuances, that vernacular, the difference between mana and the illusion of mana. ... People felt galvanised. These were people who had been looking down the barrel of poverty, unemployment, starvation, and they put all their faith in this one woman.'[66]

The unionists landed one of the heaviest blows on the Talleys in early May. By then the workers had gone ten weeks without wages.

Planning had been underway for weeks to take representatives from the various plants to Motueka to demand an audience with Peter and Michael Talley, the two brothers who ran the food-producing empire along with Peter's son Andrew. Oosterman had got prime-time television on board. The story was given top billing on the two main news channels. TV3's *Campbell Live* followed a family from Ngāruawāhia on their journey to Motueka. There was Richard, who had worked at Affco's Horotiu plant for 25 years and was locked out, and his partner Melissa, who had worked there for seven years, and was not locked out but had gone on strike in solidarity. Their three-generation household of nine lived in a small house on the outskirts of the town. All they wanted,

Richard said, was 'an honest day's wages for an honest day's work. What more can you ask for?'

The cameraman and reporter followed the family as they packed their things and joined the entourage of 40 locked-out and striking workers on the long journey south, across Cook Strait and on to beautiful Tasman Bay. It was the first time they had ever been to the South Island. Wearing their green T-shirts, the group went from mansion to grandiose mansion, turning the Talleys' locked front gates into impromptu picket lines. They asked to talk to their bosses and were, predictably, ignored. They sang, chanted and left messages tied to gates and fences, and then drove to Nelson for a march through the main street. Richard, a quiet man, found himself in the lead and on the megaphone. It was 'a proud, proud moment', he said. 'This is what it's all about – families, whānau and community.'

It was powerful, moving television. Soon afterwards Michael Talley laid a complaint with the police against Helen, who had joined the group, accusing her of inciting violence.[67] The company then tried to bar her from attending the next attempt at negotiation, alleging intimidation, aggression and bad faith on account of the Motueka protest and the pressure that had been put on Talley's international customers.

'It's sad actually for [the Talleys],' Helen emailed a contact. 'They have everything on a plate but won't be happy treating people like this.'[68]

A few days after the delegation had been to Motueka, Peter Cranney began presenting submissions in the Employment Court, seeking to have the lockout declared unlawful. The case looked strong: a lockout, like a strike, had to be in pursuit of a collective agreement. The law clearly prohibited the use of lockouts to secure individual agreements or encourage workers to quit the union.[69]

However, after a few days in court the legal arguments were suddenly aborted. The iwi leaders had used their influence to drag the company and union back into talks. 'Our motivation was the health and well-being of our whānau and the impact the lockout was having on them,' remembered Ken Mair, an iwi leader and former union official from Whanganui who took charge of the negotiations. 'Talley's motivation was … to break down the collective, the union's power base. They had a particular perspective on the world and that was that individualism was the way forward, and people getting together was undermining that.'[70]

The parties gathered at the Tainui-owned Novotel hotel at Auckland Airport. 'I said to them, "We are not leaving here until this is resolved,"' Mair said. '"We are staying on this marae until we find a way through, and if that takes two days, three days, four days without sleep, so be it, but we need to find a solution because too many people are suffering."'

Concluding that the union's officials were part of the problem, he sidelined them into another room during the later stages of the negotiations, and elevated the role of plant delegates, who knew the pain that was being experienced in their communities. Helen agreed with Mair; she took control of the union's side of the negotiations.[71] In this, she was walking a delicate line between invading the authority of the union's leaders and getting a settlement over the line.

After two marathon sessions of eleven hours, followed immediately by a further 20-hour stint, a deal was finally reached at five on the morning of May 22. It was almost three months since the first lockout notices had been issued. Helen's role had been instrumental, Mair said. 'Her intellect and her feel for the people. She could read and analyse the situation. ... a powerhouse.'

Not everyone was happy; Mike Nahu, the Meat Workers Union president, saw the settlement as a two-edged sword: concessions were made that would come to haunt the Affco workers for years afterwards. But it was a face-saving deal the union thought it could live with. And Nahu doubted the workers could have held out much longer; there was word that at some plants they were about to fold and go back in.

For his part, Cranney was frustrated that the court case had been called off. It had been going well and he thought a legal win could have put the workers in a better position.

But the key Affco demands – the removal of job security from season to season, the right to unilaterally alter production rates and therefore wages, the right to sack 'incompatible' workers without recourse – had been resisted. There was a small pay increase, and Andrew Talley had promised to work with the union to heal the wounds left by the dispute.

In a newsletter Helen drafted, the workers were advised the deal had laid the basis for 'a new relationship' to be developed between the company and the union. On balance, it looked like a reasonable resolution to a long and terrible struggle.

In the space of six months, aggressive challenges had been laid down by three powerful companies – CMP, Ports of Auckland and Affco – in industries with long union traditions. In all three cases the companies had been forced to retreat. But the union movement could hardly call them wins. In each case the outcome had been merely to hold the line, and in the CMP case to reduce the scale of cuts demanded. The three battles had shown the movement could act in solidarity to support workers whose wages and conditions were under attack, but it wasn't winning improvements.

And the environment was only going to get tougher. A few days before the Affco dispute was settled, the Key government announced yet another round of employment relations reforms. Employers would be free to walk away from negotiations without settling and to opt out of multi-employer collective bargaining. New workers would no longer be automatically covered by any applicable collective agreement for their first 30 days on the job.

Inequality had levelled out for a few years during the 2000s and in the immediate aftermath of the Global Financial Crisis, but now it was increasing again. International research was accumulating to show a strong link between declining collective bargaining power and widening inequality.[72] Yet the government was intent on reducing the ability of unions to bargain for workers; there seemed to be an expectation that the approach to industrial relations that had failed to achieve economic results in the 1990s would somehow work now.

The minister of labour, Kate Wilkinson, said the proposed changes were 'pragmatic'; they would increase productivity, create high-paying jobs, increase fairness and provide flexibility.[73] They would do nothing of the sort, Helen said. They were significant intrusions into collective bargaining rights that the government had an obligation under international law to uphold. Had these changes already been in force, they would have allowed the Ports of Auckland and Affco to simply walk away from bargaining. They were, she said, a 'dirty, dirty attack on working people'.[74]

The workload was relentless and growing. As Helen's public profile rose, more cases and disputes were drawn into the CTU's orbit but its resources were shrinking. She was constantly juggling multiple balls in the air – everything from hassling a funeral director for a receipt so Charanpreet Dhaliwal's ACC claim could be finalised to grinding through interminable hours of bargaining for the wharfies' collective agreement, intervening for workers caught in the bitter aftermath of the Affco dispute, and working on global labour standards as a New Zealand delegate to the ILO.

She flicked from one task to the next, often while curled up on the sofa late at night with an iPad on her lap and Yuffie – one of her and Steve's two cats – by her side, or on her phone as she dashed between meetings. After her hesitant first couple of years in the job, she was thriving, fuelled by outrage at the conditions for many of the workers she met and energised by the immense challenge of throwing her weight against an inequitable status quo.

There was no separation between 'work' and 'life', nor any notion of balance between the two. Work *was* life, and life was a vast network of union and political relationships, extended family ties, close friendships, backchannels, people to look after and problems to be fixed.

For years, Helen and Cath had lived two doors apart, but Cath was struggling with the difficult access to the Shannon Street house and with walking her dog Abby. It was time to move somewhere more convenient. She chose an apartment in a retirement village in the suburb of Newtown. She had always been determined that Shannon Street would remain the family home. Helen and Steve moved in; the place was much as it had been when Helen and Max were growing up. It still bore the signature of Pat's rough-and-ready handiwork and the kitchen joinery Cath had built decades earlier. Meanwhile, Max, who was living in an inner-city apartment and working in the entertainment industry, moved into the house in McIntyre Avenue.

Linda Mitchell had moved to Auckland, but Clare Wells and her partner Paul Cochrane were still next door. Every Sunday afternoon the two couples would get together before tea for a wine and a catch-up on family and neighbourhood news, local and national politics, and international affairs. The Shannon Street diary was marked with dinners,

Guy Fawkes parties and festive gatherings with friends, family, waifs and strays. Helen was loyal and attentive to old friends such as Helen Kinsella, Michelle Saban, Amanda Coulston and Clare Leniston, and there was a constant inflow of new friends, who included meat worker Terangi Wroe and actress Robyn Malcolm.

Somehow she was able to make time to take Abby to the vet and Cath to the doctor, to mentor young unionists, to visit a colleague's new kitten, to write detailed advice to non-union workers who contacted her in desperation after suffering an injustice at work. She and Steve gave practical and emotional support to Cath's elderly sister Margaret and her husband Jim Dart, who lived in Auckland and whose three sons lived overseas. Helen visited when she was in the city, helped them select and move into a retirement village when they could no longer manage the family home, and assisted with their affairs as Jim became increasingly unwell with Parkinson's.[75]

Every few weeks there was an appointment at Chop, a downtown hair salon, to tame her thick crop of dark hair, these days cut in a bob with a fringe that rested at her untrimmed eyebrows and framed a deep-dimpled face that broke easily and often into laughter. She and Clare Wells were also learning French, which Helen thought might be useful since she was spending several weeks a year in Geneva on ILO business.

What Slater had derided as 'snivelling, whinging' socialism was an applied set of values at Shannon Street. There were constantly people staying – young people starting out in Wellington, friends of friends who needed support. The door was always open, just as it had been in Pat and Cath's day. Some stayed for months at a time. 'We called it the Kelly orphanage,' Dylan said. 'When Mum saw a problem she could never leave it to someone else to solve.'[76]

Not everyone experienced the softness of her friendship. Some older unionists found her dismissive of their experience; others resented her focus on promoting younger organisers and activists. Her rapid-fire humour was part of her charm but it could also inflict glancing blows, even within the tight team at the CTU. Peter Conway was sometimes wounded by her flippant, teasing comments. The two were close; Conway's measured, risk-averse style was an essential counterweight to Helen's high-energy flair and rush to action, and she relied heavily on his judgement. He held the CTU together while she was out campaigning or negotiating.

Conway told a colleague that Helen was a once-in-a-generation talent, and that he saw his role as freeing her up to be the brilliant leader the union movement needed.[77] The two of them were yin and yang, both strategic thinkers and exceptional communicators but with vastly different personalities. 'Picture the general on a white stallion, brilliant adornment, inspiring aura, and the field commander on a sturdy steed, unadorned with baubles, directing the troops, strategically ensuring their safety as much as possible,' observed Sue Windsor of Helen's and Peter Conway's contrasting styles.[78]

The old hands at the Meat Workers Union were among those who felt the sting of Helen's judgement. Five years into her role as head of the CTU, she was increasingly frustrated by unions that had failed to adapt and modernise. Having seen the weakness of the Meat Workers Union's strategy and organising capabilities at close quarters in the CMP and Affco fights – not to mention the confusion and discontent it had caused workers caught up in the disputes – she was determined to steer the union into a programme of change.

Carol Beaumont was briefed to undertake a major review. Helen made it clear what she thought the problems were: ageing leadership, poor communication skills, lack of grassroots organising, lack of staff training, arcane branch structures. With a large membership base concentrated at big sites and enormous potential for the development of workplace leaders, it was a union that should be strong and dynamic. Instead it was slow-moving, reactive and in decline.

'My colleagues and I resented it a bit,' remembered Mike Nahu of her criticism. 'She didn't have a very high opinion of us.'[79]

Her efforts to trigger reform were unsuccessful. Beaumont consulted widely and delivered an exhaustive report late in 2012. She recommended more member participation and training, sharper focus on health and safety, stronger engagement with local communities, modernised communication, restructuring of branches and officials' roles, and development of a coherent national strategy. Given the emergence of hostile employers and a tougher bargaining environment, as well as the meat industry's decades-long problem of excess processing capacity, the need for change was 'compelling'.[80]

Beaumont's report was too much for the Meat Workers Union. They listened to the recommendations and then nothing much changed.

Helen's efforts to reform the wider movement through the Union Change programme weren't having much more success. The idea of unions collaborating on procurement and membership systems was getting nowhere. The new union to organise the unorganised, Together, was sputtering along.

Together was an ambitious project, reliant initially on the support of affiliate unions to sign up family members of existing union members. The CTU's National Affiliates Council had given it the nod of approval, but when it came to the roll-out some unions were actively hostile, or stymied it with the dead hand of disinterest.

The leaders of Unite, the upstart union that had provided some of Helen's inspiration for Together, thought it was a daft idea that would never work. If it was merely a landing pad for workers who liked the idea of a union but it wasn't able to get involved in bargaining, why would anyone bother? 'What's a union? In the end you have to front up to a work site and confront the boss and get better pay and conditions. Together was never able to do that,' said Gerard Hehir, Unite's national secretary.[81]

The EPMU – the biggest private sector union – thought Together was altogether too loose and woolly. 'You have to have an organisation and structure,' said Paul Tolich, who represented the EPMU on the National Affiliates Council. 'It doesn't have to be bureaucratic, and it can be participatory … [but] Together couldn't actually represent people. That was its flaw. We didn't go around attacking it; we just didn't promote it.'[82]

'I think there were actually very few unions who were 100 percent in support of it,' remembered Bronwynn Maxwell, who was charged, along with CTU researcher Andrew Chick, with getting Together off the ground. It was a huge undertaking – setting up the administrative systems, developing a website, trying to get affiliates to put in some effort. Both she and Chick found the experience intensely frustrating as they struggled along with inadequate resources.

'Helen was trying to shake the union movement out of its apathy and complacency [but] there was a selfish attitude from unions of "What's in it for me?" They couldn't see it benefiting their union, so why would they support it? Forget the fact that hundreds of thousands of people are being exploited.'[83]

Helen was constantly agitating for results and frustrated that her creation wasn't flourishing as intended. 'She wasn't the best at bringing people along with her,' said Maxwell. 'She was impatient, results-driven, goal-oriented.' She kept talking it up in speeches and interviews but Together never attracted more than a few hundred members – far from the 50,000 she'd hoped for.

She remained convinced that the union movement had to act in more tangible ways for all workers. It had to shrug off its insularity and defensiveness, and anchor itself in the values of equality, fairness and the right of workers to come home safely from work. It had to fight for well-funded public services and opportunities for young people. It needed to convince a generation of New Zealanders inured to the idea that business interests should prevail over workers' that it stood for things that were good for them and their families, and that it could change things for the better.[84]

In the late winter of 2012 she travelled to Dunedin to deliver a public lecture in honour of Rutherford Waddell, the Presbyterian minister who had helped expose the conditions endured by workers in the city's sweatshops in the 1880s; his campaigning had led to a royal commission that helped lay the foundation for the social and labour reforms rolled out by the Liberal government of the 1890s.

Had things changed for workers since Waddell gave his famous sermon against the 'sin of cheapness' from the pulpit of St Andrews Church in 1888? Of course, but the question was relative, said Helen from the pulpit of First Church. For many people 'working life is extremely hard and terms and conditions are on the decline'. The model of contracted labour that Charanpreet Dhaliwal had worked under the night he was killed and which the Ports of Auckland had tried to bring in was, she said, the modern sweatshop. Over 300,000 workers were on the minimum wage of $13.50 an hour – a rate recognised as insufficient to live on – and contracted workers were often paid less. Two out of five children who lived in hardship were from families where at least one adult was in full-time work.

‘This can’t be right. It can’t be the deal about work that people understand. It can’t be the deal that you can work Monday to Friday or longer and spend Saturday at the food bank. Work has to make a greater economic and social contribution than that. It is not a deal anyone I know has signed up to. It has crept up with the deregulation of the labour market in the 1990s and in particular the treatment of employment as simply a commercial transaction. It is the workers’ version of leaky homes, without the outrage …[85]

‘We [the union movement] are trying, like Waddell, to change the fundamental structural relationships in our society. If we don’t maximise our potential then those who do have the power, the money and the political dominance will be able to continue on the path they are taking, with us simply nipping at their heels.’ Her southern audience responded with rousing applause.[86]

11. Dangerous by design

No one really cares about these deaths. They are workers who can be replaced by others – no one wants to know what will keep them safe and make the industry a good place to work. *Helen Kelly, 2013*

A month after the Dunedin speech, Helen flew to Gisborne to meet local couple Caroline and Roger Callow. They had a story she wanted to hear.

She had made contact with them as a result of a chance sequence of events. Paula Bennett, the minister of social development in the National-led government, had announced plans to cut benefits to unemployed people who failed a drug test, or refused to take one, when applying for a job. Helen had called the proposal 'beneficiary bashing'; it perpetuated the myth that unemployed people were lazy. Instead of pushing the blame for high unemployment – 6.7 percent at the time – on to workers, the government ought to come up with policies that would create jobs.[1]

She was asked to debate the issue on a TV show. Her antagonist was a representative of a drug-testing company. He praised the government's planned policy and mentioned that drug testing had been a big success in the forestry industry. Helen didn't know a great deal about forestry, but she did knew that three men had been killed in one Gisborne forest over the previous 18 months. Workplace drug testing had clearly done nothing to prevent these tragedies, she said. 'It's a debacle, it's a ruse and it doesn't work.'[2]

Her stance was spectacularly unpopular with the viewing public – the show was inundated with thousands of messages criticising her.[3] Logging contractors were particularly affronted, accusing her of 'absolute ignorance'. John Stulen, chief executive of the Forest Industry Contractors Association, put out a press release claiming the sector had 'advanced workers' attitudes and their safety record' by getting drugs out of the workplace. 'Everyone in the forestry industry is far more safety conscious than most any sector in the country [*sic*].'[4]

To be cast once again as the villain on the wrong side of the debate was a source of wry amusement for Helen, but she was also furious about the forestry industry's dismissive attitude and decided to dig around for more information. It didn't take long to see that the true story about health and safety in forestry was far worse than anyone was letting on.

She came back at Stulen with a press release pointing out that four logging workers had been killed so far in 2012, and 30 had died in the previous six years. She called it 'carnage'. The industry's reliance on drug testing as a health and safety tool was a 'one-trick pony'. She mentioned again that three men had died in the Wharerata forest, just south of Gisborne, in recent times.[5]

The battle of press releases triggered media interest, including a story in the *Gisborne Herald* quoting the Forest Owners Association's health and safety committee chair, Sheldon Drummond. He said 'huge' efforts were going into worker safety, and union critics ought to be grateful for the industry's 'hard-line' approach to drug and alcohol use. He described the death of three workers in the Wharerata forest within a very short space of time as 'most unfortunate'.[6]

Caroline Callow had picked up her *Gisborne Herald* on the evening of August 27 and read Drummond's words. Her 31-year-old son Ken was one of those three dead men. Eleven terrible months had passed since he'd been killed at work. Nothing had been done and no answers provided other than an autopsy report, which noted that drugs and alcohol were not a factor, and a bloodless five-paragraph coroner's report recording that he had been felling a rotten tree that had then come down on him. Caroline and her husband Roger had been left alone with their shock and grief, and the part-time care of Ken's two little boys. Now they were reading that his death was merely 'unfortunate'.

Caroline was filled with anger. She couldn't sleep so she got up at five a.m. and typed a letter to the editor of the *Gisborne Herald* to let Drummond know of her family's outrage. 'Lend a thought to those forestry workers who are out there in the burning heat or freezing snow with minimal appropriate clothing. To wear bulky cold-weather gear can slow you down if you have to move fast to get out of the way of a rolling log. Our son did this on a daily basis, often wearing shorts in the snow. …

'As a mother it agonised me to see our son come in at the end of the day that exhausted he could not eat a meal but just fell into bed. There is huge pressure put on our forestry workers by contractors and forest owners for those men to get the wood out. Often they skip meal breaks to reach a deadline. All this you may not know, Mr Drummond, as you have your OSH policies – but in reality this is how you get your quotas. These men and women risk their lives to earn a living, yet no one gives a thought to how those logs arrive at the wharf. Spare a thought for the families, Mr Drummond. If it had been a member of your family would it still have been "unfortunate"?'[7]

The letter, full of pain and insight, somehow came to Helen's attention. She wrote to the Callows and asked if she could meet them. A few weeks later she sat at their kitchen table and listened as they talked about Ken's life – how he had started out working for logging contractors at 19, how he worked hard and played hard, and was a good father to his two sons.

Depending where his crew was working, he could be up as early as four in the morning to travel two unpaid hours to the job; sometimes he worked six days a week. There were no overtime or penal rates to compensate for the huge hours. He was a skilled tree feller, the guy who got the wood to the ground so the rest of the crew could efficiently break the logs out, haul them up the hillside to the skid and on to the back of a truck to the wharf, the guy at the start of the production line who got his crew mates their bonuses.

They told her about the stiff competition between logging contractors – most of them small outfits with a handful of workers – and about the production levels they had to meet. They described the times that Ken's crew had crossed flooded rivers to get to the block they were working on, and about how he had once urged his foreman to cease work because snow was settling on the ground, only to be told they had to carry on because there was a truck to fill.

They talked about the times he got home so tired he couldn't carry his chainsaw in the door. In the days before his death he had been under even more pressure than usual. He been put by mistake into the wrong block to fell trees in advance of the crew, and therefore felt he had to make up for lost time. They told her the industry was at liberty to work its employees as hard as it liked because there were no rules or regulations.[8]

Helen was horrified, Caroline Callow remembered. She was also shocked that the Ministry for Business, Innovation and Employment (MBIE) hadn't given the Callows a copy of the investigation report it had carried out under the Health and Safety in Employment Act.[9]

Using the Official Information Act, Helen had obtained a few of the ministry's forestry investigations, including the one into Ken's death. Her copy was the first the Callows had seen. She considered it a deficient piece of work. It paid no attention to working conditions, hours of work or production pressure. Ken had made a mistake in the way he had gone about felling the rotten tree and the investigator had therefore concluded he was 'the architect of his own demise'. The casual dismissal of their son's life, skills and worth stunned the Callows.

Ken's employer, a local contractor called Blackstump Logging, was not prosecuted. At the time of Ken's death, Blackstump was working in a forest owned by Hikurangi Forest Farms. Despite the Māori name, it was owned by Malaysian investors and was one of the larger forest owners in the country.

As they sat around the table Helen talked about making change, Caroline said. 'She talked about making the rest of the country aware of the working conditions in the forestry industry, and about the greed. She said we could help make those changes.'

The Callows knew that speaking out in a forestry town carried the risk of repercussions. 'We said we would never have been able to do it while Ken was alive, but if we could save the life of somebody else by speaking out, then we would.'

Back in Wellington Helen phoned Tony Sutorius, a film-maker

she had worked with a few times on CTU campaigns. She opened the conversation as she always did when she wanted to rope a comrade into a cause: 'Hi mate. You busy?' It was clear to Sutorius that she had been deeply affected by the Callows' story. He and Helen talked about making a film about Ken Callow. Helen also suggested a billboard.

A few weeks later Sutorius shot a haunting, visceral interview with the Callows. They sat on cheap picnic chairs amid pine-tree slash in the forest where their son was killed and talked about his work, and about the industry that had taken his life. It went live on YouTube early in February 2013. Over the next few weeks, the CTU fundraised to pay for a billboard, and in early April a giant sign went up on Auckland's busy Khyber Pass Road. It featured a black-and-white photo of Ken and an urgent question, typed in capital letters against a red strip: 'What killed Ken Callow?'

By then Helen had publicly demanded that the government set up an inquiry into the forestry industry's high rate of death and injury. In late 2012 the Royal Commission on the Pike River Coal Mine Tragedy had published a damning report that had identified the root causes of that disaster – the failure of the mine company to manage its methane gas risk, its routine disregard for workers' concerns, the abysmal performance of the board of directors when it came to health and safety, the push for production at the expense of safety, the timidity of the Department of Labour, which should have shut the place down but didn't. Helen argued that the deaths in forestry warranted similar scrutiny.

The government and the industry dismissed her call. A new 'code of practice' for forestry health and safety had been released, with claims it would bring about a big improvement. Helen predicted it would fail because it didn't touch the underlying causes of death and injury. Workers had had no real say in its development. It did little to deal with fatigue, or working in severe weather and bad light. It was silent on the economic model that put workers' wages, conditions and safety under perpetual pressure because the employers – hundreds of small contractors – were competing against each other to win work from forest owners and managers.[10]

She was working with themes that were tragically familiar. Just like Charanpreet Dhaliwal, the young security guard murdered on his first

Helen was elected vice-president of the Council of Trade Unions in 2003. The CTU president, Ross Wilson, had identified her as a future leader for the union movement. Her parents Pat and Cath were present for the occasion.
Kelly family collection

Helen was appointed general secretary of the Association of University Staff in 2002. Morale in universities was poor and salaries were eroding. The union rolled out a major campaign for increased pay and a multi-employer collective agreement to cover all universities. Here, Helen speaks at a Christchurch rally in 2003. *Annette Turnbull-Dew/Stuff*

Unite Union came to prominence in 2003, with an ambition to 'organise the unorganised' in sectors such as hospitality and fast-food chains. Under the leadership of Matt McCarten (pictured) and Mike Treen, the union trod on the toes of other unions, particularly the Service and Food Workers Union, with whom Helen sided in the turf war. She would later come to admire Unite's efforts to bring ununionised workers on board. *Stuff*

When the Council of Trade Unions was formed in 1987 from the merger of the Federation of Labour and the Combined State Unions, its first president was Ken Douglas (left), with whom Pat Kelly had worked at Wellington Drivers' Union. Ross Wilson (right) succeeded Douglas in 1999, working to unite a divided and dispirited movement. When Helen became president in October 2007, she tried to reform and modernise the unions. *Kelly family collection*

Peter Conway, a dedicated and highly respected unionist, became CTU secretary in 2008. He worked alongside Helen, and like her carried an enormous workload, including managing the overstretched and under-resourced organisation. He is seen here in 2010 addressing a Fairness at Work rally. *Council of Trade Unions*

In 2010 the National Party-led government of John Key announced plans to roll back workers' rights. One of its moves was to allow employers to dismiss newly hired workers with impunity within their first 90 days. On October 20, 22,000 workers attended Fairness at Work protests around New Zealand. Here, marchers are addressed by Helen in front of Parliament. *Council of Trade Unions*

A few hours after the Wellington Fairness at Work rally, a broiling dispute between the New Zealand actors union and the producers of a proposed series of films based on J.R.R. Tolkien fantasy *The Hobbit* spilled on to the streets. Film workers believed the union's demand to negotiate terms and conditions would cost thousands of jobs and destroy the New Zealand film sector. *Stuff*

After executives from Warner Bros. flew to New Zealand, John Key, seen here addressing a media scrum, announced a law change would be passed under urgency removing film workers from the country's employment laws. Warners gained an additional $33 million on top of existing subsidies. *Stuff*

Over 100 meatworkers at the ANZCO-owned CMP Rangitikei abattoir were locked out in October 2011. The company was insisting on pay cuts. Helen threw the CTU's weight behind the workers, attending many meetings like this one, boosting picket-line support and bringing the attention of CMP's international customers, including McDonalds, Waitrose and Tesco, to the company's actions. The dispute was settled just before Christmas after 65 days.
Kelly family collection

Helen fought for justice for the family of Charanpreet Dhaliwal, a student murdered on his first night at work for a small security company contracted to construction giant Fulton Hogan. His violent death was emblematic of the situation for large numbers of workers who lacked union representation and had no bargaining power over pay or health and safety.
NZ Herald Archives

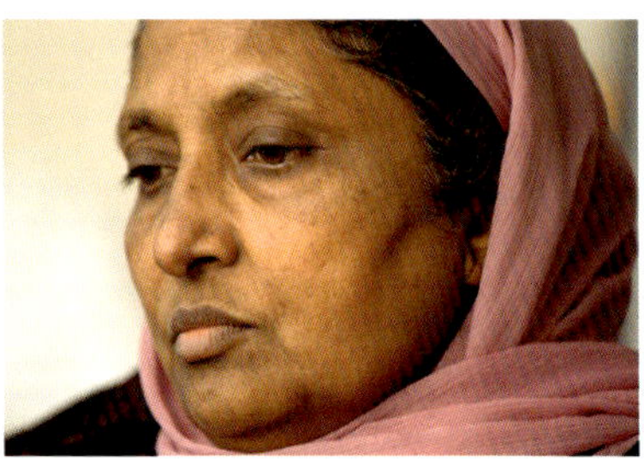

Charanpreet Dhaliwal's grieving mother came to New Zealand from India after he was killed. On June 21, 2011 she visited the building site where her son died. *Brett Phibbs/ NZ Herald Archives*

A dispute over the waterfront workers' collective agreement descended into a bitter struggle at the Ports of Auckland in early 2012. The port wanted to sack hundreds of workers and put stevedoring in the hands of contractors. Helen embedded herself with the Maritime Union to fight back against the company. Overseas unions including the International Longshore and Warehouse Union also supported the wharfies, including at this rally along the Auckland waterfront. *Maritime Union of New Zealand*

Talley's-owned Affco meat company locked out 1000 workers at six plants in the North Island in 2012 in a bid to force them to accept more flexibility and less union influence. The union movement struggled to raise funds to support so many workers. The dispute was settled with the intervention of iwi leaders after three months. Here, Helen addresses workers locked out from Affco's Rangiuru plant near Te Puke. *Simon Oosterman*

When Caroline and Roger Callow told Helen about their son Ken's death in the forestry industry, it marked the start of an intensive campaign. Helen was determined to show that long hours, poor working conditions, lack of training and facilities, low pay and 'race to the bottom' competition among contractors were behind the high rate of death and injury. This billboard went up on Auckland's Khyber Pass Road in early 2013. Pictured are Caroline and Roger Callow with Ken's sons Ali and Max. *Dean Purcell/NZ Herald Archives*

Nineteen-year old forestry worker Eramiha Pairama was killed while working alone on a hot January day in 2013. As in most cases, the government's health and safety agency did not prosecute his employer. In 2015 Helen and a team of unpaid lawyers took successful private prosecutions against the employers of both Pairama and another forestry worker, Charles Finlay. *Selena Eruera collection/NZ Herald Archives*

Forestry worker Charles Finlay was killed on a cold dark winter morning near Tokoroa in July 2013. His wife Maryanne Butler-Finlay is pictured here holding Charles' photograph and surrounded by her children Charles Jnr (left rear) and his partner Kyla and twins Sharneica and Shelby. Butler-Finlay became a tireless campaigner alongside Helen in the fight for justice for the families of dead forestry workers. *Maryanne Butler Finlay collection*

Grieving families of workers killed on the job came together on Workers Memorial Day, April 28, 2014. Craig Kidd, front left, whose son Lincoln was one of ten forestry workers killed in 2013, made the casket that was carried from Wellington Railway station to Parliament. Charles Finlay's son Charles Jnr is on the right, and behind him is Deborah McMillan, whose husband Shane Frater was killed in the forestry industry in 2009. *Council of Trade Unions*

Helen kept in close contact with her father's extended family, most of whom still lived in Wigan in the UK. She visited in 2015, after her cancer diagnosis, with husband Steve Hurring and son Dylan. Dylan is seated at centre, with Helen behind and Steve standing on the far right. *Kelly family collection*

Helen with Uncle Harold and Auntie Lolo Moss at Wigan, 2015. Lolo was Pat Kelly's only surviving sibling. The black and white photo on the wall is of their father Patrick, a Liverpool dock worker, who had no regular employment during the Depression. He died of cancer at the age of 39. *Kelly family collection*

Helen and Steve at Wigan, 2015. *Kelly family collection*

Helen stepped down as CTU president in 2015 because of her illness, although she continued to carry a heavy workload of campaigning for workers. Several months after being diagnosed, she disclosed that she was using cannabis for pain relief. Her campaign for law reform included an unsuccessful application to associate minister of health Peter Dunne. She often took to social media to tease and criticise Dunne, pictured in this cartoon. *Monique Ford/Stuff; Sharon Murdoch/Stuff*

In 2013 health and safety charges were dropped against the boss of the Pike River Mine where 29 men had lost their lives in November 2010. Helen vowed to challenge the decision, and a judicial review was taken in the names of Sonya Rockhouse (left), whose son Ben was killed, and Anna Osborne (middle), whose husband Milton was killed. Anna, like Helen, was fighting cancer. After Helen's death the Supreme Court ruled the decision to drop the charges was unlawful. *Maryanne Butler-Finlay collection*

Service and Food Workers Union national secretary John Ryall, pictured with care worker Kristine Bartlett, was instrumental in a landmark legal case taken on behalf of Bartlett for pay equity. It culminated after five years in a $2.2 billion pay settlement for workers in residential aged care, disability support services and home support services. Ryall was also an instigator of the Living Wage movement in New Zealand. *John Ryall collection*

Helen's cancer was incurable, but she was determined to live as long as she could. With treatment options in New Zealand exhausted, she and Steve travelled to Cuba in August 2016 so she could receive a novel cancer vaccine. Despite her pain, she and Steve managed to see many sights of Havana with their guide, Juan Francisco Hernández Cabrera. *Kelly family collection*

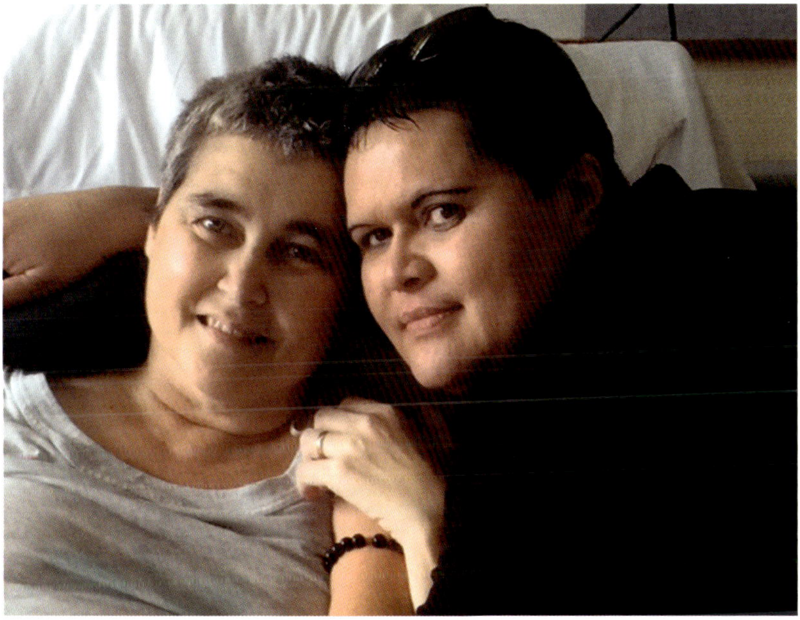

Maryanne Butler-Finlay developed a close friendship with Helen, which began in 2013 when Helen took up the case of her husband Charles, one of ten men killed at work in the forestry industry that year. Here, the two are pictured after Helen and Steve's return from Cuba. *Kelly family collection*

Helen died on October 14, 2016. She was 52. Her death led morning news bulletins and it was widely acknowledged that New Zealand had lost a remarkable leader. Here, cartoonist Sharon Murdoch acknowledges her passing. *Sharon Murdoch/Stuff*

Helen Kelly, September 19, 1964 – October 14, 2016. *Cameron Burnell/Stuff*

night at work, the forestry workers were at the bottom of the food chain. Those at the top – the owners – reaped the rewards of the workers' labour and were divorced from responsibility for the daily risks they faced.

She was almost immediately proved right about the new code. Forestry workers kept dying. Four were killed within the first four months of 2013. The youngest, Eramiha Pairama, was only 19. 'It was terrible,' Helen later told Sutorius. 'You'd get up in the morning and think, oh no, not another one.'[11]

The forestry workers were completely deunionised, but Helen saw the families of those killed on the job as natural allies in forcing change. The challenge was finding them. She set about tracking them through Facebook, searching death notices, writing to funeral homes and asking for messages to be sent on. She worked through the CTU's Māori vice-president Syd Keepa to find contacts for the many whānau affected. Some made contact with her after reading her public comments or seeing the Ken Callow video or billboard. Some workers came forward to share their experience and knowledge. Even when she went to Geneva in March 2013 for a regular meeting of the ILO's governing body, Helen carried on ferreting out contacts and emailing those with whom she'd established a connection.

She kept pumping MBIE, the Transport Authority and the police under the Official Information Act and argued with them over petty redactions. She tussled with coroners for access to files and reports. Gradually, she shook loose a mountain of paper. It was clear the enforcement agencies were not taking the industry's death and injury toll seriously enough. Prosecutions were rare and the report on Ken Callow's death was typical of many: the dead worker was often said to be at fault, usually no one else was to blame, and production pressures, long hours and other structural factors didn't get a mention.

'My view is that no one really cares about these deaths,' Helen wrote to a relative of one dead worker. 'They are workers who can be replaced by others – no one wants to know what will keep them safe and make the industry a good place to work.'[12]

In her office at the CTU, she propped up a huge noticeboard on a couple of chairs and used it to map out the personal and forensic details. Along the top were the names of workers killed in the forestry industry;

underneath were photos, timelines, extracts from reports, coloured stickers to indicate whether this or that document had yet been obtained, family contacts, pictures drawn by children who grieved for their fathers. Over time the board became densely packed. It dominated the room, which started to resemble a scene from a TV detective drama. No one who came to see her could avoid being confronted by it. Sometimes her executive assistant Julia London would find her staring at it with tears in her eyes.[13]

Workers Memorial Day was coming up in late April. It was an obvious focal point for organising. Helen wrote to the families for whom she had contact details and invited them to a gathering in Auckland. Her tone was both soft and confronting: 'I realise this letter will come as a surprise and I hope you don't mind receiving it,' she began, before writing about a death and injury toll that remained concealed from the nation, and the CTU's belief that the key to change lay with the forest owners. She encouraged the families to come together and share their stories.

The families of six dead workers came. The Maritime Union hosted the event in a meeting room. There was a memorial table with photos and mementos. A roll call was read of 26 men killed since 2007. A forestry worker spoke about the constant pressure on crews to produce more and the lack of genuine training.[14] Family members talked about their experiences, candles were lit, waiata sung. The room felt full, intimate and desperately sad.

The Callows attended and spoke about Ken. Deborah McMillan talked about her husband Shane Frater, who had been killed on May Day, 2009. The 28-year-old had left their Napier home at five that morning and travelled an hour and forty minutes with his crew to the block they were harvesting. McMillan expected him home about seven p.m. as usual. Instead, his body was loaded into the back of a vehicle and taken from the site after he suffered a fatal head injury.

Frater and his crew were working on a 33-degree slope for a logging contractor engaged by Rayonier, one of New Zealand's biggest forest owners. A broken section of tree had become snagged on the tail rope, part of the apparatus used to haul logs up a hill. As tension went on the rope the 2.3-metre chunk of debris started moving, as if on a flying fox.

The worker operating the hauler couldn't see what was happening but Frater could. He radioed up for the tension on the rope to be released. As the rope slackened the debris came loose and flew through the air, hitting him and narrowly missing another worker. The co-worker went immediately to his aid but could find no pulse; he removed his T-shirt and used it to wipe blood from Frater's face.[15]

Frater and McMillan's daughter Skyla was two when he was killed.

By 2013 Deborah McMillan had struggled for four years without answers or information. She felt lost and confused, her grief triggered every time she read in the news that another forestry worker had been killed. She happened to be searching on the internet one night when she came across the Ken Callow video. She got in contact with Caroline Callow and from her to Helen.

Helen hadn't known about Frater until McMillan phoned to ask if she could come to the Workers Memorial Day gathering. In the mounting pile of investigation reports Helen had obtained from the ministry, there was no sign of him. According to the data, Shane Frater didn't exist and his death hadn't occurred.[16] It turned out that an investigation report had been written, and at Helen's insistence the ministry unearthed it from a regional office. It described in detail the manner of Frater's death, noted the tendency of the forestry industry to be 'sorry after the fact', and recommended no one face prosecution.

For McMillan, the Workers Memorial Day event was – as it was for many of the families – the start of a journey into activism. Helen asked her to speak but she wasn't sure what to say. 'Helen said, "Write from the heart",' she remembered. 'It was a hard day, but it really got us started.'

The families were no longer alone, divided by time and distance, the collateral damage of the country's third largest export earner; they were now together as a community, each with their own line of communication to Helen. 'She was very comforting and caring,' said McMillan. 'She never forced you to do anything that you didn't want to do. She was incredibly passionate about it.'[17] And attentive: she generally started clearing her emails when she got up in the morning and was often still working through them well after eleven at night, so it seldom took more than a day for her to respond to family members like McMillan when they sought advice or reassurance.

There was no doubting Helen's empathy with the stricken families. She was pained by the stories of exhausted workers under constant production pressure literally being 'worked to death'.[18] She channelled her emotions into a campaigning zeal that linked the need for change in the forestry sector with her continued ambition for a regime of industry standard agreements that would set bottom-line wages and conditions, and with the union movement's resistance to the National-led government's latest round of changes that would further deplete workers' collective bargaining rights.

She cast the forestry industry as an exemplar of what happened in a deregulated labour market, where workers were on individual employment agreements, unable to collectively bargain and denied the ability to be heard on matters of health and safety.

'Basically, without regulation everyone takes the low road to stay competitive,' she wrote in one of a series of articles on left-wing website *The Standard*. 'Forest owners operate a model on the lowest common denominator, so they are unlikely to favour a contractor with higher costs.'

Logging workers were highly productive and harvesting more wood than ever before, yet were earning a diminishing slice of the industry's spoils. Analysis by Bill Rosenberg revealed that the share of the sector's income going to wages and salaries had been 70 percent in the late 1980s. By 2011 it had fallen below 20 percent.

Helen came up with a new slogan: the industry was 'dangerous by design'. While owners captured the profits, the risks and the cost of death and injury were pushed on to workers, families and society. An industry standard agreement could help fix this, she argued, by establishing a level playing field for all operators that set minimum pay and conditions, and maximum hours. In the New Zealand of 2013 this sounded radical, she acknowledged, but in many countries it was normal.[19]

Also in the background as the forestry campaign gathered momentum was a major review into New Zealand's health and safety system. The Independent Taskforce on Workplace Health and Safety had been set up in 2012 as part of the government's response to the Pike River tragedy, and by chance its final report was released a couple of days after

Workers Memorial Day. It pulled no punches – New Zealand's high rate of workplace harm was a 'shameful tragedy' and the situation was 'appalling, unacceptable and unsustainable'. Forestry and farming were identified as two of the country's five most deadly industries.

The taskforce sheeted the failure of the health and safety regime back to its roots, including a generation-long ethos of business self-regulation, labour market deregulation, and the massive deunionisation of the late 1980s and 1990s, which had removed the capacity for workers to be systematically involved in health and safety management. The government's health and safety inspectorate had been depleted and was weak and light-handed. Essential regulations had remained unwritten for two decades. There were gaping holes in the law as it related to contractors, fragmented supply chains and the duties of directors.

The taskforce called for a stand-alone, properly resourced health and safety regulator, tougher penalties that could reach up to the boardroom, coherent rules and true worker representation. Tripartism involving workers, employers and the regulator was essential to reduce the dreadful toll of death, injury and occupational disease.

There was an implied warning to the government not to pick the eyes out of its recommendations: its prescription for reform was an integrated package.[20]

Despite the taskforce's compelling report, forestry leaders continued to belittle Helen's commentary on their industry as a self-interested drive to recruit workers into unions. 'The grandstanding of Helen Kelly is deplorable,' said John Stulen. 'The union is desperate – they will never get crews to unionise. These are men who hunt and fish and play football together; they have a culture of their own.'[21] A forestry industry magazine, *New Zealand Logger*, repeatedly sniped at the campaign, deriding 'headline-hungry unionists', 'unions [that] want control more than safety' and who saw the industry as 'a major potential source of new members'.[22]

Helen Kelly hadn't been the first to recognise the industry's toll of death and injury. At FIRST Union – formed in 2011 from a merger of the National Distribution Union and the Finance Sector Union – general secretary Robert Reid had won the backing of his executive to start trying to organise forestry workers. As a result of union amalgamations over the years, FIRST incorporated the Wood Industries Union and had a presence in the big sawmills and pulp and paper mills, where there was a history of industrial militancy. But the workers out in the forests who harvested the radiata pine crop were completely deunionised.

It wasn't always so. Before the neoliberal revolution began in the 1980s, most were unionised employees of the state-run New Zealand Forest Service, which owned over half of the country's production forests. The Forest Service had been driven more by employment, soil and water conservation and regional development concerns than by commercial returns. It hadn't produced a trading surplus in almost seven decades, and by 1986 was being subsidised to the tune of $1.5 million a week.[23] When Labour turned it into a profit-driven state-owned corporation in 1987 there were massive job cuts. Hundreds of former wage workers became 'reluctant entrepreneurs', assisted by the new Forestry Corporation to set up as self-employed contractors using the same machines and equipment they had been using as employees.[24]

Privatisation quickly followed corporatisation, and through the late 1980s and the 1990s ownership of most state forests was hived off to multiple owners. The Employment Contracts Act completed the process of deunionisation, atomising the workforce (by then mostly employed by contractors) into individual employment contracts.

By 2013 it was estimated that half New Zealand's production forests were in the hands of institutional investors, including global hedge funds and North American pension funds.[25] For professional investors, forestry was an asset class – something that was good to have in a mixed portfolio, and more desirable since the Global Financial Crisis. At the same time, harvest volumes were growing: trees planted in the 1980s and early '90s were reaching maturity and there was strong demand from China for logs.[26] The on-the-ground reality for forestry workers on steep New Zealand hillsides, under pressure to fill log ships while prices were high, was a world away from the investors and traders who ultimately controlled their destiny.

There had been some efforts to re-unionise the workforce, but access on to privately owned forestry blocks was difficult. Even when arrangements were made for union organisers to meet with workers, they would often arrive to find nothing but a smouldering camp fire; the crews had been moved to another block.[27]

The heightened awareness of health and safety following the Pike mine disaster had motivated Robert Reid to renew efforts to organise the forestry sector. FIRST Union had got as far as describing the problem and doing some publicity when 'this sky-rocket called Helen Kelly came over, making some of the same statements and taking it a lot further', remembered Reid. 'Some unions could have been grumpy about that. We were absolutely delighted because we didn't have the resources and we knew that Helen wouldn't let something like this go. In some ways, we joined on to her coat-tails.'

Reid recalled a sense of running to catch up with her. 'There was a bit of her Dad there … Very much that old Pat thing of "I'm secure in the position I hold, so basically stuff the rest of you. I'm going to do what I believe is right."'[28]

A platform called 'FIRST Forestry Together' was set up to build a network of forestry workers and communities and share information. But the real power of the campaign came from grieving families and their relationship with Helen. Mothers, sisters, fathers and aunties became agitators under her guidance; many became confident with media interviews. They petitioned Parliament and wrote to the Transport and Industrial Relations Select Committee seeking an inquiry into the industry.

Deborah McMillan sought and gained personal meetings with the chair of the select committee, David Bennett, and minister of labour Simon Bridges. Her push for an inquiry met with resistance. A couple of weeks before her meeting with Bridges he had announced plans for a major overhaul of health and safety law, based on the taskforce report. He argued his proposals should be given time to bed in. When it came to the crisis in forestry, it seemed to McMillan he 'wasn't interested at all. He sat there flicking his pen. It seemed like he was just going through the motions. I wanted him to hear us and understand but he was saying, "I've been out there [to a logging operation] and everything is going fine."'[29]

FIRST Union had employed Edward Miller, a young law graduate. Miller's analysis of the industry's economic history and financial structure brought extra ballast to the campaign. He was able to help identify new points of leverage, including the fact that most New Zealand forests were certified by the Bonn-based Forest Stewardship Council as meeting the 'social, economic and ecological needs of present and future generations' – a standard plainly at odds with the industry's scandalous human toll.

Miller worked closely with both Reid and Helen, who he found had a 'preternatural ability to squeeze things down to the essence. I would meet with her and we would discuss something, and I would hear things that I had said to her explained by her much better two days later on the radio'. She absorbed new information instantly and used it with confidence; she didn't waste time second-guessing herself. 'It would happen in meetings too,' Miller recalled. 'I would say something to her just beforehand and it would pop up moments later in the meeting. ... She'd be, "Well, we have the research that says forest certification means you get an extra 30 percent profit as a result of what you're doing, so if [we caused you to lose] your forest certification you're going to be in a really bad position." I'd be like, "Gee, I just told you that outside."'[30]

Men kept dying in the forests. On July 19, 2013, the toll for the year reached six when Charles Finlay, a Tokoroa father of three, was killed. He had got home at six the previous night. He was picked up by his foreman at 4.15 the next morning to travel to their site. He was dead by 5.15, struck by a 50-kilogram log.

Finlay had been in the industry for 27 years and was a diligent, careful worker. After all those years – including ten with his present employer – his hourly wage was just $16, although it was boosted by non-taxable chainsaw and clothing allowances. He had been a tree feller for much of his career but in recent years had become a machine operator, loading the logs on to trucks. The job was easier on the body but involved starting at four or five in the morning, and routinely doing eleven- or 12-hour days.

Finlay's contract stipulated that he work as much overtime as the employer required, at his standard rate of $16 an hour. He had become increasingly dissatisfied with the growing pressure. The crews would receive log orders that had to be filled, and he would often be out of the vehicle and on the ground felling trees and breaking out to help meet the demand.[31] His wife Maryanne Butler-Finlay remembered he was often exhausted.[32]

It was pitch-black and cold on the site on July 19. Soon after starting work, Finlay got out of his loader and went to speak to another machine operator, who was loading logs on to a truck. He then went to get oil for his machine. He was found on the ground fifteen minutes later, close to the truck being loaded. The log he had been hit by was nearby. He had suffered a catastrophic head injury.

Messages bearing the awful news filtered out of the forest to various people around the district in the couple of hours after his death. His wife didn't learn until eight a.m., when a friend and bush contractor came to the family home.

Finlay worked for M&A Cross, a local contractor. That afternoon the owner arrived and handed her $100 in grocery vouchers from the forest manager, Hancock Forest Management.

Twelve hundred people attended Finlay's tangi. As well as shock, grief and concern for her children, Butler-Finlay was in a state of high alert in the days after her husband's death. She started to hear talk among forestry workers that Charles had been in the wrong place when he died, that it was somehow his fault. It didn't square with what she knew of him. He was methodical and safety-conscious.

Finlay's cousin-in-law, a delegate with the Engineering, Printing and Manufacturing Union, mentioned that a woman named Helen Kelly had been campaigning about forestry safety. Butler-Finlay had no idea who Helen was, but after the tangi she decided to contact her. When word got around that she had called on someone from the union movement for support, she heard that a family friend had commented, 'It better not be that bloody Helen Kelly.'

Helen was in Tokoroa within a few days. She arrived in Doc Marten-style boots, a frock and a plaid jacket, sat on the floor and heard about the man Butler-Finlay had fallen in love with when she was 19 and he was 22. Despite his wife's urging, Finlay had never been a union member. He thought it would be found out and count against him at work.

Helen met the couple's 19-year-old son Charles Jnr and nine-year old twin girls, Shelby and Sharneica. She talked about the campaign to force improvements in the forestry industry, and explained the role of MBIE in investigating Finlay's death. Butler-Finlay remembered that she cried and said, 'I'm so sorry,' as if she was in some way responsible for the family's devastating loss.

Indeed, she did feel the union movement bore a share of the blame. When membership collapsed among forestry workers in the 1990s, there had been no attempt to develop a new model of unionism that met their needs.[33] From talking to older forestry workers, she had also come to believe that a bitter internal power struggle in the late 1970s in the then Timber Workers Union, which divided communities and led to the sacking of 150 workers, had left a long shadow.[34] The legacy of a 'union elite scrapping over the power these very workers give them' meant that, even decades later, some workers were reluctant to be associated with unions. As the forestry campaign gathered force, she was getting emails from union activists keen to help with boycotts and pickets, but she was determined that, whatever form of unionism emerged from the current crisis, workers and their families must be in control of it.[35]

Her visit to Tokoroa would mark the beginning of a loyal friendship between Helen and Butler-Finlay. She became integrated into the family and came to be known as 'Aunty Helen Kelly'. Charles Finlay soon became a leading figure in Helen's public narrative about work and workers' rights. Killed in the middle of the country, in the middle of the night, in the middle of winter, he was 'a victim of poor health and safety in an industry that is dangerous by design, and designed in a manner that leaves its workforce scared of raising concerns, unorganised in health and safety, and working in conditions predicated on it getting away with being dangerous'. Not only had a family lost a father and husband, they had suffered a severe financial penalty, left to manage on ACC compensation based on 80 percent of his $16-an-hour wage.[36]

Finlay's death erased any remaining shreds of credibility in the industry's claim that its safety performance was up to scratch – let alone leading edge, as had been claimed a year earlier. The media were now running major stories on the issue, with names and context; the workers dying in the forests were no longer faceless dope-smokers but men with skills and experience, families and responsibilities. Individual deaths were no longer hidden from public awareness – one here, another one there – but aggregated into a story of catastrophic failure.

Bridges, under increasing pressure, was phoning the Forest Owners

Association demanding answers; some forest owners were getting heat from investors and directors alarmed at what was going on.[37]

Even before Finlay's death, the industry's leaders had conceded they were in an untenable position and there needed to be a health and safety review. The only question was what form such an inquiry would take. Would the industry attempt to be judge and jury in its own cause?

Some forest owners now saw Helen as the enemy. They wanted nothing to do with her or the CTU. 'A lot of words used by the CTU aggrieved a number of the large forest owners because there were allegations that they were heartless or uncaring or making profits from the blood of workers – emotive stuff like that,' remembered Bill McCallum, who was the president of the Forest Owners Association, as well as managing director of Hancock Natural Resources Group, the biggest forest owner and management company in New Zealand. However, he was convinced that any attempt to run an inquiry without having the CTU on board would lack credibility and be a worthless exercise.[38]

The upshot was a period of detailed to-and-fro communication between McCallum and Helen to nut out terms of reference for the review. The stakes were high, but McCallum said they forged a positive and respectful relationship. 'Helen was a very forthright woman. … The engagements were constructive, and Helen in every sense was helpful. There was nothing she put forward that I thought was unreasonable or unnecessary or intending to manipulate the outcomes. Her objectives were totally sincere and heartfelt in terms of what she was trying to achieve for people in the industry. She didn't have a political motivation as I saw it.'

Despite the goodwill between the two, Helen continued to come under attack. The Forest Owners Association's health and safety leader Sheldon Drummond – speaking on behalf of an industry that killed workers at 15 times the rate of other industries – accused her of exploiting bereaved families and playing fast and loose with the facts.[39]

Even as the details of the inquiry were being thrashed out, workers continued to die. By the end of 2013 four more had lost their lives in the forests. The last was Lincoln Kidd. The fit, hard-working 20-year-old was killed in a small forest block near Levin six days before Christmas, hit by a tree felled by his boss. His spine was broken and his skull smashed: he died instantly. His death left his family bereft and brought the industry's toll for the year to ten.

By early 2014 the Independent Forestry Safety Review was underway, with a wide-ranging brief and – remarkably – the backing of Simon Bridges and his departmental officials. One of its three members was Hazel Armstrong, who had become a leading advocate for workplace health and safety. In the years before Helen began to grasp the urgent need to organise around health and safety, she had often lightly mocked Armstrong's expertise. Not any more. Armstrong was keen to serve on the forestry review and Helen insisted she be there.

It was 16 months since Helen's visit to the Callows in Gisborne; 16 months of hard, hands-on campaigning had forced the industry to this point. Some contractors were now breaking ranks with the owners' lobby and talking publicly about the unregulated race to the bottom that Helen was talking about – thin margins leading to long hours, a lack of capacity for training, and insufficient time for health and safety planning on site.[40] In addition, Rotorua's coroner was planning a joint inquest into multiple forestry deaths in his region, and more and more bereaved forestry families were making contact with Helen and the CTU for support.

Genuine change to keep workers safe was not a foregone conclusion, but the grieving families had finally been acknowledged and they were a small step closer to the improvements they sought.

Helen hadn't waited for permission to launch into the forestry campaign. There were some in the union movement who doubted whether the leader of the CTU should be so obsessively focused on this issue, and who didn't think there was any hope of unionising far-flung forestry workers in remote rural areas.

But for the six years she had been in the role Helen had been trying to pull down the walls that separated the union movement from the great majority of workers. Consciously or not, by diving headlong into the forestry scandal and building up a grassroots campaign, she was demonstrating what an open, inclusive union movement could look like.

It came down to a fundamental question: What is a union? 'When [forestry workers] say, as they do, that they want a union, I say they have one,' she told the CTU's biennial conference in late 2013. 'Look at them – talking together and with their families and communities, discussing health and safety, discussing industry training, discussing wages and conditions – what else does a union look like?'[41]

But she didn't have a monopoly on innovative strategies to renovate unionism and lift the position of vulnerable workers. At the instigation of John Ryall a groundbreaking new campaign for a 'living wage' had been launched in 2012. Two experienced union organisers – Annie Newman in Auckland and Lyndy McIntyre in Wellington – had been appointed to drive it. They drew on the lessons of the UK's living wage campaign and community organising models from North America, and began building a new movement that wasn't owned or controlled by the unions, but instead founded on a partnership between workers, community groups and faith groups.

They linked up with the Family Centre Social Policy Research Unit, which would independently calculate the rate of pay that workers needed to sustain the basic necessities, live with dignity and actively participate in society. An accreditation system was developed by which companies who wanted to identify themselves as 'living wage employers' would be assessed. The rules were simple: companies must pay at least the stipulated living wage to workers they employed or who were employed by their regular contractors, and workers must have access to a union.

The first living wage was assessed in 2013 at $18.40 an hour – $4.65 more than the statutory adult minimum wage set by the government. It met with immediate pushback, even though it was entirely voluntary. There were predictions it would drive businesses under and cause a flight of newly unemployed New Zealanders to Australia. Wellington Chamber of Commerce insisted the economy needed to grow before workers got a living wage: 'employers can only pay what they can afford'. The Employers and Manufacturers Association called it a 'slippery slope'.[42]

However, the campaign had moral power in a country that had become more unequal than ever, where some working families struggled to put food on the table while multimillion-dollar chief executive salaries had become unexceptional.[43]

Helen was an enthusiastic supporter. She wasn't directly involved but the CTU backed it strongly; Peter Conway chaired a steering group which worked to get other unions on board, and Bill Rosenberg helped with economic analysis. Momentum slowly grew and over subsequent years employers ranging from city councils and boutique food manufacturers to banks and power companies signed up.

Along with Peter Cranney, Ryall was also a key driver of a series of groundbreaking campaigns using legal cases as leverage to introduce industry employment standards for low-paid workers. In the first, the Service and Food Workers were supported by the PSA in taking a case to the Employment Relations Authority, claiming the minimum wage for a worker in a disability support centre who regularly had to stay overnight to respond to residents' needs. As things stood the worker was paid between $3.40 and $4.30 an hour for this 'sleepover' time – about $7 below the minimum wage. Litigation was a high-risk strategy for the unions as they were up against both the employer (IDEA Services) and the government (the funder of disability support services). When the unions kept winning all the way up to the Court of Appeal, the employer went into voluntary liquidation. The minister of health said he might legislate to prevent the workers gaining the minimum wage.

But the unions had built up groundswell of public support along the way – through petitions, public meetings, and invitations to MPs to walk a couple of hours in support workers' shoes – and had 4000 other cases filed with the Employment Relations Authority. Finally, just before the Supreme Court was due to hear the final appeal, the government agreed to negotiate. The $150 million settlement covered back pay and future minimum wage payments, with the cost split between the government and employers in the sector. It was an outstanding win for a group of low-paid workers – all those in the health and disability sector required to be on call overnight – who ended up with an extra $270 a week.[44]

Another dispute then arose: home support workers weren't being paid for the time they spent travelling between their clients. Claims were made by the PSA and the Service and Food Workers Union for them to be paid the minimum wage for this 'in-between' travel time. After the sleepover case, the government soon decided to negotiate with the two unions, resulting in a $38 million settlement.[45] This in turn helped build momentum for a landmark case.

John Ryall and Peter Cranney had been mulling over the possibility of taking a case under the 1972 Equal Pay Act to address the chronically low wages paid to workers in the female-dominated residential aged care sector. The legislation had been on the statute books for over 40 years, but it had been assumed to apply only in cases where women were paid less for doing the same job as men in the same workforce. Ryall and Cranney were talking about taking a case that would link low pay with historic gender discrimination and undervaluation. It would involve looking at the skills, responsibilities and effort required in the job and ascertaining what a male worker would be paid for similar work.

To go ahead they would need a worker willing to endure the stress and exposure of a court challenge. The person would preferably be a long-serving employee on an individual employment agreement, who was earning around the minimum wage.

Such a person happened to pop into the Servos' Petone office one day. Kristine Bartlett was on $14.46 an hour as a senior caregiver at an aged care facility owned by TerraNova Homes and Care in the Hutt Valley. Ryall, who knew her well, said, 'Kristine, have I got an offer for you.' Bartlett listened to their proposal. She'd been slogging away for 20 years on low wages, was close to retirement and decided she was happy to lend herself to a cause that could make a difference to workers who came after her.[46]

A case in Bartlett's name was filed with the Employment Relations Authority in 2012, backed by the Service and Food Workers Union and the New Zealand Nurses Organisation.[47] It would mark the beginning of a drawn-out journey through the courts that culminated in victory in the Court of Appeal in 2014. The government would decide to negotiate rather than fight, and to extend the coverage beyond residential aged care workers like Kristine Bartlett to include home support and disability support workers. Five years after the case began, a landmark $2.2 billion pay equity settlement was reached. It delivered pay rises of 15 to 49 percent to 55,000 workers who carried out this emotionally and physically demanding work.[48]

In both the travel and pay equity cases, it was agreed the settlement would be for all workers, not just paid-up union members. All workers got to attend paid meetings to vote on whether to accept the deal; in the process the unions recruited thousands of new members. The settlements were, in effect, embryonic versions of the industry standard agreements that Helen had been pushing for.

She had not played a direct role, but had helped out whenever Ryall needed the mana of her position to secure meetings with key people or clear blockages with government. 'She was always available to hop in at the right times.'[49] She was intensely interested in the legal arguments, and in the use of strategic litigation as a way to address workplace injustices that were impervious to bargaining or political pressure.

'This is how she thought unions should operate,' Ryall said. 'Whether you got leverage through publicity, or through getting the wider community to rise up, or through the courts – [unions] needed to negotiate beyond their numerical strength.'

While the Kristine Bartlett case was slowly working its way through the courts, the justice system delivered shattering setbacks in two of the causes that had profoundly affected Helen.

In September 2013, almost two years after the death of Charanpreet Dhaliwal, the man accused of his murder was acquitted in the Auckland High Court. Dhaliwal's family had come from India for the trial and were shell-shocked by the verdict, said Sammy Singh, the Sikh community leader who worked with Helen in advocating for Dhaliwal.[50]

A month later came another terrible blow when charges brought against Dhaliwal's employer under the Health and Safety in Employment Act were dismissed by a District Court judge. Dhaliwal – clad in gear borrowed from another casual worker, shown briefly around the site late at night, and left alone with his little torch and cell phone to keep watch – was not the victim of poor health and safety oversight, ruled Judge Lisa Tremewan. The site was 'low risk' and she could not find fault with the employer. The death was 'unfortunate' but that did not alter her assessment of the employer's liability.[51]

Helen had built a relationship with Dhaliwhal's family and felt an unshakeable commitment to his case. 'I can't imagine what you think of this country – it has not cared one bit about Charanpreet's death,' she wrote to Dhaliwal's brother Chamanpreet after the failure of the health and safety charges.[52] She was determined to find a way to assert the dignity of a young life that had been spat out the bottom of a seemingly unaccountable supply chain, a life that – like that of so many forestry workers – seemed to be expendable, part of the cost of doing business.

She tore into the decision, saying it endorsed 'the worst kind of sloppy practice' and created an 'intolerably low threshold of care' for workers' safety.[53] She called (without success) for MBIE to appeal. In private, she excoriated the ministry's bosses for running a weak case that failed to emphasise the precarious nature of Dhaliwal's work – hired on the night without a contract, in a tenuous employment relationship that would have deterred him from asking questions about safety. The ministry had an effective monopoly on prosecutions under the Act and had done a poor job, she told them.[54]

She had continued to hammer away at Fulton Hogan, linking its brand with Dhaliwal's death and accusing it in speeches and submissions of walking away from its responsibilities as the beneficiary of the young man's labour. The company was fed up with her, but she and Sammy Singh had formed an effective alliance. Along with Phil Twyford, a good friend of Helen's and the Labour MP for Te Atatu – the electorate in which Dhaliwal was murdered – Singh established a more productive relationship with Fulton Hogan. After initially refusing to contribute anything more than the $4000 it had paid to help fly Dhaliwal's body back to India, by the end of 2013 the company was prepared to make a confidential compensation payment to the family.[55] The deal was packaged up in public relations spin to disguise the fact it was the result of relentless shaming by Helen, but at least Dhaliwal's family had finally got some accountability for his death.

Then, on December 12, 2013, astonishing news broke. Health and safety charges against Peter Whittall, the man who had driven the Pike River Mine development and was its chief executive at the time of the 2010 disaster, were discharged in the Christchurch District Court. Not a shred of evidence had been heard from the prosecution or the defence in relation to the 12 charges against him. Instead, a deal had been done in which the case would be abandoned in exchange for payment of $3.41 million in insurance money to the Pike victims.

It took the breath away. How was it possible that 29 workers could be killed in a preventable disaster and the person who ran the show could walk away upon the payment of money that was, in any case, already owed in compensation to the victims? Since when did the New Zealand justice system allow a defendant facing serious charges to buy his way out of a trial? Where was the accountability in all this?

There was widespread outrage, including from Helen. 'Everyone wins here except the families and … the men killed in the mine,' she wrote on *The Standard*. 'It is the Crown's job to represent them. They cannot seek justice themselves.'[56]

Exhaustion, frustration and anger laced her words. 'We [the CTU] are up to our eyeballs in legal expenses around health and safety. While money pours in from government agencies to help industries run health and safety initiatives, we are fighting on all fronts using the money paid in union fees by shop workers who stack supermarket shelves at night, to try and be the counter-voice here, be it for security guards killed on their first night at work on Fulton Hogan building sites, the families of forestry workers appearing at coronial hearings, or seeking advice on what happened today in the Christchurch District Court. It sometimes feels unsustainable against all the lawyers that corporations can afford, and with a department which does not consult or work with us on these issues.'

Sustainable or not, she had already made up her mind that the $3.41 million arrangement to abandon the charges would be challenged somehow. 'The decision announced today … cannot be left to rest.'

12. Into the breach

You have to remember it's about capitalism getting its greatest return from work – it doesn't want anything to get in the way. But collectivised labour puts a brake on that. *Helen Kelly and Peter Conway, 2014*

Peter Cranney was Helen's first port of call. She charged downstairs from the CTU office to see him at his law firm, Oakley Moran. 'We have to do something,' she said.

It wasn't clear what could be done to challenge the decision to release Pike River mine boss Peter Whittall from the charges against him. None of the reasons given seemed credible. The Ministry for Business, Innovation and Employment had advised Judge Jane Farish it would offer no evidence in relation to the 12 health and safety charges it had laid against Whittall back in late 2011. It said there were problems with the prosecution – witnesses who refused to make themselves available, 'contests between experts', 'pre-trial issues' – and asked the judge to discharge him.

The ministry said it had reviewed the case against the Solicitor-General's Prosecution Guidelines and concluded the 'public interest was not met by continuing with a long costly trial with a low probability of success.'[1]

It was three years after the disaster and this was how things stood:

29 workers lay dead inside a mine that had failed on every level to keep them safe, and somehow it was 'not in the public interest' to bring to trial the single person who was to have been called to account.

The ministry employed tortured logic. It took shelter in the fact that if Whittall was convicted he would receive only a low fine, and in the idea that the 'principal offender' behind the disaster had already been convicted by Judge Farish in July 2013. But that principal offender was the mine company, Pike River Coal Ltd (in receivership), which had gone broke less than a month after the disaster. Judge Farish had fined it $760,000 for breaches of the Health and Safety in Employment Act, and ordered it to pay $3.41 million in reparations – $110,000 to each of the 29 families and the two workers who escaped the explosion. The defunct outfit couldn't pay, and its major shareholder and directors refused to. The money recovered from the sale of the mine (to state-owned coal miner Solid Energy) and a small stockpile of coal, and from an $80 million insurance payout had already gone to Pike's secured creditors. There was only enough in the pot for the families to be paid $5000 each.[2]

There had been an attempt to get the government to pay the $3.41 million owed to the victims, but it had refused. Prime Minister John Key had told Parliament on November 12, 2013, that the government had no legal obligation to pay and had to be careful about setting precedents. Plenty of companies went broke without paying redundancy owed to workers and the government didn't step in, he said – as if this common or garden situation was somehow akin to New Zealand's worst industrial catastrophe in almost 100 years, and one that the state regulator had failed to prevent.[3]

Now, the very people who had managed and governed the catastrophically flawed mine – Whittall and the directors – were using their insurance cover to pay the $3.41 million debt to the victims, provided the charges against Whittall were dropped.

Everyone was asked to believe this was not a case of Whittall buying his way out of a prosecution. Judge Farish told the families it was a 'good outcome', and a trial was 'not in the best interests' of their community.[4] No one had asked the families what they thought. The deal was done and dusted before they knew anything about it; the money was already lodged with the court, ready to be paid into their bank accounts.

Making matters worse, the police had also shelved their criminal investigation. Five months earlier, they had called the families together to tell them they wouldn't be laying charges. Because the mine was still unaccessible it wasn't possible to establish the exact cause of the explosion; manslaughter charges therefore couldn't be sustained. While they had concluded there was enough evidence to support a charge of criminal nuisance, this would be 'double jeopardy' because MBIE was (at the time the police made their decision) already charging Whittall.[5]

As the Pike families headed towards a fourth Christmas without their men and boys, it appeared no one would be held to account. The agencies of the state charged with enforcing the law and exacting justice had investigated the calamity and concluded that nothing could be done.

The morning after Judge Farish's decision was announced, Helen went on Radio New Zealand. Justice and accountability had been 'traded off', she said. The CTU wanted to see if a judicial review was possible.[6]

Her comments made it sound as if the CTU had ample resources and standing to mount such a challenge, when in fact it was stretched in every direction. A draft of the proposed new Health and Safety Reform Bill was due, and there would be a huge amount of analysis and submission-writing to do. There was the ongoing campaign against the Key government's intention to roll back workers' rights under the Employment Relations Act. An election was coming up and there were plans for a union-wide campaign to get out the votes. There was the need to support the Living Wage Movement, and to push back against the insidious growth of precarious and insecure work. There was the forestry campaign.

But the Pike decision was an outrage. Ways and means would be found. The CTU would fundraise. Cranney, whose loyalty to Helen was anchored in his formative years under Pat, would provide his estimable legal skills for free. Helpers would be recruited. She would work every hour that God sent.

Helen's confidence was not ill-founded. She had now led the labour movement for six years and shown her skills on the traditional battle lines of the waterfront and meat industries; with her unpolished beauty and quick, combative commentary, she was seen as good talent by the media; she had the wit and charisma to inveigle supporters into her passionately argued causes. Indeed, a promising offer of help was received within a week: a highly respected Christchurch lawyer, Nigel Hampton QC – who knew the Pike story intimately, having represented the EPMU at the royal commission – wrote to say he was happy to have a look at the Whittall development, and was wondering if he could assist (pro bono) on forestry matters.

The question of the standing needed to challenge the Pike decision was quickly resolved. Sonya Rockhouse's son Ben had been killed in the mine. Another of her sons, Daniel, had survived the explosion and hauled the other survivor, Russell Smith, to safety; Helen had made a number of speeches in which she had told Daniel's harrowing story of heroism.

Sonya Rockhouse had been wary of Helen when she came across her in the first couple of years after the disaster. She had grown up in an anti-union household and her impression of Helen had been formed by the *Hobbit* dispute in October 2010. 'I was mad at her, watching her on TV going on about *The Hobbit*. I thought, why is she stirring things up?' she remembered.[7]

But Rockhouse had gradually come to see Helen as an ally in the desperate struggle for answers and accountability. Helen had tried to get to the bottom of some dodgy arrangements regarding Ben's employment with a major Pike contractor, Valley Longwall International. The company had often paid him in cash at the pub and claimed after the explosion that he had been a self-employed contractor. Valley Longwall had been implicated in the mine's poor safety management; after the disaster it been convicted on three charges under the Health and Safety in Employment Act and fined $46,800.

Rockhouse had emailed Helen the day she heard John Key tell Parliament that the government had no more responsibility to pay the court-ordered reparations owing to the Pike victims than it did to pay redundancy owed to workers of bankrupt companies. 'I said to Helen, "This is simply not right, what's happened to us."'

A month later Helen asked Rockhouse if she would be willing to be named as a plaintiff in some preliminary legal inquiries over the deal to release Whittall, with the possibility it might lead to a judicial review. She was in immediately.

Rockhouse thought Anna Osborne, whose husband Milton had been killed in the mine, might also be keen. Osborne had publicly expressed her disgust at the arrangement to let Whittall walk away from the charges and had called the $3.41 million payout 'blood money'. Yes, she told Helen, she was happy to lend her name to a legal challenge. But she was worried about how much money it would cost. She didn't have much and lawyers didn't come cheap. 'Helen said, "Don't worry about it, mate. It's all right, I'll sort it,"' remembered Osborne. 'I said, "Helen, you can't sort it. You can't go and ask lawyers to come and help us [for nothing]." She said, "Yes I can. I know someone who will do that for me."'[8]

Acting for the two women, Helen and Peter Cranney were able to make a start. On Christmas Eve 2013, Cranney wrote to the Christchurch District Court asking for the file containing all the briefs of evidence that Judge Farish had referred to in making her decision.

It had been another huge year. Helen and Steve planned a restorative summer break in the South Island. They stowed tramping boots and packs into the boot of the Daihatsu Charade and crossed on the interisland ferry on New Year's Day. They had been picking off New Zealand's celebrated Great Walks over the years, often in the company of close friends such as Linda Mitchell, Anne Goodman, Janette Kelly and her partner Alan Ware. The previous year they had done the Routeburn and then cycled the Otago Central Rail Trail. This time they were doing the Kepler, the Milford and the Rakiura North West Circuit, with a side trip to the Catlins and a pause at Kaitangata's memorial for the 34 men killed in the town's 1879 coal mining disaster.

As ever, Helen had her phone, iPad and files with her. As they drove through the verdant Southland countryside she engaged in a Twitter war with the farming lobby over the industry's terrible health and safety record, low pay and long hours for its entirely ununionised workforce. She regularly received desperate emails from farm workers and sharemilkers who had been unfairly sacked or badly treated, and had taken a strong personal interest in the case of a 19-year-old British tourist, Tom Sewell, who had been killed in a quad bike crash on his first day at work at a Katikati orchard in 2008.

She was a huge social media user, and was ramping up a one-woman campaign of pressure on the agriculture sector by looking up advertisements for farm jobs and broadcasting the miserable details. En route to Te Anau, she sat in the passenger seat and tweeted: 'farm assistant job $16.66 an hour'; 'another paying $14.33 an hour'; '18 days on for 57 hours and then 3 days off. I mean really?' Defenders of the industry tweeted affronted replies: 'Not as simple as you make out! I look after my staff and pay as much as my contract/cashflow will allow!' She had the last word: 'the emp model in agriculture is dangerous and unfair'.

After the Rakiura tramp, she and Steve got back into internet coverage to find a storm had broken out over the CTU's and Business New Zealand's long-running (but steadily shrinking) contracts with the Accident Compensation Corporation to train workplace health and safety representatives. A story had been parlayed by an outfit called the Taxpayers Union, recently set up by a National Party-aligned blogger and pollster, David Farrar, and led by Jordan Williams, an associate of Cameron Slater. The group had obtained figures about the contracts from ACC under the Official Information Act. They decried them as a 'nice little earner' and a 'worthless' scheme.[9] According to ACC minister Judith Collins, the scheme had 'all the hallmarks of a rort' and a 'scam'.[10] ACC had announced it would axe the contracts.

Peter Conway had defended the value of the training scheme in a firm but polite press statement and in media interviews. Helen sat down with the documents in Oban and hammered out a blog: 'I couldn't give a rat's arse about Jordan Williams and his new little ACT campaigning vehicle against the state, but I do care about health and safety ... the manner in which some of the media have run his latest little ruse against training health and safety representatives in the workplace is a disgrace.'

The CTU had trained 30,000 workers over the previous decade in how to exercise the duties of a workplace health and safety representative. Ditching the contracts was an assault on workers' ability to protect themselves and others on the job, she argued.[11] Even Business New Zealand was furious at the lobbyists' slur and its repetition by Collins;

chief executive Phil O'Reilly 'utterly' rejected the allegations and defended the scheme's integrity.[12]

Helen saw it as a clear political hit job and rolled with it, but Peter Conway was extremely offended. He was meticulous – a perfectionist – in all his dealings, and his work was held in high esteem across the political and economic spectrum. He felt Collins was impugning his integrity. He even called her to discuss the smear. She promised to 'try not' to repeat the defamatory words but wouldn't withdraw.[13] 'He was incredibly upset,' remembered Sue Windsor, the CTU's finance and operations manager. 'He was furious and took it very badly.'[14]

In the middle of this came news that yet another forestry worker had been killed on the job, this time in Marlborough. WorkSafe – the new post-Pike health and safety regulator that had come into being in the last days of 2013 – put out a stern statement criticising the forestry industry's 'appalling safety record … [and] ingrained systematic issues'.[15] The agency was by then running a blitz on forestry contractors and finding non-compliance everywhere; hundreds of infringement notices had been issued and some operators had been shut down.[16]

It was easy for the new regulator to talk tough now: the campaigning by Helen and the families had established an irrefutable narrative of failure, and the Independent Forestry Safety Review was going ahead. But there had been years of indifference and timidity from the old Department of Labour and then MBIE. The evidence was in Helen's enormous trove of forestry files, on the huge board in her office, and in the unresolved grief and anger of so many of the families she had come to know. The state had turned its back on justice for these families and she wasn't prepared to let it lie.

As president of the CTU Helen had started breaking down the walls of the union movement through her hands-on campaigning for ununionised workers, including Charanpreet Dhaliwal, forestry workers and those tossed aside under the 90-day fire-at-will law. Together, her union for the unorganised, wasn't working, but she was demonstrating through these campaigns what an open and community-centred workers' movement, grounded in the values of fairness and equity, might look like.

And she was taking that thinking even further. Three-quarters of

New Zealanders lived by their labour alone. They didn't have shares, investment properties or reserves of cash in the bank. The economy was dependent on their time and skills, but in the dominant political and economic narrative, unions – organisations of workers – were marginalised and derided as self-serving lobbyists interested only in harvesting membership fees. Helen was now starting to frame the union movement as the 'fifth estate', an institution that sat alongside others that operated for the public good. Just as the media, the courts, Parliament and the public service were broadly understood to be 'public institutions' that were vital to accountability, freedom and democracy, so too was the union movement.[17]

The powerful forestry industry had killed dozens of workers but the state had failed to hold it to account. Who, then, but the union movement would take action? An incompetent mine company had sent 29 workers to their deaths and the state had turned its back on justice. Who but the union movement would step into the breach?

She got back in touch with Nigel Hampton QC. Would he mind reading over the case of Eramiha Pairama, who had been killed in a Bay of Plenty forest almost exactly a year earlier? Hampton was at the beach and suggested she send him the file. No problem, she and Steve were on the road to Christchurch and would drop the file at his home on their way through.[18]

Pairama's story was heartbreaking. He was 19, a polite outgoing young man, deferential to his elders and proud of his Tūhoe, Whānau-ā-Apanui and Ngāti Porou whakapapa. He had a strong work ethic and was a good sibling to his two younger brothers. He loved kapa haka, kickboxing and music. He had spent his early years with his grandmother in the tiny East Coast community of Raukokore. He was, said his mother Selina Eruera, 'one of these very naïve country kids'.[19]

Pairama left high school in Whakatane when he was 16 to work for a local forestry contractor. By January 2013 he had three years' experience and was working at one of the industry's most hazardous tasks, breaking out trees that had been felled. Soon after going back to work after the Christmas break, he was hit on the side of the face by a branch. At home that night the wound was discoloured; he looked unwell and was taking

Panadol. Eruera, a district nurse, was worried about him and wanted to take him to the hospital, but he insisted he was fine.

On Friday, January 11, a week after the previous incident, he started work at seven a.m., attaching a strop to felled trees so they could be hauled up the slope to the skid. He worked without a break alongside his foreman until about one, when there was a half-hour smoko. He then worked on into the hot afternoon, but alone now as the foreman had gone to attend to other tasks. At about 3.15 the hauler driver didn't receive an expected communication from him. He went to investigate and found the young man on his hands and knees, coughing, gurgling and unable to walk. The log that had just been hauled had snapped and struck him. An ambulance was called but Eramiha Pairama died at the scene.

His two younger brothers were terribly affected by his death, and their schooling suffered. For Eruera, the loss of her firstborn brought confusion, despair and anger that lay over her like a dark cloak.

MBIE had six months to investigate and decide whether to prosecute. Under the Health and Safety in Employment Act, no one else was permitted to litigate while the regulator was considering action; if the regulator decided not to prosecute there was a small window for a private individual to bring charges. However, it was nine months before Eruera was advised there would be no prosecution over the death of her son.

In its report the ministry didn't explicitly describe Pairama as the architect of his own demise, but it came close. It listed the things he had 'failed' to do that contributed to the incident. The list of 'contributing causes' did not include the fact he had been left to work alone at a highly hazardous task, or that he had laboured all day in the heat with only a half-hour break, or that he had received a blow to the face a few days earlier. Everything was 'best practice'. No further action was to be taken.[20]

With the help of its vice-president Syd Keepa, the CTU had made contact with Pairama's family in October 2013. Helen met Selina Eruera for the first time in December that year, in preparation for a planned hearing by Rotorua's coroner into multiple forestry deaths in his area, including that of Pairama. Helen was convinced MBIE should have prosecuted. On New Year's Day 2014 she wrote to Eruera, asking if she was interested in the possibility of a private prosecution against her son's employer, Puketi Logging, and mentioning the 'amazing' offer from a Christchurch QC to do some work for free. 'There is no pressure here, Selina. If you want to leave it, then we understand,' she wrote. But 'this is the only chance that the company be held to account and I didn't want you to miss that if you want to proceed'.[21] Eruera did wish to proceed.

It didn't take Hampton long to conclude that Helen was right. MBIE had done a poor job of investigating. There was sufficient evidence to prosecute. It seemed to Hampton that the themes laid bare in the Pike River royal commission – a regulator that was indifferent, incompetent, lacking in specialist knowledge and overly cosy with the industry – were apparent here, too.[22]

Before long, Helen had Hampton looking at another case in which the regulator failed to prosecute – that of Charles Finlay. At the end of the six-month investigation period, the regulator had concluded the only person at fault was Finlay himself – he didn't have his hard hat on and was inside an exclusion zone. No one else was responsible for his death.[23]

As far as Helen was concerned, that investigation proved 'the modus operandi of the regulator [was] to blame the worker'.[24] How could it be acceptable for the industry to have systems so wafer-thin, so devoid of back-up and safety triggers, that a single mistake by a worker could lead to death? Surely Charles Finlay's case was another contender for a private prosecution? Again, Hampton agreed.

Helen kept pushing. She looked closely at the cases of two other forestry men, David McMurtrie and George Mahanga. Both had been killed in 2012 and the regulator had declined to prosecute. It would be much harder to convince a judge to allow private prosecutions over the deaths of these men, given the long passage of time and the strict limitation period in the statute, but she was determined to have a go.

It was a daring strategy. There had been only one other private prosecution under the Health and Safety in Employment Act.[25] The first step was to convince the court to grant leave to prosecute. Then there would be the task of marshalling evidence and legal arguments to achieve guilty verdicts. If the cases were unsuccessful, there was the risk of being hit with weighty court costs.

The whole plan relied on lawyers willing to work for nothing. A stressed Cranney pushed back at one point, telling Helen: 'Look, I just can't do it, go to hell. Your demands are too big.' She retorted that there were plenty of lawyers around, and stormed down to the ground floor to check if there were any in the building.

Simon Meikle, barrister and solicitor, was listed on the board beside the lift. Helen didn't know him and he hadn't done union work before. She went up to his office and asked if he would be willing to do unpaid work involving private prosecutions of forestry companies under the Health and Safety in Employment Act. Meikle had experience taking private prosecutions on behalf of the SPCA and had some time in his schedule. He agreed to help.[26]

Soon, another lawyer appeared. Tim Braithwaite, who practised in the forestry heartland of Rotorua and was the son of Helen's old friend Marty Braithwaite, sent her a message to say he was happy to help. Within a week she had flown him to Wellington and sent him home again with a box full of files.

By April 2014 Helen had a small army of lawyers donating their time to both the forestry cases and the still developing idea of a judicial review of the decision to let Peter Whittall off the Pike River charges.

Workers Memorial Day, April 28 – the international day of remembrance for workers killed at work – was an important rallying point, as it had been in 2013, but she wanted it to be bigger this year. There would be a memorial service and a vigil, as well as a street collection to raise money for legal advice for victims' families; there was something truly bleak and potent about the notion of volunteers shaking buckets on street corners in the cause of justice for workers killed on New Zealand job sites.

As ever, her ideas poured forth. CTU staffers scrambled to keep up and turn loosely conceived plans into action.

Forestry families came from around the country, this time to Wellington and this time in much bigger numbers. Some were billeted in the homes of unionists. Twenty of Charles Finlay's whānau stayed at Shannon Street while Helen and Steve moved out to Carol Beaumont's place.

Lincoln Kidd's family drove down from Levin; they had come into contact with Helen, Cranney and other forestry families after discovering the *What Killed Ken Callow?* video after their 20-year-old son was killed in December 2013. Lincoln's father Craig Kidd built a wooden casket; it was carried by pallbearers at the head of a 200-strong crowd that marched from the Wellington Railway Station to Parliament grounds. Lesley Kidd, Lincoln's mother, had never thought of herself as someone who would march on Parliament, speak from the steps and be interviewed by media but, empowered by the sense of solidarity, she did all these things.[27] 'As our forestry industry comes of age, are we to accept that death and injury is a part of it?' she asked. 'How long before the buyers of our wood see the sap running red with the blood of these men killed?'[28]

The number 51 was held aloft on placards and banners – the death toll of all workers killed on the job in New Zealand during 2013. 'These workers have paid the price of a deregulated, unsatisfactory health and safety system,' declared Helen to the crowd. 'A system that said the employer will self-regulate and keep these workers safe; that says if you dare to question whether you should be working eleven-and-a-half hour days in the snow and the rain with plastic bags stuffed down your boots, as we have heard from these forestry families, don't expect to work in this industry again. ... It is no coincidence that the five most dangerous industries have virtually no union organisation at all ...

'Let's be sad today,' she told the crowd. 'It is a sad day. But let's be angry too, and let's be organised.'[29]

Over the following weeks and months, the foundations were laid for three major lawsuits. The District Court granted leave to prosecute the employers of Eramiha Pairama and Charles Finlay; Helen was named as the prosecutor in both. She was holding out for permission to prosecute in the McMurtrie and Mahanga cases as well. And an application for a judicial review of the decision to discharge Peter Whittall was filed in the Wellington High Court in the names of Sonya Rockhouse and Anna Osborne.

For the families involved, Helen was a font of reassurance. 'She was our friend. She genuinely cared,' Osborne said. 'She never claimed she was going to save us. She always said this [judicial review] might not work out, but if it doesn't there's a plan B, and if that doesn't work we'll find something else, because this is too important to let lie.' Her default response to stress and worry was, '"It's okay mate, trust me." Nothing ever seemed to be a problem, even though it was huge for us.'[30]

There would be no substantive arguments heard in court on any of the cases until 2015, and there was much legal preparation to be done before then. The army of volunteers swelled. Dylan got involved with organising the exhibits in the forestry cases; law students from a newly established clinical legal programme at the University of Canterbury helped with research and sorting the voluminous files. Helen also brought her own legal analysis to bear and was constantly hunting out possibilities with Cranney. Hampton observed a sharp brain that quickly got to the heart of problems. She could be obdurate and was inclined to an 'overenthusiastic scattergun approach where she would fire as many shots in the air as she possibly could. That's no bad thing because among the shots there would be one or two that [were] valid. That's where Cranney came in.'[31]

Hampton was approaching 70. He had a distinguished career as a criminal defence lawyer behind him and had been thinking of slowing down towards retirement before he came into Helen's orbit. Now he was happily roped in across all three lawsuits. 'She had an ability to genuinely make you feel as if you had a significance that probably was greater than in reality it was. So although she would probably have disavowed it, I think she was one of the great flatterers – which is probably one of the necessary attributes of someone who is going to achieve in the sort of political positions that she was trying to achieve in. I don't think it was a designed flattery. It was something that was inherent within her and how she related to people …

'I had been in practice for nigh on 50 years. The thought that somehow someone considerably younger would light within you some of the idealism of your own youth is an interesting one, isn't it? That's what she did.'

At the CTU, things were under more strain than ever. Earlier in the year Peter Conway had become extremely unwell. The organisation was without its fiercely intelligent, principled backbone, a man who had served the union movement for almost four decades and whose judicious management of the organisation had enabled Helen to flourish and bring substance to the idea of a movement that spoke for all workers.

The previous year Conway had led groundbreaking research showing 30 percent of the workforce were now in jobs that lacked security – they had casual, zero-hour, short-term or other contracts with unstable hours and uncertain income. The contracts imposed huge stress and cost on to workers and families.[32]

A skilled musician, he had played his beloved mandolin in a gig with his political band, Not the Day Job, only a month or so before he became ill. A noted Harvard University labour scholar, Elaine Bernard, was on a teaching visit to New Zealand during March, and Conway was there to introduce her at a seminar for unionists. He had announced he would retire from his role as CTU secretary at the end of the year, leaving plenty of time for others to consider standing for the position. But suddenly he was in a living hell, struggling with a severe depressive illness.

Conway was respected across the union movement for the quality of his work and depth of his commitment. His presence was sorely missed at the CTU and everyone hoped desperately that he would recover. Meanwhile the load was spread among the small staff, who were already run ragged across so many fronts.

Helen had by then decided against standing for Parliament at the 2014 general election. She would have had to run on the Labour list because the two obvious electorates, Wellington Central and Rongotai, were occupied by sitting MPs Grant Robertson and Annette King. She had given it serious thought, but the forestry and Pike tragedies had enormously affected her. She thought it would be reckless to leave while there was so much unfinished business.[33]

Labour was enjoying a spike in the polls after the selection in September 2013 of a new leader.[34] David Cunliffe had attracted backing from unions and party members for his declared left-wing leanings. A coalition between Labour and the Green Party, the latter co-led by Helen and Steve's close friend Russel Norman, looked like a genuine possibility. Helen thought she could achieve more for workers by continuing to lead the CTU during a 'red-green' administration than she could as an MP.

Meanwhile, she was involved in the machinations behind Labour's manifesto for workers and unions. The idea of industry standard agreements – based on her draft legislation – had been adopted as party policy in 2011 and endorsed at annual conferences since. Cunliffe had embraced the policy, along with a commitment to the living wage for workers in the core public service, an end to National's 90-day fire-at-will law and an increase in the minimum wage to $15 an hour.[35]

However, industry standard agreements remained controversial, even among unionists. Some thought the proposal was far too complicated and convoluted. The former national secretary of the EPMU, Andrew Little, was Labour's industrial relations spokesman. Little had come into Parliament on the Labour list three years before. He wanted to water down the policy and push out the timetable for implementation if Labour were elected. 'My concern was … that putting this on the table as the first step was too big a chunk to bite off, and that we should start with simple processes to rebuild collective bargaining and the culture of collective bargaining before we moved to something more elaborate,' he would recall.[36]

Along with the Service and Food Workers Union's John Ryall and others on Labour's affiliates council, Helen was staunchly opposed to any dilution or delay of the policy. Recent European research on collective bargaining systems had only hardened her confidence that the industry standards model would lift wages, reduce inequality and redistribute power.[37] Little was worried about getting too far ahead of public understanding, given that a generation of workers had grown up with scant idea of unions or collective bargaining, but for Helen the fact that collective bargaining hadn't rebuilt and wages hadn't recovered since the Employment Contracts Act lay at the very heart of the case for urgent reform.

Low pay was baked into the New Zealand economy: the 2008 Global Financial Crisis and its long aftermath had reinforced that. Wages were stagnant – average pay was only 1.3 percent higher than in mid 2009 and for years had failed to rise in line even with New Zealand's lacklustre productivity growth. The share of the nation's income going to workers through wages and salaries was now one of the lowest of OECD countries – not least because New Zealand had among the weakest employment protection laws and one of the lowest levels of collective bargaining.[38] For those who did have the privilege of collective bargaining – a mere nine percent of private sector workers – pay rises were far more likely than for those who didn't.[39]

In 2014, New Zealand was billed as a 'rock star economy' because of its relatively strong growth. But if the epithet was true for dairy farmers and property owners, it was untrue for a great many families.[40] Once one of the most egalitarian countries, New Zealand was now among the most unequal in the developed world. The top one percent owned three times as much as the poorest 50 percent. Some 740,000 people were below the poverty line, many of them children and a disproportionate number Māori and Pasifika.[41]

The neoliberal promise that wealth would 'trickle down' from the rich to the poor had proved a fairy tale; the rich got richer while the poor worked harder to stand still.[42] Given that the vast majority of families relied on wages and salaries, lifting workers' pay was critical to New Zealand fixing its crisis of inequality and poverty.

Helen wasn't on the Labour Party affiliates council – effectively its industrial relations policy committee – but she was in the thick of the battle to keep the policy on industry standard agreements intact. Relations were tense as the election and the deadline for releasing policies drew closer. At one meeting she told Little that while she was a member of the Labour Party she was not beholden to it, and would go out and campaign against him if his attitude didn't shift.[43]

In the end, disagreements were plastered over and wording fudged. A policy was released stating that Labour was committed to industry standard agreements as a way of setting reasonable minimum pay and conditions; a commission of inquiry would be set up to figure out how to do this.[44]

The election on September 20, 2014 rendered it moot. Labour was thumped, achieving only 25 percent of the vote. The John Key-led National Party was voted back for a third term, unharmed by revelations that the prime minister's office had been associated with a campaign of dirty politics.[45] National entered into coalition with Act, United Future and the Māori Party.

Labour's heavy loss triggered the third leadership change in as many years. Andrew Little narrowly defeated Grant Robertson to take over from Cunliffe. Behind the scenes – as president of the CTU she couldn't publicly express a preference – Helen strongly supported Robertson's tilt. Privately, she fumed at the selection of Little.

The first law passed after the election was National's long-planned industrial relations reform. It went in the very opposite direction to the idea of industry standard agreements. The Employment Relations Amendment Bill had been introduced in early 2013, but National had been unable to muster the numbers to pass it. The election solved that, and the Bill went through with the backing of United Future and Act.

It was dubbed the tea-break law because it took away workers' mandatory right to two ten-minute breaks and a half-hour lunch. It also threw a raft of obstacles in the way of collective bargaining: employers could now walk away from negotiations without settling, and could refuse to participate in multi-employer bargaining. It made it easier for employers to hire new workers on lower pay and conditions by scrapping the requirement for them to be covered for the first 30 days by any applicable collective agreement.[46]

Another key element was a rollback of protections for the likes of cleaners, orderlies, cafeteria and laundry workers employed by companies that operated under contract. These protections had been introduced in 2004 and ensured that such workers – mostly women, mostly low-paid – could keep their jobs and transfer on their existing pay and conditions to the new employer if the contract changed. It had been a major breakthrough when introduced; the struggle to prevent workers' wages from being undermined by contractors scrapping for work went back decades. It was the same battle Pat Kelly had fought alongside striking Waiouru army cleaners in 1979. The 2004 provision had taken wages out of the mix when contractors were bidding for work, thus helping to protect jobs and incomes.[47] The Key administration was now screwing back these protections by exempting contractors with fewer than 20 workers.

Combined, the package was a lurch back towards the industrial relations code of the 1990s.[48] Even Treasury acknowledged it would 'shift the balance of power in the employers' favour'.[49] It was sold on the hoary notions of 'flexibility', 'choice' and a 'level playing field', yet even the powerful organisations that had lauded the Employment Contracts Act and championed the neoliberal theory that defined modern New Zealand – the International Monetary Fund, the OECD – had been forced by the Global Financial Crisis into a rethink. They now recognised that inequality was bad for social stability and even for economic growth. They were publishing papers arguing for strengthened collective bargaining – and therefore improved wages – as part of the solution.[50]

The CTU had expended an enormous amount of energy campaigning and submitting against National's changes, but had failed to make a dent. Although the issues were central to workers' pay packets, they came across in the media as complex and arcane.

Helen tended to hack through the jargon with sharp furious sound bites: the changes were driven by 'true blue worker hate'; '[they are] the most serious attack on the rights of working people to a fair go since 1991'; 'they're bad for us and they aim to humiliate us'. On the eve of the changes coming into effect, she scolded with the moral outrage of a teacher berating a schoolyard bully: 'The government should be ashamed of itself. They do not care about New Zealand workers and they are determined to drive wages down in this country, and removing their tea break and their lunch break is an absolute attack on every working person in this country.'[51]

She had also gone global. After the legislation was introduced into Parliament she took the microphone at the International Labour Organisation's conference in Geneva – the annual gathering of hundreds of worker, employer and government representatives from 187 countries – and condemned the performance of New Zealand, which at the time was seeking a position on the UN Security Council.

'New Zealand has a habit of turning up to international forums pretending to be the good guy. It likes to portray an image that it can no longer sustain, of an egalitarian society where everyone gets a fair go, of a liberal social agenda with strong social dialogue, and of a modern international outlook which respects and actively supports the international institutions and in particular the United Nations. … [I]n the last two decades, within this group of countries we have gone from being one of the most equal to becoming one of the most unequal. A recent OECD report notes that New Zealand's inequality is increasing faster than any other OECD country. It lays significant fault for that shameful fact on the great inequality in wages and salaries.'[52]

She told the forum the government was intent on employment law changes that its own advisers said were in breach of New Zealand's legal obligations under ILO conventions. '[I]t is not good enough to pick and choose which international obligations a country will comply with.'

Departmental advice on the changes had indeed envisaged a complaint to the ILO, although it was thought the changes were not 'significant enough to damage our international reputation'.[53] It was never put to the test. The CTU started working on a formal complaint but decided it wouldn't achieve anything; it would be better to work for change through the ballot box.

Notwithstanding that decision, Helen placed huge store on the ILO as the global meeting place of labour, capital and governments, a tripartite parliament whose founding mission was decent work and social justice. She had been an elected member of the workers' group of the ILO Governing Body since 2011, and represented New Zealand workers at its annual conference, where minimum global labour standards were agreed and allegations of labour abuses heard.[54]

Despite the ILO's dense bureaucracy and slow pace, she saw it as an essential lever for change. For workers in some countries, ILO standards were the only line of defence against slavery and child labour, and its complaints process the only means of calling to account governments that used to violence and intimidation to suppress workers' rights.

She had grown up immersed in international labour struggles; Pat was no less passionate about the conditions for Chilean workers under the brutal Pinochet regime than for New Zealand workers struggling under Muldoon's wage freeze. Likewise for Helen the plight of Charles Finlay and Eramiha Pairama – killed in the course of producing commodity logs for export – was on a continuum with Bangladeshi clothing workers killed in death-trap buildings while making cheap T-shirts for the world.[55] All were casualties of complex and unaccountable global supply chains.

Trade unions everywhere were grappling with the huge increase in precarious and informal work, erosions of collective bargaining, austerity programmes that corroded social welfare and public services, and the urgent need to forge a 'just transition' from jobs in old carbon-intensive industries to new low-carbon jobs. The challenges were profound and wickedly complex: 'How do you deal with the changing nature of work? How do you deal with global capital? What kind of tactics work in a world where you are dealing with multinational employers and not domestic employers,' said Sarah Fox, an American trade unionist who served alongside Helen on the workers' group of the ILO Governing Body.[56]

In the search for strategies and innovation, Helen was regarded as a 'bright light' in the global labour movement, Fox said. 'She was so smart and thoughtful and focused. I think people immediately saw her as the real thing.'

The process of developing new global rules was glacial – it took years to get new proposals on to the ILO agenda and negotiate towards tripartite consensus. Helen was sometimes in a lead role as the workers' spokesperson on committees negotiating a new standard or recommendation. It was a difficult task – communicating through translators with worker delegates from around the world, navigating political undercurrents between conservative and radical unionists, maintaining unity.

'Every day you caucus with your group and talk about what points you will try to achieve. … the worker spokesperson carries the water and is on her feet negotiating,' said Fox. 'It's very easy to get people in your group mad at you. But Helen was very good at making people feel listened to. There's a great skill in that. You're in a giant room full of people, most of whom you don't know. It's knowing when you should push for something and how far, knowing when you should compromise, knowing when you should take a deal because it's a good deal, knowing how to make the arguments for your position in a way that's persuasive.'

The New Zealand delegation to ILO annual conferences comprised union, employer and government representatives. They all stayed at a hotel in Ferney-Voltaire, a small French town just over the Swiss border where it was much cheaper than Geneva. Phil O'Reilly, the chief executive of Business New Zealand, often took spokesperson roles for the employers in negotiations, sometimes across the table from Helen. 'She was the most remarkable negotiator I have ever worked with in those environments. She was sharp, she was critical, she ran her side really well. She took the piss out of the opposition if she thought it deserved it. … She listened hard in order to find a point of disagreement or agreement to take it forward.'[57]

Negotiations often ran until the small hours of the morning. The New Zealanders would then climb into a shared rental car and drive back over the border. 'She hated my driving. [It was] too aggressive for her, so sometimes I'd let her drive,' O'Reilly said. The car journeys were a chance to debrief about the day – what had gone well, what had gone badly. 'We were taking global leadership roles. We took it very seriously.'

Team New Zealand occasionally had downtime to enjoy French village life. With a few hours to kill before flying out one Saturday morning, Helen and Paul Mackay, a member of the Business New Zealand delegation, took a stroll around a local market and paused to sample fresh oysters and champagne from a stallholder. The two had a good relationship, but it wouldn't do to look too comfortable and chummy. 'We agreed we wouldn't tell anyone at home that we were (a) having champagne and oysters and (b) doing it together,' remembered Mackay.

As it turned out, they ended up in the midst of a health and safety incident. The oysters were being shucked by the son of the stall owner, using a large screwdriver. He slipped and drove the tool deep into his palm. When his mother told him to put a hankerchief over the bleeding hole in his hand and keep serving customers, the New Zealanders insisted he get medical attention. Eventually the mother relented and Helen, an inveterate fixer and rescuer, marched her and her son to a doctor's surgery over the road, went inside with them and made sure they were signed in.[58]

But there were limits to the bipartisan collaboration. A bitter conflict blew up at the ILO conference in 2012 when the normal process of hearing human rights abuses committed by governments was aborted. Under the rules, the worker and employer groups would agree each year on a list of 25 cases to be heard. This time the process was brought to a halt over whether the right to strike was protected by ILO convention 87 on freedom of association and the right to organise. The employers said it wasn't; the workers said it was and had been recognised as such for decades. The employers' group then refused to include on the list any complaints relating to the right to strike. The workers' group rejected the restriction and things came to a standstill.

The upshot was that workers who had travelled from around the world with stories of violence and oppression were denied a hearing. There was widespread fury on the workers' side. To O'Reilly's chagrin, Helen wrote to each of his members throwing shame on Business New Zealand for playing a 'leading role' in an employer campaign that had resulted in the hearings being cancelled. 'The impact is devastating, especially for those brave workers that had travelled to Geneva from countries such as Guatemala (where ten union members have been murdered this year), Colombia (29 killed) and from Venezuela where there have been reports of abuses against employers,' she wrote. 'They have been left to return home exposed … In our region, the arrests of union officials and removal of work rights in Fiji was one of the cases to be heard.'[59]

Helen was re-elected in 2014 for another three-year term on the workers' group of the Governing Body. Her close friend and mentor on the international stage was Sharan Burrow, an Australian who had come up through the teacher unions to lead the Australian Council of Trade Unions, and since 2010 had been the general secretary of the International Trade Union Confederation (ITUC) – the world's largest trade union federation.

The two worked closely on global strategies, including an ITUC-led campaign using the leverage of the 2022 FIFA World Cup in Qatar to pressure the Gulf state to end its 'kafala' system of enslaving migrant workers. New tournament venues to the tune of $140 billion would be built on the backs of guest workers who were tied to a single employer, had their passports confiscated and were unable to leave the country without an exit visa signed by the boss, who routinely had wages withheld. The workers were denied the right to strike or unionise. They worked enormous hours in extreme heat, were consigned to squalid and overcrowded labour camps, barred by apartheid-like rules from public places, and died in their hundreds on building sites and other workplaces while corporations and foreign governments looked the other way.[60]

Burrow had promoted Helen's rise through the ILO and the two women had a tight and trusting relationship. 'She and I shared so many conversations about what was wrong in the world and with the [labour] movement, and where we could intervene. Because you can't do everything … We both believed in the ripple effect: if you took these actions, would it provide a broader momentum?' Burrow said. 'Helen was never constrained by dominant or historical practice. She always had her own creative thought, so you could run ideas past her, or tap her for ideas which were always left field and came at a problem in a different way.'[61]

Burrows hoped Helen would become the chair of the workers' group on the Governing Body, a position that would cast her as the strategic leader for global workers at the organisation, their primary negotiator and one of a core ILO governance group. 'It's a role she would have been well cut out for. But really I think at that point in her union career she could have done anything.'[62]

At 50, Helen was coming into her prime. There was a fork in the road ahead: a seat in Parliament for Labour or a position of global leadership for workers? She had already delayed the former, and while a bigger international role had appeal it wasn't something she would take on while Cath – by then aged 88 – needed looking after.

As it was, her ILO duties demanded three annual trips to Geneva and six weeks away from home every year. It was a punishing schedule of long-haul travel (she ended up with deep vein thrombosis on one trip), lengthy and often frustrating days in negotiating rooms, and late-night Skype sessions with New Zealand to keep on top of multiple campaigns. However, the work brought her immense intellectual satisfaction, as well as the chance to forge strong links across the global union movement.

There was the bonus, too, of sometimes tacking on a few extra days to visit Pat's family in Wigan and catch up with members of the Eichelbaum diaspora, including cousins she had holidayed with for years at Rangataua who were now living in the UK. On her trip to the ILO's mid-year conference in 2014 she met with Elisabeth Kahn, a German relative who had extensively researched the Eichelbaum family and its losses in the Holocaust.

Together, the two women went on a pilgrimage to find the grave of Sophie, the grandmother of Thomas Eichelbaum, Cath's cousin who in 1938 had fled to New Zealand with his parents. Sophie had died in 1943 in a Berlin detention centre. She had been sent there to await transportation to a death camp. In the large Weissensee Cemetery Helen and Elizabeth cut through weeds to find her unmarked grave. Later they visited the building in which Sophie had suffered her last days.

Helen wrote afterwards to Sir Thomas – by then a retired Chief Justice of New Zealand – with her typical blend of empathy and crisp practicality. 'Dearest Tom, I have been to Berlin and found Sophie's grave. It is hard to know how much you want to see and know, but I feel the need to describe my trip to you and leave it to you to decide what you want to read. It was an emotional visit and I felt the grief of our family everywhere.

'In regards to the grave site, it is this huge graveyard as you probably know and very overgrown in most parts. We took gardening tools and slashed our way in, which is what people do. The graves [are] relatively easy to find when you are with a German speaker! ... I am unsure if I am the first to visit it since she was buried there but it was nice to be there and "find her".

'It must have been so hard on you all to have left her in Berlin and I can't imagine what you all went through. The grave is unmarked and I have some information for you in case you want to put a stone on it.'[63]

A gravestone for Sophie was later erected by the family and with Elisabeth Kahn's help a stolperstein (stumbling stone) was laid.[64]

The year drew to a close with a mixture of sadness, outrage, frustration and vindication. Peter Conway had not recovered his health by the time of his retirement. The end of his long career of service was marked by the CTU's National Affiliates Council at its December meeting with a solemn message of 'heartfelt thanks, support and solidarity'.[65] Sam Huggard from FIRST Union was elected to take on the role of secretary and work alongside Helen.

The Pike River disaster continued to produce fresh betrayals for the families. A government-funded project to re-enter the mine's 2.3-kilometre tunnel to search for forensic evidence and bodies – a task in the hands of the mine's new owner Solid Energy – had been abandoned. The state-owned enterprise was under new managers and directors and in a parlous financial state. The risks, it said, couldn't be managed.[66] The families, who had been assured for months that the project was proceeding well, were given the news a few days before the fourth anniversary of the tragedy.

Helen's team of legal volunteers was continuing to work towards the judicial review of the dismissal of the Whittall charges. This now seemed even more urgent and necessary. Helen turned over every stone in search of other avenues to accountability: keeping in touch with the families, whose own mining experts said that re-entry could and should be done; demanding the police and WorkSafe take back responsibility for re-entry and berating the 'privatisation' of the task to Solid Energy; complaining to the Independent Police Complaints Authority that the police had walked away from their responsibility to investigate the disaster.[67] The complaint was dismissed.[68]

On the forestry front, hopes of adding the 2012 deaths of David McMurtrie and George Mahanga to the suite of private prosecutions were dashed by the District Court, which ruled that too much time had elapsed. On the same day, the Independent Forestry Safety Review released the report of its nine-month investigation. It was a sweeping endorsement of the campaign to bring the scandal of death and injury in the sector to light. The report descibed an industry with a 'blame culture and a weak safety culture'. It depicted a widespread attitude of contempt towards workers: 'All too often the [panel] has been told about the challenges of dealing with a "bottom of the barrel" workforce. A significant portion of the industry continues to view its workers from this perspective and consequently absolve itself of its responsibilities to do better. ... It is damaging and demeaning.'

The report confirmed the campaign's stories of inadequate training and supervision, and of workers who put in huge hours to meet production targets with little respite from the weather. It spoke of worksites without toilets, drinking water, handwashing facilities or shelter. It found that worker participation in health and safety was rare. It recommended a 'forestry leadership action group' made up of industry, workers and government, proper codes of practice and regulations, decent training, and better procedures for investigations.[69]

It looked as if change would come. Indeed, two years of incessant pressure and publicity had already made a difference; early in the new year the head of WorkSafe remarked on a milestone – 12 months had passed without a single forestry worker being killed.[70] The campaign had undoubtedly saved lives, but news of one good year begged a bitter question: if the industry could get through the last 12 months without death, surely that proved the deaths that had gone before – of Ken, Charles, Eramiha, Shane, David, Lincoln, and so many others – were entirely avoidable?

Helen and Steve headed off in the New Year of 2015 for another Great Walk, this time Lake Waikaremoana with seven of their tramping buddies. Helen was feeling generally fit, despite a lingering cough – a hangover from a bug that had gone through the office – and a sore back, for which she had been seeing a physiotherapist for months. She was conscious of the risk of osteoporosis, which Cath suffered from, and tried to keep up regular walks. She had taken up Pilates to build strength and swam when her crowded diary allowed it.

The tramp was – as she put it – 'beaut', with fabulous weather and views, good huts and the company of old friends.

In late January her cousin Ben Patrick came out from London with his wife Helen and baby Atticus. They had discovered the old family bach at Rangataua – long since sold – was available for rent, and the two families spent Waitangi weekend visiting their favourite childhood swimming spots and going up the mountain. The bach was much as it had been, although more comfortable. On the shelves were the assorted glasses they had drunk from as children, and on the sofa were Cath's cushions, albeit freshly upholstered. The new owners had also tidied up Pat's dodgy home handiwork, including a bay window that he and his mates had installed and which always leaked.

Both trips away were opportunities to recharge ahead of the relentless work ahead: preparing for the suite of court cases; building new campaigns (farming was now firmly in Helen's sights) and defending existing gains; leaning against the power of capital and the complacency of the state to advance decent pay, dignity at work and the right to come home safe at the end of the day.

13. Fight to the last

The market left uncontrolled is destroying families and will destroy the very earth we rely on to survive. We need a new way of living, a new leadership and a sharp change in the incentives to do the right thing.
Helen Kelly, 2015

A few days after the trip to Rangataua, Helen woke in the night with severe pain around her chest and lower ribs. She thought it might be a heart attack, and spent some time googling symptoms before she and Steve decided it was serious enough for them to go to the hospital.

They sat for a long time in the emergency department. An X-ray was taken. An on-duty registrar noted something of concern on her lungs. She was shifted to a medical assessment ward.

As morning came, she sent word through to the office that she wasn't well and wouldn't make it to various meetings. There was to be a farewell that afternoon for Georgie McLeod, who was leaving after several years as the CTU's communications adviser. Huia Welton, McLeod's replacement, sent a text to Helen to find out if she would be in for that. No, she replied. 'Too sick sadly!' Business New Zealand 'tried to poison me' at a function the previous night, she cracked.[1]

'No, not really,' she went on, oscillating between flippancy and gravity. 'Didn't go to party. … Have something on my lungs. Could be anything.

Lump.' She assured Welton she was fine. 'Steve looking after me and the whole ward is union so it's all good. ... Honestly it could be a scar from flu or somethin.'

'Is there anything you need?' Welton asked. 'Affco settled,' she flicked back. It wasn't an unreasonable wish, given the interminable struggle at the Talley's-owned Affco meat plants, where unionised workers had been trying to settle their expired collective pay agreement for 15 months.

At some point in the blurred hours of tests and waiting and listening, she and Steve were ushered into a room with two young doctors and told: 'This is lung cancer.'

It was impossible to absorb the news. 'I think both of us thought, "This can't be right. We'll get through this. It's just not plausible,"' remembered Steve.[2]

It was February 18. They went home to Shannon Street that night in a state of dazed shock. Ben Patrick and the family had just come back to Wellington and were at the house, unaware of any trouble. Helen Kinsella, Helen's lifelong friend from their days at Hataitai School and Wellington High, was waiting. When Helen and Steve walked in, the two women fell into each other's arms and held a long embrace.

There were more tests over the following days to confirm the diagnosis: stage four non-small cell lung cancer. There was no cure.

She had never been a smoker and it was impossible to avoid pondering possible causes. The weeks travelling in Europe with Chris immediately after the Chernobyl disaster? The car trips in a haze of Pat's roll-you-own smoke? Pumping petrol as a teenager at the Tinakori Road service station? She settled instead on the idea that it was mostly 'genes and bad luck.'[3] The critical tasks were to build knowledge of the disease, open up channels of information and advice, assess options, organise a strategy.

Word leaked out and messages of goodwill trickled in: from friend and former prime minister Helen Clark, from unionists, from old friends and colleagues, from cousins around the world. Her replies were sometimes bright and grateful, sometimes crisply realistic. 'Thanks darling cousins, I am hoping I will be fine,' she wrote to Andrew Dart. 'Basically they can't cure it,' she wrote to Tim Braithwaite.

She was supposed to be flying to Geneva for the ILO. That trip was now off. As she waited for more tests and a prognosis she carried on with work, including receiving and analysing a decision from the High Court relating to the upcoming Pike River judicial review. The legal team had tried for months to get access to the full file of documents relevant to the decision to let Peter Whittall off his health and safety charges.[4] The lawyers had managed to obtain much of the key documentation, but now the High Court had ruled they were barred by legal privilege from getting the notes of meetings and phone calls between the Crown prosecutor and Whittall's lawyer in the months leading up to the deal to discharge the mine boss on payment of $3.41 million to the victims.[5]

Helen knocked out a blog: 'MBIE is fighting hard to maintain the secrecy of the deal that saw the Crown accept money in exchange for a criminal discharge for one of this countries [*sic*] worst cases of health and safety failures,' she wrote in *The Standard*. 'The big point about yesterday's [February 24, 2015] decision is the State continues to fight all the way against the demand for justice for these families.'

There was an addendum: the latest development in the year-long struggle to obtain the documents on which Judge Jane Farish had made the decision to dismiss the Whittall charges was that parts of the District Court file had been lost.[6]

The news of Helen's diagnosis went public on February 26. She struck an upbeat note: rumours of her demise had been 'exaggerated,' she said. 'I am looking after myself and feel remarkably well all things considered.'[7]

The flow of messages from close contacts now became a steady torrent from far and wide. They came from people she knew, people she had crossed paths with in the past, and people she had never met. Almost all carried words of admiration and respect for her strong advocacy for workers' rights. She even got emails from the odd farmer, congratulating her for her ongoing social media war on poor pay, long hours, death and injury on New Zealand farms.

There was an exception from the mood of goodwill. A man calling himself Philip and claiming to be an 'unelected representative of the NZ film industry' emailed to say he hoped she would suffer a 'long and painful death. You put my family's livelihood at stake during the [*Hobbit*] … We didn't ask for your meddling. Everyone in the film industry hated you and most probably cursed you and your lungs.'[8]

Helen insisted the message not be responded to. 'Honestly, I get a few and it's water off a duck's back,' she assured her colleagues at the CTU.

She was feeling well, but it seemed each new test produced worse news. The disease had spread to her spine and pelvis. There were hopes her cancer might have a specific genetic mutation that would allow targeted treatment, but this turned out not to be the case. Standard chemotherapy was the first line of attack.[9]

She was having coffee one morning with Suzanne McNabb, a friend and colleague from her days leading the Association of University Staff, when McNabb observed that she looked dreadful. Stubborn as ever, Helen reckoned she was fine and had a dentist appointment to get to. McNabb put her foot down. She demanded Helen's car keys, ordered her into the vehicle, drove – fast – to the hospital emergency department, threw open the doors and said, 'You need to get this woman help!' Helen passed out. When she came to she was surrounded by doctors. After first thinking it was a blood clot, they diagnosed pericardial effusion – a build-up of fluid around the heart. The condition had developed as a complication of the cancer. The doctors drained two litres from the sac around her heart. Dylan later said to McNabb of her action, which likely saved Helen's life: 'Suzanne, thanks so much for standing up to Mum.'[10]

'I survived,' Helen assured friends and colleagues in an email a few days later. 'I'm good and feeling positive again and in good health.'[11]

She had been told by a specialist that her life expectancy could be a few weeks. The heart incident had brought the proximity of death into sharp relief, and with that came a major worry: what about the two private forestry prosecutions? She was named as the prosecutor, a decision that had been taken to protect the families of Charles Finlay and Eramiha Pairama from the risk of court costs. If she died before the cases got to court, the litigation would die with her. She kept these fears quiet; she didn't want the employers – who had pleaded not guilty – to be alerted to this possibility.

She was well enough to fly with Steve to Auckland for the unveiling of a memorial plaque for Charanpreet Dhaliwal. It was three and a half years since the young man's savage murder. There had been no justice for his family and Helen had refused to let his case be forgotten. The memorial ceremony was an assertion of the dignity of Dhaliwal's life and labour. Still to come, in a few months time, would be a full coronial inquest, at which the CTU would represent his mother and brother.

Within a few weeks of her diagnosis Helen decided she would have to stand down as CTU president at the biennial conference in October. All going well she would be able to perform in the job until then.

She and Steve made another monumental decision: they would get married. Father Gerard Burns, a prominent voice for social justice in Wellington who had spoken at the CTU's Fairness at Work rallies, officiated at a small private gathering at Shannon Street.

In early May they threw a wedding party with 450 family and friends at Helen's old stomping ground, Wellington Teachers' College. Max was there, as was Cath – frail and struggling to come to terms with Helen's diagnosis. Forestry families, Pike River families, meat workers, unionists, extended family, lawyers, politicians, old friends from primary school, high school and college, cousins and lifelong friends of Shannon Street attended. Don Swan led the catering effort. A collective of friends made salads by the ten-kilogram lot. Mates baked cakes, did the flowers and smoked trout. Alby White, Helen's Clyde Quay School friend who had lived for a time at Shannon Street and was now a Sydney hairdresser, did Helen's hair and make-up. The Wedding Band was put together by musician unionists, with Dylan joining them on guitar and vocals. Everyone danced.

Helen called it 'a small gathering of very, very close friends'. It was an emotional, joyous affirmation of her standing within the union movement and as a leader of the left, and of her and Steve's close and committed partnership. Dave Morgan, her 'second father' was master of ceremonies, as he had been when she and Chris married in 1988. She observed that she would need Morgan to remain available for further work: 'Two weddings and a funeral.'[12]

She was dying and everyone knew it. If she was worried, the black humour deflected it. There were so many battles still to be fought, so many injustices to be put right. Her instinct was to press her mortality into service as an organising tool. She told her friend Ged Kearney, president of the Australian Council of Trade Unions, 'I'm really fucked, Ged.'

'She said, "I'm gonna die, the disease is everywhere, it's really bad. …

It's all right, I'm not scared. But I'm going to do something good with it. I'm going to really use it." She said, "I'm not sad for me, I'm sad for my boys.'"[13]

She was approaching her fourth round of chemotherapy when the time came to assemble in the Wellington High Court to hear the legal submissions in relation to the judicial review of the dismissal of charges against Peter Whittall. The treatments tended to knock her back for a couple of days and cause fatigue, but otherwise she was tolerating them well. She joked about chemo that she was 'made for it', given that she felt so good. She still had a full head of hair, and no need yet for the knitted beanies that people had kindly donated.[14]

The court hearing was set down for May 25 and 26. It was 17 months since the day Helen had barged into Peter Cranney's office declaring that something must be done about the shock decision to let Whittall walk away. Nigel Hampton QC and Simon Meikle presented the arguments on behalf of the two applicants, Sonya Rockhouse and Anna Osborne. The challenge was fundamental – to convince Justice Brendan Brown that the decision of District Court Judge Jane Farish on December 12, 2013 to dismiss the charges was unlawful, and that MBIE's decision not to call evidence in support of the charges was also unlawful.

Even without access to all of the communications between Whittall's lawyer, Stuart Grieve QC, and the Crown prosecutor, Brent Stanaway, the available documents left no doubt that months of negotiation had gone on prior to the decision. The sequence of communication showed that what began in July 2013 as an attempt by MBIE to plea bargain – with the expectation that Whittall would plead guilty to some charges – had degenerated into a deal in which Whittall steadfastly maintained his innocence and $3.41 million in insurance money would be paid to the Pike River victims on condition that MBIE did not proceed with any of the charges.[15]

The documents made clear that Grieve would put up an aggressive defence if the charges went ahead, including a focus on the role of the Department of Labour during the life of the mine, and its successor MBIE in the handling of evidence. Grieve had pushed for an arrangement of which the 'essential feature' was the dropping of all 12 charges against

Whittall. Stanaway had hoped for a guilty plea on at least one charge and a statement of regret or apology from Whittall, but in the end even that scrap of accountability was absent.[16] The families would be paid the $3.41 million they were already owed in court-ordered reparations, *if* all the Whittall charges were dropped.[17]

The central argument of the legal team was that this amounted to a payment to stifle a prosecution and was therefore unlawful. MBIE was the only agency with the power to bring the health and safety charges, but it had 'lost its way' in agreeing to a deal that sent a message that access to money was a way for a defendant to avoid a prosecution.[18]

Justice Brown reserved his decision. Nothing more could be done on this front in the meantime. But at the very moment the legal arguments were being heard – arguments central to the pursuit of justice for the victims of the worst health and safety disaster in almost a century – news broke that the Key government was going to substantially water down the Health and Safety Reform Bill.

The Pike River disaster had triggered the reform effort; the Royal Commission on the mine tragedy and the Independent Taskforce on Workplace Health and Safety had laid bare the appalling weaknesses of the existing regime. There was broad consensus across the political spectrum that the Pike tragedy should lead to urgent and far-reaching reform. New Zealand's record of workplace death was twice as bad as Australia's and four to six times worse than the UK's.

The recommendations of the taskforce had been put forward as an integrated package, with a warning to lawmakers against cherry-picking. Of utmost importance was that the new system include robust worker participation and empowerment. This was the crucial third leg of a stool that included a strong regulator and capable employers. At Pike, all three legs of the stool had failed. Yet now the government was hacking into that third leg of the reform.

It beggared belief. The CTU had worked closely on the Bill with key business groups Business New Zealand and the Business Leaders' Health and Safety Forum. There had been broad agreement on its thrust. Each of the parties had quibbles, but all recognised that a step change was needed in the way the country managed and regulated worker health and safety. The business groups had agreed that worker participation was essential – the forum had even written to Cabinet ministers to reassure them its members supported this.[19]

However, lobbying by small business and farming interests had kicked in and some backbenchers were rebelling. Former ACC minister Judith Collins complained about the prospect of 'red tape'.[20] John Key talked about the need to balance 'safety' with 'workability'. Under the original Bill workers would have had the right to request health and safety representatives, and these representatives would have enhanced powers. It was now becoming clear that the government planned to carve out businesses with fewer than 20 workers from that requirement, unless they were in an industry classed as 'high risk'.[21] Not only was this a serious departure from the taskforce's recommendations, it would make the new law weaker than the existing one in terms of worker participation.[22]

In the midst of these revelations, Helen emailed a health update to friends and colleagues. The chemotherapy had caused some shrinkage of her tumours 'which is good because the bloody government is trying to gut the new health and safety bill. We are working hard to try and push back. … So far I think we are winning in public at least. It is incredible that they think this is ok.'[23]

The Bill was to be reported back from the select committee in two months. With an intensive campaign there was still a chance to pressure the government to reinstate the original Bill, Helen told affiliates.[24] Political lobbying got underway, including of Māori Party MPs, whose constituents were suffering disproportionately from New Zealand's failed health and safety regime and were heavily represented in the most dangerous industries.

Helen had an army of impassioned advocates – the grieving forestry and Pike families she had worked so closely with – whom she could call on to lend authenticity to the campaign. Plans were made for 291 wooden crosses, one for every workplace death in the previous five years, to be taken around the country in a series of set-piece vigils attended by widows and mothers, like Deborah McMillan and Sonya Rockhouse, whose husbands and sons had been killed at work.

She put Tony Sutorius to work on a short film harnessing the stories and images of workers killed in small businesses. Firms of the size collectively employed a third of the workforce but were to be exempted from a key part of the reform. The video led with the voice of Linda Sewell, the English mother of 19-year-old Tom Sewell, an intelligent, strapping young man who had come to New Zealand for a few weeks to watch the All Blacks play.

Sewell had got a casual job on a Katikati kiwifruit orchard alongside some friends from school. He was due to begin studying war history at Kent University the following autumn. Instead he was killed in a quad bike crash on his first day at the orchard. There was no supervision or training in the use of the vehicle. It was in an unlocked shed with the keys in the ignition. There was no crash helmet and the roll bars had been removed. When Sewell was driving the vehicle he overcorrected and hit a tree, suffering a traumatic brain injury. He returned home to the UK in a coffin.[25] There was no prosecution. Instead, blame was pushed back on to the young student for driving the vehicle 'without permission'.[26]

True to form, when Helen had heard about Tom's death she'd made contact with Linda and Ken Sewell and taken the time to visit them at their home in Surrey in 2013. They had kept in regular contact. Helen became a friend and supporter of their relentless calls for tighter regulations on the use of quad bikes, which had killed six people in the year of Tom's death.[27] Their son Tom's story had hardened her drive to subject the farming industry to the same blowtorch of scrutiny and grassroots organising as she had forestry.[28]

The campaign to stop the weakening of the health and safety Bill generated political heat and media attention, but not enough to change the government's mind. What should have been a story of crucial, consensus-based change descended into a farce when it released the list of industries considered 'high risk' (and therefore bound by the requirements for worker participation). Beef, dairy and sheep farming weren't on it, but worm-farming and mini-golf were.[29]

The CTU staffers and affiliates who campaigned furiously against the dilution of the health and safety reform did so under the weight of terrible grief. On June 9, Peter Conway died. For 15 months he had endured a black world of severe depression. He had now taken his own life. The news of his suicide was shattering.

Wellington's Wesley Methodist Church was overflowing with mourners at his funeral a week later. Friends, family, union comrades, politicians, business leaders and public servants remembered an immensely productive, analytical and compassionate man, 'soft on people but hard on issues', whose contribution to social justice included years of involvement in international development work through Oxfam and UnionAID.[30] The hardest loss was felt by his wife Liz Riddiford and children Maddy, Sean and Rosa. They spoke of a devoted and loving soulmate and father, a man who lived a life of dignity, loyalty and ideals.

Conway was described as 'no ordinary man … an inspiration of how a life of service to humanity should be lived', a man whose 'overdeveloped sense of duty and pride in, and commitment to, maintain the highest standards had accumulated into a weight of responsibility that no human being could sustain'.[31]

Helen read *So Many Different Lengths of Time* by Liverpool poet Brian Patten: 'A man lives for as long as we carry him inside us, for as long as we carry the harvest of his dreams, for as long as we ourselves live, holding memories in common, a man lives.' She and everyone at the CTU grieved for 'more chances to work with [Conway], to hear his ideas and strategies and to feel his support, to fight alongside him and to share his friendship … We will miss him always.'[32]

Everyone at the CTU continued to come to the office each day. What else could they do? There, they could weep and talk and lean on each other, and draw strength to carry on the battle for workers to which Conway had devoted his life.

At the same time, Helen's own diagnosis continued to worsen. In July an MRI scan revealed tumours on her brain. She and Steve decided on private radiotherapy in Auckland, which meant staying there for a couple of weeks. She had been told the treatment could affect her balance and joked that it might turn her into a Tory. By now she was talking and corresponding with medical researchers in New Zealand and the US who were working in the emerging field of immunotherapy. A new drug, Keytruda, appeared to hold promise but wasn't funded through the public health system.

The extended stay in Auckland gave them the chance to spend more time with their close friends Katya Paquin and Russel Norman – by then executive director of Greenpeace Aotearoa – and their three young children. They could also lend more support to Helen's increasingly frail aunt and uncle, Margaret Dart and her husband Jim. Helen had been influenced by the writing of the American physician Atul Gawande; his 2014 book *Being Mortal* had helped her think more clearly about her terminal illness. It also helped open a new conversation with Margaret and Jim about what really mattered to them in their final years. She asked Jim one day if he might like a pet. He replied immediately that he wanted a cockatiel. She took him to get one, along with an elegant cage. The bird, named Pretty Boy George, or PBG, brought huge pleasure. Helen recruited a local schoolgirl to come and clean the cage each week.[33]

She and Steve hoped to spend most of August and September in Europe, touring and spending time with friends and relatives. The plan was for Dylan to be with them for part of the trip. It would be a chance to reacquaint him with Pat's extended family in Wigan.[34] But with the disease's rapid advance everything was up in the air.

'They say this cancer thing can be a series of let-downs, hope and disaster. I'm finding that out really,' she emailed in one of her now regular health updates. She was able to travel to Tauranga District Court to observe some of the proceedings in the prosecution of Puketi Logging, the employer of Eramiha Pairama. It was the first of the two private forestry prosecutions in her name and there had been a mammoth effort to get this far. 'Seeing it in court was one of the best days I've had in this job. Hx,' she wrote to the team of lawyers.[35]

The judge's decision was issued three weeks later. Puketi Logging was found guilty of failing to take all practicable steps to provide Pairama with a safe working environment. He was a young, relatively inexperienced worker, had been inadequately trained, and should not have been left alone and out of sight on a hot tiring day, doing the dangerous work he was doing when he was killed.[36]

The second prosecution, against Charles Finlay's employer M&A Cross, was also due to be heard but it didn't get that far: the employer pleaded guilty to one charge; the others were withdrawn.

Two out of two: it was a remarkable outcome. The Helen Kelly legal team had thrown shame on the state's health and safety regulator, which had looked at the circumstances of both men's deaths and declined to enforce the law. Both men had been blamed for their own deaths, but now – with no resources other than the commitment and generosity of the lawyers, the courage of the two families and Helen's boundless organising zeal – they had proved that Eramiha Pairama and Charles Finlay had been tragically failed by their employers.

Sentences and reparations were later imposed. In the case of Charles Finlay's employer M&A Cross, a $25,000 fine was ordered and $105,000 in reparations to Maryanne Butler-Finlay and the children. For Eramiha Pairama's employer, Puketi Logging, there was a $25,000 fine and $75,000 in reparations.

Pairama's mother Selina Eruera never received the $75,000 ordered by the court. Within a month of the sentencing, Puketi's owners had put the company into liquidation. Its assets had been disposed of and there was no money, although the owners' other company, Harper Logging, continued to operate.[37] Helen tried to pressure PF Olsen, the forest management company that had contracted Puketi, as well as its investors, to pay what was owed to the young man's family.[38] They declined.

Eruera, a part-time district nurse, was unable to afford a headstone for her son's grave. The union movement fundraised for her and the attendant publicity attracted an offer of a headstone from Francis Tipene of the TV show *Casketeers*, which she gratefully accepted.[39]

By early August, Helen was undergoing more radiotherapy on her hip and spine, and had received her first infusion of Keytruda. The chance it would be effective against her cancer was low, but it seemed the best available option and she and Steve were determined to try it. The cost was enormous and wasn't met by her health insurance; she would have to empty out her KiwiSaver and superannuation accounts to cover it.

She was still feeling fit and well most of the time. Her doctors gave the okay for the overseas trip. The chief complication would be finding a specialist to administer the next couple of doses of Keytruda while they were away.

The end of the northern summer was a glorious time to travel. The trip was everything she and Steve hoped for: time with cousins in San Francisco, an enormous family gathering in Wigan, time in London, Sussex and Nice with cousins on the Eichelbaum side, sightseeing in

Rome and Paris, and a trip to Brussels to stay with Sharan Burrow. After an anxious scramble she found a doctor, Mary O'Brien, to administer two rounds of Keytruda at Royal Marsden Hospital, travelling back from Paris by train for the second treatment.

She told friends back home that she was doing 'a little bit of work' while travelling. In fact she was incorrigible. She was keeping in close contact with the broiling dispute between the Meat Workers Union and Affco, which by September saw union workers at the Wairoa plant locked out. When she popped back to London for her Keytruda infusion, she met with Britain's Unite Union to shore up their support for the Affco workers. There was regular contact with the forestry families. She was in touch with the ongoing row over the health and safety reform legislation; from the other side of the world she tweeted that the CTU would seek a judicial review of the decision to class agriculture as 'low risk'. The CTU's in-house lawyer, Jeff Sissons, was on TV doing his first live appearance at the time the news came through. When the interviewer brought the tweet to his attention he had to keep a poker face and pretend it was all part of an agreed plan.[40]

Helen and Steve spent time in Burgundy with James Ritchie – previously the national secretary of the Dairy Workers Union, who was then with the International Union of Foodworkers – and his wife Jane Lawless and their 20-year-old daughter, Kate. Helen had an easy warm rapport with young people and had long been a mentor for Kate, who was distressed by her illness. The two spent time alone talking, and somehow Helen's acceptance that she was dying had a healing effect for Kate.

They cycled along the canals, picked wild blackberries, pottered around ancient villages, and tasted wine. Helen's gallows humour was flowing thick and fast. Presented with a bottle of red on a vineyard visit, she inquired of the pontificating vintner how many years until the wine would be good to drink. Five years, she was told. 'Well, that's no bloody good for me!' At Dijon, they paused at the statue of the 15th-century duke Philip the Good: 'I'll be known as Helen the Bloody Annoying,' she predicted.[41]

She and Steve were in Scotland when they marked her 51st birthday on September 19. They flew home to Shannon Street to find the garden in immaculate condition. A collective of friends had tended it in their absence.

There was nothing triumphant about Helen's last speech as the leader of the New Zealand union movement. When she stood before the CTU's biennial conference on October 14, 2015 she talked about the hard-fought incremental gains of the previous few years. More people who hadn't previously encountered the 'collective power of working people' now knew what unions were. The Living Wage Movement and the Kristine Bartlett equal pay case had reached into communities with the message of fair wages. New collectives had formed for migrant workers and Samoan workers. A powerful campaign had been led by Unite Union against egregious zero-hour contracts.

She reflected on the epic disputes with employers who wanted it all: the Ports of Auckland, which tried to sack everyone and contract out the work; the Talleys, one of the country's richest families, with whom the meat workers seemed to be in perpetual struggle. She called New Zealand a 'fishing village', where power and control rested with a few and dissenters were ridiculed and bullied. She talked of the actors who had sought to bargain their terms and conditions on *The Hobbit* and been punished by an angry crowd, an accusatory media and a government willing to use urgency to remove basic work rights.

She had taken to using the hashtag #itsbydesign, in her social media posts. It was shorthand for an economy she saw as stacked against those who lived by their labour. As she bowed out of the CTU role, she had no illusions about what the union movement was up against. 'We are working against the design of those who hold the wealth in this country and want more of it. … We have the ability to fight back, we have shown we can, and we must be sophisticated and disciplined about doing that.'[42]

By chance, Coroner Peter Ryan had signed off his report into the murder of Charanpreet Dhaliwal the day before her speech. This young non-union migrant worker and his faraway family had been given a voice by a union leader determined that the movement act for all workers. The coroner found that Dhaliwal had been let down by a lack of regulation; he was untrained and there had been no regular checks on his safety. The security industry needed to bring in a decent system of training, a code of practice and competent risk assessments.[43] It was a bitter irony that under the government's new health and safety law, security work was classed as 'low risk'.

It was only five years since the *Hobbit* dispute, when Peter Jackson had called Helen 'clueless' and cabinet minister Gerry Brownlee had accused her of lying. Now she was an appealing, widely recognised and terminally ill public figure and the Crown wanted to pin a badge to her lapel. In November 2015 a letter arrived from Government House offering her a Companion of the New Zealand Order of Merit, one notch down from a damehood.[44]

She considered whether to accept it. 'It could be good for our movement in our sycophantic little country', she wrote to Peter Cranney. She joked about bargaining them up to 'princess' or a campaign to 'make Helen the dame she wants to be'. If she accepted the honour she would have to declare whether there was anything in her background that might bring the system into disrepute. 'I bloody hope so,' she said to Cranney.[45]

She decided to turn it down, embarrassed to have given it a second thought. In any case there were far more pressing matters to deal with. Her latest tests showed the Keytruda wasn't working; the cancer was growing in her lungs and brain. Ten days of full brain radiation therapy in Auckland lay ahead, at the same time as more chemotherapy. It would be harsh treatment, with risk to her sight, balance and speech.

In an update to friends she didn't hide her worries, but lightened the message with a sardonic jibe about important work she would be unable to do: 'Who will attend the quad bike safety forum and keep the Feds honest?'[46] She had not long taken the CTU's seat on the group, which had been set up to look at ways to reduce the death and injury toll from the lethal vehicles, but the resistance of Federated Farmers and the manufacturers of the machines ensured it was getting nowhere.

She considered not having the treatment, and reflected on Gawande's observations that modern medicine tended to overtreat patients and favour quantity of life over quality. The question of assisted dying had been thrust to the fore through a valiant High Court suit by a 42-year-old Wellington lawyer, Lecretia Seales, who had died of brain cancer that

June.[47] Helen was moved by Seales' advocacy. Like her, she feared an unbearably painful end to her life and supported a safe legal framework for assisted dying.[48] But – like Seales – she wanted to live as long as she could. She had jobs to do, problems to fix, friends and family to love and be loved by. She was constantly receiving emails from people in New Zealand and around the world bearing encouraging thoughts, prayers, solidarity, and suggestions for alternative remedies and cancer-beating diets.

The treatment was scheduled for December 3 to 16. The pace of life in the days before, during and after didn't let up. She went to Pike River for the fifth anniversary of the disaster, taking some of the forestry families with her. A week later the High Court released its decision on the application for judicial review of the dropping of the Whittall charges. Every argument put up by Nigel Hampton and Simon Meikle on behalf of Anna Osborne and Sonya Rockhouse had been rejected. It was a terrible disappointment and there was no question that the legal team would appeal.

She delivered an impassioned speech against untrammelled market forces at the People's Climate March in Wellington on the eve of the climate talks in Paris. She mined farm job advertisements to post on Twitter and Facebook – '55 hpw, $16.50 ph … Long hours, low pay & reduced safety rights. #itsbydesign'; '55 hours per week. #itstoomuch' – and called for an inquiry into farm work conditions.[49]

She also remained closely involved in the struggle between the Meat Workers Union and Affco. The latest round of hostilities had been going on for months. Affco, having been unable to get the changes it wanted through collective bargaining, told its workers they had to sign individual agreements if they wanted jobs when the new killing season started. The individual deals contained the changes Affco hadn't been able to achieve through bargaining – cuts in guaranteed minimum pay, an end to the seniority rules that provided security of employment in a seasonal industry, the ability of the company to change hours of work at will.[50]

It was a bitter situation: Affco was the first company to apply under the government's altered industrial relations law to walk away from collective bargaining. The workers had voted strongly in favour of a strike, but it had been called off after intervention by iwi leaders. The union tried and failed to get an interim injunction against the company's take-it-or-leave-it individual agreements; it then told the workers to sign and it would continue the fight through the Employment Court.

At Wairoa in northern Hawkes Bay around 200 workers defied the union and refused to sign. Affco was the main employer in the small town. The workforce had already gone through two lockouts and by 2015 the atmosphere at the plant was 'toxic', said worker Therese Turipa. 'We said, "We're not going to take it any more. No more. No more watching families leave rather than go back to the works, because of the way it was being run." … I don't want my kids working 12 hours for what I get now in 20 years.'[51]

They were locked out. Animals were killed and processed by workers prepared to sign the individual agreements.

In mid November a full bench of the Employment Court ruled emphatically that Affco's actions in forcing individual agreements on the workforce amounted to an unlawful lockout and a breach of good faith.[52] The challenge for the union now was to regroup, see that workers' original terms and conditions were restored, get the Wairoa workers back to work, and get the company back to bargaining.

A few days before she was due to start treatment in Auckland, Helen drove north with Peter Cranney to meet with Affco workers in Feilding and Whanganui to explain the court ruling and discuss strategies. Tony Sutorius was with them, in the early days of filming a documentary. Helen had decided to participate in the film because it could shine a light on the workers' causes the union movement was grappling with.[53]

At the Whanganui meeting a worker opened his shirt to reveal the scars of recent heart surgery. Five months earlier he had been shovelling offal, tonnes of which had accumulated on the ground because of damaged equipment. Some of the material had squirted into his eye, carrying with it an infection that seriously damaged his heart and required emergency surgery to replace two heart valves. Helen was appalled. The previously fit and active man was left with serious lifelong effects. It was a major health and safety incident, but WorkSafe had no knowledge of it. She reported it and kept on the case to make sure it was investigated.[54]

A few days later, between sessions of full brain radiation and chemotherapy, she attended mediation between the union and Affco to try and resolve the situation in Wairoa. The workers were still out, despite the Employment Court ruling. Affco was insisting they work night shift, which most had never done before. Affco refused to allow Helen into the mediation room. She participated from a separate room but the negotiations got nowhere. 'For me this represents a family who think they are above the law,' she said of the Talley dynasty afterwards.[55]

After Christmas she went to Wairoa for another mediation attempt. By now she had lost her hair and was becoming unsteady on her feet. The locked-out workers had been out for four months, sustained by local iwi, support from local and international unions, and a tightly organised resource centre run by Therese Turipa.

This time Affco let Helen into the room. Pete Amato, a local union delegate, was struck by her performance: 'She gets in there and she starts growling at them.' She tore strips off the mediator for bias, and for allowing the employer representatives to walk out. 'She blew us out of the water,' Amato said. 'We're pretty hearty here in Wairoa. I mean, we call a shovel a fucking shovel. After that meeting all I wanted to do was be like her.'[56]

'She came here. She cared,' said Turipa. 'Accessible to anyone and everybody. … We related to her through her humanity. That was probably the biggest thing for us. We knew she was sick and dying.'[57]

Even so, the talks failed. 'I don't have any magic fix for this,' she told the exhausted workers afterwards. 'I can't fix this for you. They will continue to pick on you in that plant as long as they have power in that plant and the only thing you guys can do is organise and stick together.'[58]

It took yet another trip to the Employment Court to force Affco to allow the workers back to their jobs.[59] It would be another three and a half years before they were finally compensated for the months they were unlawfully locked out.

'I am doing a little bit of work and have found myself in a row about medical cannabis,' Helen wrote to friends a few days after the trip to Wairoa. It was typical understatement.[60]

Helen had barely touched dope as a teenager when friends were experimenting, but now she was New Zealand's most high-profile user. People had recommended she try it to relieve the pain and nausea associated with her cancer and chemotherapy. She had been receiving a good supply of cannabis balm made by a friend of a friend. It would arrive via conduits in beautiful jars, with little hearts carved into the top of the ointment. No money ever changed hands. Cannabis oil was helping her sleep at night and reduce the need for morphine, which made her feel sick and 'gluggy'.

She had disclosed publicly around the time of her retirement from the CTU that she was using cannabis and it was making an enormous difference to her ability to function. 'Green fairies' were soon dropping stuff at the front door of Shannon Street or mailing it to the CTU: cannabis cookies, cannabis chocolate, cannabis leaf to brew into tea. All of it was illicit and all supplied by people who were putting themselves at risk of criminal charges.

Emails started arriving, too – from people with multiple sclerosis, arthritis, cancer and chronic pain who were either relying on cannabis sourced from the black market and wanted to get it legally, or who were desperate for advice on how it might relieve their symptoms and how to obtain it.

She had no background in the long-running drug reform debate, but from the moment she spoke up activists were in touch to harness her voice to the cause. She felt no choice but to climb into the campaign for legalisation of cannabis: the law was blocking products that could ease suffering and she was in a position to shift public opinion. 'It seemed to me you couldn't take illegal cannabis and let other families [be] absolutely deprived of it,' she told broadcaster John Campbell.[61]

A prominent union leader turning to cannabis made good copy, and the media was keen on the story. At her urging, Labour MP Damien O'Connor drafted a private member's Bill for a referendum on legalising medicinal cannabis; it was knocked back in caucus, the party instead adopting a policy to allow medicinal use in limited circumstances if it won the 2017 election.

Helen decided to apply through a very small regulatory window to bring in a non-pharmaceutical cannabis product from the US. There was a high threshold for approval; it would have to be signed off by the associate minister of health, Peter Dunne. If the application succeeded, it might help ease the way for other people to get what they needed. If she was turned down, it would expose an inhumane law that was forcing a dying woman to become a criminal. She thrashed the story on social media – posting a photo of herself mailing the application and teasing Dunne relentlessly with the hashtag #apersoncoulddiewaiting about the time it was taking for a response.

She didn't get approval, but the story of her stymied application simmered away in the media for months. Meanwhile, she was on television demonstrating the products she found most helpful and how and when she imbibed them. Her lawbreaking was brazen; she might as well have said to the police and justice system, 'So – what are you going to do about it?' No constable ever turned up at Shannon Street to lay charges.

'She changed the game completely,' said Abe Gray, a veteran cannabis campaigner who worked closely with Helen to shift political and public attitudes. 'She was the first living person with clout to stand up and say, "I'm using this." She got cut-through.'[62]

And there was no artifice about her claims; cannabis had become a key part of her disease management and she struggled to cope without it. In March 2016 – in the midst of ongoing chemotherapy – she flew to Geneva for a meeting of the ILO Governing Body focused on the refugee crisis crashing across Europe. She stayed with James Ritchie and Jane Lawless; as a nurse, Lawless was able to provide care and advice if anything went wrong.

Ritchie had the job of heading down to a local park populated by 'dubious characters' to secure a cannabis supply. Communicating through body language and his modest French, a deal was done. Ritchie and Lawless mixed up the cannabis in the coffee grinder and baked it into brownies. 'It took a long time to get that smell out of the coffee grinder,' Ritchie remembered.[63]

One journalist referred to Helen's cannabis campaign as a 'second act' after years as the face of the union movement.[64] It would have been more accurate to call it a double, triple or quadruple act: she was still at the centre of long-running campaigns, including on forestry and Pike River.

Three forestry inquests were due to be heard by Coroner Wallace Bain in the Bay of Plenty. They were among eight forestry deaths that Bain was investigating. Hearings into five others had already been held, and these last three – into the deaths of Charles Finlay, Eramiha Pairama and David McMurtrie – had been delayed because of the private prosecutions.

All three men had been blamed for their own deaths, and the three families were looking to the Coroner's Court for answers, for the opportunity to be heard, and to clear their loved ones' names. For Donna McMurtrie, this was her only chance for justice because the courts had refused to allow a private prosecution over her husband's 2012 death.

David had worked in forestry most of his life and was killed harvesting trees he had planted in the steep country around the small town of Ōpōtiki. He worked for a local contractor, as did two of the couple's sons, Luke and Eli. A hung-up branch had come down on Luke in 2010, causing a fractured vertebrae, and it seemed to Donna that the accident had not been adequately investigated and the blame heaped on Luke.

David McMurtrie's hours and conditions were typical of the industry: very early starts, long hours, working on through rain and hail. He was increasingly unhappy about production pressures, poor quality management decisions, and the deployment of inadequately trained workers on to tasks beyond their skill levels. He often complained that safety issues raised by workers were not followed up.[65]

On a cold, wet morning in June 2012 he had left home as usual at about 5.30 and travelled with his crew to log trees on steep muddy uneven ground. As was common, he had supermarket plastic bags over his socks to keep his feet dry; he wasn't provided with wet-weather gear.[66] He had been labouring in these demanding conditions for three and a half hours without a break when, as he cut a tree, a branch hung up in the canopy came down on him. He died at 10.30 a.m.

Donna wasn't told until three in the afternoon, and even then the burden was put on other family members to break the news to her. David's body was not recovered until almost dark. Luke and Eli cradled their lifeless father through the long hours he lay at the scene.

The Department of Labour investigation had concluded his death was down to a 'failure by Mr McMurtrie to identify overhead hazards'. Four years later, the inquest before Coroner Bain was providing an opportunity to establish the full facts. 'I had my say there,' Donna McMurtrie said. 'I wanted to clear my husband of any wrongdoing beause I knew how safe he was.'[67]

A lack of systematic hazard assessment, fatigue, lack of shelter and warmth on the site, the employer's failure to learn from other near misses and from the incident that had nearly killed Luke, inadequate clothing, and other underlying causes were presented. 'The Court, on the balance of probabilities, finds no fault with Mr McMurtie,' Coroner Bain ruled.[68]

Preparation of submissions for the three inquests had required a huge amount of work by the families, the lawyers and Helen, who roped in Anne Goodman, an old friend of Shannon Street, to help. Throughout the hearings Helen suffered badly from nausea and tiredness caused by chemotherapy. She was vomiting so often she had to keep a container handy. At one point Coroner Bain paused to pay tribute to her work in bringing the deaths in the forestry industry to light. 'It became apparent she was quite ill,' he remembered. 'It was important to thank her in front of everyone.' It was evident to him that she had a close bond with the bereaved families: 'She led the way for them.'[69]

By July it had become difficult for Helen to manage while Steve was at work during the day. She couldn't walk without a stick, couldn't drive, and was having breathing difficulties. The tumours had fractured her spine; she had been rushed in for emergency radiation to stop them spreading to her spinal cord. However, cannabis was keeping pain and anxiety at bay and enabling her to sleep. She managed to remain positive. 'I myself am doing well,' she wrote to friends. 'I enjoyed the 100th celebrations for the Labour Party here and even danced on Saturday night.'[70]

Huia Welton set up a roster of friends to be with her each day. There were about a dozen in 'Helen's Team', which was run through a private Facebook page. Morning and afternoon, someone would arrive at Shannon Street to make cups of tea, chat, massage cannabis balm into her back, take her to appointments, run errands, cook, clean. Among the carers' periodic tasks was taking her to the post office to despatch parcels of cannabis products to desperate people who had contacted her. She was being supplied with more than she needed and had plenty to share.[71] Other friends looked after the garden, gave the bathroom a much-needed paint, made stews for the freezer. She was wrapped in love and support.

She was still carrying a complex workload. The appeal against the High Court's refusal to allow a judicial review of the decision to drop the Whittall charges was heard in August. Helen sat through the proceedings with Anna Osborne and Sonya Rockhouse. Osborne was battling Hodgkin lymphoma and, like Helen, was self-medicating with cannabis. The two cancer sufferers wore beanies on their bald heads and cracked jokes about who would die first.

Helen, Peter Cranney and the Pike families were also pursuing compensation and resolution from the Crown over the failures of regulatory oversight at the mine. Attorney-General Chris Finlayson had been disgusted by the dropping of the Whittall charges and was sympathetic to the families' position. He supported a package of measures: the payment of compensation, a Parliamentary acknowledgement in which the names of the 29 dead would be read into the record, and a process that would allow mine re-entry to be considered at a later date if new technology, such as drones, enabled it.[72]

Finlayson floated the proposal to the power brokers in Cabinet, but the idea of compensation was strongly opposed and the package went nowhere.[73]

Helen could have chosen to retreat from these causes, but she was still highly productive and the work was keeping her happy. 'There was a therapeutic element to it,' said Cranney. 'She felt lucky to have the work to do. It wasn't a delusional happiness.'[74]

She knew she had only months left. She had already far exceeded her initial prognosis. The cancer was aggressive and chemotherapy had been abandoned back in May. She wanted to eke out every additional day possible but the New Zealand health system had no further treatment to offer.

There was one last option. Early in 2016 the ambassador for Cuba had made contact to tell her about a cancer vaccine that had been developed in his country. He undertook to get more information about whether she could be a suitable candidate. She didn't want to chase rainbows but she kept in touch with him, read the results of trials on the novel treatment, and discussed it with her doctors and with researchers at the Malaghan Institute of Medical Research in Wellington.

By August she and Steve were looking at how to get the treatment, Cimavax, transported to New Zealand. Possibly one of her US cousins would collect it from Cuba and fly over with it, or Steve could travel to get it. Her doctors were supportive of her trying it but thought the risk of her travelling to Cuba was too great.

The process of getting the necessary information and approval to bring it to New Zealand was slow and complex. She and Steve decided they would fly to Cuba. She would receive the first round of treatment there and hopefully bring the rest home. It was risky, but – as Steve later said – she wasn't going to just sit around and die. She wanted to do something.

By August 23 they were in residence at La Pradera medical complex outside Havana. Her wider family had helped to fund the trip. Helen had farewelled Dylan, Max, Cath and friends with no certainty of when or if she would be back. She might be back soon with the drugs, she might have to stay for months to have the full treatment, or she could die there. 'I really have tried everything and am getting sicker by the day … [Cimavax] is experimental, but all patients are getting an advantage and I am lucky to have access,' she wrote to friends before she and Steve left.[75]

La Pradera was tranquil, a medical resort with expansive gardens, a swimming pool with a drinks hut, meals, piped Latin American music and very sick guests. When it rained heavily the roof leaked and the power went out. It had been set up originally to provide medical assistance to workers from poor countries.

'It's a beaut place we are in,' Helen wrote on Facebook on the second day. 'Nice staff etc. Internet connection intermittent but phone vaguely working but too expensive to use really. Worse things can happen eh? I feel very pleased and very privileged to be here.'[76]

She needed a wheelchair by then, was in great deal of pain and was getting little sleep. There was no way to source cannabis and she hadn't dared bring a supply from home. After the first Cimavax treatment – four injections – it was 14 days until the next one, during which she continued to figure out what was required to bring the rest home. Word had gone out through the global union network that she and Steve were in residence, and offers of assistance and translation came forward. They had been recommended a guide, Juan Francisco Hernández Cabrera, who showed them the sites of Havana, and Helen shopped for gifts for a long list of friends and family. It was beautiful and interesting – particularly the Museum of the Revolution – but being driven around in a mid-20th-century vintage vehicle with no suspension was uncomfortable and aggravated her pain.

It was stressful for Steve to have Helen so ill and so far from home. But it was also a precious time of peace and quiet together, although Helen kept in touch with various projects, including a campaign to run Affco meatworkers as candidates in the 2016 local body elections, and developing a budget and rough campaign plan for a citizens-initiated referendum on cannabis reform.[77]

They flew out from Havana after almost three weeks. Helen had had two treatments. The remainer of the course of drugs was in vials packed into a chiller bag. 'So grateful to the Govt and people of Cuba and my beautiful cousins for a chance,' she posted on Facebook. 'Even if I don't respond it's such an opportunity and I know it might be placebo or maybe just rest and [warmth] but I feel good and I am very alive! Thanks everyone for the support.'[78]

Helen wanted to spend a few days in the US on the way home. They landed in New York and spent half a day looking around the Manhattan sights before boarding an Amtrak train to Washington to stay with Sarah Fox, Helen's friend and colleague from the ILO Governing Body. By then she was relying on morphine every four hours. She had planned to meet with the AFL-CIO, the major union federation in the US, but was in such a bad way she had to pull out.

'I need my cannabis and am more determined than ever to campaign for it,' she posted. 'Sorry to have negative news. It stresses people out but I have been probably too optimistic and am trying to be honest.'

She had hoped to be able to source cannabis legally in Washington and bring it back into New Zealand through a loophole that had recently been discovered in the law, and was upset to discover access was restricted to residents.[79] At home, a new poll showed 75 percent support for medicinal cannabis; she posted the results on social media hashtagged '#noshitsherlock' and '#gettingimpatientnow'.[80]

She and Steve landed in Auckland on her 52nd birthday. They were met by Customs officers plainly expecting her to be carrying cannabis.

Back in Wellington, she was almost immediately admitted to Mary Potter Hospice to bring her pain under control. The staff administered her third dose of the Cuban treatment. '[S]truggling a bit is the summary,' she posted on Facebook. 'Cuba may be over but it was beautiful and let's hope the medicine does something and ya gotta live to die right?'[81] She reminded people to get out and vote for the meatworker candidates in the local body elections.[82]

Her hospice room was bedecked with teacher union campaign messages about school funding.[83] There was a constant troop of people wanting to visit. 'Helen would never turn anyone away,' Steve said.[84]

She got back home to Shannon Street and the roster of carers swung back into action. She was in demand from the media – a beacon now not only for workers' rights but for drug reform. Journalist Russell Brown came to Shannon Street for an interview about cannabis on October 7 and found her 'focused, good-humoured and thoughtful'. She displayed and shared the range of illicit chocolate, oil, tea and balm that she was using in conjunction with morphine. Her voice had lost its strength and she was breathless, but she talked about the struggle faced by others who were severely ill and the state of the campaign for reform.

She was still fighting, still defiant, still positive.

Four days later she wrote to friends: 'Hey I am writing because doctors told us yesterday I am now quite rapidly dying and only … have a few months or even weeks to live.' Pain had forced her back to the hospice, but she hoped to get back home again 'for a few months! … I am hoping the Cuban drug [does] break through. … I haven't given up!!!'[85]

Friends and family rallied to make sure she was never alone. 'When can I go home?' she asked one of the hospice doctors. 'Oh Helen, you can't go home,' she was told. 'If you are here, we can help you.'[86] It was October 13, a Thursday. Huia Welton had come in with the first peonies of the season. They were Helen's favourite flower.

Just after midnight, with Steve at her side, Helen died. Steve phoned to break the news to Dylan, who came to be with his mother in the small hours of the morning. Steve remained with her through the night, and sent word as daylight came.

News leaked out quickly. Her death led the morning news bulletins. She had become public property. On Parliament's next sitting day, the following Tuesday, business was interrupted to mark her passing. Andrew Little, John Key, Winston Peters, Denise Roche and Marama Fox eulogised. Politicians on all sides stood together to sing 'He Hōnore'.

There was a public memorial in Wellington's Michael Fowler Centre, attended by a thousand or more and viewed via live stream by 65,000 people in 106 countries.[87]

Before this, there had been a private farewell. At the Lychgate Funeral Home, close friends and family came together in a tight knot of love and sorrow, free from cameras and reporters and social media posts. Max wrapped an arm around Cath in the front row. Chris and Dylan sang Carole King's 'You've Got a Friend' and Dylan – recalling a Leonard Cohen concert that he and Helen had gone to – sang 'Hey, That's No Way to Say Goodbye'. Steve spoke of the empathy and compassion that underpinned every one of her campaigns, and of the nights at her laptop helping ununionised workers find resolution to workplace grievances. Her cousin Bill Rosenberg said what others were saying in newspaper tributes and blogs: that had she lived she would one day have become prime minister.[88]

Stories were told of two generations of Shannon Street politics, of a childhood full of friendship and opportunity, of extended family holidays jammed into the Rangataua bach and roaming free through the landscape, of a little girl full of loyalty, kindness, confidence and intelligence, who built on those foundations as she grew into a leader of courage, authority and fortitude; a warrior who was outraged by injustice and who could not witness suffering without seeking to solve it.

Peter Cranney had been part of the household since he was 18 and she 13. He knew her mind and motives as well as anyone. 'It's a very hard blow to lose her,' he said to the gathering. 'She became just an extraordinary political leader. She became a powerful voice, a strong voice, for the poor, for the dispossessed; for the humiliated meat workers, for the forestry workers, the miners, the women workers, the cleaners, the low paid, the impoverished …

‘She was a great person to have as a friend. She was a great person to have shoulder to shoulder in a struggle, when you needed someone reliable. You didn’t need to check with her. She was a sound fighter.’

Helen lay in a closed coffin at the front of the bland, intimate room. ‘We will carry you out of here today. We will shed tears, not of bitterness and defeat but of justice and solidarity and freedom.’

Epilogue

Pat had been gone 12 years by the time of Helen's death. Cath never recovered from the loss of her beloved daughter. By Christmas 2016 she had had enough; she was depressed and had no appetite, and ended up in Kenepuru Hospital. From there she went to Te Hopai, a rest home in Wellington's Newtown. She continued to fade and died peacefully on March 13, 2017, five months after Helen and three days after her 91st birthday. Max and Dave Morgan were by her side.

Those who knew Shannon Street always saw in Helen the inheritance of both parents: Pat's oratory, wit and passion; Cath's steely, brusque conviction. The stories from both sides of the family moulded her understanding of the world: the cruelty of poverty, hunger and unemployment; the power of compassion, belief and defiance to bring change.

She was primed to fight, just as she had seen them fight for an end to apartheid in South Africa, an end to war in Vietnam, an end to fascism in Chile, for good wages and a decent life for workers in New Zealand. She was schooled in the certainty that nothing worthwhile happened without organisation and relentless hard work.

But she wasn't just her parents' daughter. She took the attributes and values she was bequeathed, absorbed the advice of her many mentors, and sharpened her skills through experience and study, trial and error. For 52 years she was a deeply loved child of Shannon Street, and that love underpinned her confidence, resilience and daring. For workers and families in distress and grief, her empathy was real and the quality of her care was solid and practical. They didn't have to doubt that she was on their side, and that made them braver and more ready to fight.

In her last days, as Anna Osborne and Sonya Rockhouse massaged cannabis oil into her temples and legs, Helen said to them of the struggle for justice over the Pike River tragedy, 'Never give up the fight.'

'She gave us the strength to carry on,' said Osborne.[1] Within a month of Helen's death the two women – one a high school teacher aide, the other seriously ill with Hodgkin lymphoma – were sitting on camp chairs blocking the access gates to Pike. Solid Energy had been preparing to permanently seal the mine with 30 metres of concrete. Osborne and Rockhouse were determined to stop that from happening, and to make one more push for the mine to be re-entered and searched for forensic evidence and any remains of the the 29 dead men.

They borrowed a pop-top caravan and parked it across the road, and soon a legion of supporters were providing food, security and solidarity. The protesters were visited by dignitaries, politicians and activists.

Osborne phoned Solid Energy's concrete supplier and asked it not to work on the mine sealing. The company agreed. No other concrete contractor was willing to do the work. 'Sonya and I would sit in the caravan and say, "Helen, we hope you're proud of us,"' remembered Osborne. 'She worked so hard and got so much done before she died that we weren't going to let her down.'

The occupation was maintained for 107 days, forcing open a window of political opportunity for re-entry into the mine's 2.3-kilometre access tunnel. A month before the 2017 general election, all parties other than National and Act pledged a commitment to re-entry. When a Labour-led coalition took office in October and an agency was set up to develop a re-entry plan, it seemed accountability could finally be within reach.[2]

Around the same time, the justice system issued its final verdict on the 2013 decision to drop health and safety charges against Peter Whittall. Both the High Court and the Court of Appeal had rejected the bid for judicial review of the decision; the Court of Appeal ruling had come four months after Helen's death. The lawyers had resolved to fight on to the highest court in the country.

Now, four years after Helen had declared to Peter Cranney, 'We have to do something', the Supreme Court had vindicated her outrage. The court's decision of November 23, 2017 was unanimous: the deal to drop the charges against Whittall was unlawful. WorkSafe had entered into an arrangement in which the $3.41 million would be paid on condition that it enter no evidence to support the charges. It was a bargain to stifle a prosecution.[3]

The decision made no material change to the pursuit of justice – the charges against Whittall would not be reinstated. But it was a profound moral victory, and a testament to Helen's capacity to inspire others.

But wins for workers and their families were only as good as the ability to defend them. In early 2015, Gordon MacDonald, the head of WorkSafe, had celebrated 12 months without the death of a single forestry worker. Helen was proud of the campaign to bring the industry's carnage to light, but knew it had relied too heavily on her own hands-on involvement. There remained an enormous task to win basic protections and representation for forestry workers employed by hundreds of contractors on remote logging sites.

That responsibility was taken on by FIRST Union and funded by its members from other sectors.[4] In the meantime, without the glare of publicity that Helen had generated, the number of workers dying in the forests rose again. In the three years after her death, 20 were killed.[5] Across the supply chain, 44 died between 2014 and 2020, with WorkSafe prosecuting in only seven of these cases.[6] Helen would have been bitterly disappointed, but probably not surprised.

Her ambition was Herculean: she wanted to change the way working people were treated, and she wanted to wrap the arms of the union movement around those who were powerless and isolated. But there was no totemic endpoint, no towering legacy. How could there be? No single leader, no matter how talented, could re-engineer an economy that had shaped itself for a generation around low wages, and where a job was no antidote to poverty.[7] No single leader, no matter how forceful, could reform a union movement that had adapted and survived by focusing primarily on the private needs of a minority of workers.

When change didn't come quickly enough through conference remits and discussion groups, she went out to the forestry towns and the meeting halls full of locked-out workers and demonstrated how she thought an inclusive movement based on the values of solidarity, fairness and community could look and sound.

All the while she dug away at the deep-rooted assumptions that had set the boundaries of political possibility throughout her adult life: that the market was the best arbiter of what workers were worth; that unions were dinosaurs; that workers were lucky to have a job, even if that job left them maimed or didn't pay enough to keep their children warm and fed. She stood alongside those with stories of disempowerment, poverty wages and death, and people began to listen because it was evident that these stories were true, and because they resonated with their own experience of long hours, with wages that didn't keep up, with the humiliation in their child's eyes when sacked without cause from their first job after 89 days.

But advocacy and organising weren't enough. Even as Helen gave the union movement a public profile it hadn't had for decades, its ranks continued to thin.[8] Together, her union for the unrepresented, didn't succeed and was deregistered after her death and turned into a social media campaigning platform.

No matter how persuasive her message, for the vast majority of workers collective action and genuine wage bargaining remained out of reach.

She regarded law change as essential. Early in her tenure as CTU president she had written her draft Bill on industry standard agreements, which would enable minimum wages and conditions to be negotiated for whole sectors of otherwise low-paid workers. When the Labour-led government took power in 2017, this policy was on its manifesto, but now it was simplified and went by a new name: Fair Pay Agreements.

In 2018 a working group was established to figure out how these agreements might work. It was chaired by Jim Bolger, the former prime minister whose National government had enacted radical labour market deregulation in 1991, and who had latterly declared the neoliberal revolution a failure and lamented the shrunken state of trade unions (but who continued to insist the Employment Contracts Act had been necessary).[9]

The Bolger-led group concluded that Fair Pay Agreements would help prevent 'race to the bottom' competition that depressed wages and conditions.[10] Two years later, with Labour re-elected in a landslide in the midst of the Covid-19 pandemic, Fair Pay Agreements remained a political promise, yet to be implemented.

The story that had first thrust Helen on to prime-time news – the *Hobbit* dispute – also continued to reverberate. It carried lessons she never forgot – how easy it was to lose control of the narrative, how readily a sycophantic state would please big business at the expense of workers' basic rights. Despite talk by Labour after it formed the 2017 coalition government that legislation to repeal the *Hobbit* law would be before Parliament within 100 days, three years later the law remained in place. Instead of a simple repeal, a compromise Bill was drafted. It would continue to deem film workers independent contractors, but permit them to bargain collectively without the right to strike.

Had she lived, Helen would likely have been a member of the Labour-led government that took office on October 26, 2017, probably as the MP for Rongotai. She would have gone straight into Cabinet without the usual period of apprenticeship for junior MPs.[11] Without doubt, she would have been a formidable presence around the Cabinet table, and impatient with the inertia of government and the turgid pace of change. She was a rarity in that, as her influence and stature grew, she became more radical, not less. The more she heard from struggling workers and families, the more she saw of an economy tuned to favour capital at the expense of those who live by their labour, the more compelled she was to fight for change.

'We don't give up and we push back,' she said. 'Eventually there must be a point where working people say, "Actually, we are going to look for a different model, a social democratic model where our role in society, the respect for us, is recognised."'[12]

She didn't use the word 'I'; it was always 'us' and 'we' and 'our'. The fight for a society that distributes its wealth fairly and assures dignity and participation was not hers alone to win or lose; that fight was and is a collective one. But her place in it was a calling, to which she brought a fierce, bright and inspiring energy. Hers was a life of loyalty, love and duty, fully lived, a life of public service, to which she could have given no more.

Supporters and sources

Being a full-time writer of non-fiction in New Zealand is a huge financial challenge, but I have been luckier than many. I wouldn't have had the confidence to leave my salaried job at the *Listener* to write this book for Awa Press if not for an offer by the CTU to fundraise for a writer's fellowship to assist me. This raised $70,000, which was held in trust and administered by the Labour History Project. I don't know who or what organisations donated, but my sincere thanks to those who made this funding possible. Thanks also to the Labour History Project and its committee.

In December 2018 I was awarded $8500 by the New Zealand History Research Trust Fund, administered by the Ministry of Culture and Heritage, to help cover travel and research costs. I also received the $25,000 Copyright Licensing New Zealand/New Zealand Society of Authors' Writer's Award for 2020. I'm very grateful for these sources of support.

In researching the book, I was able to draw on a wide range of primary and secondary source material, and for this there are many people to thank. I am indebted to Anne Goodman and Pat Webster, who had conducted lengthy interviews with Helen's parents Pat and Cath and gave me this invaluable material. It is not possible to tell Helen's story without also telling her parents' and I could not have done that without Anne and Pat's generosity with their tapes and transcripts. Clare Wells and Lesley Hall had also conducted interviews with Cath for their respective academic work, and it was a huge bonus to find Clare's oral history and Lesley's full interview transcript among the papers at Shannon Street. Hazel Armstrong and Bob Kerr had copies of autobiographical stories that Pat had written about his childhood and these were also full of rich detail.

To Steve Hurring, my deep thanks for allowing me to dig through the boxes of archive material stored in wardrobes and cupboards at Shannon Street. This enabled me to get a deeper insight into the activism and outlook of Pat and Cath and the quality of the environment in which Helen and Max were immersed from birth. It seemed that nothing had been thrown out over the decades, and so I was able to reference a trove of letters, diaries, pamphlets, CVs, academic records, photos, scrapbooks and yellowed newspaper clippings to help fill out the story.

During the course of my research Max Kelly applied for Pat and Cath's SIS files. Cath's full file and part of Pat's have so far been released. My thanks to Max for making these available to me, as well as for the family documents that he shared.

Steve and Max both provided a large number of photos, met with me on many occasions, and answered my countless phone calls, emails and texts seeking further details or clarification. To both of you, my eternal gratitude for your fortitude and patience.

Helen's extended family helped me to better understand her heritage by providing detailed family trees and access to correspondence relating to the situation for members of the Eichelbaum family under the Nazis. Thanks in particular to Bill and George Rosenberg for this. On a trip to the UK in 2018, Helen's son Dylan recorded a conversation with Pat's only surviving sibling, Lolo Moss. Dylan, thank you for sharing this with me.

Peter Franks and John Hughes both sat down with me soon after I began the project and, possibly without knowing it, helped calm my fears. They also shared research material and pointed me in the direction of texts that I wouldn't have known to look for or that I had forgotten existed. My thanks to both of them for their generosity.

To Karl Zohrab, my thanks for the unpublished footage of your interview with Pat Kelly. My gratitude also to Tony Sutorius, who allowed me the use of his interview footage with Helen, shot in 2015 and 2016 when he was filming *Helen Kelly – Together.* Gordon Anderson dug into his files for academic work that Helen had worked on towards a Master of Laws, material that was important in understanding the development of her views of how the union movement needed to change. Thank you, Gordon.

Many other people helped with documents of various types – legal submissions and rulings, speech notes, newsletters written in the thick of various disputes, union annual reports, briefings, notes of conversations with Helen, email and text threads, academic papers, books, journal articles, government papers, photos, voice recordings and videos. At the risk of leaving someone out, my grateful thanks to Ken Douglas, Ralph McAllister, Bill Rosenberg, Gerald Sutton, Margaret Wilson, Laila Harré, Liz Riddiford, John Ryall, Lyndy McIntyre, Graeme Clarke, Paul Goulter, Cybèle Locke, Jim McAloon, Darien Fenton, Hazel Armstrong, Linda Mitchell, Clare Wells, Marty Braithwaite, Brent Edwards, Stan Rodger, Grant Duncan, Jennifer Ward-Lealand, Craig Harrison, Linda Sewell, Nigel Hampton, Steve Hurring, Peter Cranney, Fleur Fitzsimmons, Huia Welton, Camilla Belich, Paul Mackay, Abe Gray, Selina Eruera and Sonya Rockhouse.

I lost track of the number of times I emailed pleadingly to Peter Bateman at *Safeguard* magazine for this or that article he'd published relating to workplace health and safety and Helen's campaigning work. He would promptly send me what I was after, attached to an email that invariably bore his typically droll observations on life. My huge appreciation also to Sue Ryall for guiding me through the research collection at the Centre for Labour, Employment, and Work at Victoria University and pulling out and sending me the papers I wanted.

As mentioned in the Author's Note, I had extensive access to Helen's CTU papers, and this was essential to the project, particularly in terms of understanding the disputes she got involved in, the campaigns she led, and the scale of her workload. My special thanks to Richard Wagstaff and Steve Hurring for this, and to Huia Welton, Sue Windsor, Belinda Heffron and Julia London, who dug out specific details and documents that I needed to fill gaps.

To the librarians who helped me navigate your catalogues, you are wonderful and your skill is a taonga. At the Alexander Turnbull Library, I tapped into the archives of Pat's old union, the Wellington and Taranaki Caretakers, Cleaners and Lift Attendants and Watchmen's Industrial Union of Workers (held as part of the Service Workers Union of Aotearoa's records); the Combined Early Childhood Union of Aotearoa and its legacy unions, the Kindergarten Teachers Association and Early Childhood Workers Union, where Helen started her union career; and the Campaign Against Rising Prices, the movement that Cath devoted years to. The CTU archive, also held at the Turnbull, was an important reference source, as were various New Zealand Employers' Federation and New Zealand Business Roundtable files (thanks to Oliver Hartwich for facilitating access to the latter). Items in the Trade Union Oral History Project were also helpful, in particular the interview with Angela Foulkes. Collections lodged at the Turnbull by Bert Roth and Ron Smith provided important context.

Thanks to the staff of the Parliamentary Library, the Macmillan Brown and law libraries at the University of Canterbury, the JC Beaglehole Room at Victoria University, and at Ngā Taonga Sound and Vision. Thanks also to Rewa Wehipeihana and Sharn Riggs at the Tertiary Education Union and Jenny Whyte at NZEI Te Riu Roa for documents and facilitating access to archives, and to Jeanette Harford at Coronial Services for her help.

Tūranga, Christchurch's beautiful new library and one of the best things to happen to the city since the February 2011 earthquake, opened while I was working on the project. It was wonderful to have access to this space and its excellent librarians, who helped me out on so many occasions, not least by guiding me to sources I didn't know existed and by hauling in trolleys groaning with bound volumes of *National Business Review* and *New Zealand Listener* and box files of *New Zealand Journal of Industrial Relations*.

Some 400 interviews with more than 200 people form the backbone of this book. Several people sat through three or more interviews as I canvassed different periods of Helen's life and that of her family, and significant events and phases for the labour movement. Some put their thoughts and recollections into lengthy email replies, and kindly responded to my follow-up phone calls and emails. Again at risk of accidentally leaving someone out, my great thanks to the following people (in no special order) for sharing their knowledge and views: Steve Hurring, Max Kelly, Dylan Kelly, Hazel Armstrong, Peter Cranney, Russel Norman, Jennifer Ward-Lealand, Robyn Malcolm, Tandi Wright, Robert Reid, Warwick McKee, John Barnett, David Long, Marty Braithwaite, Rob Egan, Carol Beaumont, Simon Whipp, Anne James, Margaret Legerton, John Ryall, Jackie Ford, Karin Currie, Belinda Heffron, Helen Kinsella, Julia London, Anne Goodman, Clare Wells, Georgie McLeod, Sue Windsor, John McGuire, Don Swan, Richard

Bluck, Frances Walsh, Richard Fletcher, Tom Ryan, Chris Wratt, Ken Douglas, Jeff Sissons, Tom Patrick, Rachel Patrick, Ben Patrick, Angus Dart (by email), Miriam Long, Ross Wilson, Paul Goulter, Jean Marending, Henry Stubbs, James Ritchie, Michelle Saban, Therese O'Connell, Paul Tolich, Andrew Campbell, Phil O'Reilly, Clare Leniston, Jackie Matthews, Eileen Brown, Nanette Cormack, Ralph McAllister, Bill Rosenberg, George Rosenberg, Amanda Coulston, Rosslyn Noonan, Sam Huggard, Richard Wagstaff, Gerry Brownlee, Sir John Key, Erin Polaczuk, Andrew Chick, Maxine Gay, Karl Andersen, Sammy Singh, Linda Mitchell, Annie Newman, Huia Welton, Sue Piper, Annette King, Meg Bailey, Joanna Beresford, Ross Teppett, Grant Duncan, Andrew Little, Gerard Burns, Stephen Blackburn, Nigel Haworth, Pat Webster, Nigel Hampton, Trevor Mallard, Kristen Thompson, Alby White, Rob Fyfe, Mike Sweeney, Gordon Dryden, Bernie Monk, Carol Rose, Alison Saunders, Darien Fenton, Jon Johansson, Rob McKeen, Brownwynn Maxwell, Stan Rodger, Anne Rodger, Tom Doherty, Shelley Lee, Laila Harré, Simon Oosterman, Doug Catley, Dennis O'Reilly, Michael Law (by email), Alan Ware, Janette Kelly, Jane Adams, Matt McCarten, Mike Treen, Gerard Hehir, Trevor Richards, Russell Mayn, Craig Harrison, Joe Fleetwood, Rob Campbell, Graeme Clarke, Rob Haultain, Liz Baldwin-Featherstone, Parks White, Margaret Wilson, Peter Dunne, Mike Paltridge, Fran Wilde, Brenda Pilott, Rebecca Wright, Mike Smith, Suzanne McNabb, Lee Cooper, Steph Doyle, Allan Marsden, Fleur Fitzsimons, Maryanne Butler-Finlay, Tina McIvor, Ruth Dyson, Peter Monteith, Selina Eruera, Donna McMurtrie, Deborah McMillan, Therese Turipa, Pete Amato, Caroline and Roger Callow, Camilla Belich, Denise Roche, Helen Baxter, Rick Barker, Paul Bell, Ian Hodgetts, Gerald Sutton, Jane Benefield, Philippa Branthwaite, Lyndy McIntyre, Ian Fraser, Ruth Richardson, Guy Reynolds, Peter Donelan (by email), Suze Wilson, Lynne Bruce, Doug Martin, Ralph Stockdill, Sharan Burrow, Graeme Whimp, Grant Robertson, Anna Osborne, Sonya Rockhouse, Marian Hobbs, Steve Maharey, Rebecca Matthews, Maureen Montgomery, Sir Michael Cullen, Sir David Skegg, Roy Sharp, David Small, Peter Wills, Steve Poletti, Andrew Casidy, Maryann Kaka, Terangi Wroe, Dave Eastlake, Mike Nahu, Mike Paltridge, Eric Mischefski, Syd Keepa, Paora Stanley, Ken Mair, Tali Williams, Murray Free, Phil Twyford, Linda

Sewell, Katya Paquin, Edward Miller, Chris Gallivan, Wallace Bain, Paul Mackay, Sarah Fox, Kevan Nelson, Lynne Collins, Ged Kearney, Abe Gray, Damien O'Connor, Craig and Lesley Kidd, Louisa Jones, Bill McCallum, Charles Finny, Chris Finlayson, Jim Bolger and David Rhodes. Thanks also to Tim Braithwaite and Mike Paltridge for helping me connect with several people who were important to Helen's story.

I was honoured to interview Sir Thomas Eichelbaum, who died in October 2018, and Dave Morgan, who died in November 2019. It was also a privilege to visit Simon Meikle, who died in October 2020.

A small number of people declined to be interviewed or didn't respond, and it is worth noting the most significant of these for the record: Sir Peter Jackson, Sir Richard Taylor, Dave Gibson, Stuart McCutcheon and Tony Gibson.

My goal has been to write a story that is readable, accurate, and accessible to those who might not normally be drawn to a book about a trade union leader. If I have succeeded in that, it is due in no small part to the people who read and gave me feedback on the draft manuscript, or large parts of it, as I went along. To Ian Reddington, Graeme Whimp, John Ryall, Hazel Armstrong, Steve Hurring, Peter Cranney, Max Kelly, Ross Wilson, Huia Welton, Don Swan, my father Bob and my daughter Grace – my heartfelt appreciation for your time and insights. Thank you for the suggestions and comments that kept me going during the long months of isolation at my laptop, and saving me from numerous inaccuracies and blunders.

Mary Varnham of Awa Press has been steadfast in her backing for this project. She stuck with me when the first deadline went up in smoke, and kept sticking with me whenever I told her forlornly that I just didn't know how long it would take. Mary was also a firm, collaborative and respectful editor and, along with Sarah Bennett, who guided the book through its production phases, was fantastic to work with. My thanks also to Lee Slater for his brilliant indexing, to Neil Pardington for his striking cover design, to Tina Delceg for her careful and dedicated typesetting, to Chris Cessford for photo research, and to Hagen Hopkins and the *Listener* for the cover photo.

Also part of the wairua of this book are the many friends and family members who supported me in all sorts of ways – putting me up during my research trips away, lending me their cars and houses, feeding and watering me, forcing me to take a break by dragging me out tramping and biking, listening at the end of the phone when I was feeling overwhelmed. It's hard to name everyone wthout filling pages, but my loving thanks especially to Hazel and Bob, Jane and Tom, Grace and Ash, Charles and Laura, Ian and Sally, Russell and Caroline, Charles and Raewyn, Jessie, Tony, Roger, Francie, Justin, Katherine, Ruth, Susie, Ian, Delwynne, Cate, Jo, Jacqui, Binny, Huia, Graeme and Peter. There were few days when I didn't wish for a good long chat with Caroline, who would have been intensely interested in Helen's story and whom I and so many others miss dearly. Most of all, thanks to Neil for his love and support, and for believing in this book.

Endnotes

Prologue

1 Video, Fairness at Work rally, Parliament Grounds, October 20, 2010. Retrieved from YouTube, October 27, 2020.

2 Ministry of Economic Development, 'Growth and Dynamics of the New Zealand Screen Industry', April 2012.

3 Federation of International Actors, correspondence to Robert Fisher and David Sagal, directors of 3 Foot 7 Limited, the Warner Bros. subsidiary set up to make the films.

4 Peter Jackson, statement, September 27, 2010; Simpson Grierson, legal advice to MEAA, September 17, 2010.

5 Ministry of Culture and Heritage, aide memoire for minister of arts, culture and heritage Chris Finlayson, September 27, 2010.

6 Julia London, author interview, May 2018.

7 Peter Jackson, email to Tim Hurdle, October 18, 2010; email thread between Screen Actors' Guild, Warner Bros. and MEAA between October 17 and 19, 2010.

8 Printed handout given to workers at Stone Street Studios, Wellington, October 20, 2010.

9 Ibid.

10 CTU staff, author interviews, May 2018.

11 Robyn Malcolm, author interview, May 2018.

12 Jennifer Ward-Lealand, speech, 2013.

13 Frances Walsh, author interview, October 2018.

14 Anonymous, email to Helen Kelly, May 25, 2015.

15 Three News, October 21, 2010; Sheryl Cadman and Tom Ryan, eyewitness accounts provided to the author.

16 Tom Ryan, author interview, June 2018.

17 Tim Hurdle, email exchanges with Rick Abercrombie, New Line Cinema, October 20 and 21, 2010.

18 Newstalk ZB, October 21, 2010. Ngā Taonga Sound and Vision.

19 *Close Up*, TVNZ, October 21, 2010. Ngā Taonga Sound and Vision.

20 Kiran Chug, Antonio Bradley, Michael Fox and Tom Cardy, 'The Hobbit looks headed overseas', *The Dominion Post*, October 21, 2010; Tom Cardy, 'We may as well not live here', The Dominion Post, October 22, 2010.

21 *One News*, Television New Zealand, October 29, 2010. Ngā Taonga Sound and Vision.

22 Employers and Manufacturers' Association, press release, 'Call not to Hobbit the Rugby World Cup', October 22, 2010.

23 Pam Nuttall, 'Where the shadows lie: Confusions, misunderstandings and misinformation about workplace status', NZJER, 2011, 36 (73–90).

24 Sir John Key, author interview, September 2018; Tim Hurdle, email to officials with notes of meeting between Peter Jackson and Minister of Arts, Culture and Heritage and Attorney-General Chris Finlayson, September 28, 2010.

25 Chris Finlayson and Gerry Brownlee, letter to Peter Jackson and Fran Walsh (undated).

26 *Close Up*, TV One, October 21, 2010. Ngā Taonga Sound and Vision.

27 Sir John Key, author interview.

28 Briar Chamley, email to Joanna Holden and Tim Smith, October 26, 2010.

29 Department of Labour, briefing to Hon. Kate Wilkinson, October 26, 2010.

30 Britton Broun and Tracy Watkins, 'Hobbit fans warned we could lose it all', *The Dominion Post*, October 26, 2010.

31 James Weir, 'Hobbit to kick life into Wellington', *The Press,* October 29, 2010.

32 New Zealand National Party, special press conference on the *Hobbit* film, October 27, 2010. Retrieved from YouTube, November 2, 2018.

33 Carol Beaumont, author interview, May 2018.

34 *New Zealand Parliamentary Debates*, October 28, 2010, Week 58, Volume 668.

35 Helen Kelly, letter to John Key, October 27, 2010. CTU files.

36 Michele Hewitson, 'Interview: Andrew Little', *The New Zealand Herald,* October 29, 2010. Retrieved from nzherald.co.nz, October 27, 2020.

37 'New Zealander of the Year 2010: Readers' choice', *The New Zealand Herald*, December 11, 2010. Retrieved from nzherald.co.nz, October 27, 2020.

38 Keith Lynch and Giles Brown, 'Mine chief "should have apologised"', *The Press*, December 6, 2010. Retrieved from stuff.co.nz, October 27, 2020.

39 *Kiwiblog*, December 6, 2010.

40 Anonymous, email to Helen Kelly, December 6, 2010. Helen Kelly papers.

41 Helen Kelly, 'The Hobbit Dispute', *Scoop*, April 12, 2011.

Chapter 1

1 Helen Kelly, interview with Richard Langstone, Radio New Zealand, October 28, 2013.

2 Rebecca Kitteridge, Director-General of Security, New Zealand Security Intelligence Service, letter to Max Kelly, October 30, 2019. Cath Kelly was under state surveillance from 1951 until 1989, and Pat Kelly from 1957 until 1990.

3 *NZ Truth*, 'Red Siren Behind Communist Infiltration Plan', October 25, 1960. Cath was not named in the article as the Red Siren, but a note in her SIS file confirms that she was the subject. Cath Eichelbaum SIS file note, November 4, 1960. Declassifed May 28, 2020.

4 Cath Kelly, interview with Pat Webster. Provided to author by Pat Webster.

5 Sir Thomas Eichelbaum, author interview, May 2018. Cath's oldest sister Ann married a prominent left-wing economist and lawyer, Wolfgang Rosenberg.

6 Eichelbaum family archives; *The Evening Post*, August 19, 1952.

7 Cath Kelly, interview with Pat Webster.

8 Letter from Charles Patrick to Dr W.I. Axford, August 3, 1985. Eichelbaum family archives.

9 Gordon Dryden, author interview, October 2018.

10 Bill Rosenberg, memorial speech for Helen Kelly, October 14, 2017.

11 Ibid.

12 Peter Spiller, *The Chapman Legal Family,* Victoria University Press, 1992. Henry Samuel Chapman was a businessman, pamphleteer and radical journalist who supported free trade and opposed Britain's corn laws, before becoming a lawyer in London. He was a close associate of Edward Gibbon Wakefield and shared his friend's enthusiasm for colonisation, advancing his views through the *New Zealand Journal*, a publication he launched in 1839 with backing from Wakefield's New Zealand Company. In 1843 he was appointed a judge of the Supreme Court of New Zealand for the southern district (which included Wellington, Nelson, New Plymouth and later Christchurch). He had a house built for his family in Karori, and called it Homewood. The house was later extended and since 1958 has been the residence of the British High Commissioner. The carpenter hired by Chapman to build his home was Samuel Parnell, who by then had made his celebrated stand for workers' rights in 1840 by refusing to work more than eight hours a day. Chapman was briefly the colonial secretary of Van Diemen Land (Tasmania), but was sacked after refusing to uphold the imperial government's policy of transporting convicts to the then penal colony. He later returned to New

Zealand as a judge of the Supreme Court in Dunedin.

13 Cath Kelly, interview with Lesley Hall, conducted as part of Hall's research for 'Better Red than Wed? Gender Relations and the Role of Women in the Communist Party of New Zealand, 1921–1970', PhD thesis, Victoria University, 2003. Kelly family archives.

14 Cath Kelly, interview with Pat Webster.

15 Siegfried Eichelbaum, letter to Walter Eichelbaum, December 16, 1935. Eichelbaum family archives.

16 Sir Thomas Eichelbaum, author interview, May 2018.

17 Eichelbaum family archives.

18 Sir Thomas Eichelbaum, author interview.

19 Walter and Frida were the nearest that Helen and Max Kelly had to grandparents, as Siegfried and Vera died long before they were born. There were frequent family outings from Shannon Street to visit them in Lower Hutt. On a trip to Berlin in 2014, Helen found the unmarked grave of Thomas's grandmother Sophie, who died in 1943 in a collection centre for Jews awaiting transportation to a concentration camp. A headstone and Stolperstein (stumbling stone) were later laid for her. The Stolpersteine project was started in 1996 by German artist Gunter Demnig. A Stolperstein is a small concrete cube with a brass inscription, laid at the place where a victim of Nazism last freely lived. As at October 2018, 70,000 Stolpersteine have been laid, making it the largest decentralised memorial in the world.

20 Queen Margaret College, testimonial for Catherine Eichelbaum, December 10, 1942. Kelly family archives.

21 Cath Kelly, interview with Pat Webster.

22 Ibid.

23 Ibid.

24 Cath Kelly, interview with Lesley Hall.

25 Ibid.

26 Ibid.

27 Cath was heavily involved in fundraising for and supporting small rural aid projects in Vietnam from 1990. In 2005 the president of Vietnam awarded her the Friendship Order and she maintained close links with the Vietnam Embassy in Wellington after it opened in 2003.

28 SIS, file note on Cath Eichelbaum, March 16, 1953.

29 George Fraser, *Seeing Red: Undercover in 1950s New Zealand,* Dunmore Press, 1995.

30 SIS, file notes on Cath Eichelbaum, November 8, 1951–April 22, 1957.

31 Cath Kelly, interview with Lesley Hall.

32 Ibid.

33 Ibid. Cath told Hall she was barred from getting a job as a vocational guidance officer, which she applied for again and again over three years, because she was a communist. Eventually, with the Public Service Association's backing, she appealed and won.

34 Gordon Dryden, *Out of the Red,* Collins, 1978.

35 Birchfield tried to resign, but the party rejected her resignation so that it could instead expel her for 'factionalism'. Maureen Birchfield, *She Dared to Speak: Connie Birchfield's Story,* University of Otago Press, 1998.

36 Cath Kelly, interview with Lesley Hall.

37 Stan Rodger, former president of the PSA, author interview, December 2018.

38 Margaret Brand later married Dan Long, a rising star in the PSA who was also heavily involved in the equal pay campaign. Long became PSA president in 1958 and general secretary in 1960.

39 Cath Kelly, interview with Anne Goodman. Provided to author by Anne Goodman.

40 Surveillance was a constant concern for Communist Party members. For instance, a Special District Circular put out by the Wellington district executive of the party in June 1955 warned of 'security pimps and informers on jobs where progressive work' was occurring, the risk of 'raids on people's

homes … [and] grabbing of documents', and telephone tapping for which 'up-to the-minute machinery … is in N.Z. and is in use'.

41 In 1974 Sutch was alleged by the SIS to be spying for the Russians. He was charged and acquitted.

42 Mark Derby, *White Collar Radical: Dan Long and the rise of the white collar unions.* Craig Potton Publishing, 2013.

43 Margaret Corner, *No Easy Victory: Towards Equal Pay for Women in the Government Service, 1890–1960*, New Zealand Public Service Association, Dan Long Trust, 1988.

44 Mark Derby, *White Collar Radical.*

45 Cath Kelly, interview with Lesley Hall.

46 Ken Douglas, author interview, July 2018.

47 Cath Kelly, interview with Pat Webster.

48 This is likely to be at least partly true, as the party saw the 'moral behaviour' of members as a security concern. In a 1955 Wellington District Circular entitled 'Sharpen Working Class Vigilance in the Ranks of Our Party', the district secretary, Ken Stanton, wrote that vigilance included 'frank and specific criticism of the moral behaviour of party members – eg, excess drinking, abnormal sex life, gambling, lying, irresponsible personal behaviour, consistant unpunctuality, etc'. Ronald Smith, 1921–1995: Papers, MS-Group-0327 94-189-1/3, ATL.

49 Lesley Hall, 'Better Red than Wed'.

50 Meg Bailey, author interview, November 2018.

51 Cath Kelly, interview with Pat Webster.

52 'Red Siren Behind Communist Infiltration Plan', *NZ Truth*, October 25, 1960.

53 Letters between Cath Kelly and Pat Kelly. Kelly family archives.

Chapter 2

1 Frank Deegan, *There's No Other Way: An Autobiography*, Toulouse Press, 1980.

2 Pat Kelly, interview with Pat Webster.

3 Britain's National Health Service, which provided universal free medical treatment, was not introduced until 1948, eight years after Patrick Kelly's death.

4 Pat Kelly, interview with Pat Webster.

5 Ibid.

6 Ibid.

7 Pat Kelly, unpublished. Pat wrote several vignettes of his childhood with the goal of self-publishing them. Provided to author by Hazel Armstrong.

8 Pat Kelly, interview with Pat Webster.

9 Pat Kelly, unpublished stories.

10 *Ten Pound Poms*, Ninox Films, 1997.

11 Pat Kelly, unpublished stories.

12 Ibid.

13 Pat Kelly, interview with Pat Webster. In an interview with Linda Fleming in 1979 Pat claimed to have thrown bricks at Mosley.

14 Ibid. Pat's childhood impression is supported by Owen's friend and fellow communist Frank Deegan, who wrote in his memoir *There's No Other Way* that 'money meant little to him; his life's work was helping his class'.

15 Frank Deegan, *There's No Other Way.*

16 Juliet Gardiner, *Wartime: Britain 1939–1945*, Headline, 2004.

17 Lolo Moss, recorded conversation with Dylan Kelly, 2018. Lolo was born Nora, but went by Lolo as Pat couldn't say her name. Provided to author by Dylan Kelly.

18 Merseyside Maritime Museum, National Museums Liverpool, 'Spirit of the Blitz'.

19 Lolo Moss, recorded conversation.

20 Pat Kelly, unpublished stories.

21 Ibid.

22 Lolo Moss, recorded conversation.

23 Max Kelly, author interview, April 2018.

24 Ibid.

25 Pat Kelly, interview with Pat Webster.

26 https://nzhistory.govt.nz/culture/assisted-immigration/administration; *Ten Pound Poms.*

27 *Ten Pound Poms.*

28 J.D. Gould, *The Rake's Progress? The New Zealand economy since 1945*, Hodder and Stoughton, 1982. By the same measure – GDP per capita – New Zealand's ranking had dropped to eighth by 1965 and 17th by 1970.

29 Assisted migrants had no idea where they would be posted until told their destination and their employer's name on arrival in New Zealand. Megan Hutching, *Long Journey for Sevenpence: An oral history of assisted immigration to New Zealand from the United Kingdom 1947 to 1975*, Victoria University Press in association with Historical Branch, Department of Internal Affairs, 1999.

30 Pat Kelly, interview with Geoff Robinson, Broadcasting Corporation of New Zealand, August 14, 1986, Ngā Taonga Sound and Vision.

31 Tony Endres, 'The New Zealand full employment goal: A survey of changing attitudes 1950 to 1980', *New Zealand Journal of Industrial Relations*, Volume 9, No. 1, May 1984.

32 Tim Pankhurst, 'Pat Kelly fights his good fight', *The New Zealand Sunday Times*, August 24, 1986.

33 *Ten Pound Poms.*

34 Tim Pankhurst, 'Pat Kelly fights his good fight'

35 Al Morrison, 'Kelly: When the cloth cap fits', *The Dominion*, March 6, 1993.

36 Pat Kelly, interview with Pat Webster.

37 Pat Kelly, interview with Geoff Robinson.

38 'Trades Council head Pat Kelly aims at removing Government', *The Dominion*, March 24, 1977.

39 Declassified SIS documents relating to Bill Andersen. Provided to author by Cybèle Locke.

40 'Aufait', 'Off the Record', *Zealandia*, April 17, 1958. Pat told interviewer Linda Fleming in 1979 that the church 'left him' in 1957 when he joined the Communist Party.

41 In a 1959 circular from the party's national secretariat, members were instructed: 'While a study of the Marxist classics must be vigorously pursued, Branch education should not sink to the level of mere academic recitals, but must be the living theory and stuff of class-struggle today.' 'Ronald Smith, 1921–1995', Papers, MS-Group-0327 94-189-1/3, ATL.

42 Pat Kelly, interview with Geoff Robinson.

43 Cath Kelly, interview with Pat Webster.

44 Ibid.

Chapter 3

1 Cath Kelly, interview with Lesley Hall.

2 Suffrage Day, September 19, marks the day in 1893 when New Zealand women became the first in any country to gain the right to vote.

3 Cath Kelly, interview with Pat Webster.

4 Ibid.

5 Cath Kelly, interview with Megan Cook. 'Women in the anti-Vietnam War movement' oral history project, 1996. OHInt-0452/07. ATL.

6 Roberto Giorgio Rabel, *New Zealand and the Vietnam War: Politics and Diplomacy*, Auckland University Press, 2005; Freda Cook, *A Tribute; Letters from Vietnam, 1961–1968*, The Fund, 1991.

7 Roberto Giorgio Rabel, *New Zealand and the Vietnam War.*

8 'Slogan-painting couple caught', *The Evening Post*, August 19, 1966. The person caught and fined with Cath was fellow Communist Party member and anti-Vietnam War activist George Goddard; The Committee on Vietnam was a 'shaky alliance of various tendencies, sects, pacifists, quakers, and assorted former [Communist Party] and similar members', according to Michael Law, who was installed as a young ex-student leader as chair of the committee in 1971. Cath and Pat were almost certainly party to his election, which was designed to block a member of Trotskyist Socialist Action League from being elected to the chair. Email correspondence with Michael Law, April 20, 2019.

9 Max Kelly, author interview, May 2018.

10 Ken Douglas, author interview, January 2019.

11 Bert Roth, *Trade Unions in New Zealand, Past and Present*, Reed Education, 1973.

12 Walsh was a foundation member of the Communist Party of New Zealand in 1921, but by the 1940s he was a vigorous anti-communist. He was vice-president of the Federation of Labour at the time of the 1951 waterfront lockout, and president from 1952 until his death in 1963. Pat Walsh, 'Fintan Patrick Walsh', *Te Ara*, 1998; Graeme Hunt, *Black Prince: The Biography of Fintan Patrick Walsh*, Penguin, 2004.

13 The curtain-raiser to the 151-day lockout was a decision by Labour prime minister Peter Fraser's government to deregister the communist-led Carpenters' Union in 1949 after it imposed a go-slow. That opened up a schism within the wider union movement between those, such as Walsh, who supported the government's punitive action against the communists, and militant unions, who split from the FOL in protest to form the rival Trade Union Congress.

14 Jim McAloon, 'New Zealand Since the War', in *New Zealand Government and Politics*, edited by Raymond Miller, Oxford University Press, 2010; Cybèle Locke, *Workers in the Margins: Union Radicals in Post-War New Zealand*, Bridget Williams Books, 2012; Bert Roth, *Trade Unions in New Zealand*.

15 Bert Roth, *Trade Unions in New Zealand.*

16 Receivers were sent in to seize its assets, and when the union secretary refused to hand over the property, he was arrested, charged and fined £50. With government and employer backing, several small unions – derided as 'scab' outfits – were set up to replace and foil the militancy of the deregistered drivers' union.

17 Bert Roth, *Trade Unions in New Zealand.*

18 Cath Kelly, interview with Pat Webster.

19 David Grant, 'Rona Bailey', *Foreign Control Watchdog* 110, December 2005.

20 Mark Derby, *White Collar Radical.*

21 Rob Campbell, *The Only Weapon: 75 Years of the Wellington Drivers' Union*, Wellington Drivers' Union, 1976.

22 Ken Douglas, author interview, January 2019.

23 to come

23 During the 1950s and 1960s General Wage Orders were issued about every two years. Pat Walsh, 'An Unholy Alliance: The 1968 Nil Wage Order', *New Zealand Journal of History*, 1994, Vol 28, No 2. In 1936 the Labour government made union membership compulsory for workers covered by awards. In 1961 compulsory membership was theoretically abolished, but replaced with the 'unqualified preference' clause. These clauses were negotiated as part of awards and required all workers who were covered to join the union – which effectively meant that compulsory membership continued.

24 Bert Roth, *Trade Unions in New Zealand.*

25 Melanie Nolan and Pat Walsh, 'Labour's Leg-iron? Assessing Trade Unions and Arbitration in New Zealand', in *Trade Unions, Work and Society; A Century of the Arbitration System*, Dunmore Press, 1994.

26 Brian Roper, 'The Fire Last Time: The rise of class struggle and progressive social movements in Aotearoa/New Zealand, 1968 to 1977', *Marxist Interventions 3, 2011.*

27 Noel Woods, *Industrial Conciliation and Arbitration in New Zealand*, Government Printer, 1963.

28 Brian Roper, 'The Fire Last Time; Pat Walsh, 'The State and Industrial Relations in New Zealand', in *State and Economy in New Zealand*, edited by Brian Roper and Chris Rudd, Otago University Press, 1993.

29 Stevan Eldred-Grigg, *New Zealand Working People, 1890–1990*, Dunmore Press, 1990.

30 Helen Kelly, interview with John Cowan, Newstalk ZB, July 27, 2015.

31 Cath Kelly, interview with Pat Webster.

32 Ken Douglas, author interview, January 2019.

33 Trevor Richards, author interview, April 2019.

34 Helen Kelly, eulogy for Pat Kelly, 2004. Kelly family recording.

35 Ibid.

36 Helen Kelly, interview with John Cowan.

37 Ibid.

38 Max Kelly, author interview, April 2018.

39 Ibid.

40 Rebecca Macfie, 'The final campaign', *New Zealand Listener*, May 16, 2015.

41 Cath Kelly, interview with Megan Cook.

42 J.D. Gould, *The Rake's Progress?*; Michael Reddell and Cath Sleeman, 'Some perspectives on past recessions', *Reserve Bank of New Zealand Bulletin*, Vol 71, No 2, June 2008; Paul Dalziel, 'New Zealand's Economic Reforms: An assessment', *Review of Political Economy*, Volume 14, Number 1, 2002.

43 Cath Kelly, interviews with Pat Webster and Anne Goodman.

44 'Reds seen everywhere, Carp says', *The Dominion*, August 9, 1971.

45 Unions won wage increases of 24 percent between 1969 and 1973, compared with only two percent between 1955 and 1966. Ryan Bodman, 'The Public Have Had a Gutsful and So Have We', *New Zealand Journal of History* 48, 2014.

46 Anne James, author interview, May 2018; Anne Rodger, author interview, December 2018; Clare Wells, oral history of Cath Kelly. Kelly family archives; Cath Kelly, interview with Pat Webster.

47 Rebecca Macfie, 'The final campaign'; Helen Kelly, interviewed by Tony Sutorious for documentary *Helen Kelly – Together*, 2016.

48 George Rosenberg, author interview, May 2019.

49 Max Kelly, author interview.

50 Ibid.

51 Rebecca Macfie, 'The final campaign'.

52 Dave Morgan, author interview, May 2018.

53 Matthew Dearnaley, 'Retiring Union Leader says he'll continue to fight', *The New Zealand Herald*, October 30, 2003. Retrieved from nzherald.co.nz, January 21, 2020); 'Dave Morgan: Maritime unionist and working class leader', *The Maritimes*, December 2004.

54 Dave Morgan, author interview.

55 Alby White, author interview, December 2018.

56 Jackie Ford, author interview, May 2018.

57 Shelley Hopper, author interview, December 2018.

58 Ken Douglas, author interview.

59 Jackie Ford, author interview.

60 David Long, comment to author, July 2019.

61 Tom Patrick, author interview, October 2018.

62 Max Kelly, author interview.

63 Evan Smith, 'Peking Review and global anti-imperialist networks in the 1960s', https://hatfulofhistory.wordpress.com/category/new-zealand/.

64 *People's Voice*, February 9, 1966.

65 Ron Smith, *Working Class Son: My fight against capitalism and war*. R.J. Smith, 1994.

66 Cath Kelly, interview with Pat Webster.

67 Pat Kelly, letters. Kelly family archives.

68 *People's Voice*, January 2, 1970.

69 Cath Kelly, interview with Pat Webster.

70 Tommy Jefferson, 'Pat Kelly: Labour's Modern Gadfly', *Labour Network*, Volume IV 3 (Winter 1986).

71 Ron Smith, *Working Class Son*.

72 Ibid.

73 Cath Kelly, interview with Anne Goodman.

74 Cath Kelly, interview with Lesley Hall.

Chapter 4

1 Alison Saunders, author interview, December 2018.

2 Max Kelly, author interview.

3 Helen Kinsella, author interview, May 2018.

4 Tom Patrick, author interview, October 2018.

5 Stephen Blackburn went on to become the head of production of the World of Wearable Arts.

6 Stephen Blackburn, author interview, October 2018.

7 Rob McKeen, author interview, December 2018.

8 Tom Docherty, author interview, December 2018.

9 Alison Saunders, author interview.

10 Ibid.

11 Helen Kelly, interview with Tony Sutorius, filmed at the Shannon Street house in 2016. With thanks to Tony Sutorius for the use of out-take files from the documentary *Helen Kelly – Together.*

12 Referred to hereafter as Cleaners Union.

13 Cath Kelly, letter to Ann and Wolfgang Rosenberg, March 12, 1981. Kelly family archives.

14 Helen Kelly, diaries 1979, 1981. Kelly family archives.

15 Pat Kelly, interview with Karl Zohrab. Provided to author by Karl Zohrab.

16 Helen Kelly, interview with Tony Sutorius.

17 Don Swan, author interview, April 2019.

18 Helen Kelly, diary, 1981. Kelly family archives. Muldoon was widely referred to as 'Piggy'.

19 Helen Kelly, diary, 1981. Kelly family archives.

20 Now Year 12.

21 Helen Kelly, Wellington High School leaving certificate, December 1981. Kelly family archives.

22 Max Kelly, author interview.

23 Cath Kelly, interview with Anne Goodman.

24 Annette King, author interview, October 2018.

25 Pat Kelly, interview with Karl Zohrab.

26 Pat Kelly, interview with Pat Webster.

27 Ken Douglas, author interview.

28 Hazel Armstrong, author interview, July 2018.

29 Peter Cranney, author interview, May 2018.

30 *Advance*, December 1979.

31 *Advance*, January 1979.

32 Wellington and Taranaki Caretakers, Cleaners and Lift Attendants and Watchmen's Industrial Union of Workers minutes. MS-Group-0491, MSY-4200, ATL; Brosnan, Peter & Wilkinson, Frank, 'Low pay and industrial relations: The case of contract cleaning', *New Zealand Journal of Industrial Relations*, 1989 (14) 83–89.

33 *Advance*, April 1986. By 1986 arbitration was no longer compulsory.

34 Don Swan, author interview.

35 Pat told journalist Tim Pankhurst in 1986 that he'd been blocked from getting on to the FOL executive because he was seen as a maverick. 'What they really mean is I don't toe their line,' he said. *New Zealand Times*, August 24, 1986.

36 The roots of the industry stretched back to the 1920s and had been nurtured by decades of protective government policies designed to maintain full employment, build New Zealand's industrial base and help control the country's balance of payments.

37 Peter Cranney, author interview.

38 Robert Reid, author interview, April 2019. New Zealand withdrew from the Vietnam War in 1972.

39 John Ryall, email correspondence with author, April 28, 2018.

40 Peter Cranney, author interview.

41 Wellington and Taranaki Caretakers, Cleaners and Lift Attendants and Watchmen's Industrial Union of Workers minutes. MS-Group-0491, MSY-4157, ATL.

42 Don Swan, author interview, October 2019.

43 Ryan Bodman, 'The public have had a gutsful and so have we: The alienation of organised labour in New Zealand, 1968–1975', *New Zealand Journal of History*, 48, 2014.

44 Department of Statistics, 'Work Stoppages and Industrial Unions 1978–1983'.

45 Wool prices crashed in December 1966, triggering a recession in 1967 and prompting the government to cut food subsidies, hike the cost of state housing and other charges, increase taxes on alcohol, tobacco and petrol, and devalue the New Zealand dollar

to increase the cost of imports and improve returns for exporters.

46 The 1973 oil shock quadrupled New Zealand's oil costs. New Zealand suffered as part of a global crisis when the Middle Eastern oil-exporting countries imposed an embargo targeting nations that had supported Israel in the Yom Kippur War. The 1979 oil shock followed the Iranian Revolution, after which oil production dropped and prices soared; James Belich notes that the 40 percent deterioration in New Zealand's terms of trade in the mid '70s was similar to the decline in the Depression. *Paradise Reforged, A history of the New Zealanders, from 1880 to the year 2000,* Allen Lane, 2001.

47 Department of Statistics, 'Work Stoppages and Industrial Unions 1978–1983'.

48 Bryce Fraser (ed), *The New Zealand Book of Events*, Reed Methuen, 1986; Alison Rudd, 'Remembering the day farmers took action', *Otago Daily Times*, June 11, 2013. Retrieved from odt.co.nz, October 15, 2020.

49 Jim McAloon, *Judgements of All Kinds*, Victoria University Press, 2013; James Belich, *Paradise Reforged*. Muldoon introduced universal national superannuation in 1978. Supplementary Minimum Prices – just one of a range of taxpayer-funded payments to farmers during this period – were introduced in 1978. They put a floor under the prices farmers received for meat, wool and dairy products. Muldoon greatly increased the handouts to farmers from 1981.

50 Brian Roper, 'The Fire Last Time'.

51 Pat Kelly, interview with Linda Fleming. Kelly family archives.

52 Helen Kelly, diary, 1979. Kelly family archives.

53 Raymond Harbridge, 'The 1980 Federation of Labour Conference', *New Zealand Journal of Industrial Relations,* 1980, 5.

54 Cath Kelly, letter to Ann and Wolfgang Rosenberg, March 12, 1981. Kelly family archives.

55 Helen Kelly, diary, 1981. Kelly family archives.

56 Helen Kinsella, author interview, June 2018.

57 Jim McAloon, *Judgements of All Kinds.* McAloon describes a proposal developed in 1980 by the Federation of Labour and Employers' Federation for a 'bold new set of proposals' on wage-fixing reform, in which the Arbitration Court would set a minimum single adult wage, then unions would negotiate on top of that. There would be a shift from occupational awards to industry agreements, which promised to break rigid pay relativities. However, Treasury was 'unenthusiastic', and the government did not accept crucial details of the proposal. The possibility of reform at a critical moment was therefore lost. The FOL then rejected proposals by Muldoon for a wage-tax trade-off that purported to maintain real incomes without sharp wage rises. The FOL thought the proposal would end up harming low-paid workers.

58 Statistics New Zealand, Long Term Data Series, Table B2.2.

59 Wellington and Taranaki Caretakers, Cleaners and Lift Attendants and Watchmen's Industrial Union of Workers minutes. MS-Group-0491, MSY-4198, ATL.

60 Helen Kelly, diary, 1982. Kelly family archives.

61 New Zealand Official Yearbook 1985.

Chapter 5

1 Clare Leniston and Ralph McAllister, author interviews, August 2018.

2 Ernie's first dog, Patch, was infamous for having jumped off the roof of Trades Hall in pursuit of a seagull. He survived, with a limp.

3 Clare Leniston, author interview.

4 Raymond Harbridge, 'The 1983 Federation of Labour Conference', *New Zealand Journal of Industrial Relations,* 1983, 8; Raymond Harbridge and Don Edwards, 'The Federation of Labour's right to bargain campaign: Its background, impact and effectiveness', *New Zealand Journal of Industrial Relations,* 1985, 10.

5 Raymond Harbridge and Don Edwards,

'The Federation of Labour's right to bargain campaign'; *The Press*, March 27, 1984.

6 Ibid. Over the course of the 'right to bargain' campaign from March 26 to June 20, 1984, over 57,000 workers took industrial action, Half were meat workers or waterfront workers. A key objective of the campaign was to help bring about a change of government as an election was due in November. Harbridge and Edwards report that, apart from the 1951 waterfront lockout, it was the largest ever industrial dispute in New Zealand in terms of the number of workers who took part and the number of working days lost.

7 Bert Roth, 'Chronicles', *New Zealand Journal of Industrial Relations*, 1983, 8. 'The rich had grown richer while the poor had grown poorer,' Roth wrote. Real disposable incomes of the top fifth of income earners rose 7.8 percent from December 1981 to December 1982, while those of the lowest paid declined 4.6 percent.

8 Bert Roth, 'Chronicles', *New Zealand Journal of Industrial Relations*, 1982, 7.

9 Department of Statistics, New Zealand Long Run Data Series, Labour Market Series, Table B.2.2. Chapple series.

10 Bert Roth, 'Chronicles', *New Zealand Journal of Industrial Relations*, 1982, 7; Roth, 'Chronicles', 1983, 8.

11 Department of Statistics, 'Work Stoppages and Industrial Unions, 1983–84'.

12 Bert Roth, 'Chronicles', *New Zealand Journal of Industrial Relations*, 1984, 9. Roth lists strikes by railway, carpet mill, newspaper, hotel and brewing workers in response to fellow workers quitting their unions.

13 Helen Kelly, interview with Tony Sutorius.

14 Max Kelly, author interview; 'Twelve Questions', *The New Zealand Herald*, August 9, 2012.

15 *Cold Case: Ernie Abbott, Trades Hall Bombing 1984*, Screentime, June 2019.

16 Graeme Clarke, author interview, May 2019.

17 Henry Stubbs, author interview, August 2018.

18 Graeme Clarke, author interview.

19 Detective Senior Sergeant Warwick McKee, author interview, May 2018.

20 Tim Donoghue, 'Kelly considered picking up case', *The Dominion*, April 6, 1984.

21 Graeme Whimp, email correspondence with author, January 27, 2020. Whimp was one of a number of out-of-town unionists who were in Wellington that day.

22 Henry Stubbs, author interview; Unions Wellington, Facebook post, '35 Year Anniversary of Trades Hall bombing', https://www.facebook.com/UnionsWellington/posts/35-years-ago-today-ernie-abbott-murdered-in-anti-union-terrorist-attack-on-welli/1267485223399589/.

23 Helen Kelly, interview with Jesse Mulligan, Radio New Zealand, October 26, 2014.

24 Susan Arthur, 'Bomber called paranoid loner', *The Dominion*, May 1, 1984.

25 Helen Kelly, interview with Tony Sutorius.

26 Ibid.

27 *The Hatred Campaign*, Vanguard Films, 1985.

28 A line derived from a working-class poem, 'We have fed you all for a thousand years'.

29 *The Hatred Campaign*.

30 Doug Catley, author interview, December 2018. Catley respected and trusted Pat. 'The man had integrity,' Catley said. 'Pat Kelly's word was his word.'

31 Helen Kelly, interview with Tony Sutorius.

32 Chris Wratt, author interview, July 2018.

33 Clare Leniston, author interview, August 2018.

34 'Wellington Trades Hall Bombing – Papers', Wellington and Taranaki Caretakers, Cleaners and Lift Attendants and Watchmen's Industrial Union of Workers. MS-Group-0419, 96-235-12/1. ATL.

35 This campaign was part of the long-running effort by the Cleaners Union to gain pay parity between public sector and school cleaners and cleaners employed by private contractors, which was won with the 30 percent pay rise

awarded by the Arbitration Court in 1986 (see Chapter 4). Other unions levied their members to support the striking cleaners, and when three workers at Todd Motors refused to pay the $4 a week levy, 350 workers went on strike. Debbie Hannan and Tim Donoghue, 'War on wage freeze widens', *The Dominion*, May 16, 1984; Ian Hodgetts, author interview, October 2019.

36 Helen Kelly, interview with Jesse Mulligan.

37 Liz Baldwin-Featherstone, author interview, October 2018.

38 Ralph McAllister, email correspondence with author, August 2019.

39 Ralph McAllister, author interview, August 2018.

40 Nicholas Carroll, 'Principles and Philosophy Underpinning the Teaching Practice of Ralph McAllister', 1997.

41 Allan Marsden, author interview, July 2019.

42 Chris Wratt, email correspondence with author, June 2019.

43 Michelle Saban, author interview, August 2018.

44 Ralph McAllister, email correspondence with the author, August 2019.

45 'University of Life: Learning the importance of being a great teacher', *The Dominion Post*, August 2, 2010.

46 Parks White, author interview, June 2019.

47 Ibid.

48 Robert Reid, author interview.

49 Wellington Teachers' College Council minutes, 1984.

50 Marilyn Waring, *The Political Years*, Bridget Williams Books, 2019. Waring had been told the government would refuse to recommend to the governor-general that he give the Bill the royal assent.

51 Waring gives a detailed and gripping account of the days and hours leading up to Muldoon's snap election announcement in *The Political Years*, pp 335–345.

52 Anne Goodman, author interview, June 2019.

53 Fran Wilde, author interview, July 2019.

54 *Little World*, March 26, 1984.

55 Parks White, email correspondence with author, June 2019.

56 Jim McAloon and Peter Franks, *The New Zealand Labour Party, 1916–2016*, Victoria University Press, 2016.

57 Barry Gustafson, *His Way; A Biography of Robert Muldoon*, Auckland University Press, 2000.

58 Hugh W. Oliver, 'The Labour Caucus and Economic Policy Formation, 1981 to 1984', in *The Making of Rogernomics*, edited by Brian Easton, Auckland University Press, 1989. Oliver notes that highly interventionist and regulatory policies were characteristic of Douglas's proposals throughout the early 1980s, including government assistance for small business and new industries, and using tax, exchange rate and protection policies to influence the business environment. His attitude to the removal of industry protections was cautious and gradualist, and he thought there needed to be positive policies to retrain and re-educate the workforce, and an active labour market policy. By the end of 1983 his views had shifted to the right and 'increasingly Douglas came to see state intervention as the root of all economic evil'. Malcolm McKinnon, in *Treasury: The New Zealand Treasury 1840–2000*, Auckland University Press, 2003, describes Douglas's *There's Got to Be a Better Way!*, published in 1980, as 'an eclectic ABC of commentaries on a variety of economic issues' and says by 1984 Douglas's thinking had 'become more coherent'. 'New Right' was the epithet commonly used at the time as shorthand for the suite of market liberalisation and deregulation policies associated with Roger Douglas. In later years the term neoliberal became the standard label for these policies and associated theories.

59 Ibid.

60 Colin James, *The Quiet Revolution*, Allen and Unwin, 1986.

61 Wellington and Taranaki Caretakers, Cleaners

and Lift Attendants and Watchmen's Industrial Union of Workers, Secretary's Report, July 30, 1984. MS-Group-0491, MSY-4199. ATL.

62 *Little World*, July 23, 1984.

63 Malcolm McKinnon, *Treasury: The New Zealand Treasury 1840–2000*. Auckland University Press, 2003.

64 Wellington and Taranaki Caretakers, Cleaners and Lift Attendants and Watchmen's Industrial Union of Workers, Secretary's report, December 10, 1984. MS-Group-0491, MSY-4199. ATL.

65 Michael Bassett, *Working with David: Inside the Lange Cabinet*, Hodder Moa, 2008.

66 Reserve Bank of New Zealand, 'Retail interest rates: Weighted average lending and deposits' – B3.

67 Stan Rodger, email correspondence with author, September 2019. Rodger wrote in 1985 that he had been concerned that voluntary unionism had the greatest impact on workers in small scattered workplaces where unions found it hard to recruit, and that it was the more moderate rather than the militant unions that were most affected. Stan Rodger, 'The Government's Role in Industrial Relations', *New Zealand Journal of Industrial Relations*, 1985, 10. The mechanism for compulsory union membership was the 'unqualified preference clause' in registered awards, which required every adult worker covered by that document to join the relevant union within 14 days (provided they were actually asked to join). Under Labour's restoration of compulsory unionism, unions had to ballot members every three years on whether to retain the union membership clause in their awards. Raymond Harbridge and Susan Webber,'Trends in Official Union Membership, 1983–1985', *New Zealand Journal of Industrial Relations*, 1987, 12.

68 Wellington and Taranaki Caretakers, Cleaners and Lift Attendants and Watchmen's Industrial Union of Workers, Annual Report, 1985. MS-Group-0491, MSY-4199. ATL.

69 Colin James, *The Quiet Revolution*.

70 Wellington and Taranaki Caretakers, Cleaners and Lift Attendants and Watchmen's Industrial Union of Workers, Secretary's Report, September 1985. MS-Group-0491, MSY-4199. ATL.

71 Don Swan, author interview, July 2019.

72 Chris Trotter, *No Left Turn*, Random House, 2007.

73 Margaret Wilson, author interview, July 2018.

74 Cath Kelly, interview with Anne Goodman.

75 Peter Dunne, author interview, June 2019.

76 Chris Wratt, author interview, July 2018.

77 Helen Kelly, diary, 1986. Kelly family archives.

78 Ibid.

79 Chris Wratt, author interview.

80 Wellington Teachers' College, Personal and Professional Report, Helen Margaret Kelly. Kelly family archives.

81 Tom Patrick, author interview, July 2018

82 Jean Marending, author interview, August 2018.

83 Bruce Jesson, 'A Study in Blue', *Metro*, December 1989.

84 Chris Wratt, author interview.

85 Rebecca Wright, author interview, July 2019.

86 Richard Willis, 'Ten years of change in New Zealand manufacturing employment', *Labour, Employment and Work in New Zealand*, 1994.

87 P. Brosnan and D. Rea, 'Rogernomics and the Labour Market', Industrial Relations Centre, Victoria University, Working paper 3/91, 1991.

88 Ibid.

89 Malcolm McKinnon, *Treasury: The New Zealand Treasury 1840–2000.*

90 P. Brosnan and D. Rea, 'Rogernomics and the Labour Market'.

91 Simon Collins, 'Rogernomics: The Economic Aftermath' in *The Making of Rogernomics*, edited by Brian Easton, Auckland University Press, 1989.

92 Robin Shave, 'Kelly fears impact from policies', *The Dominion*, July 28, 1986.

93 Wellington and Taranaki Caretakers, Cleaners and Lift Attendants and Watchmen's Industrial Union of Workers, Secretary's Report, *Annual Report*, 1986. MS-Group-0491, MSY-4200. ATL.

94 Ruth Dyson, author interview, August 2019.

95 Mike Smith, author interview, July 2019; Michael Law and Gemma Piercy, 'The Carmichael vision and training reform: Some insights from across the Tasman', Arts and Social Sciences Papers, University of Waikato, 2000.

96 Stan Rodger, author interview, December 2018; Stan Rodger, 'The Government's Role in Industrial Relations', *New Zealand Journal of Industrial Relations*, 1985, 10.

97 Rodger's State Sector Act drew massive protests from public sector unions and Rodger was stripped temporarily of his life membership of the PSA.

98 Stan Rodger, author interview.

99 Association of Consumers and Taxpayers, a political party formed in 1993 by Roger Douglas and former National Party MP, Derek Quigley, espousing New Right (neoliberal) policies.

100 Pat Webster, author interview, July 2019.

101 Pat Kelly, speech to affiliates council, 1989.

102 Ruth Dyson, author interview, August 2019.

103 Brenda Pilott, author interview, July 2019.

104 Max Kelly, comment to author, November 2020.

105 Johnsonville School, Helen Kelly: Mid-year report, Std 1–2 class, Room 5. Kelly family archives.

106 Chris Wratt, email correspondence with author, September 12, 2019.

107 Helen Kelly and Chris Wratt, wedding service sheet. Kelly family archives.

Chapter 6

1 Sonja Davies, quoted in 'Fighting for Recognition of Childcare as Real Work' by Helen May in *Trade Unions, Work and Society: The Centenary of the Arbitration System*, edited by Pat Walsh, Dunmore Press, 1994.

2 The president of the New Zealand Free Kindergarten Association, Elizabeth Hamilton, commented of her members in 1952: 'Our girls are very attractive and none of them contemplates teaching for very long. Consequently it is rather difficult to get them to take a wider view of their profession.' In the 1960s, because of a shortage of kindergarten teachers, married women were encouraged to apply for the courses run by the country's four kindergarten training centres, provided they met various requirements including 'that her marital status does not interfere with her training' and 'suitable arrangements are made for the care of her children'. Quoted in *Women Together: A history of women's organisations in New Zealand* edited by Anne Else, Department of Internal Affairs, 1993.

3 Helen May, 'Fighting for Recognition of Childcare as Real Work'.

4 Helen May, 'Twenty Years of Consenting Parties: The politics of "teaching" and "working" in childcare, 1985–2005', NZEI Te Riu Roa, 2005.

5 Kindergarten teachers were the first in the early childhood sector to undertake pre-service training provided by the government, and were state sector employees. After the State Sector Act in 1988 they, like other state employees, had to obtain an award under the Labour Relations Act, which occurred in 1989.

6 Helen May, 'Fighting for recognition'; Helen May, 'Twenty Years of Consenting Parties'. The early childhood workers' national award was not unusual in containing low pay. A study by Raymond Harbridge found that when the statutory minimum wage was increased in September 1990, 31 registered awards contained adult pay rates below the new minimum. The Minimum Wage Act took precedence over any rate set in an award. Raymond Harbridge, 'Flexibility in Collective Wage Bargaining in New Zealand: Facts and Folklore', *New Zealand Journal of Industrial Relations*, 1990 (15).

7 Clare Wells, 'The Impact of Change – Against the Odds', paper to Early Childhood Education Convention, Dunedin 1991, citing Treasury's *Briefing to the Incoming Government*, 1987, Volume II. Treasury also warned that the move towards 'professionalism' in early childhood education could have costs that 'exceed the benefits'; Sandy Farquhar and Andrew Gibbons, 'Early childhood education policy pathways: A learning story' in *Successful Public Policy: Lessons from Australia and New Zealand*, edited by Joannah Luetjens, Michael Mintrom and Paul 't Hart, ANU Press, Australian National University, 2019.

8 Helen Baxter, author interview, August 2019.

9 Hazel Armstrong, author interview, August 2019.

10 Helen Baxter, email correspondence with author, November 2019.

11 Linda Mitchell, author interview, October 2018.

12 Clare Wells, author interview, June 2018.

13 Linda Mitchell, author interview.

14 Clare Wells, author interview, January 2020. The Wellington Media Collective ran from 1978 until 1998, and was a confederation of designers, artists, printers and photographers that produced material for unions and community and activist groups.

15 Clare Wells, email correspondence with author, September 2019.

16 Helen Baxter, author interview, October 2019.

17 Helen Baxter, author interview, August 2019.

18 Clare Wells, author interview.

19 Clare Wells, 'In whose interests?: Looking back – thinking forward', paper to the 11th Early Childhood Convention, Rotorua, 2015.

20 'High time for a fair deal', Joint Issue: *KTA News* and *Roundabout*, September 1989.

21 It's not clear how this trip came about. It was not paid for by TUEA. However, Ken Douglas, who was president of the CTU at the time, said trips like this were sometimes sponsored by unions in the host country.

22 Helen Kelly, USSR journal. Kelly family archives.

23 Helen Kelly, letter to Pat and Cath Kelly, April 10, 1990. Kelly family archives.

24 Mike Jaspers, 'Rich richer, poor poorer', *National Business Review*, November 22, 1990. The story was reporting on a New Zealand Planning Council report that noted lower tax rates for top earners, the introduction of GST, rising unemployment and hard times among the self-employed were key drivers of the trend towards greater inequality.

25 Peter Franks and Jim McAloon, *The New Zealand Labour Party, 1916–2016*, Victoria University Press, 2016.

26 Ruth Dyson, author interview.

27 *Double Take*, July 1990.

28 *Double Take*, August 1990.

29 Douglas Myers, 'Labour Market Reform: Getting it Right', business and news media briefing, Wellington, June 23, 1987, in *Labour Markets and Employment*, New Zealand Business Roundtable, April 1988.

30 Douglas Myers, 'New Zealand Labour Market: Breaking Moulds', speech to Conference of Engineering Employers, Auckland, September 18, 1988, in *Labour Markets and Employment*.

31 Roger Kerr, 'The New Zealand Business Roundtable: Roles and Goals', speech to Auckland Rotary Club, November 12, 1990.

32 Anthony Hubbard, 'Crusader of the Roundtable', *New Zealand Listener*, May 4, 1992.

33 Roger Kerr, 'Seven deadly economic sins of the twentieth century', New Zealand Post College of Business Jubilee Lecture, August 6, 1997. Other sins, in Kerr's view, were special interest lobbying, inflation, unemployment and protection.

34 Roger Kerr, memorandum to Sir Ron Trotter, '1990/91 Budget', April 4, 1990. MS-Group-2154, 2013-038-044. ATL.

35 Roger Kerr, 'New Zealand Business Roundtable: Roles and Goals'.

36 Paul Harris and Linda Twinnane, *First Knights:*

An Investigation of the New Zealand Business Roundtable, Howling at the Moon Publishing, 1998. For example, Air New Zealand leader Jim Scott received a black mark, with Kerr noting he gave 'an appalling speech full of Muldoonist lines'. MS-Group-2154, 2013-038-045. ATL.

37 Roger Kerr, memorandum, 'NZBR Communications Strategy', to Sir Ron Trotter, Roderick Deane, Alan Gibbs, David Richwhite, Peter Troughton, cc to Barry Dineen, Peter Menzies, Colin Jenkins, March 26, 1990. MS-Group-2154, 2013-038-044. ATL.

38 For instance, an *Auckland Star* editorial that warned against trying to improve New Zealand's competitiveness through low wages 'could have been written by Karl Marx ... Like Marx's work, it abounded with errors,' Kerr wrote in reply on July 27, 1990. Brian Easton, a prominent economist who challenged the prevailing New Right ethos, was dismissed as 'removed from the mainstream of economic thinking' in a letter from Kerr to the editor of the New Zealand Press Association complaining about the selection of economists quoted in an article about the value of the New Zealand dollar. Kerr sneered at the work of economist Bryan Philpott; in a letter on March 29, 1990, to Ken Baker of the Enterprise New Zealand Trust, who had made reference to Philpott in a new publication called *Economic Alert*, Kerr wrote that ideas based on Philpott's 'research' (the quote marks were Kerr's) were 'garbage'. MS-Group-2154, 2003-038-044/046/050. ATL. Philpott referred to the Business Roundtable as 'ayatollahs': Brian Fallow, 'Obituary: Bryan Philpott', *The New Zealand Herald*, July 21, 2000. Retrieved January 20, 2020.

39 Stan Rodger, author interview.

40 Douglas Myers, 'Labour Market Reform: Getting it Right'.

41 Rebecca Macfie, 'Labour prepared unions for blast of deregulation', *National Business Review*, July 2, 1990. Clark's amendment also brought back compulsory arbitration to resolve long-stalled award negotiations.

42 Rebecca Macfie, 'Wage rounds more flexible, survey shows', *National Business Review*, January 15, 1991; Ellen Dannin, *Working Free: The Origins and Impact of the Employment Relations Act*, Auckland University Press, 1997.

43 Rebecca Macfie, 'Market flexibility not complete answer', *Christchurch Star*, February 28, 1990.

44 Ellen Dannin, *Working Free*. Dannin's point was underscored when, in 1996, one of the experts engaged by the Business Roundtable, Charles Baird, bemoaned the state of labour law in the US, complaining particularly about the fact that if the majority of workers in a site voted to be represented by a union, the union had the right to represent all the workers there, and that employers had a legal duty to bargain in good faith. 'Deregulation of the New Zealand Labour Market: Things Done and Left Undone', Charles W. Baird, California State University, speech to *Moving Forward* conference to mark the 5th anniversary of the Employment Contracts Act, May 15, 1996.

45 Douglas Myers, 'Where to Now in Labour Relations?', speech to 'Managing Change in Industrial Relations' conference, Institute for International Research, Auckland, July 3, 1990; Rebecca Macfie, 'Labour law update vital, says Myers', *National Business Review*, August 1, 1990.

46 New Zealand Business Roundtable, Submission to the Minister of Labour on the Report of the Committee of Enquiry into Industrial Democracy, February 1990; Roger Kerr, 'Common law and common sense: The Employment Contracts Bill', speech to the HR Nicholls Society, Melbourne, April 13, 1991.

47 Raymond Harbridge, 'Flexibility in Collective Wage Bargaining in New Zealand: Facts and Folklore', *New Zealand Journal of Industrial Relations*, 1990, 15; Rebecca Macfie, 'Radicalism sets reform pace', *National Business Review*, January 30, 1991. Wally Gardner, the head of the Manufacturers Association, said the majority of employers enjoyed the security provided by the award system of knowing what their competitors were paying.

48 Ellen Dannin, *Working Free.*

49 Ibid.

50 Penelope Brook, *Freedom at Work: The case for reforming labour law in New Zealand*, Oxford University Press, Auckland, 1990.

51 Ellen Dannin, *Working Free.*

52 'National Party Policies for the 1990s: Creating a Decent Society', authorised by Cindy Flook, Secretary General, New Zealand National Party, 1990.

53 Ruth Richardson, *Making a Difference*, Shoal Bay Press, 1995. In outlining the ideological tussle within National, Richardson wrote that by early 1990 Birch was proposing a balloting-out mechanism for workers covered by existing awards, although he was prepared to allow individual contracts for new entrants into the labour market. 'Right up until the time we took office, Bill [Birch] was still thinking in terms of simply amending the Labour Relations Act.'

54 Ruth Richardson, author interview, November 2019.

55 For instance, Roger Kerr, confidential memorandum to Bill Birch, John Luxton, Warren Kyd, Roger Maxwell, Murray McCully, Ross Meurant, Maurice Williamson, cc to Ken Bania, Alan Jones, Anne Knowles, Steve Marshall, Roseanne Meo, Penelope Brook, 'Reform of Labour Market Legislation in New Zealand', July 16, 1990. MS-Group-2154, 2013-038-046. ATL; 'NZBR Meeting with National Party Front Bench', August 17, 1990, 'Agenda'. MS-Group-2154, 2013-038-047. ATL.

56 Roger Kerr, memorandum to Sir Ron Trotter, Barry Dineen, Alan Gibbs, Colin Jenkins, David Richwhite and Peter Troughton, March 7, 1990. MS-Group-2154, 2013-038-044. ATL.

57 Roger Kerr, memorandum to Douglas Myers, 'National Party Position on Employment Equity', July 2, 1990. MS-Group-2154, 2013-038-046. ATL.

58 NZBR Meeting with National Party Front Bench, August 17, 1990, Aide Memoire, August 16, 1990. MS-Group-2154, 2013-038-047. ATL.

59 Pat Walsh and Rose Ryan, 'The making of the Employment Contracts Act', in *Employment Contracts: New Zealand Experiences*, edited by Raymond Harbridge, Victoria University Press, 1993; Ellen Dannin, *Working Free;* Rebecca Macfie, 'Birch gets rolling on reforms', *National Business Review*, November 8, 1990.

60 Paul Bell, author interview, September 2019.

61 Roger Kerr memorandum to Ron Trotter, 'Preparation for New Labour Legislation', June 5, 1990; Roger Kerr, letter to Jim Farmer, 'Labour Law Project', July 11, 1990. MS-Group-2154, 2013-038-046. ATL; Ruth Richardson, author interview.

62 Roger Kerr memorandum to Bill Birch, John Luxton, Warren Kyd, Roger Maxwell, Murray McCully, Ross Meurant, Maurice Williamson, cc Ken Bania, Alan Jones, Anne Knowles, Steve Marshall, Roseanne Meo, Penelope Brook, July 16, 1990. MS-Group-2154, 2013-038-046.ATL.

63 Bert Roth, 'Chronicles', *New Zealand Journal of Industrial Relations*, 1990, 15.

64 Owen Harvey, 'The Unions and the Government: The Rise and Fall of the Compact', in *Controlling Interests: Business, the State and Society in New Zealand*, edited by John Deeks, Auckland University Press, 1992.

65 Roger Kerr, article for *The Examiner*, October 17, 1990. MS-Group-2154, 2013-038-047.ATL.

66 Rebecca Macfie, 'Pay freeze planned: Douglas', *National Business Review*, September 18, 1990.

67 *Double Take*, October 1990.

68 Malcolm McKinnon, *Treasury: The New Zealand Treasury 1840–2000.*

69 Ruth Richardson, author interview.

70 Ibid. The two Treasury secondees working with Richardson on the labour market were Doug Andrew and Alex Sundakov.

71 Ruth Richardson, *Making a Difference.*

72 Brad Tattersfield, *Bill Birch: Minister of Everything*, Mary Egan Publishing, 2020.

73 Roger Kerr, memorandum to Douglas Myers, 'Meeting with Bill Birch', November 22, 1990. MS-Group-2154, 2013-038-048. ATL.

74 Ruth Richardson, author interview.

75 Roger Kerr, letter to Jim Farmer, December 5, 1990. MS-Group-2154, 2013-038-049. ATL.

76 Ralph Stockdill, author interview, January 2020. Stockdill commented that of the 12 or 13 ministers he had worked with in his career in the public service, Birch was the most effective at getting things through Cabinet. 'He was a master at it.'

77 Ralph Stockdill, author interview. Stockdill said the law drafters had initially set a lower bar for meeting the 'harsh and oppressive' test.

78 David Barber, 'A dose of stiff medicine', *National Business Review*, December 20, 1990; Jane Kelsey, *The New Zealand Experiment*, Auckland University Press, 1995; Ellen Dannin, *Working Free.*

79 'What Richardson said', *National Business Review*, December 20, 1990.

80 Jane Kelsey in *The New Zealand Experiment*, quoting the minister of social welfare Jenny Shipley in *The Dominion*, February 20, 1991.

81 Colin James, 'Captain Richardson and her starship enterprise,' *National Business Review*, January 16, 1991.

82 Ibid.

83 Roger Kerr, memorandum to members of the New Zealand Business Roundtable, January 17, 1991. MS-Group-2154, 2013-038-049. ATL.

84 Roger Kerr, letter to Richard Epstein, January 7, 1991. MS-Group-2154, 2013-038-049. ATL.

85 Gordon Campbell, 'Leading from the rear', *New Zealand Listener*, June 3, 1991. CTU president Ken Douglas told Campbell a lot of people were 'shellshocked' when they saw the Employment Contracts Bill, and an affiliates meeting of the CTU on December 20, 1990 was 'freaked' by it.

86 Angela Foulkes, interview for *Trade Union Oral History Project*. OHLC-003395 – 003398. ATL.

87 *Double Take*, January 1991.

88 Ibid.

89 Helen Baxter, email correspondence with author, November 2019.

90 Ellen Dannin, *Working Free.*

91 *Double Take*, April 1991.

92 Amanda Coulston, author interview, September 2018.

93 Office of the Minister of Labour, 'The Employment Contracts Bill: Questions and Answers', 1991.

94 Rebecca Macfie, 'Unions fold under pressure', *National Business Review*, March 20, 1991.

95 Ellen Dannin, 'We Can't Overcome? A case study in freedom of contract and labor law reform', *Berkeley Journal of Employment and Labor Law*, Vol 16, Number 1, 1995.

96 Wellington and Taranaki Caretakers, Cleaners and Lift Attendants and Watchmen's Industrial Union of Workers, Secretary's Report, April 16, 1991. MS-Group 0491, MSY 4201. ATL.

97 Chris Trotter, 'Blood on the streets?' *National Business Review*, April 17, 1990.

98 Brad Tattersfield, 'CTU calls for week of protests', *National Business Review*, February 22, 1991.

99 Bill Birch had dismissed the Compact as an 'old-style accord promoting centralised wage fixing'.

100 Brad Tattersfield, 'CTU calls for week of protests'.

101 *The Dominion*, April 16, 17, 18 and 19, 1991.

102 Between 1986 and 1991, 378 out of 21,654 sailings were cancelled because of industrial action. Weather and mechanical problems caused more sailing cancellations. 'Strikes and strandings', https://nzhistory.govt.nz/culture/cook-strait-rail-ferries/strikes-and-strandings, updated May 17, 2017.

103 *The Dominion*, April 17, 1991. Interviewed in 1999, Angela Foulkes described Douglas's Hokitika comment as 'foolish … What we [the CTU] were saying was people were doing things and were considering what more to do … But [Douglas's comment] enabled those who couldn't have done anything to say the

CTU had decided there shouldn't be a general strike.' Angela Foulkes, interview for *Trade Union Oral History Project.*

104 Herbert Otto Roth collection, 'Minutes of a Special Meeting of Affiliates', April 18, 1991. ATL-Group 00304, 94 106-60/07. ATL.

105 *Insight*, Radio New Zealand, January 24, 1992. Ngā Taonga Sound and Vision.

106 Rick Barker, author interview, September 2019.

107 Ken Douglas, author interview, June 2018; Gordon Campbell, 'Leading from the rear'.

108 Angela Foulkes, interview for *Trade Union Oral History Project.*

109 Rick Barker, author interview.

110 Sarah Heal, 'The Struggle over the Employment Contracts Act, 1987–1991', *Labour, Employment and Work in New Zealand,* 1994.

111 Combined Early Childhood Union of Aotearoa, *Annual Report*, August 1991. 96-196-04/3. ATL

112 Helen Baxter, email correspondence with author.

113 Sarah Heal, 'The Struggle over the Employment Contracts Act, 1987–1991'.

114 *Someone Else's Country*, written and directed by Alister Barry, Vanguard Films and Community Media Trust, 1996.

115 Jane Benefield, author interview, October 2019.

116 CECUA, minutes of National Executive Meeting, April 20–21, 1991. 96-196-02/1. ATL.

117 50,000 in national Bill protest', *The* Press, May 1, 1991; Sarah Heal, 'The Struggle over the Employment Contracts Act, 1987–1991'.

118 *New Zealand Parliamentary Debates*, Volume 514.

119 Roger Kerr, letter to Bill Birch regarding the future of the Labour Court, mediation service and personal grievance rules in the Employment Contracts Bill, January 22, 1991. Kerr said the Law Commission and Court of Appeal were also guilty of trying to bring 'fairness' into employment matters. Treasury argued strongly that there was no case for a specialist court, and that employment contract matters should be dealt with in the civil courts, just like other contracts. Birch accepted the arguments of Department of Labour officials, who argued for the retention of specialist employment law institutions. Pat Walsh and Rose Ryan,'The Making of the Employment Contracts Act'.

120 Walter Grills, 'The Impact of the Employment Contracts Act on Labour Law: Implications for Unions', *New Zealand Journal of Industrial Relations*, 1994, 19, 1.

121 'Report of the Minority of the Labour Select Committee on the Inquiry into the Effects of the Employment Contracts Act' (September 1993) stated that the award rate for early childhood workers had been $7.16 an hour; by 1993 the committee found the going rate for childcare workers under 20 was $4 an hour.

122 Clare Wells, author interview.

123 Philip Macalister, '60 richest people in New Zealand', *The Dominion*, May 17, 1991.

124 Bert Roth, 'Chronicles', *New Zealand Journal of Industrial Relations*, 1991, 16.

125 Ibid; 'Staff told union powerless', *The Press*, May 11, 1991.

126 Rick Barker, author interview.

Chapter 7

1 Lynne Bruce, author interview, January 2020.

2 Ruth Richardson, *Making a Difference*. Richardson writes in her memoir that the phrase was suggested by television reporter Ross Stevens. It alluded to Saddam Hussein's recent 'mother of all battles' in the Gulf War. Richardson agreed that it was an appropriate epithet and the name stuck.

3 The student loans scheme was established the following year, 1992.

4 David Barber, 'Help yourself Budget chips back welfarism', *National Business Review*, July 31, 1991.

5 Ruth Richardson, Budget speech, *National Business Review*, July 31, 1991.

6 Linda Mitchell, 'Influencing policy change through collective action'. The kindergartens were still bound by a national collective, but the combination of bulk funding and the Employment Contracts Act led to it splintering into regional contracts.

7 *Double Take*, October 1991.

8 Janette Kelly, author interview, April 2019.

9 Janette Kelly, author interview, November 2019.

10 Jane Benefield, email correspondence with author, October 2019.

11 A study by early childhood researcher Anne Smith in 1993/4 showed private centres tended to pay lower wages and provide poorer conditions than community-owned centres. Cited in New Zealand Council for Educational Research, Occasional Paper 2002/2, by Linda Mitchell, senior NZCER researcher. *https://www.nzcer.org.nz/system/files/11743.pdf*. The Early Childhood Council had welcomed the Employment Contracts Act because 'people will be able to express their choice in bargaining without heavies coming in to influence it'. Ross Penman in *Double Take*, March 1991.

12 Jane Benefield, author interview, October 2019.

13 Author interviews with Linda Mitchell, Helen Baxter, and Jane Benefield. CECUA developed a resource kit, 'Preventing the Sexual Abuse of Children within Early Childhood Services'.

14 Philippa Branthwaite, author interview, November 2019.

15 Chris Wratt, author interview, June 2018; Chris Wratt, email correspondence with author, September 2019.

16 Margaret Legerton, author interview, May 2018.

17 Cath Kelly, interview with Anne Goodman; Gerald Sutton, video of Cath Kelly's involvement in Vietnam, 2012.

18 In 2005 Cath was awarded the Friendship Order by the president of Vietnam. In 2010 she was invited by the leaders of Ho Chi Minh City to attend the 35th anniversary of the reunification of Vietnam and was treated as a special guest. Gerald Sutton, obituary for Cath Kelly, March 21, 2017.

19 Linda Hill and Rosemary Du Plessis, 'Tracing the Similarities, Identifying the Differences: Women and the Employment Contracts Act', *New Zealand Journal of Industrial Relations*, 1993 18, 1.

20 Ian Hodgetts, author interview, October, 2019.

21 Ellen Dannin, *Working Free*, citing *The Dominion Sunday Times*, October 20, 1991.

22 John Ryall, author interview, May 2018.

23 John Ryall, speech to Fabian Society, September 2019.

24 Annie Newman, author interview, October 2018.

25 Linda Hill and Rosemary Du Plessis, 'Tracing the Similarities, Identifying the Differences', cited in Jane Kelsey, *The New Zealand Experiment*.

26 John Ryall, email correspondence with author, December 14, 2019.

27 John Ryall, author interview, December 2019; Jason Barber, 'Kelly retires only to go back to union work', *The Dominion*, January 28, 1993; Al Morrison, 'Kelly: When the cloth cap fits', *The Dominion*, March 6, 1993.

28 David McEwan, 'Penal rates take brunt under employment Act', *National Business Review*, September 4, 1992; Raymond Harbridge and Andrew Honeybone, 'Working Time and the Application of Penal Rates of Pay: A Gender and Industry Analysis in the 1993/94 year', *Labour, Employment and Work in New Zealand*, 1994.

29 Kevin Hince and Raymond Harbridge, 'The Employment Contracts Act: An interim assessment', *New Zealand Journal of Industrial Relations*, 1994, 19, 3.

30 David McEwan, 'Penal rates take brunt under employment Act'.

31 Janet Hector, Jon Henning and Mary Hubble, 'Industrial Relations in the Non-food Retail Sector, 1991–1992, *New Zealand Journal of Industrial Relations*, 1993, 18, 3.

32 Alistair Pringle, 'The Pursuit of Flexibility in the New Zealand Supermarket: The Employment Contracts Act, Continuities and Discontinuities', *New Zealand Journal of Industrial Relations*, 1993, 18, 3.

33 The National Distribution Union was formed from the merger of the Northern Distribution Union and the New Zealand Distribution and General Workers Union. It represented workers in the retail, transport, energy, storage, textile and food sectors. It was one of many amalgamations in this period.

34 The stand-down period for the dole was reduced from 26 weeks to 13 weeks in 1997.

35 Peter Conway, 'Wage Bargaining Theory, Decentralisation, the Employment Contracts Act and the Supermarket Sector', Masters thesis, Massey University, 1998.

36 Ibid. Conway cited S. Hammond and R. Harbridge, 'Industrial relations and collective bargaining in the retail sector: A comparative analysis of trends in Australia and New Zealand', presented at ACCIRT seminar, University of Sydney, May 12, 1995.

37 CTU, Submissions to International Labour Organisation Direct Contact Mission, Submission of NDU. 2003-361-05/1. ATL.

38 Peter Conway, 'Wage Bargaining Theory, Decentralisation, the Employment Contracts Act and the Supermarket Sector'.

39 Berice Edwards, letter to Department of Labour, January 1, 1994, in 'National Distribution Union submission to the International Labour Organisation'. 2003-361-05/1. ATL.

40 Raymond Harbridge and Maryan Street, 'Labour Market Adjustment and Women in the Service Industry: A Survey', *New Zealand Journal of Industrial Relations*, 1995, 20, 1.

41 Mark Gosche, National Secretary of the Service Workers Union, submission to the International Labour Organisation. 2003-361-05/1. ATL.

42 Ian McAndrew and Matt Ballard, 'Negotiation and Dictation in Employment Contract Formation', *New Zealand Journal of Industrial Relations*, 1995, 20, 2.

43 https://en.wikipedia.org/wiki/Minimum_wage_law#New_Zealand.

44 Kevin Hince and Raymond Harbridge, 'The Employment Contracts Act: An interim assessment'.

45 Ken Douglas, 'Getting the most from employment law and structures in an expanding economy', speech to Institute for International Research, Industrial Relations Conference, Auckland, March 1995.

46 Paul Dalziel, 'New Zealand's Economic Reforms: An assessment', *Review of Political Economy*, Volume 14, Number 1, 2002.

47 Jane Kelsey, *The New Zealand Experiment*.

48 *Insight*, Radio New Zealand, January 24, 1992, Ngā Taonga Sound and Vision.

49 *Double Take*, October 1992; Statistics NZ; Bert Roth, 'Chronicles', *New Zealand Journal of Industrial Relations*, 18, 2.

50 Ellen Dannin, *Working Free;* Rebecca Macfie, 'Employers' use of lockouts under the Employment Contracts Act: A new balance of power?' *New Zealand Journal of Industrial Relations*, 1992, 17, 3; John Hughes, 'Govt watches as employers exploit Contracts Act flaw', *The Press*, June 8, 1992.

51 Ellen Dannin, *Working Free*.

52 John Hughes, 'Govt watches as employers exploit Contracts Act flaw'.

53 Ellen Dannin, *Working Free*.

54 Ibid; Gordon Anderson in *Butterworth's Employment Law Guide: 4th Edition*, 1998, edited by Christopher Osman, LexisNexis Butterworths, 1998.

55 David Grant, *Man for all Seasons: The Life and Times of Ken Douglas*, Random House, 2010.

56 *NZEI Rourou*, December 15, 1992.

57 Maxine Gay, author interview, October 2018;

Cybèle Locke, *Workers in the Margins: Union Radicals in Post-War New Zealand*, Bridget Williams Books, 2012; Murray Horton, *Foreign Control Watchdog*, April 2001.

58 Bert Roth, 'Chronicles', *New Zealand Journal of Industrial Relations*, 18, 2.

59 Murray Horton, 'The State of the Unions', *Political Review*, September/October 1996.

60 CTU, Submission to the International Labour Organisation. 2003-361-05/1. ATL.

61 Nigel Haworth and Stephen Hughes, 'Under Scrutiny: The ECA, the ILO and the NZCTU Complaint', *New Zealand Journal of Industrial Relations*, 1995, 20, 2.

62 Bert Roth, 'Chronicles', *New Zealand Journal of Industrial Relations*, 18, 3.

63 The Council of Trade Unions' economist, Peter Harris, reported in 1999 that over the previous ten years full-time employment had increased four percent, and part-time 56 percent, while the level of involuntary underemployment had trebled in the 1990s. Between 1987 and 1997, the number of people working more than one job increased from 59,000 to 79,000. Peter Harris, speech to the EPMU, March 29, 1999, 'Why we need to change the government'. 2003-361-17/27. ATL

64 Jim Bolger, speech to New Zealand Employers' Federation and Combined Business Organisations *Moving Forward* conference. From the same conference: Simon Holdsworth, President New Zealand Employers' Federation, 'The Employment Contracts Act: A Permanent Fixture'; John Savage and John Yeabsley, NZIER, 'What do we know about the economic impacts of the Employment Contracts Act?' Savage and Yeabsley point to research by Tim Maloney showing one-sixth of the job growth was attributable to the Employment Contracts Act; they also puzzle over New Zealand's poor productivity performance since the Act. Other references regarding the ECA and labour productivity growth: Brian Easton, 'Productivity Puzzle', *New Zealand Listener*, July 27, 1996; Tim Maloney, 'Five Years After: The New Zealand Labour Market and the Employment Contracts Act', Institute of Policy Studies, 1998. Maloney concluded average annual growth in labour productivity declined from 1.47 percent in the five years before the Employment Contracts Act to 0.25 percent in the five years following the Act; Paul Dalziel, 'New Zealand's Economic Reforms: An assessment', *Review of Political Economy*, Volume 14, Number 1, 2002. Dalziel calculates Australian workers increased their productivity by 21.9 percentage points between 1990 and 1998, while New Zealand workers increased theirs over the same period by only 5.2 percentage points.

65 Brian Easton, 'The Economic Impact of the Employment Contracts Act', Symposium on New Zealand's ECA 1991, *Californian International Journal*, Volume 28, No. 1, Fall 1997.

66 Roger Kerr, 'Employment, Productivity and Growth all Blossom under the Employment Contracts Act', *The New Zealand Herald*, October 5, 1996.

67 Charles Baird, California State University, 'Deregulation of the New Zealand Labour Market: Things Done and Left Undone', speech to *Moving Forward* conference.

68 Gordon Anderson, John Hughes and Dawn Duncan, *Employment Law in New Zealand, 2nd edition*, LexisNexis, 2017; Jane Kelsey, *The New Zealand Experiment.*

69 Employers' Federation, correspondence with the minister of labour. 2001-129-28/3. ATL.

70 Linda Mitchell, author interview, October 2019.

71 Janette Kelly, author interview, November 2019.

72 Rosslyn Noonan, reference for Helen Kelly, March 23, 1994. Kelly family archives.

73 Annie Newman, author interview; Therese O'Connell, author interview, August 2018.

74 Chris Wratt, email correspondence with author, October 2020.

75 Chris Wratt, email correspondence with author, December 2018.

76 Clare Wells, author interview, May 2018.

77 At the beginning of the 1980s only 20 percent of school leavers went on to tertiary studies, with just ten percent going to university. By 1991, 39 percent of school leavers were opting for tertiary education, with 21 percent going to a university, 17 percent to a polytechnic and two percent to a college of education. Department of Statistics, 'New Zealand Social Trends: Work', Wellington, 1993.

78 Academic pay was previously centrally determined by the Higher Salaries Commission. Universities were brought under the State Sector Act by Labour in 1989.

79 Guy Reynolds, author interview, November 2019.

80 Peter Donelan, email correspondence with author, August 2019.

81 Joanna Beresford, email correspondence with author, December 2019.

82 'Better Teachers for Better Learning', Education Forum, March 1992; 'Better Teachers and Employment Contracts', Education Forum, September 1992. Bargaining in the public health sector had quickly been broken down to the level of district health boards. Labour minister Bill Birch had made it clear he did not expect to see national employment contracts renewed in the education sector.

83 Joanna Beresford, author interview, September 2018.

84 Harvey McQueen and Anne Else, *A Question of Shoe Size: The Campaign for Pay Parity for Primary Teachers, 1994–1998*, NZEI Te Riu Roa, 2001.

85 Peter Monteith, author interview, August 2019.

86 *NZEI Rourou*, June 17, 1997.

87 Suze Wilson, author interview, December 2019.

88 Helen became assistant national secretary of the NZEI in January 2001.

89 Harvey McQueen and Anne Else, *A Question of Shoe Size.*

90 *NZEI Rourou*, March 10, 1998.

91 John Deeks and Erling Rasmussen, *Employment Relations in New Zealand*, Pearson Educational, 2002. In 1998, 62.3 percent of workers had no choice in whether they would be covered by an individual or a collective contract, and 9.6 percent didn't know.

92 Deeks and Rasmussen reported a 'significant increase' in average weekly hours between 1990 and 1996, which then declined slightly from 1996–1998 as a result of the economic slowdown. In 1998, 21 percent of employees usually worked more than 50 hours a week, compared with 17 percent in 1987.

93 Ibid.

94 Bill Rosenberg, 'A Brief History of Labour's Share of Income in New Zealand 1939–2016' in *Transforming Workplace Relations In New Zealand 1976–2016*, edited by Gordon Anderson, with Alan Geare, Erling Rasmussen and Margaret Wilson, Victoria University Press, 2017; Inequality in New Zealand increased significantly between the mid 1980s and mid 1990s, as measured by the Gini coefficient, a technical measure in which 0 would indicate a completely equal society, and 1 would be a society in which a single person has all the wealth. New Zealand went from a measure of 0.264 in the mid '80s to 0.331 in the mid '90s – a 'far larger change' than recorded by any other society for which figures were available, reported CTU economist Peter Harris in 'Why we need to change the government', speech to the EPMU, March 29, 1999; John Deeks and Erling Rasmussen, *Employment Relations in New Zealand.*

95 John Ryall, author interview, December 2019; Alistair Duncan, 'Lions into Lambs', *Political Review*, September 1997.

96 Darien Fenton, author interview, August 2019.

97 Ken Douglas, author interview, July 2019.

98 Ross Wilson, author interview, July 2018.

99 Joanna Beresford, email correspondence with author, September 2018.

100 The Alliance was formed at the end of 1991 from an amalgam of Anderton's original

breakaway NewLabour Party and the Mana Motuhake, Green and Democrat Parties. By the 1999 election the Greens had left the Alliance.

Chapter 8

1 Marian Hobbs, author interview, January 2020.

2 Clare Wells, 'Future Directions: Shaping Early Childhood Education Policy for the 21st Century – A Personal Perspective', *New Zealand Annual Review of Education*, 8, 1999; Helen May, 'Twenty Years of the Consenting Parties: The politics of "working" and "teaching" in childcare 1985–2005', NZEI Te Riu Roa, 2005.

3 Trevor Mallard, author interview, November 2018.

4 Ibid.

5 'No kindy pay parity – Smith', *The Dominion*, August 26, 1999.

6 Amanda Coulston, author interview, February 2020.

7 Clare Wells, author interview, January 2020.

8 Stan Rodger, author interview.

9 Lynne Bruce, author interview, January 2020.

10 The early childhood sector had dozens of site-based pay agreements, and thousands of workers were still on individual contracts following the collapse of the national award after the Employment Contracts Act, all of which made for a complicated environment in which to achieve pay parity for teachers. Two decades on from the kindergarten pay parity settlement, the struggle for fair pay for early childhood workers continued. See, for instance, 'Teachers are teachers: Early childhood teachers call for pay parity' by Josephine Franks, *Stuff*, July 15, 2019.

11 Author interview with Chris Wratt, June 2018.

12 Author interview with Linda Mitchell, October 2019.

13 Author interview with Dylan Kelly, May 2020.

14 Chris Wratt remarried and had three more children.

15 Jane Phare, 'The good life in the red', *The New Zealand Herald*, January 31, 2009. Retrieved from nzherald.co.nz, January 30, 2020.

16 Steve Poletti, author interview, April 2020.

17 Denise Roche, author interview, August 2019.

18 Anthony Giddens, description of the New Zealand reforms, in introduction to a speech to the London School of Economics by Helen Clark, February 21, 2002.

19 Jane Kelsey, *The FIRE Economy*, Bridget Williams Books, 2015, citing Bryan Perry, *Household Incomes In New Zealand: Trends in Indicators of Inequality and Hardship 1982–2013*, Ministry of Social Development, 2014; Bruce Ansley, 'Human Values', *New Zealand Listener*, March 25, 2000; Council of Trade Unions, 'Damage done by Employment Contracts Act', press release, September 22, 2003, citing results of survey by Canadian Centre for the Study of Living Standards, showing a 6.5 percent fall in real wages in New Zealand from 1980 to 2001, the worst outcome for 16 OECD countries surveyed; Peter Conway, *CTU Economic Bulletin* 3/00. Conway noted foreign ownership of the New Zealand share market had gone from 19 percent in 1989 to 61 percent in 1996, and household indebtedness had risen from 55 percent of annual household income in 1991 to 98 percent in 1999; Peter Conway, *CTU Bulletin* 6/00. Conway cited analysis by Brian Gaynor showing that the privatisation of 40 state assets since 1987 had returned \$19.1 billion to the government, and that by August 1999 those assets were worth \$35.7 billion, with 79 percent of that increase going to overseas investors; Bob Edlin, 'Economic projection shows deficit reaching crisis point,' *The Independent Business Weekly*, October 27, 1999. Edlin described the projected current account deficit for the year to March 2000, at 8.3 percent of GDP, as of 'basketcase' proportions; Bob Edlin, '"Four years going backwards" – manufacturing in crisis', *The Independent Business Weekly*, October 27, 1999.

20 Bruce Ansley, 'Human Values'.

21 Steve Maharey, minister of social development and employment, 'The Third Way and how I got on to it', lecture to 'New Zealand Society' course, Massey University, June 4, 2003.

22 Helen Clark, 'Implementing a progressive agenda in a small country after 15 years of neoliberalism: The New Zealand experience', speech to London School of Economics, February 21, 2002. 'Baby with the bathwater' comment quoted in Jane Kelsey, *At the Crossroads*, Bridget Williams Books, 2002.

23 CTU National Affiliates Council, minutes, March 2000. CTU files. When the Employment Relations Bill was introduced to Parliament, the NAC welcomed it and noted it was a 'substantial implementation of CTU policy'.

24 NZ Council of Trade Unions, Papers relating to the Workplace Relations Bill, May 1998. 2003-361-18/21. ATL.

25 Lorraine Skiffington, 'The Making of the ER Act – a recipe for success', *Employment Law Bulletin,* March 2001.

26 Laila Harré, author interview, January 2019. Harré was elected as an Alliance MP in 1996 and became associate minister of labour in 1999. The Alliance took the view that collective agreements should have universal coverage and proposed a bargaining fee regime whereby the majority in a workplace could vote that those who didn't join the union would pay the fee. The 30-day rule was the 'best compromise we could achieve in the direction of universal coverage of collective agreements', Harré said.

27 Gordon Anderson, 'Employment Law Reform: Is it really that bad?', *Employment Law Bulletin,* March 2004; Charles Chauvel and Paul Pringle, 'Margaret Wilson: Minister of Labour 1999–2004', *Employment Law Bulletin,* April 2004.

28 Gordon Campbell, 'Workers of the world', *New Zealand Listener*, September 9, 2000. In 1998 National had opened ACC work-related injury coverage up to the private insurance market.

29 Rebecca Macfie, 'Reactions to the new Employment Relations Bill', *Employment Law Bulletin,* April 2000.

30 John Hughes, 'Hot-spots and damp squibs', *Employment Law Bulletin,* October 2000.

31 Roger Kerr, 'Make work not war: business asks for reason to prevail', *The Independent Business Weekly,* March 22, 2000.

32 'Debate on controversial law bill continues', *The New Zealand Herald*, August 21, 2000. Retrieved from nzherald.co.nz March 4, 2020.

33 For instance, Ian Llewellyn, 'Govt to beef up anti-boss bill', *The Independent Business Weekly,* July 12, 2000.

34 Ross Wilson, author interview, January 2019.

35 The Labour-led government watered down the original Employment Relations Bill in six key areas: protections for dependent contractors; protection for workers when the company they worked for was sold or the work was contracted out; protections relating to fixed-term contracts; good faith bargaining obligations; disclosure of information relevant to collective bargaining; and liability of directors for unpaid wages; John Hughes, 'Hot-spots and damp squibs'.

36 Rebecca Macfie, 'Employment News in Brief', *Employment Law Bulletin,* September 2000.

37 Peter Conway, *CTU Economic Bulletin*, 2/00.

38 The first major dispute to flare after Ross Wilson and Paul Goulter moved into the leadership of the CTU was between the Lyttelton Waterside Workers' Union and the Port of Lyttelton, which planned to contract out coal loading work. The union picketed both entrances to the port. Christine Clarke, a 45-year-old social justice campaigner and mother of two children, joined the picket, along with about 140 others. She was struck by a vehicle driven through the picket by local businessman Derek Powell. She died of her injuries two days later, on New Years' Eve, 1999. Christine Clarke's story is told by Peter Clayworth in *Labour History Bulletin,* No. 78, April 2020.

39 Carol Beaumont, author interview, December

2018; Erin Polaczuk, author interview, October 2018.

40 Ross Wilson, author interview, July 2018.

41 Darien Fenton, author interview. Fenton said she was unhappy with how it was handled but her relationship with Helen didn't suffer.

42 John Ryall, email correspondence with author, April 2018.

43 Max Kelly, author interview, February 2020.

44 Don Swan, author interview.

45 Steve Hurring, author interview, January 2020.

46 Recording of Pat Kelly's funeral, Kelly family archives.

47 Amanda Coulston, author interview.

48 Doug Martin, author interview, January 2020.

49 Grant Duncan, interviews with author, September 2018 and February 2020.

50 Karin Currie, Margaret Ledgerton, Marty Braithwaite, Bronwynn Maxwell, Suzanne McNabb, Grant Duncan, author interviews. Three of the union staffers known to have opposed Helen's appointment declined to be interviewed.

51 Marty Braithwaite, author interview, May 2018.

52 *Tertiary Update*, May 23, 2002, citing lawyer Stephen Kos at the Massey University capping ceremony.

53 Bill Rosenberg, 'Quality the real issue in salary claims', *Education Review*, October 1–8, 2003.

54 Paper to the Universities Tripartite Forum Working Group from the NZVCC, AUS, PSA and ASTE, December 2005. Provided to author by the Tertiary Education Union.

55 The government subsidy per student fell in real terms by 12 percent between 1994 and 2004. Paper to the Universities Tripartite Forum Working Group from the NZVCC, AUS, PSA and ASTE – Draft, December 2005. Provided to author by the Tertiary Education Union; Ruth Butterworth and Nicholas Tarling, *A Shakeup Anyway: Government and the Universities in New Zealand in a Decade of Reform*, Auckland University Press, 1994.

56 Michelle Nixon, 'Sell, sell, sell – TEIs put marketing strategies to work', *Education Review*, September 29 –October 5, 2004; John Gerritsen, 'How class sizes balance budgets', *Education Review*, June 4–10, 2003.

57 *Tertiary Update*, August 23, 2001, quoting former AUS president Neville Blampied.

58 Helen Kelly, memo to branch presidents, November 4, 2000, 'Conference Paper on Multi-employer Bargaining'. Provided to the author by the Tertiary Education Union.

59 *Tertiary Update*, February 12, 2004. In 1979 vice chancellors were paid 2.09 times more than senior lecturers; by 2002, that ratio had doubled. Rob Crozier, 'From AUT to AUS, 1979–2002', *AUS Bulletin*, No. 54, July 2002.

60 Grant Duncan, author interview; *Tertiary Update*, June 27, 2002.

61 Helen Kelly, 'AUS proposal for bargaining and funding strategies including a Multi-Employer Collective Agreement (MECA)', August 21, 2002. Provided to the author by the Tertiary Education Union.

62 'To MECA or Not to MECA?', *AUS Bulletin*, No. 55, October 2002. The article is not bylined, but replicates the language used in Helen Kelly's August 21, 2002 strategy paper.

63 Tom Ryan, author interview, March 2020.

64 *Tertiary Update*, October 3, 2002; October 7, 2002; October 31, 2002; March 3, 2003.

65 Bill Rosenberg, 'Quality the real issue in salary claims'.

66 John Gerritsen, 'First steps to a showdown', *Education Review*, June 2–8, 2003.

67 *Tertiary Update*, April 8, 2004.

68 Association of University Staff v Vice Chancellor of the University of Auckland, Employment Court of New Zealand, May 4, 2005.

69 The Employment Relations Act was amended in 2004 to strengthen collective bargaining and provide greater protection to vulnerable workers. It brought in a requirement that where work (such as cleaning and catering)

was contracted out, workers had the right to transfer to the new employer on their current terms and conditions; allowed for bargaining fees to be deducted (subject to a majority vote of workers) where non-union workers received the same terms and conditions as set down in union-negotiated collective agreements; and slightly strengthened good faith bargaining provisions and employers' obligation to negotiate for collective contracts (but with no requirement to settle if there was a genuine reason not to).

70 *Tertiary Update,* April 7, 2005. The strike was called off after the Employment Court decision, see *Tertiary Update,* May 5, 2005.

71 General Secretary's Report to AUS Annual Conference, December 2005. Provided to author by the Tertiary Education Union.

72 Association of University Staff v Vice Chancellor of the University of Auckland, Employment Court of New Zealand, May 4, 2005, AC 19/05.

73 Ibid.

74 Trevor Mallard, author interview, March 2020.

75 *Tertiary Update,* September 1, 2005.

76 Other unions representing staff in universities, including the Association of Staff in Tertiary Education and the PSA, were also involved in the tripartite talks, but AUS took the lead.

77 Grant Duncan, author interview, February 2020.

78 *Tertiary Update,* May 29, 2008.

79 Ibid. In 2008 a Deloitte's report on university salaries noted New Zealand was still significantly behind Australia, Canada, the US and the UK.

80 Peter Wills, author interview, March 2020.

81 Roy Sharp, author interview, February 2020.

82 Michael Cullen, author interview, February 2020.

83 Andrew Campbell, author interview, August 2018.

84 The three were AUS, Association of Staff in Tertiary Institutes (ASTE) and Technical Institutes Allied Staff Association (TIASA).

85 For instance, one vocal opponent was Victoria University law professor Gordon Anderson, an expert in industrial relations law, see 'Some arguments against union amalgamation'. Retrieved from https://teucanterbury.wordpress.com/category/aus-aste-merger/, March 2020.

86 Maureen Montgomery, author interview, February 2020.

87 Marty Braithwaite, author interview, December 2018.

88 Helen Kelly graduated with a Bachelor of Laws from Victoria University in 2006.

89 Dylan Kelly, author interview, May 2020.

90 Suzanne McNabb, author interview, July 2019.

91 Peter Monteith, author interview.

92 The number of unions and union members had risen after the Employment Relations Act was introduced, but the percentage of an expanding workforce that belonged to unions – 'union density' – had scarcely budged since the last days of the Employment Contracts Act. In December 2003 union density was 21.4 percent, compared with 21.1 percent in December 1999. The number of union members had increased 13 percent in that time. See Robyn May, Pat Walsh and Catherine Otto, 'Unions and Union Membership in New Zealand: Annual Review for 2003', Centre for Labour, Employment and Work.

93 Robert Reid, author interview, April 2019. Unite was formed in 1998 to organise vulnerable and unemployed workers after the National-led government introduced a work-for-the-dole scheme. After the break-up of the Alliance Party, when Matt McCarten and Mike Treen wanted to set up a new union to organise vulnerable workers, Unite's president Robert Reid suggested they use the Auckland branch of Unite as their vehicle.

94 Mike Treen, 'A short history of the Unite Union in New Zealand', 2014. https://unite.org.nz/assets/Uploads/Publications/A_short_history_of_Unite_PDF.pdf

95 Mike Treen, author interview, April 2019.

96 Peter Malcouronne, 'Workers Unite', *Metro*, July 1, 2004; Sue Allen, 'New union puts muscle behind low-paid workers', *The Press*, February 2, 2006.

97 Malcouronne, 'Workers Unite'.

98 Mike Treen, 'A short history of Unite Union in New Zealand'; Mike Treen, author interview; Peter Malcouronne, 'Workers Unite'.

99 John Ryall, author interview, April 2020.

100 John Ryall, author interview; Darien Fenton, author interview.

101 Darien Fenton, 'Backgrounder from SFWU re SkyCity', December 2004.

102 Mike Treen, author interview.

103 Matt McCarten, author interview, April 2019.

104 John Ryall, author interview.

105 Ross Wilson, author interview, January 2019.

106 CTU National National Affiliates Council minutes, February 24, 2005.

107 Ross Wilson, author interview, July 2019.

108 Graeme Whimp , author interview, January 2020.

109 Michelle Saban, author interview.

110 Bronwynn Maxwell, author interview, December 2018.

111 Bill Rosenberg, author interview, August 2018.

112 Andrew Campbell, author interview, August 2018.

113 Erin Polaczuk, author interview.

114 Fleur Fitzsimons, author interview, July 2019.

115 John Ryall, email correspondence with author, April 29, 2020.

116 Nigel Haworth, author interview, October 2018.

117 University of Canterbury historian Maureen Montgomery defeated fellow Cantabrian and education academic David Small in the 2007 contest for the presidency. The merger of the AUS and ASTE was backed by membership ballots of both unions, and consummated after Helen had left the AUS to take over leadership of the CTU. The merged union was named the Tertiary Education Union. The third contender for the merger, the Technical Institutes Allied Staff Association, voted not to join.

118 Ross Wilson, author interview, July 2018.

119 Karin Currie, author interview, September 2018.

120 Doug Martin, author interview.

121 John Ryall, author interview, September 2018.

122 Paul Tolich, author interview, August 2018. Carol Beaumont became the Labour Party candidate for Maungakiekie and entered Parliament at the 2008 election.

123 Audrey Young, 'Union "royalty" out to right the wrongs', *The New Zealand Herald*, August 3, 2007. Retrieved from nzherald.co.nz, March 31, 2020.

124 The controversy involved the appointment of a new communications manager to the Ministry for the Environment. The appointee was the partner of the chief press secretary to National Party leader John Key. After Steve raised the matter with the chief executive of the ministry, the appointee lost her job. There were allegations from Key that it was a sign of political interference in the public service. The removal of the appointee from the role was supported by the deputy State Services Commissioner because she was working in an area sensitive to the government.

125 CTU press release, 'New CTU leadership', July 6, 2007.

126 Grant Robertson, author interview, January 2020. Robertson was selected as Labour's candidate for Wellington Central in November 2007. See 'Labour selects Wellington Central candidate', *Scoop*, November 18, 2007. Retrieved from scoop.co.nz, November 3, 2020.

127 Helen Kelly, 'Fairness and respect at work; Unions make the difference', speech to CTU Conference, October 17, 2007.

Chapter 9

1 James Buchan and Nicola North, 'Pay Jolt: The 2004/5 New Zealand Nurses Employment Agreement', April 2008. The campaign also achieved a multi-employer collective agreement (MECA), bringing all district health boards into one agreement for the first time since the introduction of the Employment Contracts Act and the radical health reforms of the 1990s.

2 Mike Treen, *A Short History of the Unite Union in New Zealand*; Simon Oosterman, author interview, January 2019; Mike Treen, author interview; Matt McCarten, 'Union clinches better deal with food giant', *The New Zealand Herald,* March 25, 2006. Retrieved from nzherald.co.nz, April 8, 2020. Restaurant Brands owned Starbucks, Pizza Hut and KFC in New Zealand.

3 Matt McCarten, 'Union clinches better deal with food giant'.

4 'Campaign sees 85pc of workers get 5pc increases', *The New Zealand Herald*, September 20, 2005. Retrieved from nzherald.co.nz, April 9, 2020.

5 In 2003, Progressive had shut distribution centres in Auckland and Christchurch, and rehired many of the same workers on lower pay at alternative sites.

6 Laila Harré and Frances Hancock, 'Reinventing Unionism as a Community-based Social Movement: Case Study of the Union Campaign at Progressive Enterprises Limited', in *Community Development in New Zealand: Exploring Good Practice*', edited by Love M. Chile, AUT University, 2007.

7 'Winning Shelf Respect', *The Maritimes,* Issue 15, October 2006.

8 Laila Harré and Frances Hancock, 'Reinventing Unionism as a Community-based Social Movement'.

9 Lindy Laird, 'Employment Court declares hospital lockout illegal', *Northern Advocate,* July 24, 2007. Retrieved from nzherald.co.nz, April 13, 2020.

10 John Ryall, email correspondence with author, April 12, 2020.

11 Erling Rasmussen and Colin Ross, 'Chronicles', *New Zealand Journal of Employment Relations,* 33, 2.

12 Māori unemployment by the end of 2007 was 7.7 percent percent, and for Pasifika workers 6.5 percent percent. Ministry of Social Development, 'The Social Report, 2008'.

13 New Zealand Skills Strategy, 2008–2012, Discussion Paper. The paper cited the December 2007 *Quarterly Survey of Business Opinion* showing 46 percent of firms had difficulty finding skilled staff, 33 percent had difficulty finding unskilled staff, and a shortage of labour was the main constraint on expansion for 21 percent.

14 Peter Conway, CTU *Monthly Economic Bulletin*, No.81, June 2007; Peter Conway, 'Unions, Productivity and Worker Participation', December 2006. Conway was citing Treasury work showing New Zealand wages had fallen from roughly level with Australia in the 1980s to 60 percent percent by 2002, and that 'with labour relatively cheaper in relation to capital than in Australia, it appears that New Zealand firms have opted for a lower level of capital intensity'.

15 Peter Conway, CTU press release, February 5, 2008. Wages in 2007 rose 3.3 percent, while food and groceries were up 7.8 percent, petrol 17 percent and house prices ten percent. Retrieved from scoop.co.nz, April 9, 2020. Peter Conway, 'Unions, Productivity and Worker Participation'.

16 Between 1992 and 1999, when the Employment Contracts Act was in force and unemployment never dropped below six percent, 351,708 working days were lost to industrial stoppages. Between 2000 and 2007, with unemployment steadily falling, the Employment Relations Act in force and a serious labour shortage emerging, only 195,408 working days were lost to industrial stoppages. Statistics New Zealand, Work Stoppages.

17 Stephen Blumenfeld and Sue Ryall, 'Unions and Union Membership in New Zealand, Annual Review for 2008', Working Paper 1/10, Victoria University Centre for Labour, Employment and Work. Union density in agriculture, fishing and forestry was four percent; in construction 5.6 percent; in retail, wholesale, restaurants and hotels 4.6 percent. In the public sector, 55.3 percent of government administration and defence workers were union members, as were 50.3 percent of education workers and 45.9 percent of health and community services workers.

18 Helen Kelly, 'Challenges and opportunities in New Zealand employment relations: A CTU perspective', in *Employment Relationships: workers, unions and employers in New Zealand*, edited by Erling Rasmussen, Auckland University Press, 2010.

19 Jean-Marc Burniaux, Flavio Padrini and Nicola Brandt, 'Labour Market Performance, Income Inequality and Poverty in OECD Countries', Economic Department Working Paper No. 500, July 17, 2006. Helen Kelly papers.

20 Helen Kelly, research proposal towards Master of Laws, 2007. Paper provided to author by Gordon Anderson. Research by Peter Haynes, Peter Boxall and Keith Macky at the University of Auckland had shown that almost 18 percent of the workforce would join a union if they could. The demand was greater among younger and lower paid workers in smaller private sector organisations. *Journal of Industrial Relations*, 48, 2.

21 A remit from the CTU's 2007 biennial conference called for a review of the industrial relations system, including amendment of the Employment Relations Act to achieve, among other things, a process for establishing industry-wide collective agreements, and mechanisms to significantly increase the incidence of multi-employer collective agreements and industry agreements. Helen Kelly – Union Leaders Forum – February 2008. Helen Kelly papers.

22 Helen Kelly, 'Unions make the difference', speech to CTU conference, October 17, 2007.

23 Audrey Young, 'Union royalty out to right the wrongs', *The New Zealand Herald*, August 3, 2007. Retrieved from nzherald.co.nz, March 31, 2020.)

24 John Ryall, email correspondence with author, April 28, 2018.

25 Helen Kelly, email to Gordon Anderson, November 27, 2007. Helen Kelly papers.

26 Helen Kelly, paper to Union Leaders Forum, February 2008. Helen Kelly papers.

27 Helen Kelly to National Affiliates Council, CTU NAC No: 2008-50, November 3, 2008. Helen Kelly papers.

28 Helen Kelly to National Affiliates Council, CTU NAC: 2009-15, May 11, 2009. Helen Kelly papers.

29 Ross Wilson, author interview.

30 Helen Kelly to CTU Biennial Conference 2009, 'Union Change'. Helen Kelly papers.

31 Ibid.

32 Ibid.

33 Rosenberg had degrees in economics and mathematics and a PhD in mathematical psychology.

34 Alan Bollard, the governor of the Reserve Bank of New Zealand at the time of the Global Financial Crisis, described it as a 'financial plague' and titled a series of talks on the topic 'Bring Out Your Dead'. Likening it to the bubonic plague of 650 years earlier, he wrote in a memoir of the crisis that 'the new plague had spread from the United States (or, some might argue, again from China), rampantly infecting European domestic markets; within a year or two it had spread infection across money, equity, commodity, foreign exchange, capital and sovereign funding markets. … Initially, diagnosis was tricky. The authorities did not understand what caused or spread the disease – they had thought that they had good principles of financial health in place. They tried to contain the outbreak by isolating institutions and guaranteeing funds, but the germs still spread.' Alan Bollard with Sarah Gaitanos, *Crisis: One central bank governor*

and the global financial collapse, Auckland University Press, 2010.

35 Ibid.

36 Alan Bollard with Sarah Gaitanos, *Crisis: One central bank governor and the global financial collapse*. By the end of October 2008, world equity markets had lost half of their value from the start of the year – about US$30 trillion.

37 Dene Mackenzie, 'Govts act to protect bank deposits', *Otago Daily Times*, October 13, 2008. Retrieved from odt.co.nz, April 17, 2020.

38 Reserve Bank of New Zealand, *Financial Stability Report*, November 2009.

39 John Ryall, email correspondence with author, April 28, 2018.

40 TV One, *Q&A*, July 20, 2009. Transcript retrieved from scoop.co.nz, April 21, 2020; James Ritchie, author interview, May 2020; Joanna Beresford, author interview, September 2018.

41 Sir John Key, author interview, September 2018.

42 'Nat's policy will hit wages, say Govt and unions', *The New Zealand Herald*, July 24, 2008. Retrieved from nzherald.co.nz, April 17, 2020.

43 Ross Wilson was sacked as chair; Wayne Butson of the Rail, Maritime and Transport Workers Union was also dumped.

44 Prime Minister John Key, speech to the CTU Biennial Conference, October 21, 2009.

45 The 2010 Budget delivered personal tax cuts at every threshold level. The top personal tax rate fell from 38 percent to 33; tax on income between $48,000 and $70,000 fell from 33 percent to 30. There was a new 17.5 percent rate for income between $14,000 and $48,000, down from 21 percent, and 10.5 percent on income up to $14,000. Company tax dropped from 30 percent to 28. GST rose from 12.5 percent to 15, with a 2.002 percent compensating increase for beneficiaries, pensioners, and recipients of Working for Families tax credits. Pattrick Smellie, 'Biggest tax package in a generation', May 10, 2010. Retrieved from business.scoop.co.nz, May 19, 2020.

46 'Budget fundamentally unfair', CTU press release, May 20, 2010. Retrieved from scoop.co.nz, April 21, 2020.

47 '$100 million cuts in health services on cards', CTU press release, June 3, 2010. Retrieved from scoop.co.nz, April 21, 2020. By July 2017, Rosenberg calculated an extra $2 billion was needed to restore health funding to the level it had been in 2009/10. Bill Rosenberg, 'Working Paper on Health', Number 18, July 1, 2017.

48 The government cited a Department of Labour survey into how the 90-day scheme had worked out for employers of fewer than 20 workers. The survey found one in five workers hired under the rule had been sacked within the 90-day period. Some of those workers said they had no idea why they had lost their jobs. The report was unable to point to evidence of an overall increase in employment. 'One in five workers sacked under 90 day scheme', Radio New Zealand, July 18, 2010. Retrieved from rnz.co.nz, April 22, 2020; Derek Cheng, 'Report on 90-day rule at odds with Govt line', *The New Zealand Herald*, July 19, 2010. Retrieved from nzherald.co.nz, April 22, 2020.)

49 John Key, speech to National Party Conference, July 18, 2010. Retrieved from nzherald.co.nz, April 21, 2020; 'Sick leave change not major', *The New Zealand Herald*, July 19, 2010. Retrieved from nzherald.co.nz, April 21, 2020.

50 Chris Trotter, 'Tragedy-hit CTU cannot survive a farce', July 23, 2010, stuff.co.nz. Retrieved from stuff.co.nz, April 21, 2020.

51 Claire Trevett, 'PM broke his word to unions, says Kelly', *The New Zealand Herald*, July 27, 2010. Retrieved from nzherald.co.nz, April 18, 2020.

52 Radio New Zealand *Nine to Noon*, July 16, 2010, interview with Peter Conway, Peter Townsend and John Hannan. Retrieved from rnz.co.nz, April 18, 2020; Helen Kelly, letter to Prime Minister John Key, July 21, 2010. CTU files.

53 Fleur Fitzsimons, author interview, July 2019.

54 https://www.youtube.com/watch?v=P3yTjbkxEdw.

55 Heather Smith v Stokes Valley Pharmacy (2009) Ltd, NZEMPC 111, WRC 14/10.

56 Ray Bianchi, email to Helen Kelly, March 3, 2009. Helen Kelly papers.

57 This is made clear in an email thread between the MEAA, the Screen Actors Guild and Warners between October 17–19, 2010.

58 Helen Kelly, 'The Hobbit Dispute', scoop.co.nz, April 12, 2011.

59 Flyer given to film industry workers who were called to the Stone Street studios in Miramar on the afternoon of October 20, 2010.

60 Newstalk ZB, October 21, 2010.

61 Dylan Kelly, author interview, June 2020.

62 David Farrar, 'CTU Criticism', *Kiwiblog*, October 23, 2010. Farrar was quoting blogger Danyl McLauchlan. Retrieved from kiwiblog.co.nz, May 14, 2020.

63 James Ritchie, author interview, May 2020.

64 Helen Kelly, email to Peter Jackson, October 22, 2010. Helen Kelly papers.

65 Dylan wrote in 2017 that he doubted Helen regretted calling Jackson a spoilt brat. 'On a new government, kindness and the (unfinished) legacy of my mother, Helen Kelly', *The Spinoff*, November 1, 2017.

66 Various members of the public to Helen Kelly. Helen Kelly papers.

67 Julia London, author interview, May 2018.

68 Catherine Harris, 'Bettors latest players in location saga', *The Dominion Post*, October 23, 2010.

69 TV One, *Q&A*, October 24, 2010. Retrieved from YouTube April 23, 2020.

70 Marty Braithwaite, author interview, May 2018.

71 *The Dominion Post*, October 28, 2010.

72 Frances Walsh, author interview, October 2018; Andrew Little, author interview, October 2018; Helen Kelly, letter to Andrew Little, October 29, 2010. Helen Kelly papers.

73 For instance, Phil Taylor, 'Pike River: Man of the moment for miners', November 27, 2010. Retrieved from nzherald.co.nz, May 6, 2020.

74 Keith Lynch and Giles Brown, 'Mine chief "should have apologised"', *The Press*, December 6, 2010. Retrieved from stuff.co.nz, April 25, 2020.

75 Workplace Health and Safety Council, minutes, May 12, 2010. Retrieved from ndhadeliver.natlib.govt.nz, May 14, 2020.

76 Royal Commission on the Pike River Coal Mine Tragedy, Volume 2, Part 2.

77 Tina McIvor, author interview, April 2020; Tina McIvor, 'Legal Viewpoint – Sidesteps?', *Safeguard*, January/February 2011.

78 Dylan Kelly, author interview, June 2020.

79 Key made the comment at a meeting with the families on September 22, 2011.

80 CTU, press release, 'Workers' wages are not keeping up with costs', May 3, 2011, citing a *New Zealand Herald* report that chief executive pay had gone up 14 percent in 2010, while workers' wage rises were being outstripped by inflation.

81 Deidre Mussen, 'CTU wades into union over strike', *The Sunday Star-Times*, April 27, 2008; Bryce Edwards, 'Matt McCarten – a right bastard', *Liberation*, May 6, 2008. Retrieved from liberation.typepad.com, April 24, 2020. In 2008, when the Labour government was still in power, Helen had come out against a strike led by the Resident Doctors' Association, saying: 'There are alternatives to getting workplace issues resolved ... I hope it doesn't give unions a bad name.' Among those who criticised her were Matt McCarten, the organisation Socialist Aotearoa and political commentator Bryce Edwards. The suggestion was made that she was advancing the interests of the Labour Party at the expense of workers. Edwards, commenting on McCarten's attack on Helen, wrote: 'Although everyone active in the union movement might already know that Helen Kelly is more concerned with her own personal ambition than with the interests

of workers, it's not something that is often publicly stated.' Edwards bracketed her as a Labour Party 'lackey'.

82 Helen Kelly, speech for International Workers Memorial Day, April 28, 2011.

83 Helen Kelly, 'The Hobbit Dispute', scoop.co.nz, April 12, 2011.

84 Helen Kelly, paper to CTU affiliates, February 8, 2011. NAC 2011-03. Helen Kelly papers.

85 Richard Wagstaff, author interview, September 2018.

86 John Ryall, email correspondence with author, April 12, 2020.

87 'A Matter of Access: Addressing the employment needs of workers currently beyond the reach of unions', Report to NDU, SFWU, Unite, CTU Project Steering Group, July 2009.

88 Bronwynn Maxwell, author interview, December 2018.

89 CTU, Regional Briefings, 'Background Paper', August 2010. Helen Kelly papers.

90 James Ritchie, author interview.

91 Helen Kelly, email to Ray Bianchi, January 27, 2011. Helen Kelly papers.

92 John Ryall, author interview, May 2018.

93 European Foundation for the Improvement of Living and Working Conditions, 'Extension of Collective Bargaining Agreements in the EU: Background paper', 2011. Helen Kelly papers.

94 For example, Susan Hayter and Bradley Weinberg, 'Mind the Gap: Collective bargaining and wage inequality', in *The Role of Collective Bargaining in the Global Economy*, edited by Susan Hayter, Edwin Elgar Publishing, 2011. Helen Kelly papers.

95 Bill Rosenberg, CTU *Monthly Economic Bulletin*, October 2011.

96 John Ryall, author interview, September 2018.

97 Labour Party, 'Own Our Future', manifesto, 2011.

98 Business New Zealand, 'National Awards and Strikes come with Labour's employment policy', October 18, 2011. Retrieved from businessnz.org.nz, May 5, 2020; Employers and Manufacturers Association, 'Industry Standard Agreements would take us back 50 years', press release, October 18, 2011. Retrieved from scoop.co.nz, May 5, 2020.

99 James Ritchie, author interview.

100 Ibid.

101 Ian Fraser, email to Helen Kelly, May 16, 2011. Provided to author by Ian Fraser.

102 Ian Fraser, author interview, May 2020.

103 Claire Trevett, 'Food parcel families made poor choices, says Key', February 17, 2011, *The New Zealand Herald*. Retrieved from nzherald.co.nz, May 5, 2020.

104 Staff writers, 'All things being equal', *New Zealand Listener*, May 1–7, 2010.

105 Helen Kelly, 'Mine tragedy shows time for shift in dynamics of power', *The Dominion Post*, September 12, 2011.

106 *Q&A*, TV One, August 21, 2011. Transcript retrieved from scoop.co.nz, May 11, 2020.

107 Terangi Wroe, author interview, May 2020.

108 Ibid. Wroe remembered he was offered $2000 to go back to work, but he resisted.

109 Maryann Kaka, author interview, May 2020.

110 Helen Kelly, email to Robbie Magee, Dave Eastlake, Peter Conway, Simon Mitchell, October 30, 2011. Helen Kelly papers.

111 Tali Williams, author interview, May 2020.

112 Dave Eastlake, author interview, May 2020.

113 Sarah Harvey, 'Meatworkers lockout "threatens reputation"', *The Sunday Star-Times*, December 4, 2011. Retrieved from stuff.co.nz, May 11, 2020.

114 Vicki Waterhouse, 'Good news for locked out workers', *Manawatū Standard*, December 5, 2011. Retrieved from stuff.co.nz, May 11, 2020.

115 Sue Windsor, author interview and email correspondence, May 2020.

116 'NZ union boss not welcome in Fiji', *Otago Daily Times*, December 16, 2011.

117 'Pike River CEO will fight being scapegoated',

press release from Minter Ellison Rudd Watts, Lawyers, November 11, 2011.

Chapter 10

1 Details describing Dhaliwal's arrival at the site, induction and death are drawn from the report of Coroner JP Ryan, October 15, 2015, CSU-2011-AUK-001532.

2 'Guard dies on first day at work', *Herald on Sunday,* November 20, 2011. Retrieved from nzherald.co.nz, May 8, 2020.

3 Rebecca Macfie, 'The Final Campaign', *New Zealand Listener,* May 16, 2015.

4 Helen Kelly, email to Daljit Singh, November 22, 2011. Helen Kelly papers.

5 Georgie McLeod, author interview, September 2018.

6 Sammy Singh, author interview, October 2018.

7 Sarah Daniell, 'Twelve questions: Helen Kelly', *The New Zealand Herald,* August 9, 2012.

8 Helen Kelly, Rutherford Waddell speech, August 28, 2012.

9 Murray Free, author interview, May 2020.

10 Department of Labour, letter to Helen Kelly, July 4, 2011. Helen Kelly papers.

11 Helen Kelly, email to Daljit Singh and Sammy Singh, July 18, 2012. Helen Kelly papers.

12 Helen Kelly, correspondence with Fulton Hogan, March 20, 2011 and April 12, 2012. Helen Kelly papers.

13 *AWUNZ/Fulton Hogan News, Confidential Internal Newsletter of the Northern Amalgamated Workers Union,* Issue 1, March 2012.

14 *The Northern News,* newsletter of the Northern Amalgamated Workers Union, June/July 2013.

15 Ports of Auckland Ltd, 2012–2016 Business Plan.

16 Ports of Auckland, 'Negotiation Timeline'. Undated.

17 Four jobs shuttling containers between the port's two container berths had been contracted out to a company called Conlinxx, which was set up and majority-owned by Ports of Auckland Ltd. in 2009. By 2011 POAL owned 90 percent of its shares, subsequently increasing to 100 percent.

18 'Dock workers threatening to go on strike at New Year', *The New Zealand Herald,* December 16, 2011; Maria Slade, 'Wharfie war hits stalemate', *The Sunday Star-Times,* December 18, 2011.

19 Jenny Keown, 'Port says threat to contract out labour for real', *Southland Times,* January 10, 2012.

20 'Port seeking three new contractors', *The New Zealand Herald,* January 10, 2012.

21 Maritime Union of New Zealand v Ports of Auckland, NZEmpC54.

22 CTU and MUNZ, 'Port of Auckland Dispute Fact Sheet', January 8, 2012.

23 Damien Grant, 'It's time to stop port rort', *The New Zealand Herald,* January 1, 2012; Katherine Rich, 'Port strikes risk permanent damage', *The New Zealand Herald,* December 27, 2011.

24 'Govt should tackle ports union "problem" – report', *The New Zealand Herald,* January 12, 2012. The final report of the Productivity Commission significantly softened its recommendations on industrial relations reform.

25 Joe Fleetwood, author interview, June 2020.

26 Russell Mayn, author interview, June 2020.

27 Maritime Union of New Zealand v Ports of Auckland Ltd, Plaintiff's opening submissions, March 27, 2012. Submissions referred extensively to internal Ports of Auckland documents showing that Rob Campbell and chair Richard Pearson were pushing for contracting out. Campbell, for instance, wanted to 'show and create their [the union's] irrelevancy' and said they should be given 'no recognition or room to move'.

28 Rob Campbell, author interview, June 2020.

29 Save Our Port, *Ports of Auckland: Setting the record straight.* Retrieved from YouTube https://www.youtube.com/watch?v=nTsm90fuXdM.

30 Jenny Keown, 'Accusations fly over Auckland port strike', *Stuff*, February 27, 2012. Retrieved from stuff.co.nz, June 20, 2020.

31 Jenny Keown, 'Port says threat to contract labour for real', *Southland Times*, January 10, 2012.

32 Helen Kelly, 'Modern voice of business includes principles in its vision for port', *The Dominion Post*, February 20, 2012.

33 Helen Kelly, on Ports of Auckland dispute, January 25, 2012. https://www.youtube.com/watch?v=e9zMlvqHjG8

34 The author is grateful to Jon Johansson for this observation about Helen.

35 Kiri Gillespie, 'Safety fears raised at Tauranga port', *The New Zealand Herald*, February 22, 2012. Retrieved from nzherald.co.nz, June 11, 2020.

36 Peter Cranney, letter to Keily Thomson Caisley, March 6, 2012. Helen Kelly papers.

37 Nicky Hager, *Dirty Politics*, Craig Potton Publishing, 2014.

38 Ibid.

39 Numerous posts on *Whale Oil* through 2012.

40 Dylan Kelly and Steve Hurring, author interviews, June 2020.

41 Russell Mayn, author interview.

42 'Wharfies vote unanimously in favour of partial strike', *The New Zealand Herald*, February 1, 2012.

43 Chris Trotter, 'MUNZ – Won: POAL – Nil', www.bowallyroad.blogspot.com, March 31, 2012.

44 Maritime Union of New Zealand v Ports of Auckland, Minute of Judge B.S. Travis, March 15, 2012.

45 'Provocation move wrong route for port', *The New Zealand Herald*, March 23, 2012.

46 Maritime Union of New Zealand v Ports of Auckland, Minute of Judge B.S. Travis.

47 Matt Nippert, 'Rift clear in Campbell's departure', *Waikato Times*, March 31, 2012.

48 Matt McCarten, 'Honourable unionist fights by the rules', *The New Zealand Herald*, April 15, 2012.

49 Eric Mischefski, submission to the Transport and Industrial Relations Select Committee on the Employment Relations Amendment Bill, 2013.

50 United Food Workers v Talley, Employment Court, September 24, 1992. WEC 44/92.

51 New Zealand Dairy Workers Union v Open Country Cheese, Court of Appeal, March 9, 2011. NZCA 56.

52 Jon Morgan, 'Talleys immovable in dispute', *Manawatū Standard*, May 12, 2012. Retrieved from stuff.co.nz, May 20, 2020.

53 Therese Turipa, author interview, August 2019; Pete Amato, author interview, August 2019; Ross Webb, 'Jobs that Count': The Fight against Precarious Work at Affco Wairoa: An Oral History', *Labour History Project Bulletin*, November 2017; *Te Karere*, May 23, 2010.

54 Therese Turipa, author interview.

55 Mike Nahu, author interviews, December 2018 and June 2020.

56 Eric Mischefski, Submission to the Transport and Industrial Relations Select Committee on the Employment Relations Amendment Bill.

57 New Zealand Meat Workers and Related Trades Union v Affco New Zealand Ltd, Plaintiff's opening submission, May 15, 2012.

58 Jill Galloway, 'Affco Easter pay decision "shaky"', *Manawatū Standard*, March 31, 2012; Matt Nippert, 'Affco seeks to undermine union, Employment Court told', *The Press*, May 17, 2012.

59 Laurie Nankivell, Meat Workers Union Moerewa shed secretary, speaking on *The Union Report*, Triangle TV, May 14, 1012; 'Talley's/Affco Fact Sheet', Meat Workers Union and Council of Trade Unions, May 2, 2011. Helen Kelly papers.

60 Basic hourly rates ranged from $13.48 to $15.76 an hour. On top of this, workers were paid a rate based on the number of animals killed. If the 'tally' for the day was reached, wages would range from $27 to $31 an hour

provided there was enough stock to kill. 'Talley's Affco Fact Sheet', Meat Workers Union and CTU.

61 Jon Morgan, 'Talleys immovable in dispute'; 'Talley's Affco Fact Sheet', April 11, 2012, Meat Workers Union and Council of Trade Unions; *The Union Report*, Triangle TV, May 14, 2012; Graham Cooke, Meat Workers Union newsletter to members, May 8, 2012. Helen Kelly papers.

62 Serious Fraud Office, media statement, 'SFO not pursuing complaint against Meat Workers Union', April 12, 2012.

63 Alison McCulloch, 'A Broader Union', *Werewolf*, October 11, 2012.

64 Affco NZ, press release, May 11, 2012.

65 *The Union Report*, Triangle TV, April 23, 2012; Helen Kelly, speech, April 23, 2012; Helen Kelly, 'We need to share the fruits of the land more fairly', *The Dominion Post*, April 23, 2012.

66 Paora Stanley, author interview, June 2020.

67 Michael Talley, letter to Senior Sargent [*sic*] Robert Crawford, May 10, 2012. Helen Kelly papers.

68 Helen Kelly, email, May 13, 2012. Helen Kelly papers.

69 New Zealand Meat and Related Trades Union v Affco New Zealand, Plaintiff's opening submission, May 15, 2012.

70 Ken Mair, author interview, July 2020.

71 Mike Nahu, author interview, June 2020.

72 Bill Rosenberg, *CTU Economic Bulletin*, January 2012, citing Michael Kumhof and Romain Ranciere, 'Unequal = Indebted', International Monetary Fund, September 2011; Bruce Western and Jake Rosenfeld, 'Unions, Norms and the Rise in American Wage Inequality', *American Sociological Review*, March 2011; *International Journal of Labour Research*, 2011, Volume 3.

73 Kate Wilkinson, 'Improvements to employment law announced', government press release, May 15, 2012.

74 Mathew Grocott, 'Job law reform "dirty attack"', *Manawatū Standard*, May 15, 2012.

75 Andrew Dart, email correspondence with author, July 2, 2020.

76 Dylan Kelly, author interview.

77 Jeff Sisson, written reflections provided to author, July 2018.

78 Sue Windsor, 'Presentation Document for assessment and consideration for Bachelor of Applied Management', June 2015. Provided to author by Sue Windsor.

79 Mike Nahu, author interview, December 2018.

80 Carol Beaumont, 'Review of the Meatworkers and Related Trades Union', 2012. Helen Kelly papers.

81 Gerard Hehir, author interview, April 2019.

82 Paul Tolich, author interview, January 2019.

83 Bronwynn Maxwell, author interview, December 2018.

84 Helen Kelly, 'The New Zealand Union Movement – Fly Buys scheme or a social movement?', presentation to NAC strategic planning day, February 21, 2012. Helen Kelly papers.

85 Helen Kelly, Rutherford Waddell speech, August 28, 2012; Bruce Munro, 'Waging the good fight' *Otago Daily Times*, August 27, 2012.

86 Rebecca Fox, 'Workers "expected to be grateful"', *Otago Daily Times*, August 30, 2012. Retrieved July 2, 2020.

Chapter 11

1 'Drug testing beneficiaries attempt to blame the unemployed', CTU press release, August 15, 2012.

2 *Close Up*, TV One, August 17, 2012. Retrieved from YouTube, July 20, 2020.

3 Helen Kelly, interview with Tony Sutorius, 2016. Provided to author by Tony Sutorius.

4 'Union drug-testing comments show ignorance of forestry', Forest Industry Contractors Association press release August 22, 2012. Retrieved from scoop.co.nz, July 20, 2020.

5 'Forestry sector's "one trick pony" won't end

workplace toll', CTU press release, August 22, 2012. Retrieved from scoop.co.nz, July 20, 2020.

6 Marino Harker-Smith, 'NZ forest accident rate "dreadful"', first published in *Gisborne Herald*, August 27, 2012. Retrieved from nzherald.co.nz, July 20, 2020.

7 Caroline Callow, original text of letter to *Gisborne Herald*. Provided to author by the Callow family.

8 Caroline Callow and Roger Callow, author interview, August 2019.

9 This was a new 'mega-ministry' set up 2012. It incorporated the old Department of Labour and its health and safety inspectorate.

10 Helen Kelly, letter to Chris Finlayson, acting minister of labour, December 21, 2012. Helen Kelly papers.

11 Helen Kelly, interview with Tony Sutorius.

12 Helen Kelly, email to family member of deceased forestry worker, March 2, 2013. Helen Kelly papers.

13 Julia London, author interview, July 2020.

14 *The Transport Worker*, Journal of the Rail and Maritime Transport Union, June 2013.

15 Department of Labour, investigation report and witness statements into the death of Shane Frater. Helen Kelly papers.

16 Helen Kelly, 'Tale two – The Death of Shane Frater, Killed 1 May, 2009', *The Standard*, July 16, 2013.

17 Deborah McMillan, author interview, July 2020.

18 Helen Kelly, speech to Post Primary Teachers' Association, October 2013.

19 Helen Kelly, 'No traffic jam on the high road', *The Standard*, June 22, 2013.

20 'The Report of the Independent Taskforce on Workplace Health and Safety He Korowai Whakaruruhau', April 30, 2013.

21 Geoff Cumming, 'Logging the perils', *The New Zealand Herald*, August 24, 2013. Retrieved from nzherald.co.nz, July 20, 2020.

22 CTU, Submission to the Transport and Industrial Relations Select Committee on the Health and Safety Reform Bill, May 2014, citing *NZ Logger*, August, September and October 2013.

23 Reg Birchfield and Ian Grant, *Out of the Woods: The restructuring and sale of New Zealand's state forests*, GP Publications, 1993.

24 Ibid; Peter Berg, 'The events of 1987: Corporatising and privatising the state's forests', *New Zealand Journal of Forestry*, May 2013, Vol 58, No 1.

25 Edward Miller, 'Health and Safety in New Zealand Forestry: A Union Response', FIRST Forestry Together, 2014. Helen Kelly papers.

26 Andres Katz, 'A strategic review of New Zealand log exports', *New Zealand Journal of Forestry*, November 2013, Vol 58, No 3; Edward Miller, 'Health and Safety in New Zealand Forestry: A Union Response'.

27 Robert Reid, author interview, July 2020.

28 Robert Reid, author interview, April 2019.

29 Deborah McMillan, author interview.

30 Edward Miller, author interview, June 2020.

31 Breaking out involves workers hooking steel cables or a mechanical grapple around trees so they can be pulled by a hauler to the skid (landing) site.

32 Maryanne Butler-Finlay, author interview, July 2019.

33 Helen Kelly, speech to Australian Council of Trade Unions, February 2014.

34 The Timber Workers Union later merged with the Pulp and Paper Workers Union to become the Wood Industries Union. The documentary *Wildcat: The struggle for democracy in the New Zealand Timber Workers Union*, Vanguard Films, 1981, tells the story of the internal battle in the union.

35 Helen Kelly, speech to CTU biennial conference, October 9, 2013.

36 Helen Kelly, speech to Labour Party conference, November 2, 2013.

37 Bill McCallum, author interview, July 2020.

38 Ibid.

39 The Independent Forestry Safety Review found that the fatality rate in forestry between 2006 and 2012 was 48.5 per 100,000 workers, compared with a fatality rate of 3.2 per 100,000 workers in all sectors. See *Independent Forestry Safety Review*, October 2014; Forest Owners Association, 'Forest owners ask critics to help', press release, November 3, 2013. Retrieved from scoop.co.nz, August 4, 2020.

40 Steve Kilgallon, 'Why is forestry so deadly?', *Stuff*, December 15, 2013. Retrieved from stuff.co.nz, January 14, 2014.

41 Helen Kelly, speech to CTU biennial conference, October 9, 2013.

42 For instance, Whitehead Group, 'Look out Australia, living wage will drive Kiwis your way', press release, March 11, 2013. Retrieved from scoop.co.nz, August 3, 2013; Wellington Chamber of Commerce, '"Living Wage" depends on stronger economy', press release, February 12, 2013. Retrieved from scoop.co.nz, August 3, 2020, Employers and Manufacturers Association, 'Living wage a feel good, wrong idea', press release, November 21, 2013. Retrieved from scoop.co.nz, August 3, 2020.

43 Bill Rosenberg, *CTU Economic Bulletin*, August 2012, citing 'Household Incomes in New Zealand: Trends in indicators of inequality and hardship 1982 to 2011' prepared by Bryan Perry, Ministry of Social Development, August 2012.

44 John Ryall, speech to Fabian Society, September 2019; John Ryall, 'Leverage and organisation in the struggle against the undervaluation of care and support workers', *Labour History Project Bulletin*, November 2019.

45 John Ryall, 'Leverage and organisation'. The settlement was implemented into law with the Home and Community Support (Payment for Travel Between Clients) Settlement Act 2016.

46 John Ryall, email correspondence with author.

47 About half of unionised aged care workers were members of the New Zealand Nurses Organisation.

48 The Service and Food Workers Union, PSA, New Zealand Nurses Organisation and CTU were represented in the negotiations with Crown negotiator Doug Martin. The Care and Support Workers Pay Equity (Settlement) Act was passed in 2017. Kristine Bartlett was named New Zealander of the Year in 2018 in recognition of her role in achieving the landmark settlement.

49 John Ryall, email correspondence with author.

50 Amy Maas, 'Acquittal in security guard death', *The New Zealand Herald*, September 12, 2013.

51 MBIE v CNE Security, District Court at Waitakere, CRI-2012-090-003047.

52 Helen Kelly, email to Chamanpreet Dhaliwal, October 16, 2013. Helen Kelly papers.

53 CTU, 'District Court wrong on Charanpreet Dhaliwal's death', press release, October 15, 2013.

54 Helen Kelly, email to Lesley Haines and David Smol, October 17, 2013. Helen Kelly papers.

55 Fulton Hogan, 'Compensation made to Charanpreet Singh Dhaliwal's family', press release, December 20, 2013. Retrieved from scoop.co.nz, August 6, 2020.

56 Helen Kelly, 'On Pike', *The Standard*, December 12, 2013.

Chapter 12

1 Ministry of Business, Innovation and Employment, 'Charges against former Pike River CEO not proceeding', press release, December 12, 2013.

2 Rebecca Macfie, '*Tragedy at Pike River Mine: How and why 29 men died*', Awa Press, 2013.

3 *New Zealand Parliamentary Debates*, November 12, 2013, Week 59, Volume 694.

4 Department of Labour v Peter Whittall, Christchurch District Court, December 12, 2013, CRI 2012-018-000821.

5 Rebecca Macfie, *Tragedy at Pike River Mine.*

6 'CTU wants to take a closer look at the deal', Radio New Zealand, December 13, 2013.

7 Sonya Rockhouse, author interview, January 2020.

8 Anna Osborne, author interview, May 2018.

9 'ACC wastes big money on cosy deal with big business and unions', Taxpayers Union, January 14, 2014.

10 'ACC programme a cosy deal, says minister', Radio New Zealand, January 15, 2014. Retrieved from rnz.co.nz August 20, 2020; Marie McNicholas, 'Angry Collins lashes out at business boss', Newsroom, January 16, 2014.

11 Helen Kelly, 'Health and safety rep training – a cut by any other name', *The Standard,* January 14, 2014. Retrieved from thestandard.org.nz, August 20, 2020.

12 Business New Zealand, 'ACC training claims overblown', press release, January 16, 2014. Retrieved from scoop.co.nz, November 9, 2020.

13 Marie McNicholas, 'Angry Collins lashes out at business boss'.

14 Sue Windsor, author interview, August 2018.

15 'Forestry worker killed by falling log in Wairau Valley; concern at safety record', *Scoop,* January 16, 2014. Retrieved from scoop.co.nz, August 20, 2020.

16 WorkSafe New Zealand, 'Interim industry report back – Cable logging assessment results', December 23, 2013.

17 Rebecca Macfie, 'The final campaign', *New Zealand Listener,* May 16, 2015.

18 Nigel Hampton, author interview, November 2018.

19 Selina Eruera, author interview, August 2019.

20 Department of Labour, Summary of Evidence, Investigation into death of Eramiha Pairama, undated. Document provided to author by Selina Eruera.

21 Helen Kelly, email to Selina Eruera, January 1, 2013. Documents provided to author by Selina Eruera.

22 Nigel Hampton, author interview; Nigel Hampton, 'Going private', *Safeguard,* January/February 2016.

23 Ministry of Business, Innovation and Employment, Summary of Evidence, Charles Harrison Finlay.

24 Helen Kelly, 'If it were someone you loved', *The Standard,* May 9, 2014.

25 'CTU forestry prosecution a tall order', Radio New Zealand, May 12, 2014.

26 Peter Cranney, author interview, September 2018; Simon Meikle, conversation with author, October 2020.

27 Lesley Kidd and Craig Kidd, author interview, November 2020.

28 Anne Russell, '200 in silent march to Parliament for Workers Memorial Day', Scoop, April 28, 2014. Retrieved from scoop.co.nz, August 25, 2020. Lincoln Kidd's employer, Paul Burr, was later charged by police with manslaughter over Lincoln's death, but found not guilty. Burr and his company were charged by WorkSafe and pleaded guilty to breaching the Health and Safety in Employment Act. Coroner Tim Scott concluded in January 2017 'dangerous and sloppy work practices' had contributed to Lincoln's death.

29 Ibid.

30 Anna Osborne, author interview.

31 Nigel Hampton, author interview.

32 Council of Trade Unions, 'Under Pressure: A detailed report into insecure work in New Zealand', October 2013.

33 Rebecca Macfie, 'The final campaign'.

34 Stephen Mills, 'Survey Findings and the 2014 General Election', in *Moments of Truth: The New Zealand General Election of 2014*, edited by Jon Johansson and Stephen Levine, Victoria University Press 2015.

35 John Armstrong, 'Cunliffe delivering the wow factor', *The New Zealand Herald,* October 12, 2013. Retrieved from nzherald.co.nz, September 4, 2020.

36 Andrew Little , author interview, October 2018.

37 Helen Kelly, email to colleagues, February 19, 2014, discussing Jelle Visser, 'Wage Bargaining Institutions – from crisis to crisis', European Commission, Economic Papers 488/April 2013.

38 Bill Rosenberg, CTU *Monthly Economic Bulletins*, March 2014 and July 2014. Between March 2007 and March 2013 labour productivity rose 9.3 percent, but private sector real wages rose only 3.8 percent; Jim Stanford, 'A View From Afar', in *Beyond the Free Market;* 'An International Perspective on the New Zealand Productivity Paradox', New Zealand Productivity Commission WP 2014/1. Three decades on from the start of New Zealand's textbook neoliberal reforms, the country's productivity growth remained one of the lowest in the OECD. Economists such as the authors of this Productivity Commission report puzzled over why New Zealand's economic policy, 'considered broadly conducive to good economic performance', had not delivered the expected results.

39 Bill Rosenberg, CTU *Monthly Economic Bulletin*, August 2014. Data showing reasons for pay rises released with Statistics New Zealand's Labour Cost Index implied jobs subject to collective employment agreements were twice as likely to receive a pay rise compared with those on individual agreements.

40 HSBC economist Paul Bloxham coined the 'rockstar' label, reasoning that high prices for dairy commodities, a booming housing market fuelled by low interest rates and high immigration, and building activity after the catastrophic 2011 Christchurch earthquake was fuelling faster economic growth than in most other countries. https://www.cnbc.com/2014/01/05/rockstar_economy_2014.html

41 Max Rashbrooke (ed), *Inequality: A New Zealand crisis*, Bridget Williams Books, 2013.

42 Bill Rosenberg, CTU *Monthly Economic Bulletin*, July 2014. Around two out of every three two-parent families were dual-earner families from 2007–2013, compared with one in two in the early 1980s, reported Rosenberg, citing Bryan Perry, 'Household Incomes in New Zealand: Trends in indicators of inequality and hardship, 1982 to 2013', Wellington, Ministry of Social Development.

43 John Ryall, author interview, September 2018.

44 Labour, Policy 2014, 'A fair day's pay for a fair day's work'.

45 Nicky Hager, *Dirty Politics.*

46 Cabinet Employment Growth and Infrastructure Committee: Employment Relations Amendment Bill, 2012; 'Paper One – Collective Bargaining and Flexible Working Arrangements'.

47 Department of Labour, 'Review of Part 6A: Continuity of Employment', October 2012.

48 Stephen Blumenfeld, 'Law changes aim to focus power in employers' hands', *The Dominion Post,* November 18, 2014.

49 The Treasury, Cabinet Committee Briefing: Employment Relations Amendment Bill 2012: 'Paper One – Collective Bargaining and Flexible Working Arrangements'.

50 For instance, Michael Kumhof and Romain Rancière, 'Leveraging Inequality', *Finance and Development,* December 2010; Olivier Blanchard, Florence Jaumotte and Prakash Loungani, 'Labour Market Policies and IMF Advice in Advancing Economies During the Great Recession', IMF Staff Discussion Note, March 2013.

51 Helen Kelly, 'True blue worker hate', *The Standard,* April 9, 2013; Helen Kelly, 'Massive changes to employment legislation announced today', *The Standard,* April 26, 2013; Shane Cowlishaw, 'Workers rail at "humilating" law plans', *The Dominion Post,* August 21, 2013; Amelia Langford, 'Concerns over new flexi law – CTU', Radio New Zealand, March 6, 2015. Retrieved from rnz.co.nz, September 3, 2020.

52 International Labour Conference, 'Record of Proceedings, One Hundred and Second Session, Geneva, 2013'.

53 Cabinet Employment Growth and Infrastructure Committee: Employment

Relations Amendment Bill, 2012; The Treasury, Cabinet Committee Briefing: Employment Relations Amendment Bill 2012.

54 The ILO Governing Body is made up of elected worker, employer and government representatives. It sets strategy, priorities and agenda for the annual International Labour Conference. The ILO is unique within the UN system as a tripartite decision-making body.

55 In 2013, 1132 workers were killed when the Rana Plaza building, housing five garment factories, collapsed. Five months earlier, 112 workers had been killed when they were trapped inside the burning Tazreen factory outside Dhaka.

56 Sarah Fox, author interview, August 2020.

57 Phil O'Reilly, author interview, August 2018.

58 Paul Mackay, author interview, September 2020.

59 Helen Kelly, letter to Business New Zealand members, September 20, 2012. CTU files.

60 'The Case Against Qatar', ITUC Special Report, March 2014.

61 Sharan Burrow, author interview, January 2020.

62 Sharan Burrow, author interview, September 2020.

63 Helen Kelly, email to Sir Thomas Eichelbaum, June 9, 2014. Helen Kelly papers.

64 Sir Thomas Eichelbaum, author interview, July 2018.

65 CTU National Affiliates Council, minutes, December 4, 2014. CTU files.

66 Rebecca Macfie, 'Now and forever', *New Zealand Listener,* October 11, 2014; Nicole Matthewson and Hamish Rutherford, 'Solid Energy announces voluntary administration ahead of sale', *Stuff,* August 13, 2015. Retrieved from stuff.co.nz, September 14, 2020.

67 Helen Kelly, letter to Independent Police Conduct Authority, November 21, 2014. Helen Kelly papers.

68 Judge David Carruthers, chair, Independent Police Conduct Authority, letter to Helen Kelly, April 9, 2015. Helen Kelly papers.

69 'Independent Forestry Safety Review: An agenda for change in the forestry sector', October 2014.

70 Gordon MacDonald, letter to Helen Kelly, February 12, 2015. Helen Kelly papers.

Chapter 13

1 Helen Kelly, text exchanges with Huia Welton, February 18, 2015. Provided to author by Huia Welton.

2 Steve Hurring, author interview, September 2020.

3 Ben Heather, 'Union stalward on cancer, dying, and bad access to good medicine', *The Sunday Star-Times,* June 5, 2015. Retrieved from stuff.co.nz, September 29, 2020.

4 Whittall strongly objected to the release of the District Court file: Ministry of Business, Innovation and Employment v Peter Whittall, Supplemental memorandum of counsel for Peter Whittall in response to application to access court file, Wellington District Court, May 30, 2014. Helen Kelly papers.

5 Anna Osborne and Sonya Rockhouse v WorkSafe New Zealand and District Court at Wellington, February 24, 2015, Wellington High Court.

6 Helen Kelly, 'The continuing fight for justice at Pike River', *The Standard,* February 25, 2015.

7 'Helen Kelly diagnosed with lung cancer', *Stuff,* February 26, 2015. Retrieved from stuff.co.nz, September 28, 2020.

8 Anonymous, email to Helen Kelly, May 22, 2015. Helen Kelly papers.

9 Helen Kelly, email to friends, March 23, 2015. Helen Kelly papers.

10 Suzanne McNabb, author interview.

11 Helen Kelly, email to friends, March 29, 2015. Helen Kelly papers.

12 Helen Kelly, speech to wedding party. Video provided to author by Huia Welton.

13 Ged Kearney, author interview, September 2020.

14 Helen Kelly, email to friends and colleagues, May 29, 2015. Helen Kelly papers.

15 Anna Osborne and Sonya Rockhouse v WorkSafe New Zealand and District Court at Wellington, Applicants' Synopsis.

16 Rebecca Macfie, 'Without prejudice', *New Zealand Listener*, March 4, 2017.

17 Anna Osborne and Sonya Rockhouse v WorkSafe New Zealand and District Court at Wellington, Applicants' Synopsis.

18 Ibid.

19 Jeff Sissons, 'A bad day at the sausage factory', *New Zealand Journal of Employment Relations*, 2016, 41 (2), citing letter from the Business Leaders Health and Safety Forum to Cabinet, June 2013.

20 Audrey Young, 'Health and safety law overhaul delayed', *The New Zealand Herald*, May 27, 2015. Retrieved from nzherald.co.nz, October 1, 2020.

21 Vernon Small, 'Pike River health and safety law changes set to be watered down', *Stuff*, May 25, 2015. Retrieved from stuff.co.nz, September 29, 2020.

22 Under the existing Health and Safety in Employment Act, all workplaces with more than 30 workers had to have worker health and safety representatives, and workers had the right to request them in all smaller workplaces.

23 Helen Kelly, email to friends and colleagues, May 29, 2015. Helen Kelly papers.

24 CTU President to National Affiliates Council, 'Health and Safety in Employment Bill Campaign', June 3, 2015. Helen Kelly papers.

25 Coroner Wallace Bain, Written findings on the death of Thomas Sewell, November 30, 2009; Department of Labour, Summary of Evidence, Investigation into the death of Thomas Sewell. Helen Kelly papers; Linda and Ken Sewell, Inquest statement, January 2013. Provided to author by Linda Sewell; Laura Proto, 'Weybridge Vandals player died in tragic New Zealand accident, coroner rules', *Sutton & Croydon Guardian*, February 5, 2013; 'Killed in a small business', YouTube, June 12, 2015.

26 Simon Bridges, minister of labour, letter to Linda Sewell, April 14, 2014. Provided to author by Linda Sewell.

27 Marty Sharpe, 'Hawkes Bay quad bike death comes on back of worst statistics for a decade', *Stuff*, January 21, 2016. Retrieved from stuff.co.nz, October 9, 2020. Sharpe reported WorkSafe figures showing that in the ten years from 2006 there were an average of 4.6 deaths attributed to quad bikes annually.

28 Gordon MacDonald with Helen Kelly and Phil O'Reilly, 'Exit interview', *Safeguard*, July/August 2015.

29 Chris Bramwell, 'Workplace safety plans open can of worms', Radio New Zealand, August 21, 2015. Retrieved from rnz.co.nz, October 7, 2020; 'Benedict Collins, 'Minister defends safety risk classifications', Radio New Zealand, August 25, 2015. Retrieved from rnz.co.nz, October 7, 2020.

30 Ross Wilson, eulogy at the funeral of Peter Conway, June 17, 2015.

31 Ibid.

32 Helen Kelly, reading at the funeral of Peter Conway, June 17, 2015.

33 Andrew Dart, email correspondence with author, July 3, 2020; Helen Kelly, email to Atul Gawande via Anne O'Brien, December 23, 2015. Helen Kelly papers.

34 The Kelly family went back to England in 1996 and various relatives from Pat's side had been to New Zealand.

35 Helen Kelly, email to Nigel Hampton, Peter Cranney, Simon Meikle and Tim Braithwaite, July 25, 2015. Helen Kelly papers.

36 Helen Kelly v Puketi Logging, Tauranga District Court, August 12, 2015, NZDC 15206.

37 Puketi Logging Ltd (in Liquidation), First Liquidator's Report, November 2, 2015; Tony Wall, 'Logging company thrives while mum of dead forestry worker can't afford headstone', *The Sunday Star-Times*, February 11, 2018. Retrieved from stuff.co.nz, October 5, 2020.

38 Helen Kelly, letter to PF Olsen, June 1, 2016; Helen Kelly, letter to Public Sector Pension

Investment Board and Canadian Union of Public Employees, June 1, 2016. Helen Kelly papers.

39 'Union raises $6k for mother who couldn't afford son's headstone', *The New Zealand Herald*, February 12, 2018. Retrieved from nzherald.co.nz, October 5, 2020.; Tony Wall, 'Francis Tipene of Casketeers fame is among those helping mother of dead forestry worker', *Stuff*, February 18, 2018. Retrieved from stuff.co.nz, November 2, 2020.

40 Jeff Sissons, author interview, July 2018.

41 James Ritchie, author interview, October 2020.

42 Helen Kelly, speech to CTU biennial conference, October 14, 2015.

43 Coroner JP Ryan, report on death of Charanpreet Dhaliwal, October 13, 2015.

44 Gregory Baughen, Official Secretary, Government House, letter to Helen Kelly, November 10, 2015. Helen Kelly papers.

45 Helen Kelly, WhatsApp correspondence with Peter Cranney, November 2015. Provided to author by Peter Cranney.

46 Helen Kelly, updates to friends and colleagues, November 26, 2015, December 18, 2015. Helen Kelly papers.

47 Seales sought declarations from the High Court to determine if her doctor could lawfully administer a drug to end her life or provide her with a drug to enable her to end her own life. In the alternative, she sought declarations that the offence provisions of the Crimes Act breached her rights under section 8 and 9 of the New Zealand Bill of Rights Act. The court declined to grant the declarations and said only Parliament could make such decisions. Seales died the day after her family received the High Court decision.

48 Helen Kelly, 'Euthanasia debate: "Why can't I have the option of assisted dying?"', *Stuff*, January 27, 2016. Retrieved from stuff.co.nz, November 19, 2020.

49 Helen Kelly, Facebook posts, December 28, 2015.

50 New Zealand Meat Workers and Related Trades Union v Affco New Zealand, Employment Court, Judgement of the Full Court, November 18, 2015, NZEmpC 204.

51 Therese Turipa, author interview.

52 New Zealand Meat Workers and Related Trades Union v Affco New Zealand, 2015, NZEmpC 204.

53 Tony Sutorius's documentary *Helen Kelly – Together* was released in 2019.

54 The case resulted in Affco being prosecuted and eventually pleading guilty in 2020. It was one of the last cases prosecuted under the old Health and Safety in Employment Act. Affco was fined $46,000 and ordered to pay $50,000 in reparations. WorkSafe New Zealand v Affco New Zealand, Whanganui District Court, July 8, 2020, NZDC 12998; WorkSafe investigation report, May 2, 2016; Helen Kelly, various emails to WorkSafe, Helen Kelly papers.

55 Jonathan Underhill, 'Affco baulks at having former union chief in mediation sessions', *National Business Review*, December 8, 2015. Retrieved from nbr.co.nz, October 13, 2020.

56 Pete Amato, author interview.

57 Therese Turipa, author interview.

58 *Helen Kelly – Together*, Unreal Films, 2019.

59 New Zealand Meat Workers and Related Trades Union v Affco New Zealand Ltd, 2016, NZEmpC 7. Auckland Employment Court, February 11, 2016.

60 Helen Kelly, update to friends, January 22, 2016. Helen Kelly papers.

61 Radio New Zealand, *Checkpoint*, January 28, 2016.

62 Abe Gray, author interview, October 2020.

63 James Ritchie, author interview.

64 Steve Braunias, 'The real oil on Helen Kelly', *The New Zealand Herald*, April 9, 2016. Retrieved from nzherald.co.nz, October 5, 2020.

65 CTU, submission to Coroner's Inquiries into the Deaths of Charles Finlay, Eramiha Pairama and David McMurtrie, July 5, 2016. Helen Kelly papers.

66 Donna McMurtie, author interview, August 2019; CTU, submission to Coroner's Inquiry into the Death of David McMurtrie, April 5, 2016. Helen Kelly papers.

67 Donna McMurtie, author interview; Hazel Armstrong, brief of evidence, May 5, 2016. Helen Kelly papers.

68 Katie Holland, 'Coroner: Forestry worker not to blame for his death', *Rotorua Daily Post,* November 30, 2016. Retrieved from nzherald.co.nz, October 10, 2020.

69 Wallace Bain, author interview, August 2020.

70 Helen Kelly email to friends, July 13, 2016. Helen Kelly papers.

71 Huia Welton, author interview, October 2020.

72 Chris Finlayson, author interview, October 2020.

73 Peter Cranney, author interview, October 2020; Chris Finlayson, author interview, October 2020.

74 Peter Cranney, author interview.

75 Helen Kelly, email to friends, August 16, 2016. Helen Kelly papers.

76 Helen Kelly, Facebook post, August 24, 2016.

77 Helen Kelly, email to Abe Gray, September 8, 2016. Provided to author by Abe Gray.

78 Helen Kelly, Facebook post, September 13, 2016.

79 Helen Kelly, Facebook post, September 13, 2016.

80 Helen Kelly, Facebook post, September 17, 2016.

81 Helen Kelly, Facebook post, September 23, 2016.

82 Helen Kelly Facebook posts, September 29 and 30, 2016.

83 Helen Kelly, Facebook post, September 30, 2016.

84 Steve Hurring, author interview.

85 Helen Kelly, email to friends, October 11, 2016. Helen Kelly papers.

86 Huia Welton, recollection. Welton was with Helen.

87 Richard Naylor, email to Belinda Heffron, final stats for Helen Kelly Memorial, October 29, 2016.

88 For instance, Isaac Davidson, 'Helen Kelly a relentless changemaker', *The New Zealand Herald,* October 14, 2016. Retrieved from nzherald.co.nz, October 15, 2020; Chris Trotter, 'Giving workers what they want; Honouring the legacy of Helen Kelly', October 16, 2016, *The Daily Blog*. Retrieved from thedailyblog.co.nz, October 15, 2020; Bryce Edwards, 'Helen Kelly, former President of the New Zealand Council of Trade Unions', *The New Zealand Herald,* October 17, 2016.

Epilogue

1 Author interview with Anna Osborne, November 2020.

2 By the end of 2020, the Pike River Recovery Agency had recovered the mine drift to 2.24 kilometres. The final few metres of the drift would be forensically searched, along with mine machinery stationed at an area called pit bottom in stone, in 2021. A police team was investigating culpability for the disaster.

3 Anna Osborne and Sonya Rockhouse v WorkSafe New Zealand and District Court at Wellington, Supreme Court of New Zealand, November 23, 2017 NZSC 175.

4 The Forestry Industry Safety Council (FISC) began introducing a certified contractor scheme in 2020. The objective is for contractors to show they meet health and safety standards and minimum employment standards. FIRST Union was also working towards a claim for above-minimum employment standards, which would be rolled out through the FISC certified contractor scheme. The goal is that forest owners agree to allow only certified contractors to work in their forests.

5 Forest Industry Safety Council, *Annual Report,* 2019.

6 Hazel Armstrong, 'Seven out of 44', *Safeguard,* July/August 2020.

7 If real wages in New Zealand had risen at the same rate as labour productivity since 1989, the average hourly wage would have been 26 percent higher by March 2018 ($37.68 rather than $29.80). If the share of the economy's income going to wages and salaries had remained as it was in 1981, average annual wages would have been $11,800 higher in 2018. Bill Rosenberg, *CTU Economic Bulletin*, March 2019; Alexander Plum, Gail Pacheco and Rod Hick, 'In-Work Poverty in New Zealand', AUT New Zealand Work Research Institute, 2019.

8 Sue Ryall and Stephen Blumenfeld, 'Unions and Union Membership in New Zealand – Report on 2017 survey', Victoria University, Centre for Labour, Employment and Work. Union density was 19.9 percent in December 2007, rose to 21.5 percent in 2009, and was 17.9 percent in December 2015. The latest figures at the time of writing, published by the Centre for Labour, Employment and Work on May 25, 2020, showed union density was 17.7 percent in the year to December 2018.

9 Author interview with Sir Jim Bolger, November 2020; Radio New Zealand, *The 9th Floor*, April 21, 2017.

10 'Fair Pay Agreements: Supporting workers and firms to drive productivity growth and share the benefits', Recommendations of the Fair Pay Agreement Working Group, 2018.

11 Prime Minister Jacinda Ardern, conversation with author, May 2019.

12 Helen Kelly, interview with Kathryn Ryan, *Nine to Noon*, Radio New Zealand, May 22, 2015.

Index

Bold denotes illustrations.
i, ii, iii, iv etc refer to picture section page numbers.